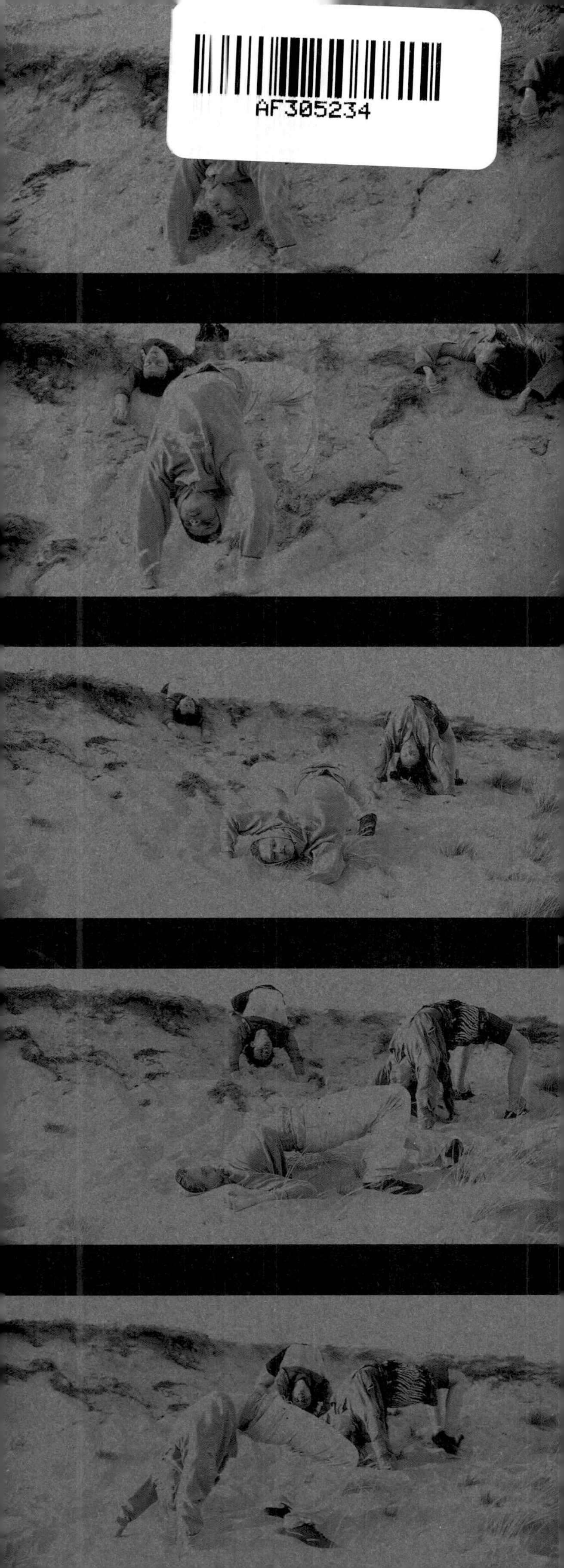

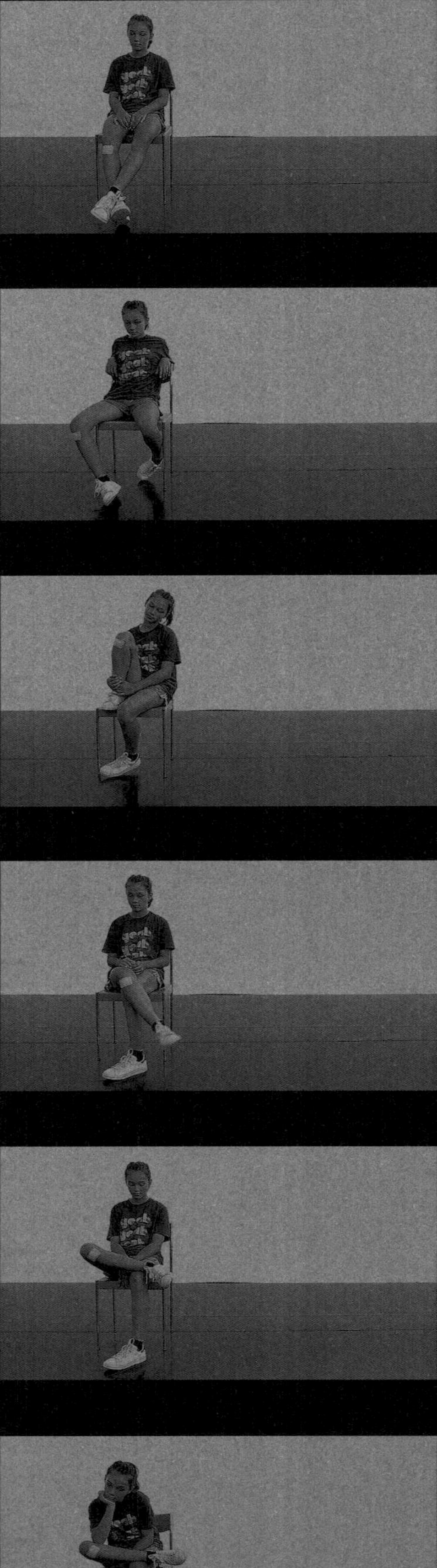

# Moving Bodies, Moving Images

Whitechapel Gallery

# Introduction

Lydia Yee and Grace Storey

Set against a backdrop of climate change, social justice movements and a global pandemic, the eight recent moving-image works featured in the exhibition 'Moving Bodies, Moving Images', unfold across multiple continents in a range of settings from the streets of Recife, Brazil and a London autobody repair shop to islands in the Arabian Gulf and the Caribbean. Dance or choreographed movement are at the heart of each film. Why have visual artists taken a new interest in choreography and its attendant focus on the body in recent years?

This engagement with dance among visual artists signals a shift away from what André Lepecki has termed the 'choreographic turn', which began in the 1950s with choreographer Merce Cunningham and the subsequent generation of postmodern choreographers he influenced, including Trisha Brown, Lucinda Childs, Steve Paxton and Yvonne Rainer, among others.[1] The impact of this period, which culminated in the experimental collaboration among dancers, composers and visual artists at Judson Dance Theater in the early 1960s, continues to reverberate six decades later and had been examined in exhibitions and publications, including 'Move: Choreographing You' (2010–11) at the Hayward Gallery, London; 'Danser sa vie' (2011–12) at the Centre Pompidou, Paris; 'Judson Dance Theater: The Work is Never Done' (2018–19) at The Museum of Modern Art, New York and the volume *Dance* (2012) from the series Documents of Contemporary Art, published by Whitechapel Gallery and The MIT Press.

Postmodern choreographers embraced abstract and conceptual approaches associated with visual art and rejected those that emphasised expression and narrative. Their choreography was often based on simple instructions, tasks and scores; they focused on everyday movement and gestures and their pieces were more likely to be performed in galleries, studios or the street rather than on a proscenium stage; they used film or video cameras primarily to document their performances or make work by performing for the camera. By contrast, the works featured in 'Moving Bodies, Moving Images' are more aligned with recent concerns around the body, storytelling and social issues. Bodies, particularly those of women, people of colour and LGBTQIA+ individuals, have been the focal point of a great deal of social and political debate, conflict, resistance and pride as well as a prevalent subject in recent art.

Muscles hold the memory of pain and joy, trauma and pleasure, and dance transfers this memory from body to body. The body can communicate things that words alone cannot. The physicality of dance highlights the body's strength and flexibility but also its fragility. Dance also carries stories across time and place. There are long-established traditions of dance and storytelling in many cultures, from Kathak, a classical dance form that originate among travelling bards in northern India, to European narrative ballet, to the elaborate dance routines in music videos.

Film is the primary medium for many of the artists in 'Moving Bodies, Moving Images'. They have all made films previously and most work with a regular group of collaborators, including choreographers, dancers, cinematographers, editors, sound designers and musicians, bringing together a wide range of expertise, knowledge and perspectives. Dance choreographed for film is distinct from any performance on stage, in a theatre or in the streets. 'The dance that is realized in dancefilm,' Erin Brannigan writes in *Dancefilm: Choreography and the Moving Image*, 'did not exist prior to film and needs to be considered entirely in terms of its cinematic manifestation.'[2] Film enables choreography and settings that are not otherwise possible in theatrical performances staged for an audience. Audiences expect that a dancer could magically appear or disappear on film or reappear instantaneously with an elaborate costume change. Moreover, the techniques of montage enable filmmakers to bring together a heterogenous admixture of dance, music, voiceover narration, textural elements and other material into a composite whole.

'Moving Bodies, Moving Images' is presented across two floors of Whitechapel Gallery, with four moving-image works on each level, which form two thematic groups. Rather than presenting films in isolation in individual viewing spaces, the works are presented in an open display across a range of projections and screens suspended throughout the two galleries, which play in choreographed sequences. This decision is both an ecological consideration, to minimise exhibition build, and a curatorial conceit which allows films to be viewed individually and forms a dialogue between them as the exhibition unfolds. In turn, the viewer becomes increasingly aware of their own body as they move between the different installations.

The first section of the exhibition explores the relationship between the human body and the landscape, with works filmed predominantly outdoors in forests, mountains, beaches and gardens in Lithuania, France, Iran, Barbados, South Africa and the UK. A number of the films were made during and in the wake of the COVID-19 pandemic, when many people found new ways of working together amid lockdowns and travel restrictions and spent an increased amount of time outdoors, developing a greater appreciation for nature. In Alberta Whittle's *RESET* (2020), elements of the natural world recur throughout as symbols of healing in the wake of the murder of George Floyd and Black Lives Matter protests; she says they 'contain a desire for my witnesses to slow down and find moments to connect with a more meditative state'. The performers in *RESET* are pictured indoors at rest and outside, dancing in an idyllic garden. In Éric Minh Cuong Castaing's *Form(s) of Life* (2021), the sounds and sensations of nature across a sprawling national park offer new possibilities of movement and ways of engaging with the landscape for performers suffering from degenerative illnesses. *Songs from the Compost: mutating bodies, imploding stars* (2020) by Eglė Budvytytė in collaboration with Marija Olšauskaitė and Julija Steponaitytė proposes a permeability between humans and the environment, as performers relate to nature in a non-human-centred manner. In Alia Farid's *At the Time of the Ebb* (2019), residents of the Iranian island of Qeshm enact ancient customs – chanting indoors, dancing on the beach in handmade costumes and processing over the mountains – which honour the sea and its importance to their livelihoods as they celebrate Nowruz Sayadeen (Fishermen's New Year) at the summer solstice.

The second section of the exhibition brings together films that focus on the movement of bodies in human-made urban environments, such as the street, the club, the gymnasium, and other spaces shaped by vernacular cultures. In Bárbara Wagner and Benjamin de Burca's *Faz Que Vai* (Set to Go, 2015), projected on a screen suspended high, gender fluid dancers perform improvisational frevo and frevoguing in the street and atop a roof in Recife, and the urban landscape of tower blocks and skyscrapers visible behind them in the distance includes the less desirable, more neglected parts of the city, spaces well-trodden by the dancers. In Pauline Boudry/Renate Lorenz's two-channel installation *Les Gayrillères* (2022), a group of six dancers perform in the dark wearing partially illuminated costumes and move across a reflective dance floor to a soundtrack that helps evoke the atmosphere of a nightclub. In Hetain Patel's *Trinity* (2021), performers connect in scenes of combat, suggesting the 'communicative possibilities of the body, beyond spoken language', showing the ability of gesture and sign language to express things that words cannot. In the final space, viewers can recline on Alexandra Bachzetsis' *Catapult* (2018), a set of AirTrack gymnastics mats, as they observe differences in the body language of the adolescent protagonists in her two-screen film *An Ideal for Living* (2018), enacting everyday gestures in a gymnasium, reading books, playing football and reciting song lyrics.

An additional gallery contains material related to the research and production of each film. These materials – including books, images and a film clip used for research by Bachzetsis and Wagner and de Burca; notes, scores, lyrics and sketches from Budvytytė, Castaing and Whittle; mood boards and production stills from Farid and Patel, along with costumes from Boudry/Lorenz and Whittle – reveal the diverse sources of inspiration and the creative collaborations behind these eight remarkable films.

1.  André Lepecki, 'Introduction', *Dance* (Documents of Contemporary Art), ed. André Lepecki (London and Cambridge, MA: Whitechapel Gallery and The MIT Press, 2012), 14–23.

2.  Erin Brannigan, *Dancefilm: Choreography and the Moving Image* (Oxford: Oxford University Press, 2011), viii.

# Pray for a life without plot, a day without narrative: Notes on 'Moving Bodies, Moving Images'

Jemma Desai

I

In French-Algerian visual artist Kader Attia's video *The Body's Legacies, Pt. 2: The Postcolonial Body* (2018), philosopher Dr Norman Ajari quotes a track by hip hop act PNL to articulate the differences in response to images of police brutality on Black bodies between descendants of colonised and enslaved people and those who are not descended from subjugation:

*They have the image without the memory, we have the image after the memory.*

In cinema such a punctum[1] can remind us of our bodies, clearing space for us to respond with all of the subjectivities of it. What we see and feel will depend on what our bodies have seen and felt before, but also on the repository in which the puncture intervenes.


II

My first memories are of watching bodies on screen. In Hollywood black-and-white and Bollywood technicolour I watched star-crossed lovers, ballerinas and showgirls navigate beauty, status, desire. Their dances propelled the force of passing narrative, one within the film but also dependent on the offscreen narratives I already knew, or would soon learn.

I sat upstairs watching a small screen as dancers moved to music, for pleasure, for validation, for beauty, for love. Downstairs my parents moved for something else. Frenetically paced movements contorted their bodies into gestures that turned cash into carrying and back into cash again. Hands counted out change or held out bags, mouths formed English words and eyes moved into deference and politeness. Legs bent to unload heavy boxes and arms stretched to stack the contents onto shelves.

This choreography that put food on the table, savings in the bank and money to send home also opened out a hernia in one of their stomachs as they loaded their bodies too heavily, and cracked open one of their skulls when a customer became an assailant.

*

Kinaesthetic contagion is a term for the ways that movement can be used to capture a body watching a body. This contagion can be used to propel a well-worn narrative, but sometimes it can also be used to halt it. It can lead to pleasure, but it can also lead to the withholding of it. The bodies I watched on and off screen taught me something of what I already knew about what movement was possible in different contexts and different bodies, but they left me with questions.

*What directions, formations, autonomies were possible for immigrant bodies, labouring bodies, and other bodies?*

Later, as a film programmer, I watched different cinema that again evoked feelings of above and below. In these films, girls who were lost, poor, alone, danced not on stages or on fantastical sets, but in a suspension of time and narrative. In the films of Western European directors like Céline Sciamma, Andrea Arnold and others, dance arrives as puncture, a sharp halt in narrative or story or a signal for a different way of engaging for the viewer.

To me, the dancing girls[2] appeared to be turning the linear arrow of story into a circular carrier, a container, a receptacle – a cradle capable of holding multitudes.

*What happens when we arrange our movements not at the service of narrative or the interruption of it? What if movement comes before language, and language is only at the service of movement?*

In 2020, dance scholars Anurima Banerji and Royona Mitra edited a special issue of the journal *Conversations Across the Field of Dance Studies* dedicated to the theme of 'Decolonizing Dance Discourses', framed by critiques of anti-Black racism and caste injustice in dance and dance studies.

In a contribution titled 'Discussing the Undiscussable, Part 2; or, This Might Hurt Your Feelings', Nadine George-Graves shares her hopes to open a conversation on the field's inability to address racism. The piece consists of a short introduction on the impossibility of this conversation, followed by a startling blank page.

I think of this article when I watch Hetain Patel's *Trinity* (2021). A mother speaks to her daughter in Gujarati, her daughter replies in English, they repeat. Every time something is lost. It is only when her mother sees her move her body, imagining something that she had also imagined, and that others had imagined before her, that we see a connection.

III

*'Continue walking, one foot forward, another foot forward, one step back.'* – Ashanti Harris

In June 2022, I participated in Ashanti Harris' performance *An Archive: The Rehearsal*, a collaboration with Mele Broomes (the dancer in Alberta Whittle's *RESET*, 2020). Harris and Broomes conceived of the 'moving dancing body as a repository of incorporated histories; a transformative archive which can only be accessed through the physical teaching and sharing from body to body.'[3] The participatory piece was accompanied by a voice-over riffing on the phrase 'one step forward and two steps back', inviting us to move to the instructions of the phrase in an effort to find new meaning in it.

Like in *Form(s) of Life* (2021), Éric Minh Cuong Castaing's work with palliative care patients with degenerative ilnesses, Harris' performance took place outside, in between trees that rustled the music of leaves and bathed us in viridescent light. Alone together in nature, we, the participants, like the dancers in *Form(s) of Life,* searched for a way beyond language – towards bodily intuition. Through embodied trust a possibility opened: leading us to a movement we already knew, but sought to know again, differently.

IV

*'Rhythm does not privilege singular ways of being but rather insists in advance, that collaborative engagement is necessary to who and what we are.'*[4] – Katherine McKittrick, Frances H. O'Shaughnessy, Kendall Witaszek

Jamaican novelist, dramatist, critic, philosopher, essayist and dancer Sylvia Wynter has a concept called the 'science of the word'. A heavy idea, loaded with many meanings and theoretical underpinnings, it is also fluid, connecting and un-disciplining, rather than delimiting and defining.

A form of theorising that offers a dance rather than an argument.

Reframing the work of theory as dance provides us with an invitation not just to reimagine narrative, or character, but to draw attention – through a new kinetic register – to the ways that we (the spectator, the dancer, the writer, the director, the actor, the character) might make meaning together; what Katherine McKittrick, scholar and friend of Wynter calls 'a witnessing through rather than witnessing about'.

As a writer who sometimes dances, but does not consider themselves a dancer, I struggle to convey the affect of dancing moments, significant exactly because they reveal the ways that life is composed of so many instances where language fails us and when something else, an embodied or spiritual connection, must be sought.

It is hard to be a writer and to begin to lose faith in words, but perhaps to be a writer with a healthy distrust of words is to write (or not write) like a dancer. Perhaps to dance-write is to understand the capacious nature of language, to understand that poetry is birthed in the space where narrative is interrupted and kinetic registers enter. It is akin to the moments that film turns into a dance and dance turns into poetry.

Wordlessness as a dancer is a rhythm with which to rewire and remix our understanding. This sense-making is not written outside the body of the spectator, as plot or story, but within it – a form of embodied knowledge woven together through different acts of moving, making and watching. Wordlessness turned into dance, turned into rhythm, invites collaboration.

In *Les Gayrillères* (2022), the artist duo Pauline Boudry and Renate Lorenz restrain the ways that film elicits movement contagion. Using music sparingly and allowing light only through light fixtures attached to the dancers' costumes, they use dance to explore not just a unification or coherence but autonomy and opacity. These techniques expand what movement can invite us to do on screen. An alternative bidding, an alternative cognitive schema: if not traditional narrative then at least with the intention and awareness of the ways that ethical relations can be conducted by and with the body.

V

*'I am waiting for them to stop talking about the "other", to stop even describing how important it is to be able to speak about differences… This "we" is that "us" in the margins, that "we" who inhabit marginal space that is not a site of domination but a place of resistance. Enter that space.'*[5] – bell hooks

In *Disidentifications: Queers of Color and the Performance of Politics* theorist José Esteban Muñoz describes the political encoding of queer performance:

> There is a certain lure to the spectacle of one queer standing on stage alone, with or without props, bent on the project of opening up a world of queer language, lyricism, perceptions, dreams, visions, aesthetics and politics. Solo performance speaks to the reality of being queer at this particular moment.[6]

*Faz Que Vai* (Set to Go, 2015) by Bárbara Wagner and Benjamin de Burca is named after a frevo step (a dance and musical style originating from Recife, traditionally associated with Brazilian Carnival). The word frevo means 'to boil', evoking the image of crabs thrown into a pot of boiling water. In his book *Frevo, Capoeira e "Passo"*, Valdemar de Oliveira writes, 'Frevo doesn't invite you. It drags you. Its effervescent rhythm is something magnetic, against which it is difficult to resist.'[7]

Recognised as an important part of Brazilian history, in 2012 frevo was included in UNESCO's Representative List of Intangible Cultural Heritage. It is also a dance of resistance, able to narrate complex notions of identity beyond recognised national cultural configurations. In Wagner and de Burca's film, the social norms of frevo are upended through the gender fluidity of four dancers who bring together elements from capoeira, drag and voguing.

If dance encapsulates body, action, space, time and energy, then in *Faz Que Vai* we feel through the frenetic use of all these elements the truth both of bell hooks' assertion that it is in the margins that there is a space of radical openness and of Muñoz's observation on the 'lure' of queer spectacle. In the film we are commanded into this space even as we know this openness cannot fully be felt second-hand.

It is only through dancing *with*, playing *with* or even fighting *with* one another that such a dance of resistance can truly be actualised.

VI

The words 'Pray for a day without plot, a day without narrative' appear in Dionne Brand's book *A Map to the Door of No Return*. Brand says she cannot be sure what these words, written by Saint Lucian poet Derek Walcott, mean, but to her 'they describe perfectly my desire for relief from the persistent trope of colonialism. To be without the story of captivity, to dis-remember it, or to have this story forget me, would be heavenly.'[8]

In a book about maps and bodies, about action and spaces, the passing of time and of energy, Brand's words appear to me like dance appears to me on screen: a gesture towards the possibilities of what a body can imagine that words cannot convey.

The desire to use the body to dis-remember (which is to fail or refuse to remember but never to lose remembrance: not ever to forget) surfaces repeatedly in the works in 'Moving Bodies, Moving Images'.

In Alia Farid's work *At the Time of the Ebb* (2019) a man excitedly dances on screen. Alongside the other performances of local residents on the Iranian island of Qeshm during the celebration of Nowruz Sayadeen (Fishermen's New Year), he is performing a local custom and tradition but this was not immediately apparent to the filmmaker, whose interaction with this dancing passed through multiple formats before its significance (re)appeared to her:

> I met Farzad buying a watermelon. He saw me struggling to count the money I had and figured I wasn't from the island. He asked what I was doing and I signalled that I was filming by holding up an invisible camera. [...] We exchanged phone numbers and later that night he sent me a video of him dancing in a

room much like in *At the Time of the Ebb*. I thought it was a strange thing to send someone you just met and became unsure about working with him. The next morning, he showed up and tagged along all day and again in the days that followed. He knew Baba Gholam, the owner of the house with the pink room where I filmed the indoor scenes—everyone knew everyone—and at some point he got in front of the camera while we were all in the next room having tea and began shimmying. He'd been wanting to dance for the camera the whole time. I later understood that dancing for guests was a form of hospitality, and remembered it was also something practiced in the Gulf before the advent of oil and modernity. I didn't have a script or strict idea of what I was there to film. I was interested in learning and being shown, and with that, remembering.[9]

In Whittle's *RESET*, a man repeatedly performs a dance beneath a car with Cuban registration plates. I watched this section, transfixed, but unable to name his movement. I moved my body through the same motions: arching my back, moving up and then down.

As I moved, my mouth formed 'limbo'.

On the significance of limbo to the film, British-Barbadian visual artist, writer and researcher Harvey Dimond writes:

> Whittle's disruption of historical events into contemporary discourse starkly presents us with the afterlives of slavery. One such example is Whittle's incorporation of limbo, a dance which first emerged in Trinidad in the 19th century that recalls the enslaved African people entering the low galleys of a ship while also turning their gaze up towards spirits which have crossed into the next life.[10]

Whittle's film takes mourning as its baseline. Mourning cannot rely on a linear three act structure: it is a never ending circle. Even as it glides upwards towards the heights of somatic and spiritual release, it moves downwards into the depths of anger.

The limbo – presented here as repetition rather than completed action – is movement as puncture. This is puncture not at the service of interrupting the plot of Black grief that cannot be interrupted, or ended, but rather a *punctum* to pin in place a dissensus of feeling – of remembering and dis-remembering.

In this moment we might find all the possibilities of what a moving body on screen is and can be: movement in different directions that remembers captivity even as it reaches beyond it.


1.  Roland Barthes described punctum in photography as 'that accident which pricks me (but also bruises me, is poignant to me)'. Roland Barthes, *Camera Lucida*, translated by Richard Howard (London: Vintage, 1993 [1980]).

2.  Alice Pember, *The Dancing Girl & Contemporary Cinema* (Edinburgh: Edinburgh University Press, forthcoming).

3.  Peter Amoore, '12 Hour Sit-in Revel: Cooper Gallery at Dundee Botanic Garden' (9 August 2022), https://learningspaces.dundee.ac.uk/dundeeuniculture/2022/08/ 09/12-hour-sit-in-revel-cooper-gallery-at- dundee-botanic-garden/

4.  Katherine McKittrick, Frances H. O'Shaughnessy, and Kendall Witaszek, 'Rhythm, or On Sylvia Wynter's Science of the Word', *American Quarterly* 70, no. 4, (December 2019).

5.  bell hooks, 'Choosing the Margin as a Space of Radical Openness', *Framework: The Journal of Cinema and Media* 36 (1989): 15–23.

6.  José Esteban Muñoz, *Disidentifications: Queers of Color and the Performance of Politics* (Minneapolis: University of Minnesota Press, 1999).

7.  Valdemar de Oliveira, *Frevo, capoeira e "passo"* (Recife: Companhia Editôra de Pernambuco, 1985 [2007]).

8.  Dionne Brand, *A Map to the Door of No Return: Notes to Belonging* (New York: Penguin, 2002).

9.  Claire Tancons, 'Conversation with Alia Farid', *Vdrome* (5 May 2020), https://www.vdrome.org/ alia-farid/

10. Harvey Dimond, 'Alberta Whittle: RESET', *Art Monthly* (2020), https://www.artmonthly.co.uk/ magazine/site/article/alberta-whittle-reset-by-harvey-dimond-2020

# Alexandra Bachzetsis
## *An Ideal for Living*, 2018

## Two-channel video, colour, sound; 22:46 minutes

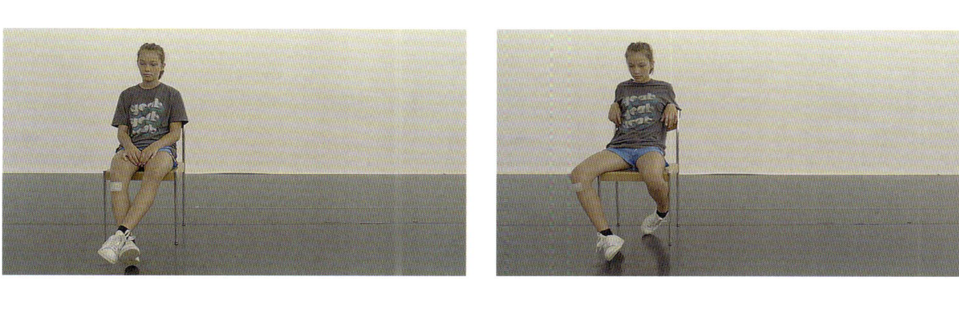
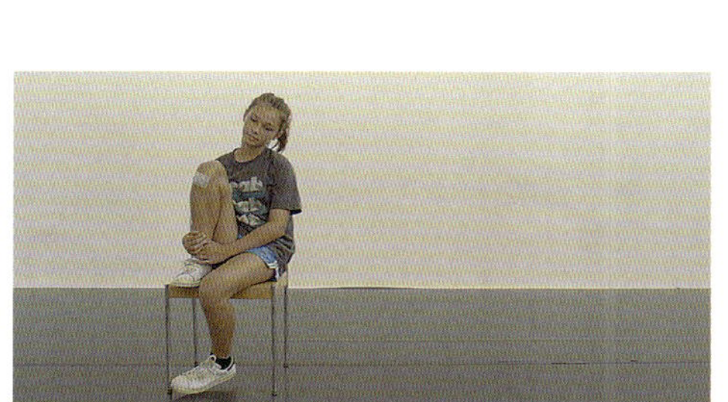
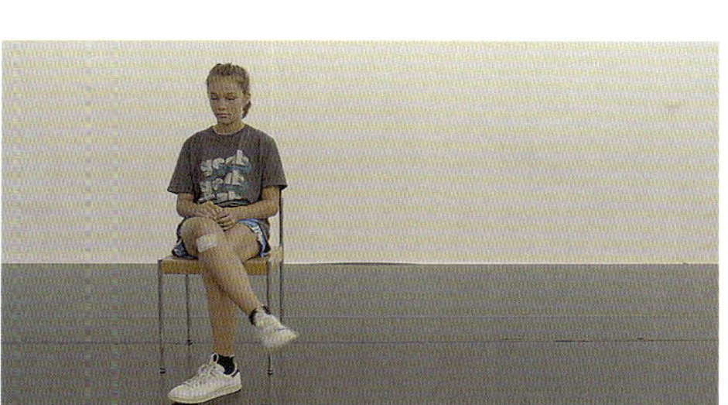
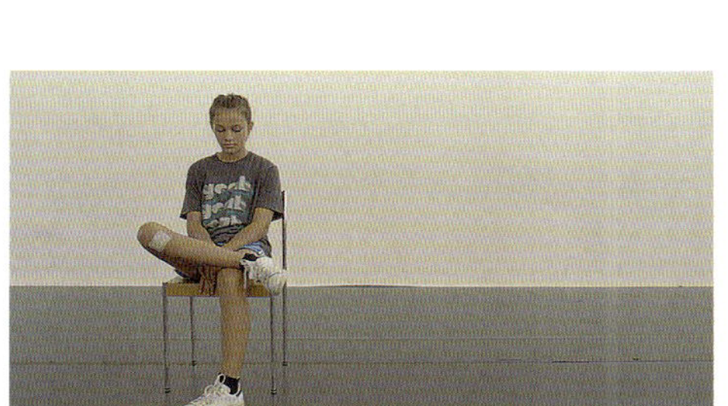
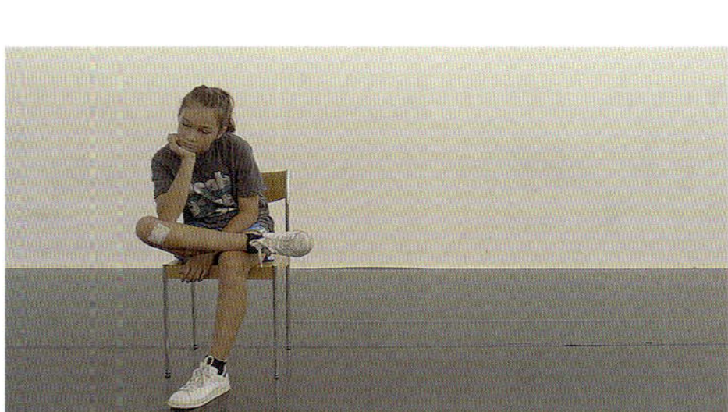

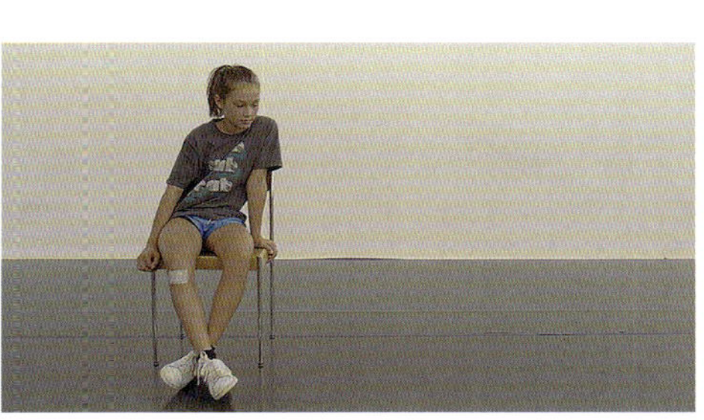
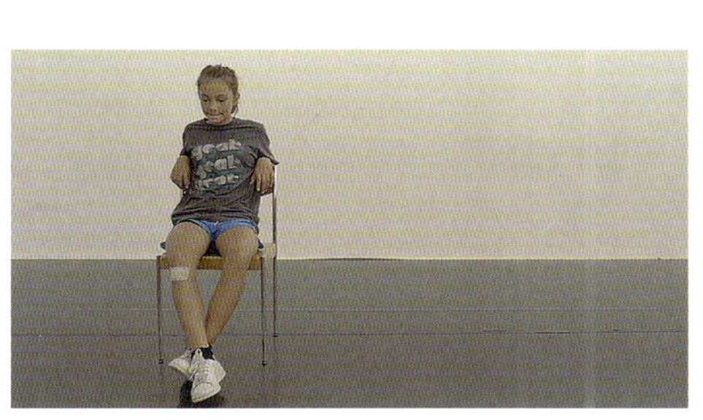
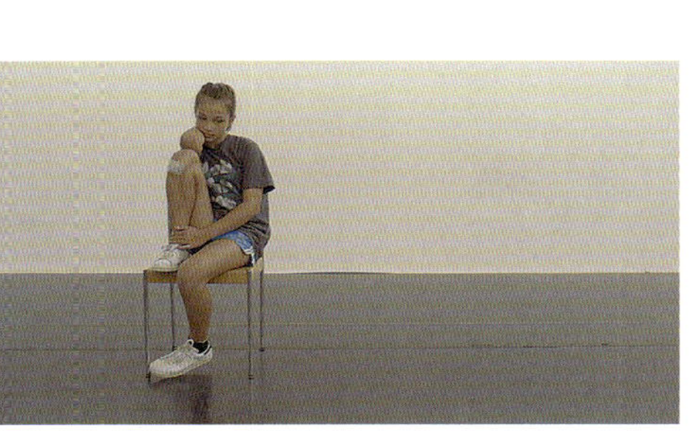

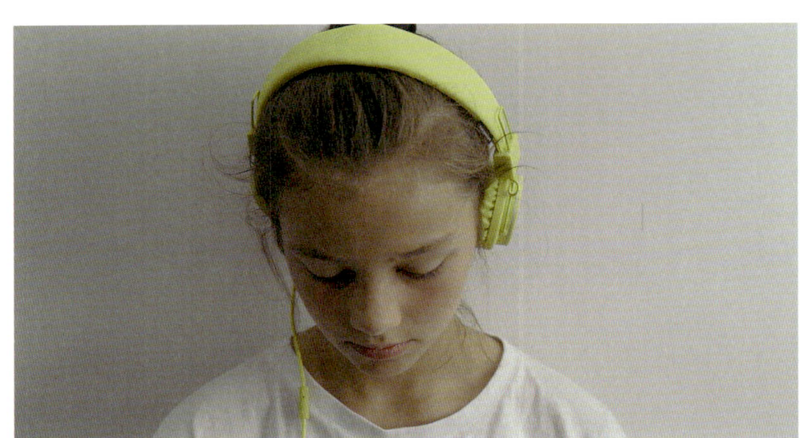
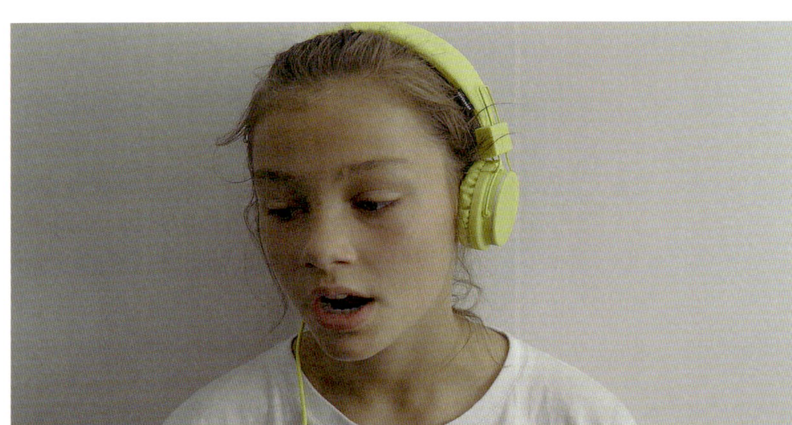
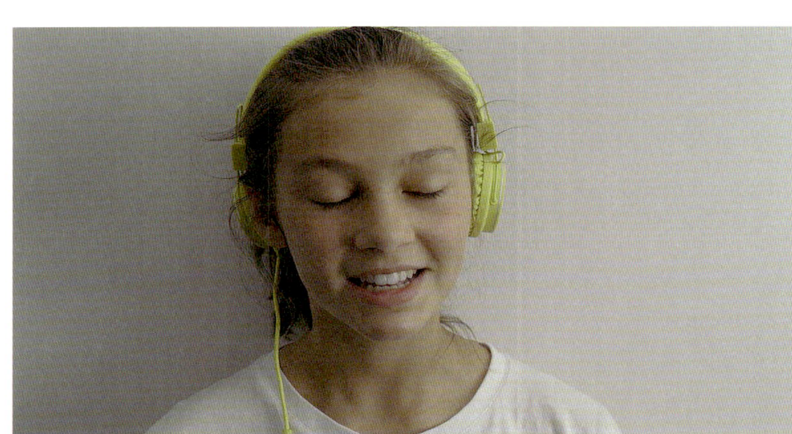
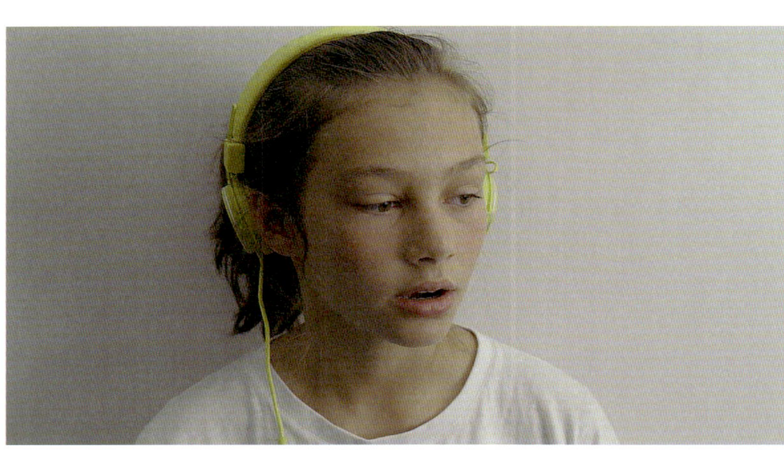

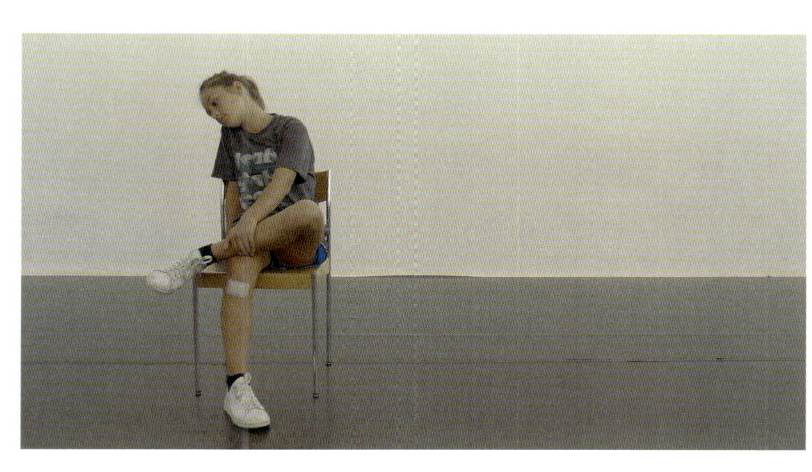
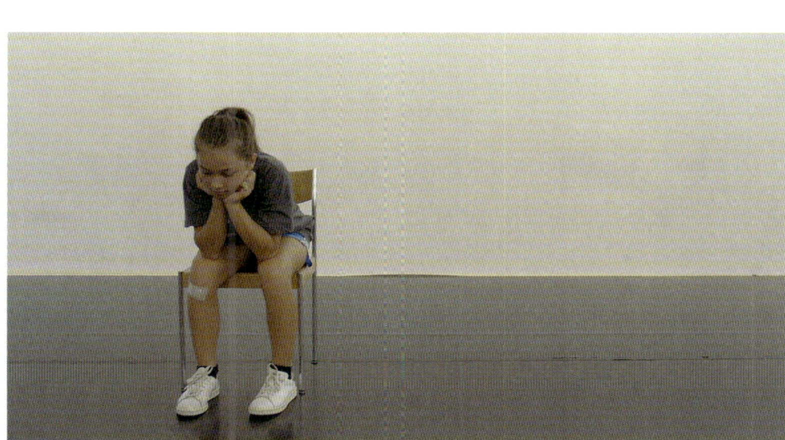
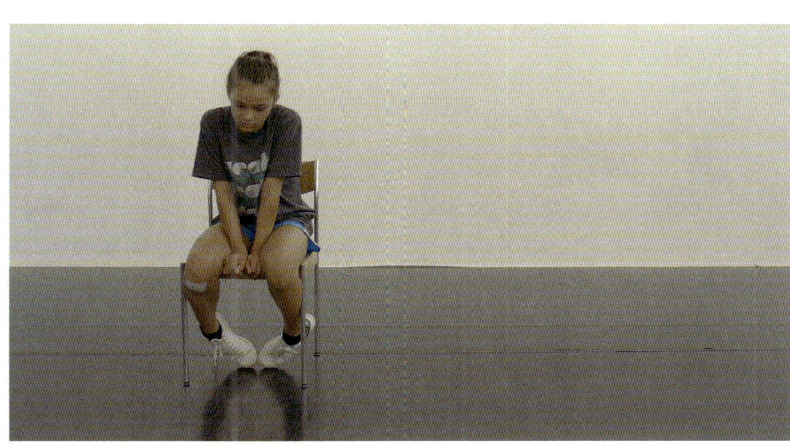
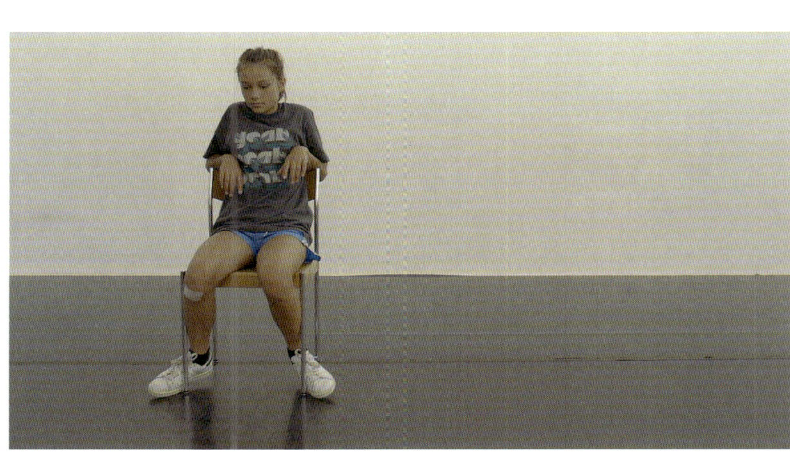

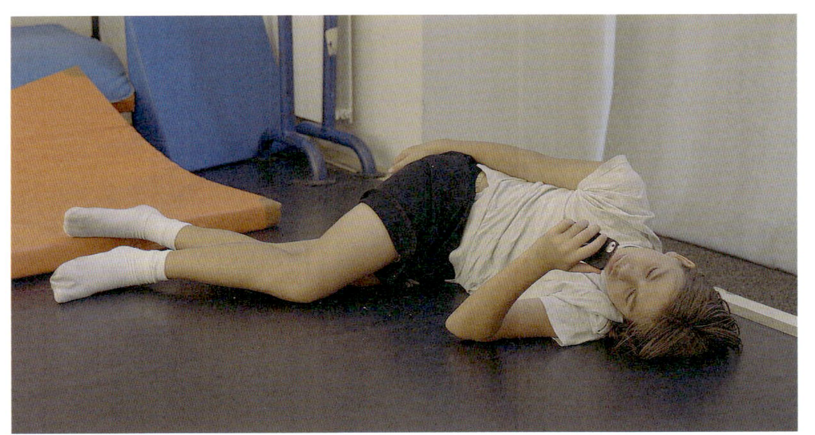

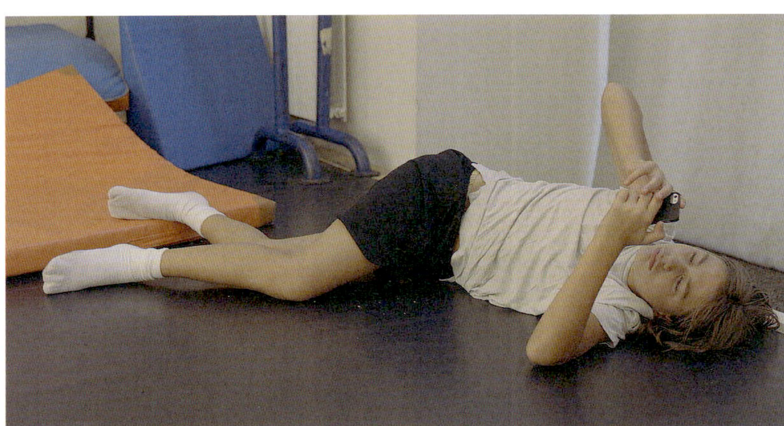

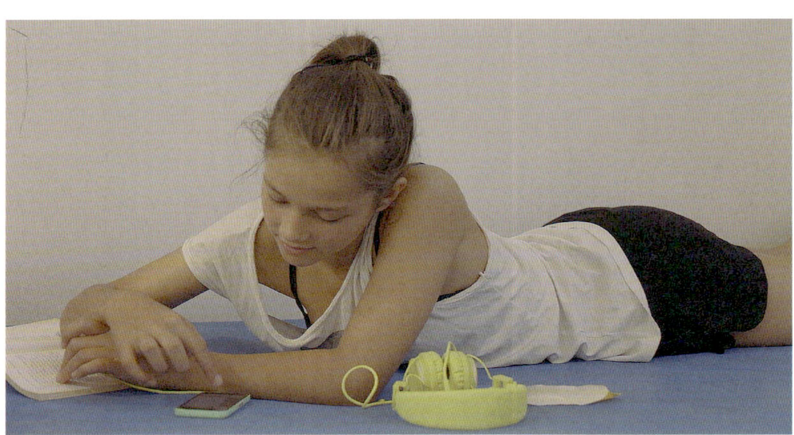

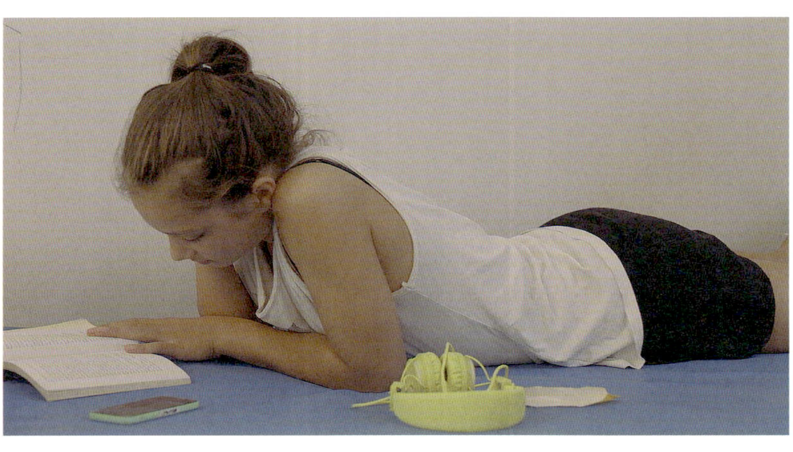

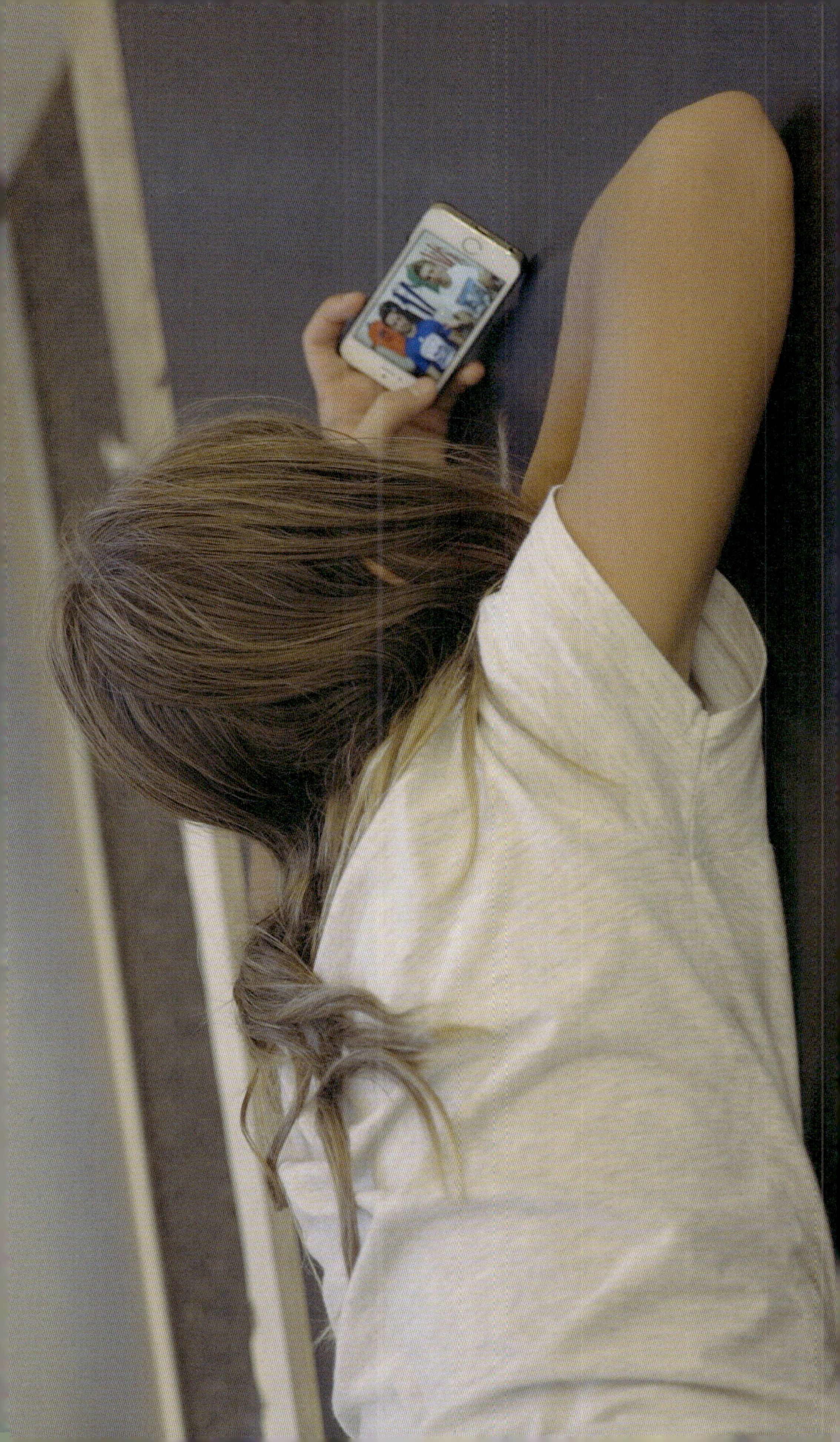

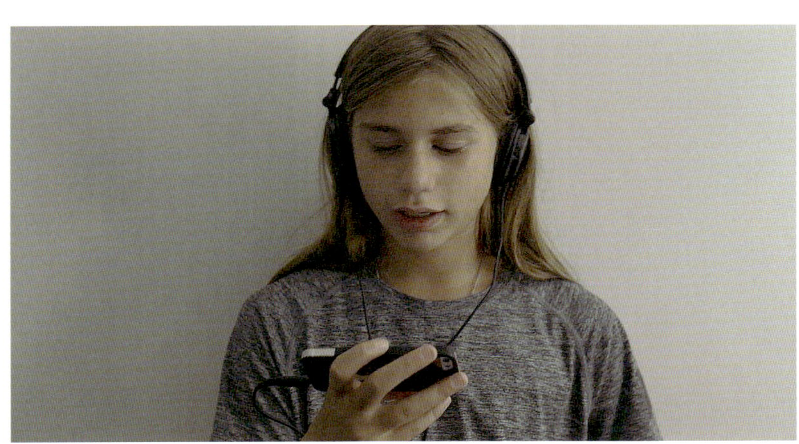

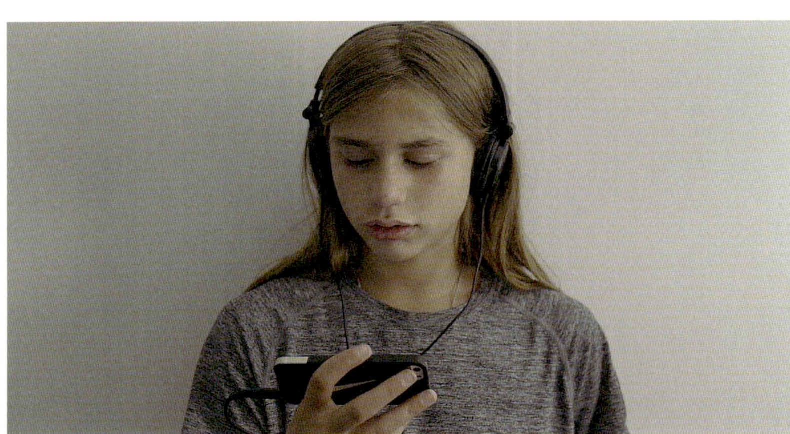

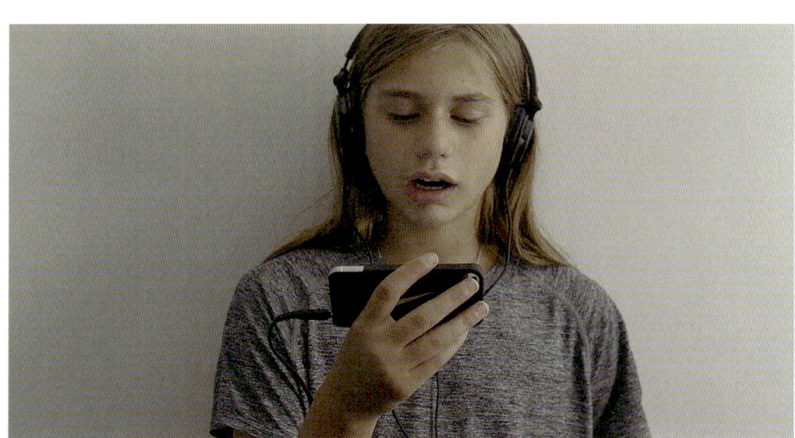

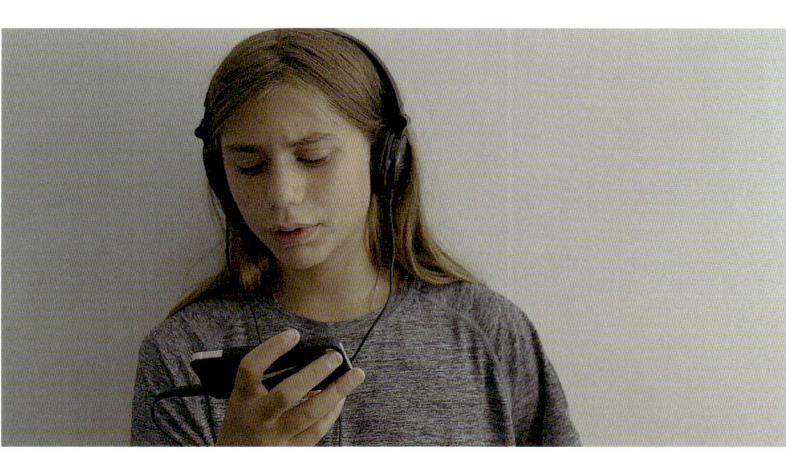

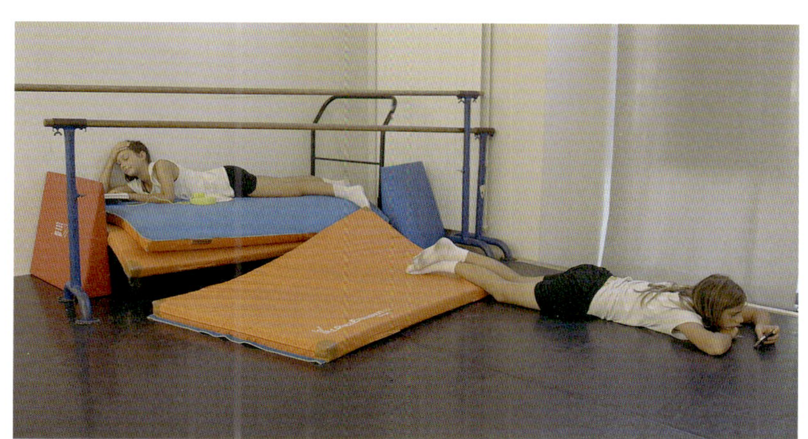

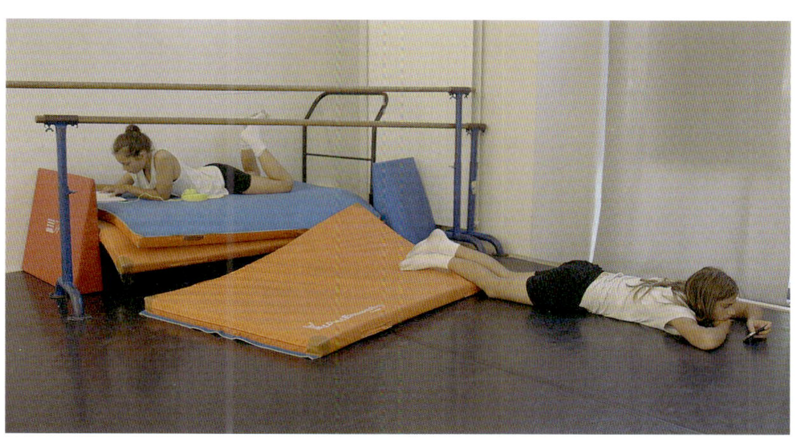

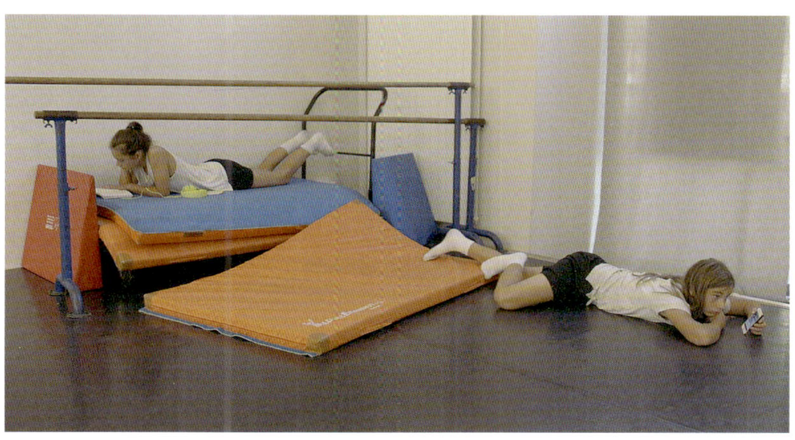

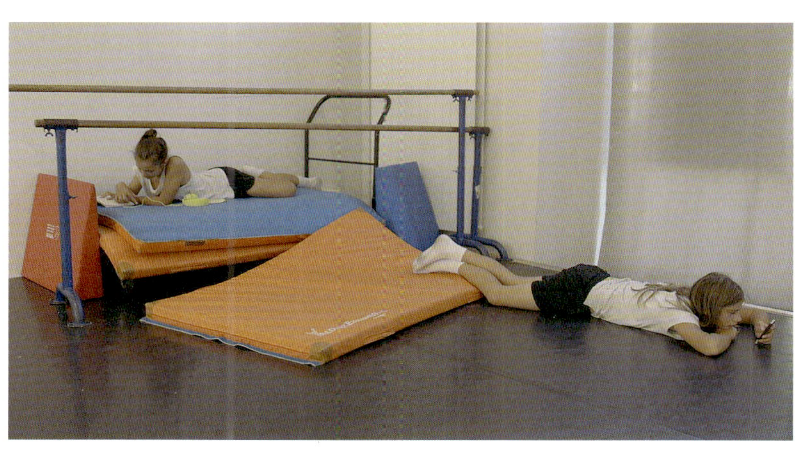

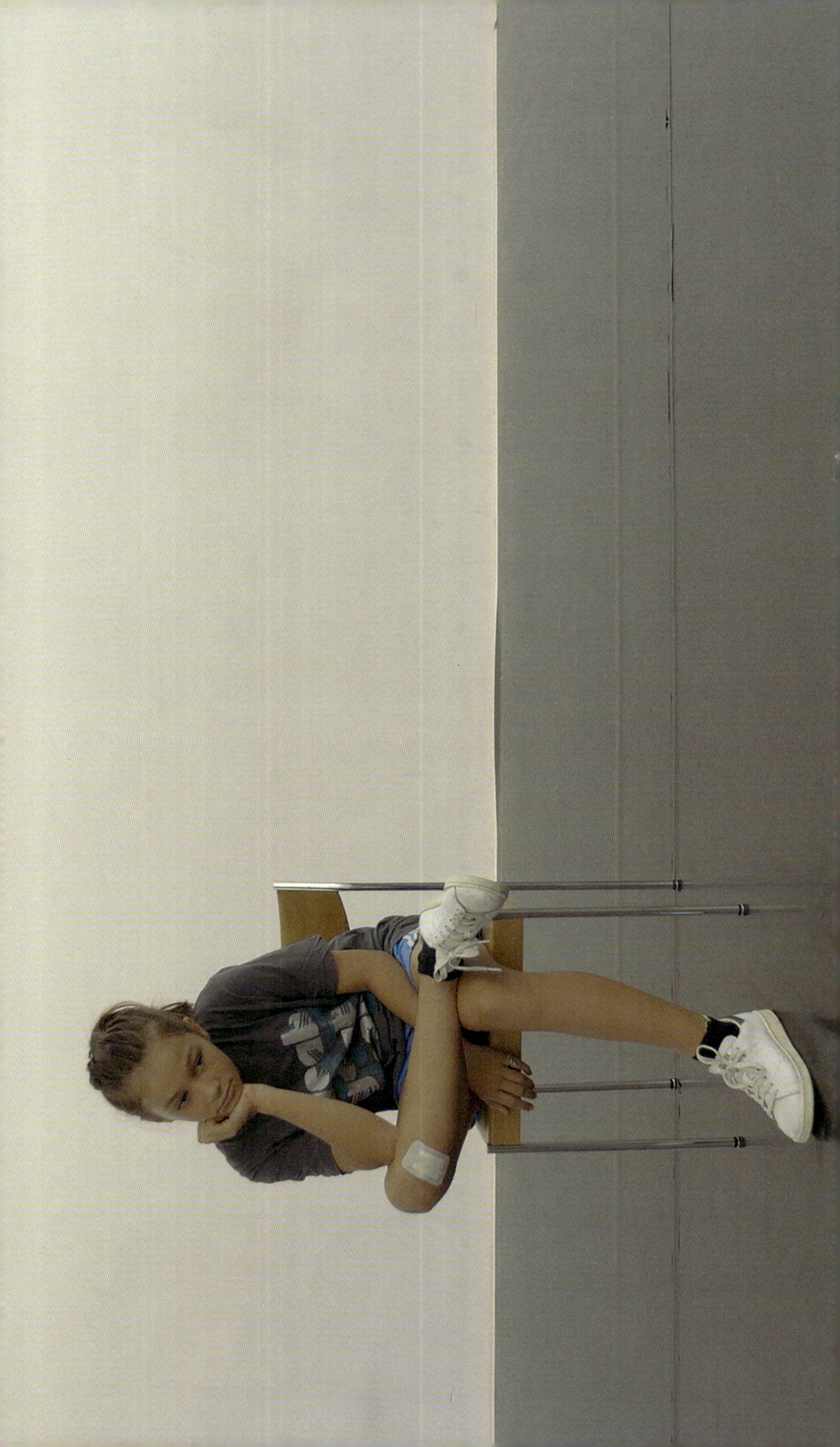

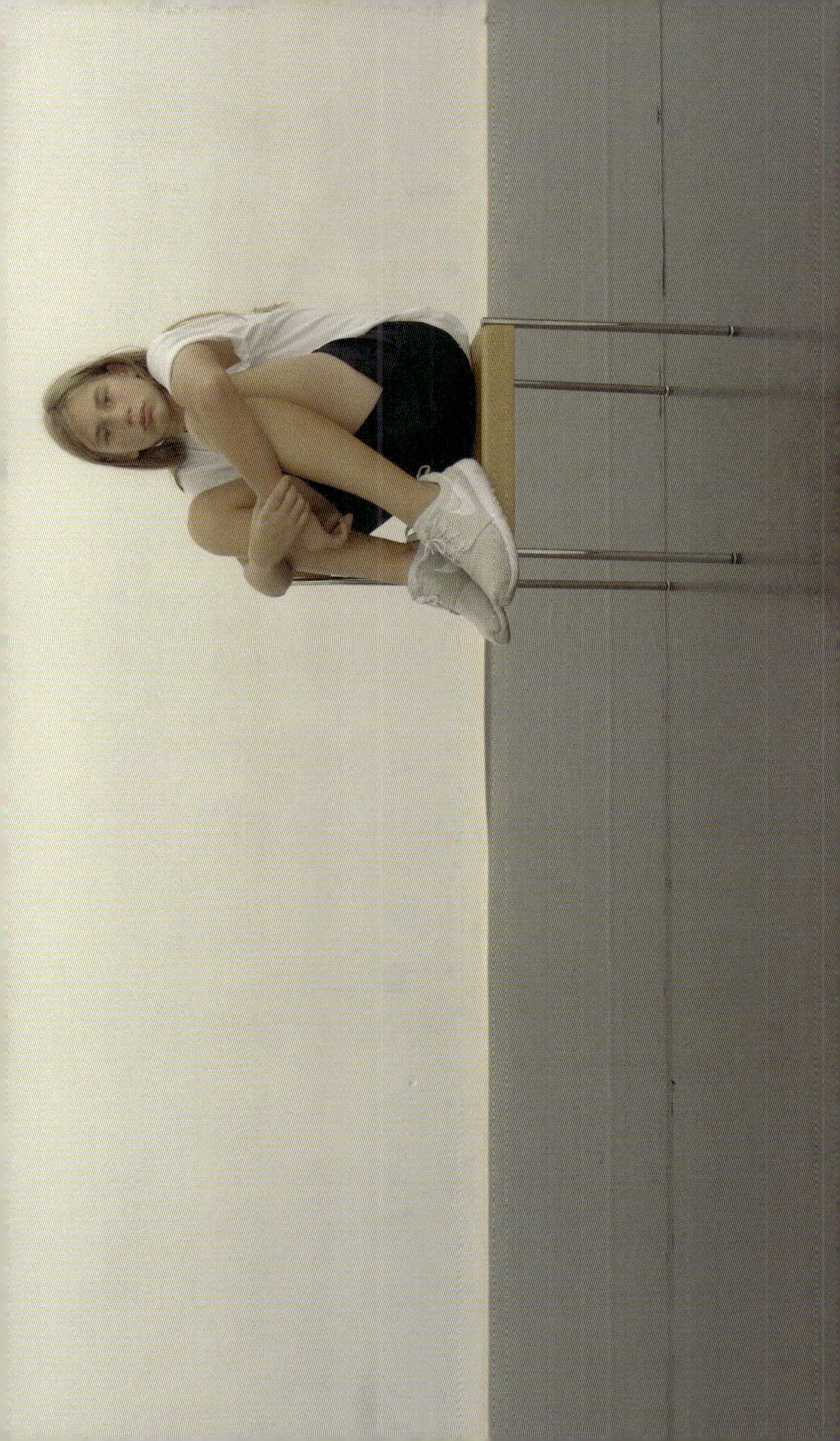

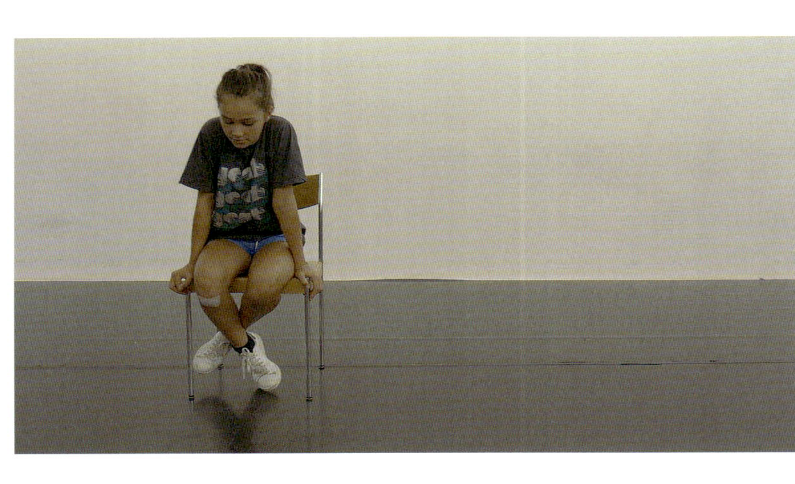

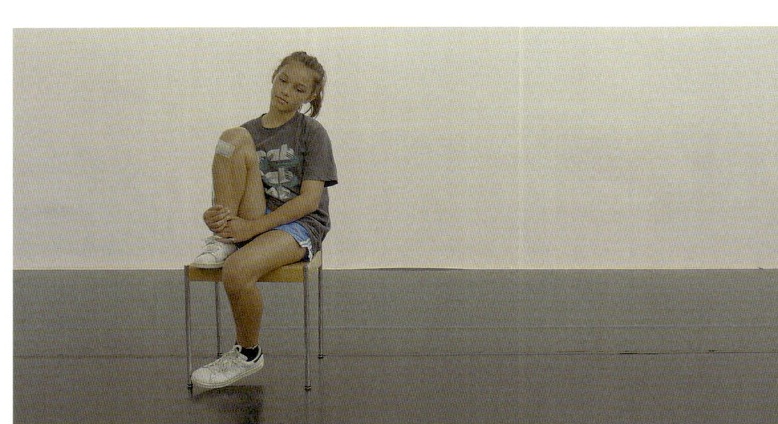

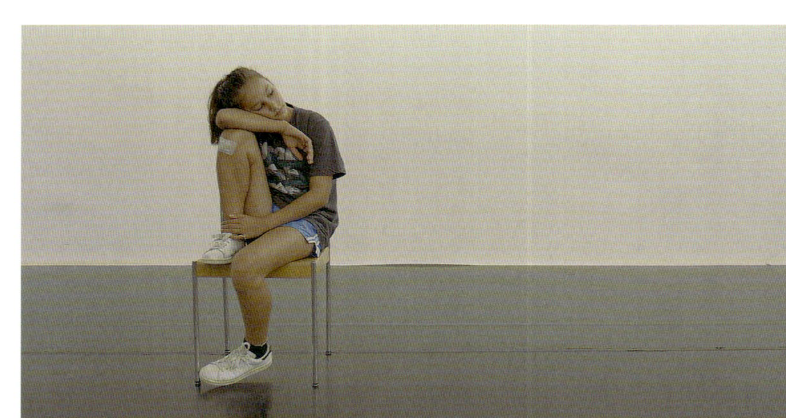

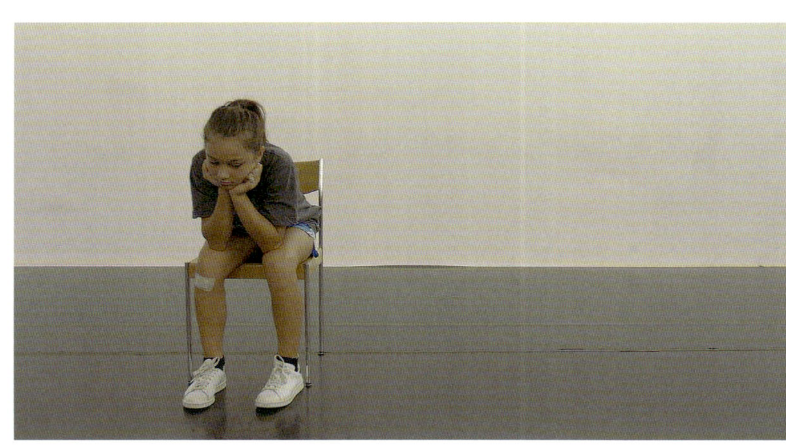

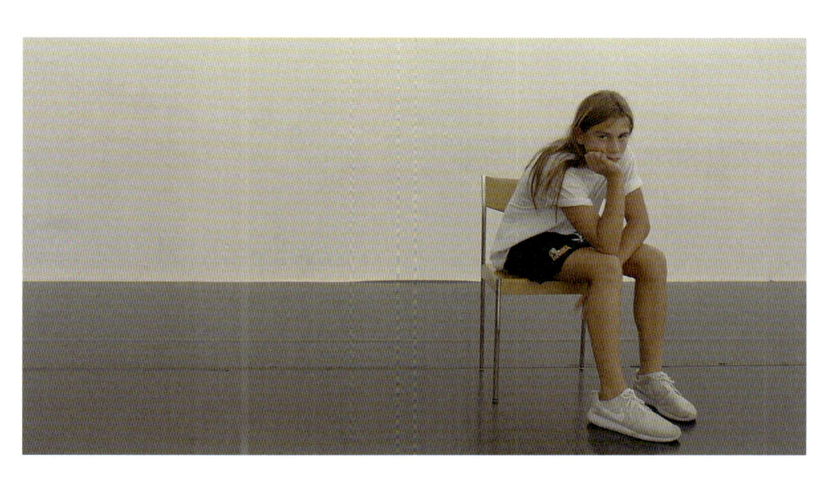

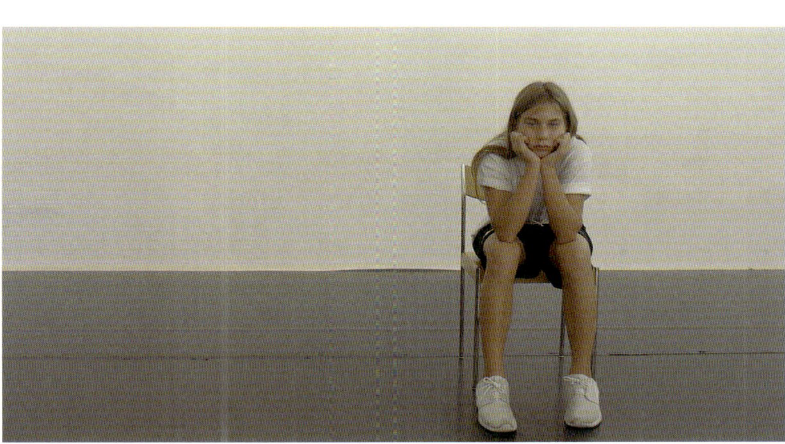

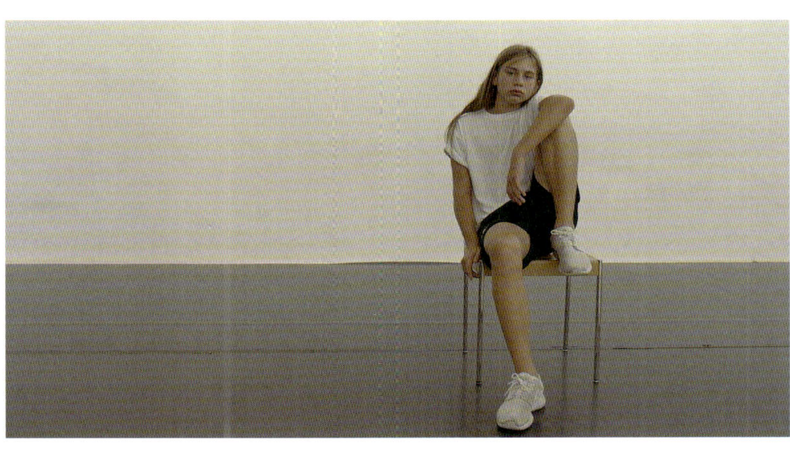

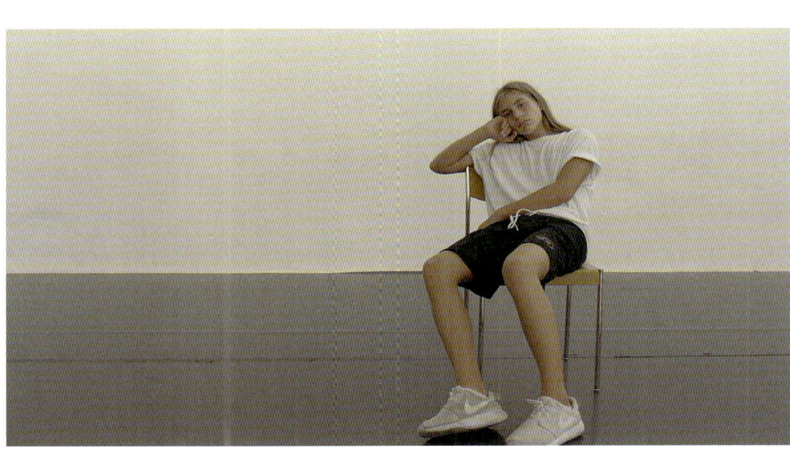

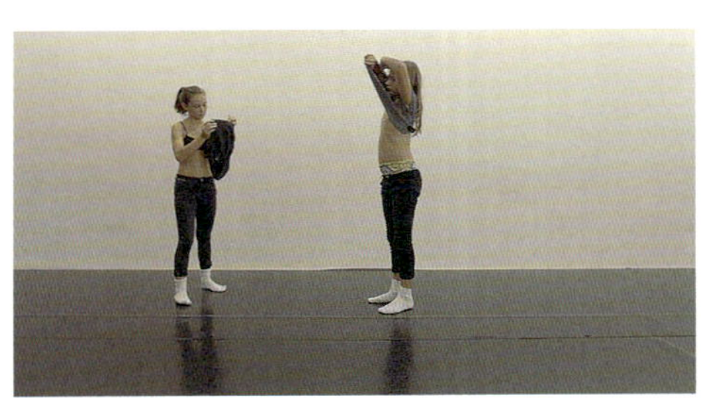
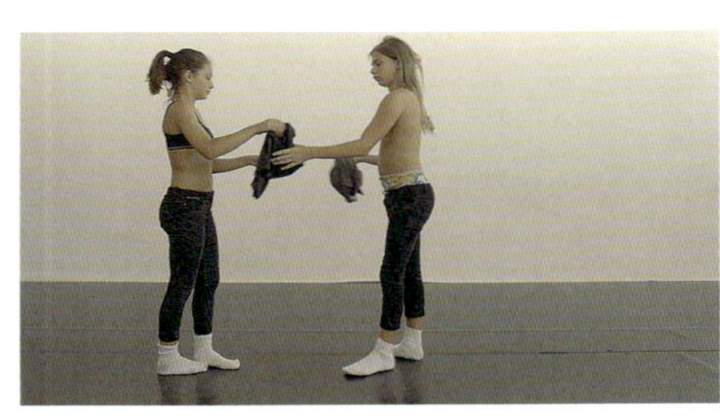
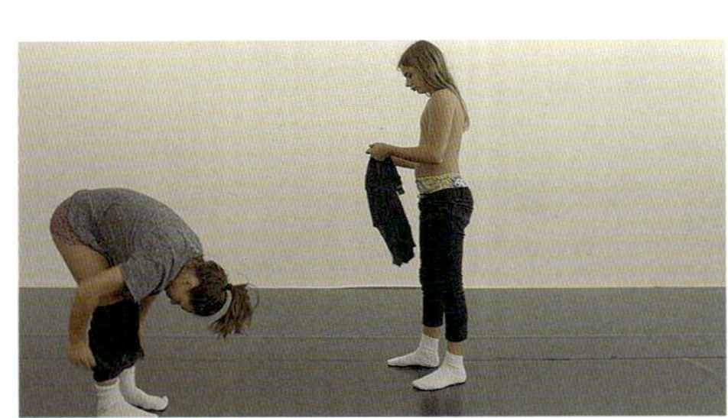
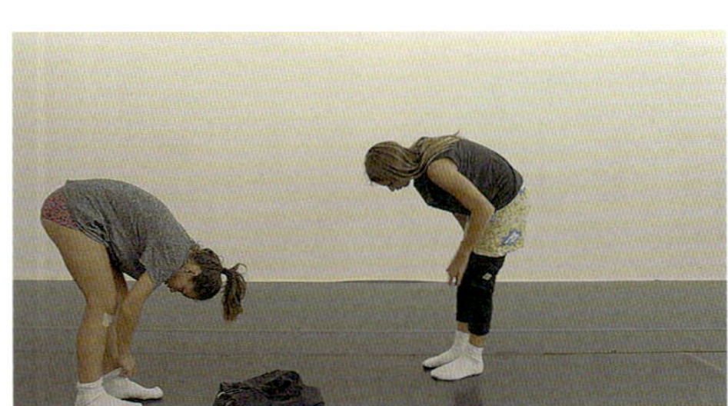
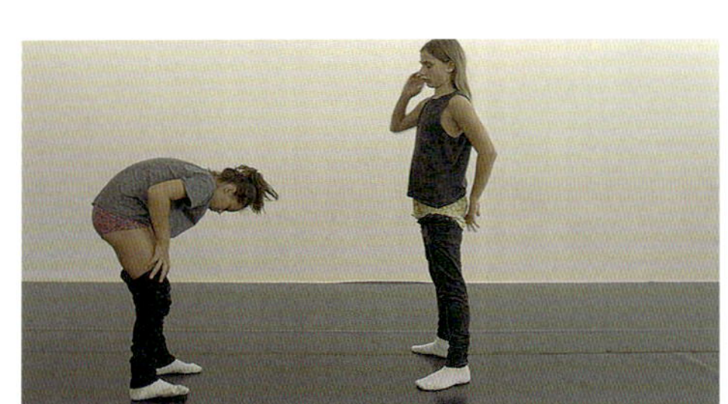
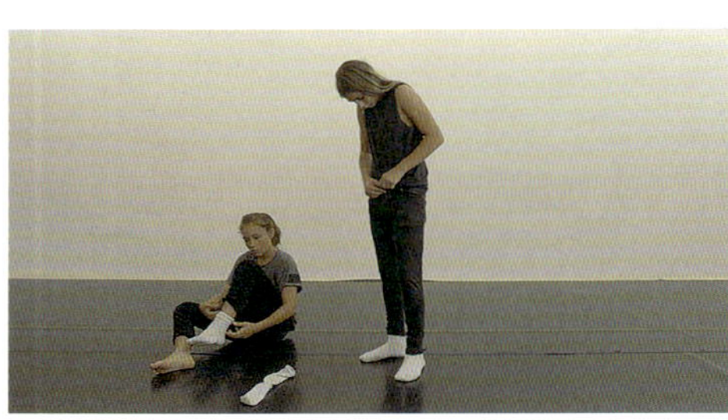
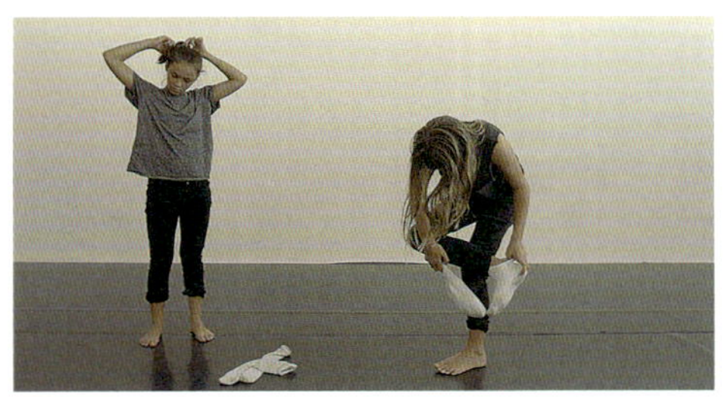
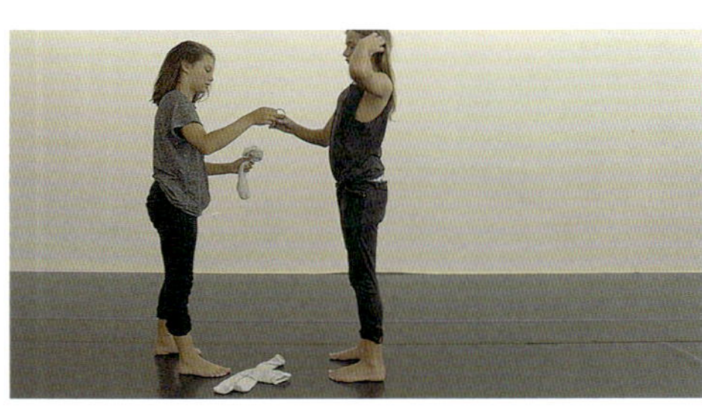

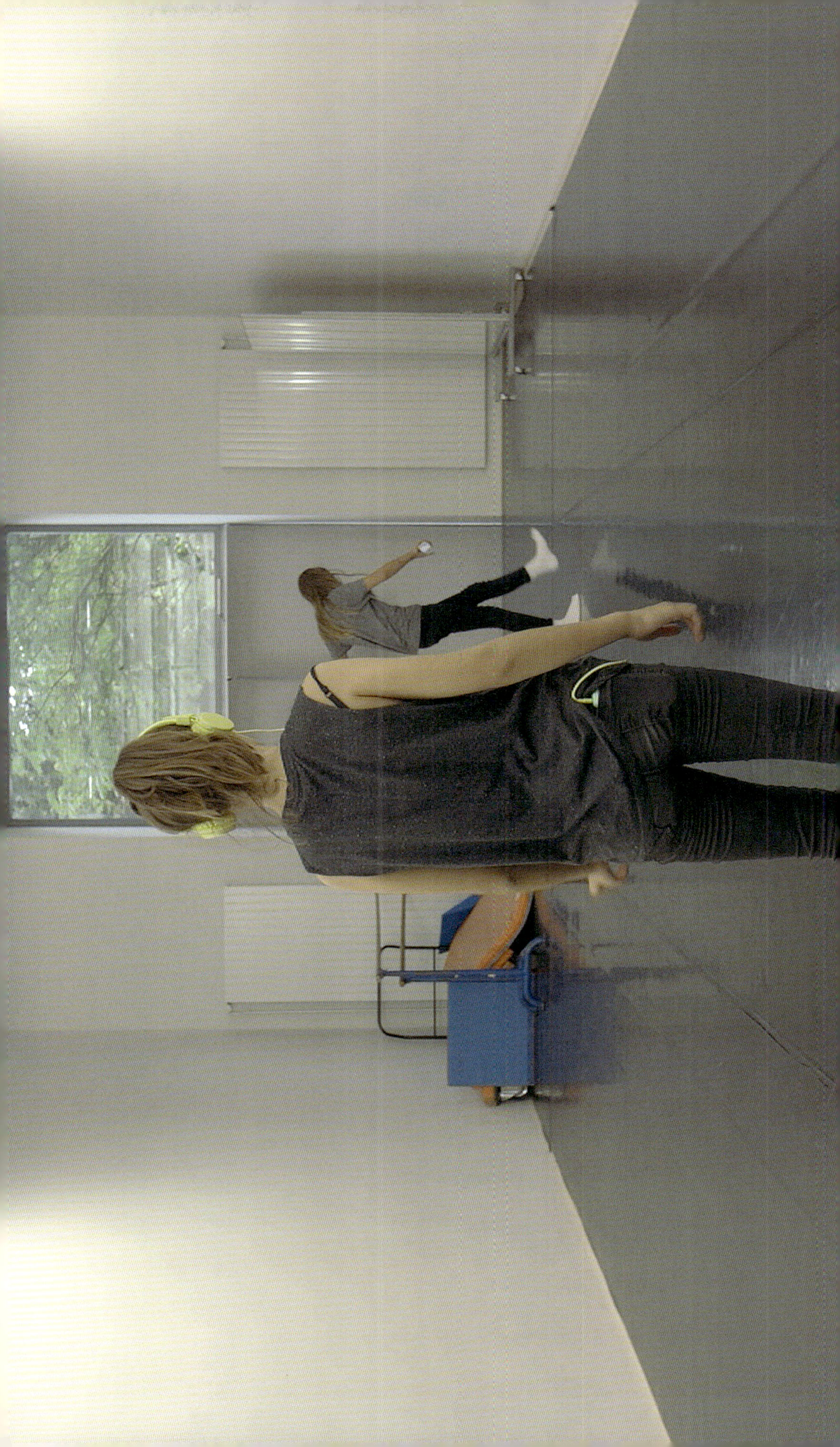

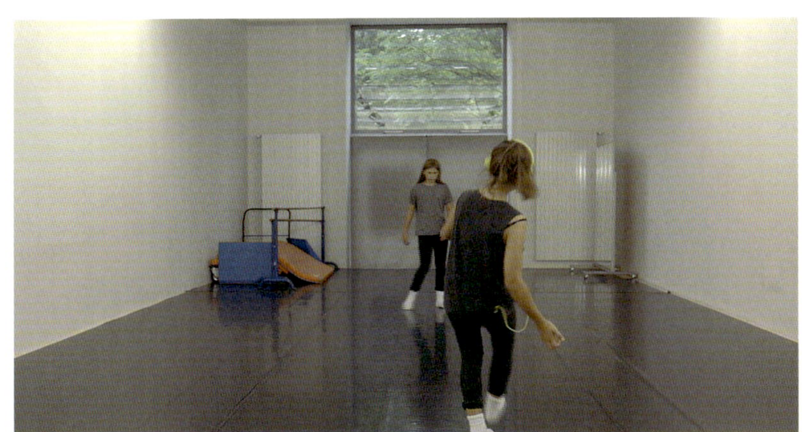

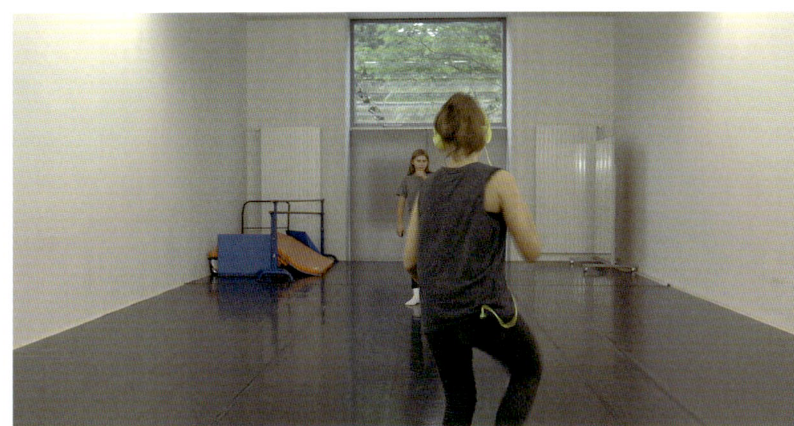

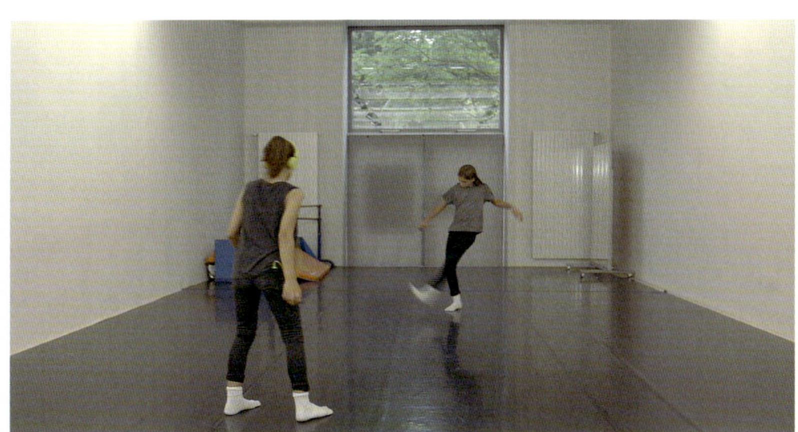

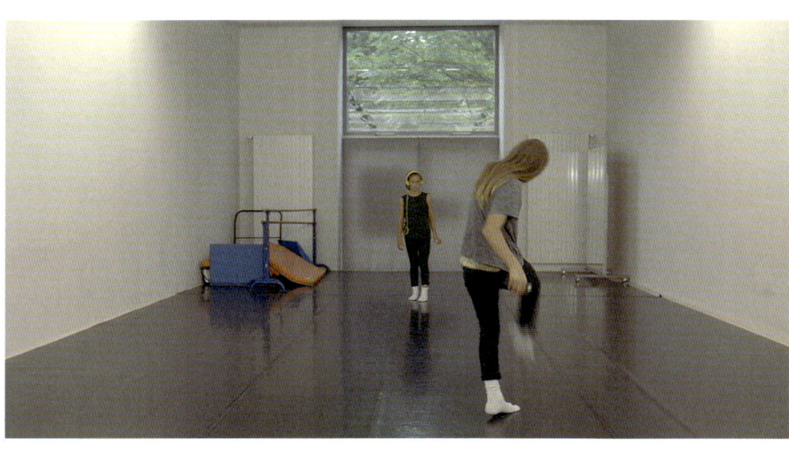

For *An Ideal for Living* (2018), Alexandra Bachzetsis cast two adolescents, one female and one male, to examine gender performance through body language, posture and gesture. Filmed against neutral backgrounds with simple props, such as a chair or gym mats, the two-channel video has the appearance of an anthropological or psychological experiment. In many ways, the two androgynous youths look remarkably similar – both are lanky, have long blonde hair and dress in activewear – yet subtle differences emerge as they perform a series of everyday activities, from sitting in a chair or listening to music and singing along to reading, watching videos or pretending to play football in a gym. The seemingly banal actions slowly unfold across the two screens and invite comparison. Sometimes one of the youths occupies both screens; sometimes they are both in the same frame and sometimes they are seen side by side. The teenage girl fidgets while sitting, restlessly shifting positions in a chair – right foot up with her left hand holding her ankle and her right arm resting on her knee; crossing and uncrossing her legs; leaning forward with her hands supporting her head and her elbows propped on her knees. Her body language is self-conscious, her posture contained. By contrast, her male counterpart sits with a more open, relaxed posture and has a much more casual demeanour.

Bachzetsis' video is related to the task-oriented experiments of the 1960s by Trisha Brown, Simone Forti, Yvonne Rainer and other Judson Dance Theater choreographers who used scores and everyday movements and gestures in dance. She also drew inspiration from Marianne Wex's 1979 book *'Let's Take Back Our Space': "Female" and "Male" Body Language as a Result of Patriarchal Structures*, based on her 1977 photographic project in which Wex collected thousands of images of female and male figures from German newspapers, fashion magazines, advertising and art history, as well as photographs she took in the streets of Hamburg, grouping them to reveal how body language has been shaped by gender conventions over millennia. Wex's photo essay builds a rigorous argument, but she also includes the occasional outlier, a figure who does not fit these norms, and also suggests that body language changed over the centuries as patriarchal structures evolved. Writing about Wex's project, the critic David Campany has noted, 'The few groups of children and young adolescents are very telling, we can sense how the gender and sexuality-neutral body language of early youth is soon conventionalized into familiar patterns.'[1]

The two adolescents in *An Ideal for Living* are starting to assume these gendered patterns, particularly when their relationship to the camera is very proximate. In a close-up, the girl, wearing chartreuse yellow headphones and a white T-shirt, sings along to 'Demons' (2013) by the American pop rock band Imagine Dragons; she appears to have memorised the lyrics and her performance seems rehearsed. Casually singing along to A\$AP Rocky's 'Ghetto Symphony' (2013), the boy has not committed the rap lyrics to memory and is unselfconsciously reading them off his phone. When both are involved in the more generic task of swapping nearly identical items of clothing, they are less cognizant of the camera and their gestures and movements are less distinct.

Are gestures learned? Are they enacted in accordance with gender expectations? Does the presence of the camera or an audience have an effect on the degree to which gender stereotypes are performed? Have these conventions become ingrained in choreography? Bachzetsis provides a set of AirTrack gym mats for viewers to sit on while watching *An Ideal for Living*. By doing so, she is also giving viewers the opportunity to assume their own poses or observe the body language and gestures of others.

Lydia Yee

---

1. David Campany, 'Marianne Wex: Let's Take Back Our Space, 1979', *Aperture* no. 213 (Winter 2013).

Alexandra Bachzetsis, *An Ideal for Living*, installation view, Centre Cultural Suisse, Paris, 2018
Alexandra Bachzetsis, *Catapult*, installation view, Centre Cultural Suisse, Paris, 2018

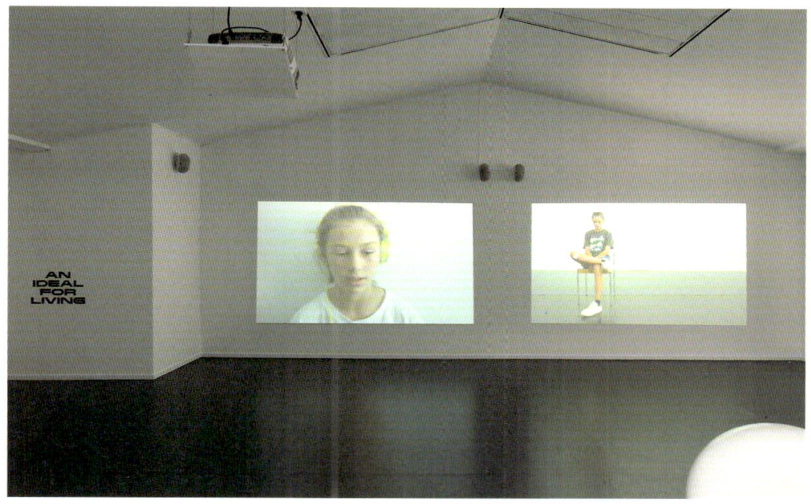


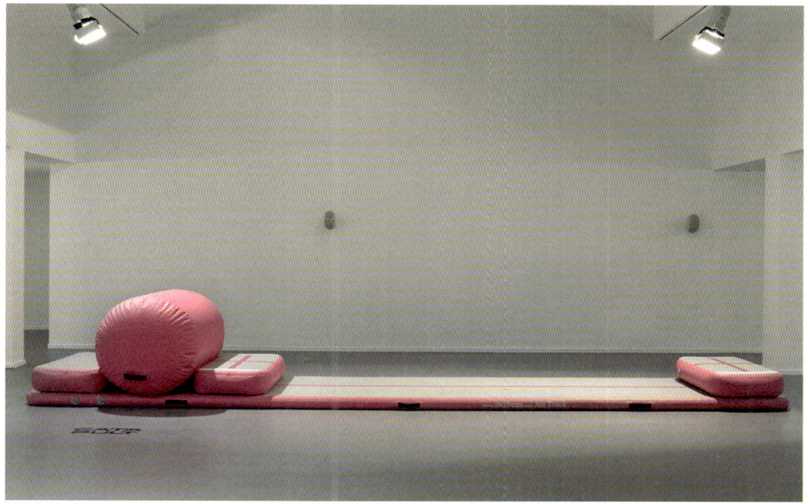

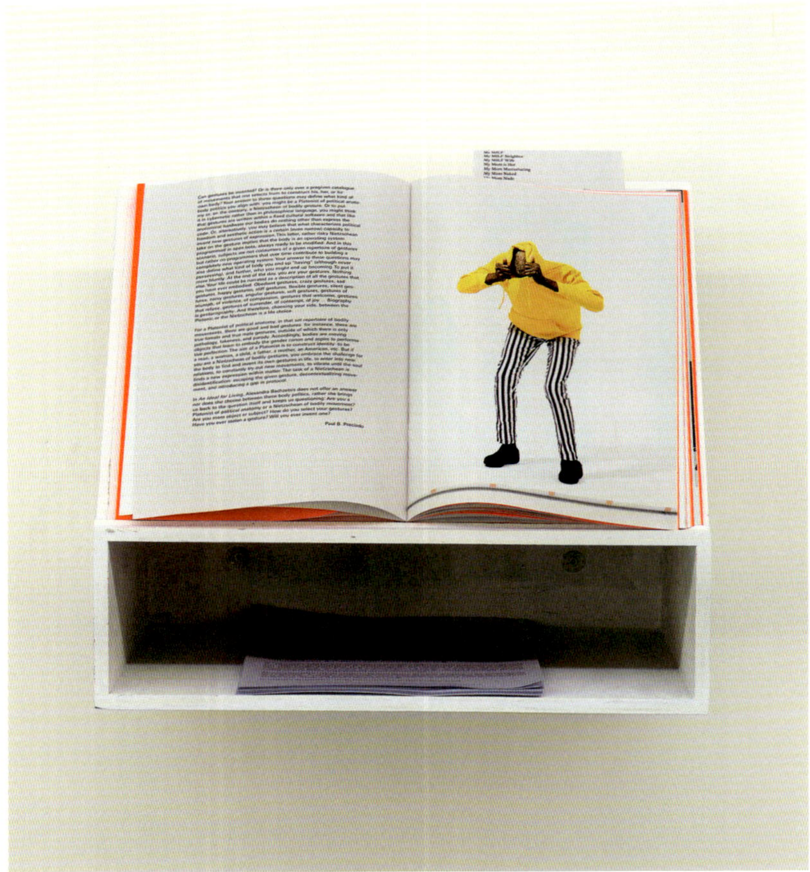

Marianne Wex

# 'LET'S TAKE BACK OUR SPACE'

## "Female" and "Male" Body Language as a Result of Patriarchal Structures

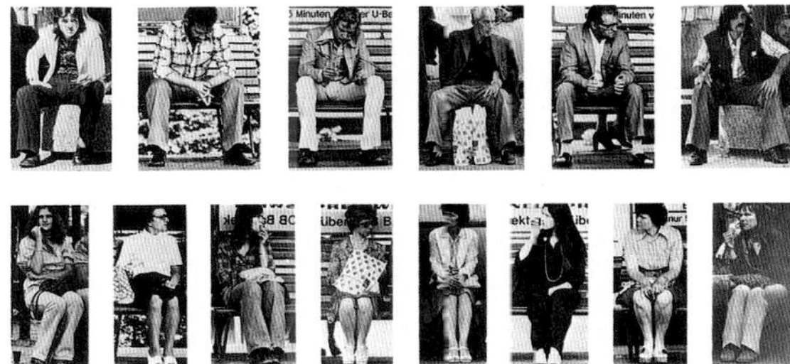

with 2037 photographs

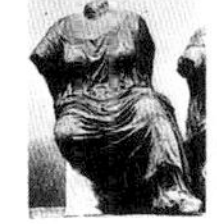
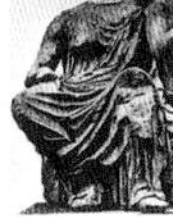
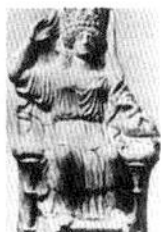

In the second part of the book:

Man's struggle against womanpower and the effects upon body language throughout the course of history.

39

Arm and hand positions

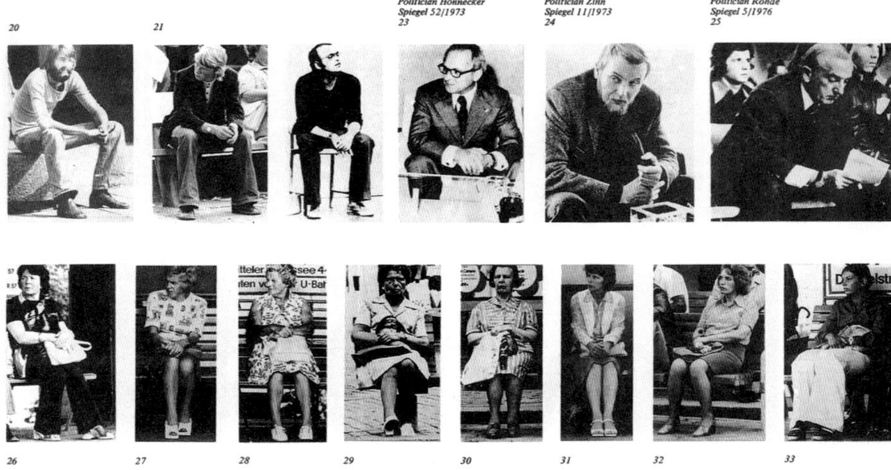



20    21

26    27    28    29    30    31    32    33

54

**Greek sculptures. Seated figures.**

*About 580 BOT*
*Figure of a man,*
*London*
*British Museum*
*1*

*About 500 BOT*
*Dionysus,*
*Athens,*
*National Museum*
*2*

*About 500 BOT*
*Zeus,*
*Athens,*
*National Museum*
*3*

*About 470 BOT*
*so-called Orpheus,*
*Leningrad,*
*Erimitage*
*4*

*460 - 450 BOT*
*Zeus,*
*Palermo,*
*National Museum*
*5*

*About 440 BOT*
*Poseidon and Apollo,*
*Athens,*
*Acropolis Museum*
*6*

*About 410 BOT*
*Xeniades,*
*Athens,*
*National Museum*
*7*

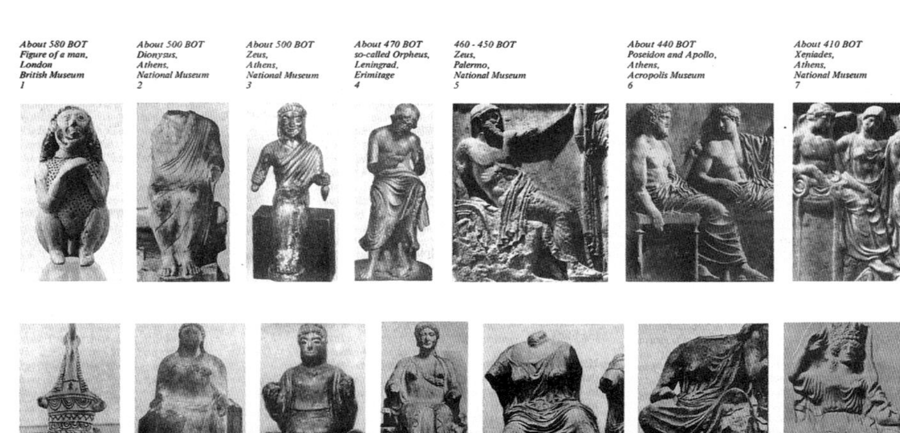

*14*
*About 580 BOT*
*Goddess statuette,*
*London,*
*British Museum*

*15*
*About 570 BOT*
*One of the Branchides*
*from the holy street lead-*
*ing to the Apollo temple*
*in Didyma by Miletus,*
*London,*
*British Museum*

*16*
*About 500 BOT*
*Demeter,*
*Athens,*
*National Museum*

*17*
*About 480 BOT*
*Goddess from*
*Tarentum,*
*East Berlin,*
*Staatl. Museum*

*18*
*About 440 BOT*
*Hestia,*
*East gable of the Parthenon*
*London,*
*British Museum*

*19*
*About 440 BOT*
*Demeter,*
*Eastern gable of the*
*Parthenon, London*
*British Museum*

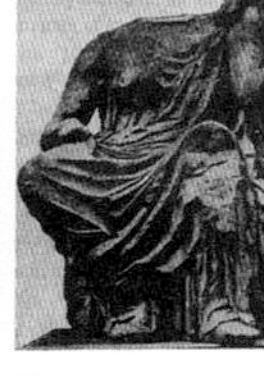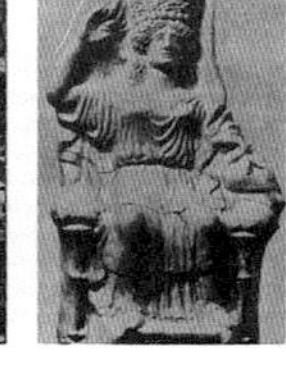

*20*
*After 400 BOT*
*Aphrodite,*
*Syracuse,*
*Museo Nazionale*
*Archeologico*

(BOT = before our time reckoning,
IOT = in our time reckoning)

238

40

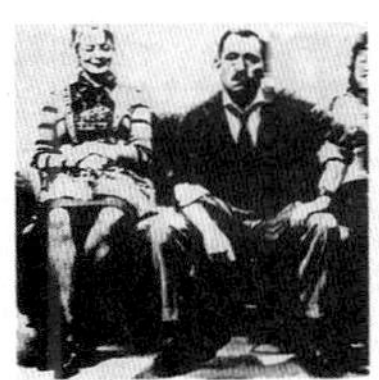

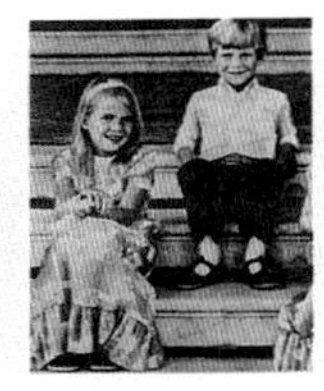

36
TV-"Disgusting Alfred and wife"
Spiegel 38/1977

37
Children of
Juan Carlos of Spain
Neue Revue 49/1975
Photo:Action Press

Couples.

*Beginning as children, men are encouraged on all levels to make themselves broad, especially in front of women while the intimidation of women leads them to take up as little space as possible.*

55

About 380 BOT
Epidaurus votive relief,
Athens, National Museum
8

About 330 BOT
so-called
"Ares Ludovisi",
Rome,
Museo Nazionale
Romano
9

About 320 BOT
Sarapis,
Alexandria,
Museum
10

3rd century BOT
Philosopher
Paris
Bibliotheque
Nationale
11

About 290 BOT
so-called
"Menander"
Rome,
Vatican Museum
12

1st century BOT
Boxer,
Rome,
Museo Nazionale
Romano
13

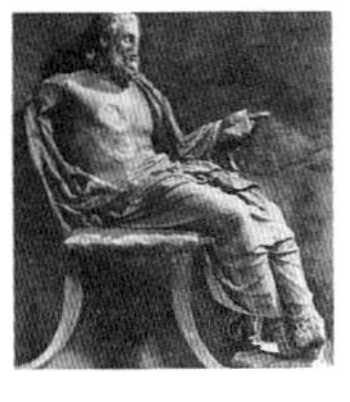
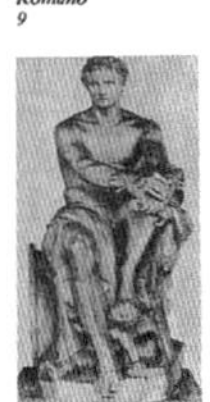
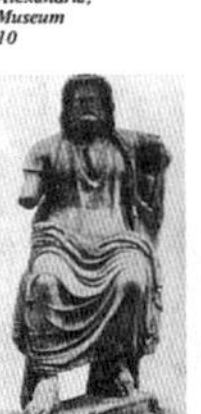
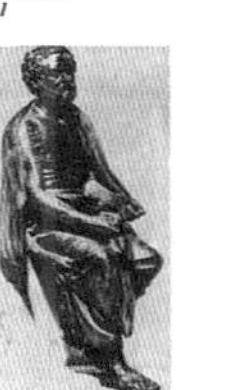
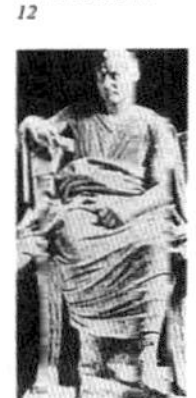
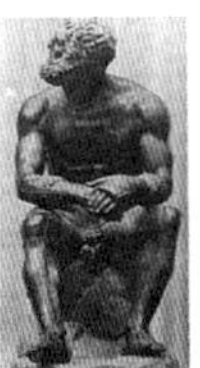

*It was exceptionally difficult to find any illustrations at all from the time before 400 BOT of sitting (this being equivalent to ruling) men. I only found them squatting in illustrations from the earliest times.*

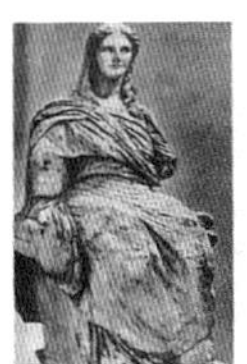
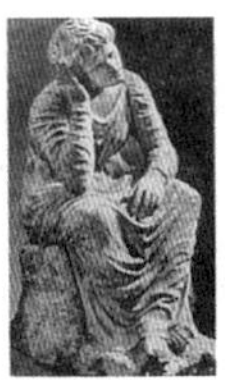
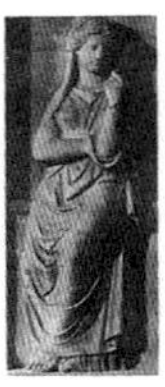
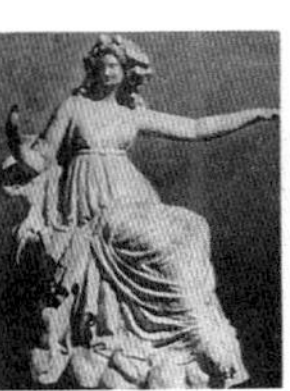
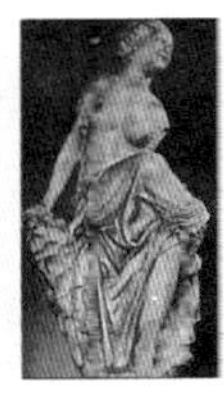
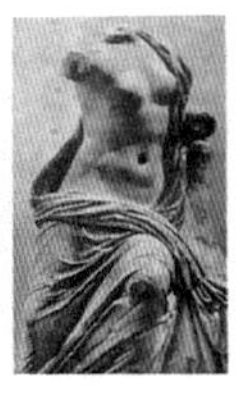

*The body posture of the sitting (ruling) women are in general broader, and appear more self-assured, compared to the postures of the seated men up until 400 BOT. After this time, the situation begins to reverse itself.*

21
340 - 333 BOT
Demeter,
London,
British Museum

22
4th century BOT
Statue on a
woman's grave
Berlin,
Staatl. Museum

23
360 - 350 BOT
Mourner,
Istanbul,
Archaeological
Museum

24
2nd century BOT
Statuette of a
woman of Ma'in
Paris, Louvre

25
2nd century BOT
Nymph statuette
Geneva, Musèe
d'Art et d'Histoire

26
About 150 BOT
Nymph statuette,
Rhodes,
Archaeological Museum

239

41

# Pauline Boudry /
# Renate Lorenz
## *Les Gayrillères*, 2022

**Installation with
two-channel video
(projection and LED),
colour, sound;
18 minutes**

42

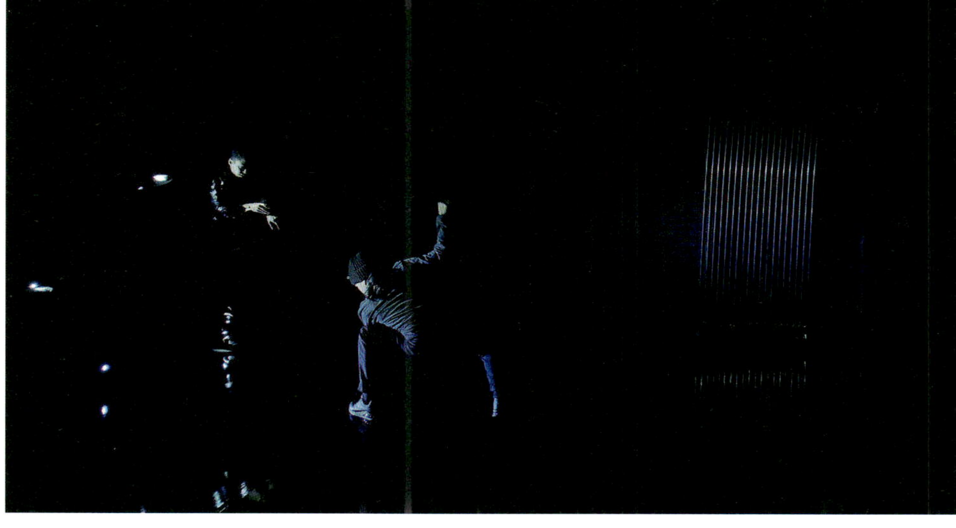

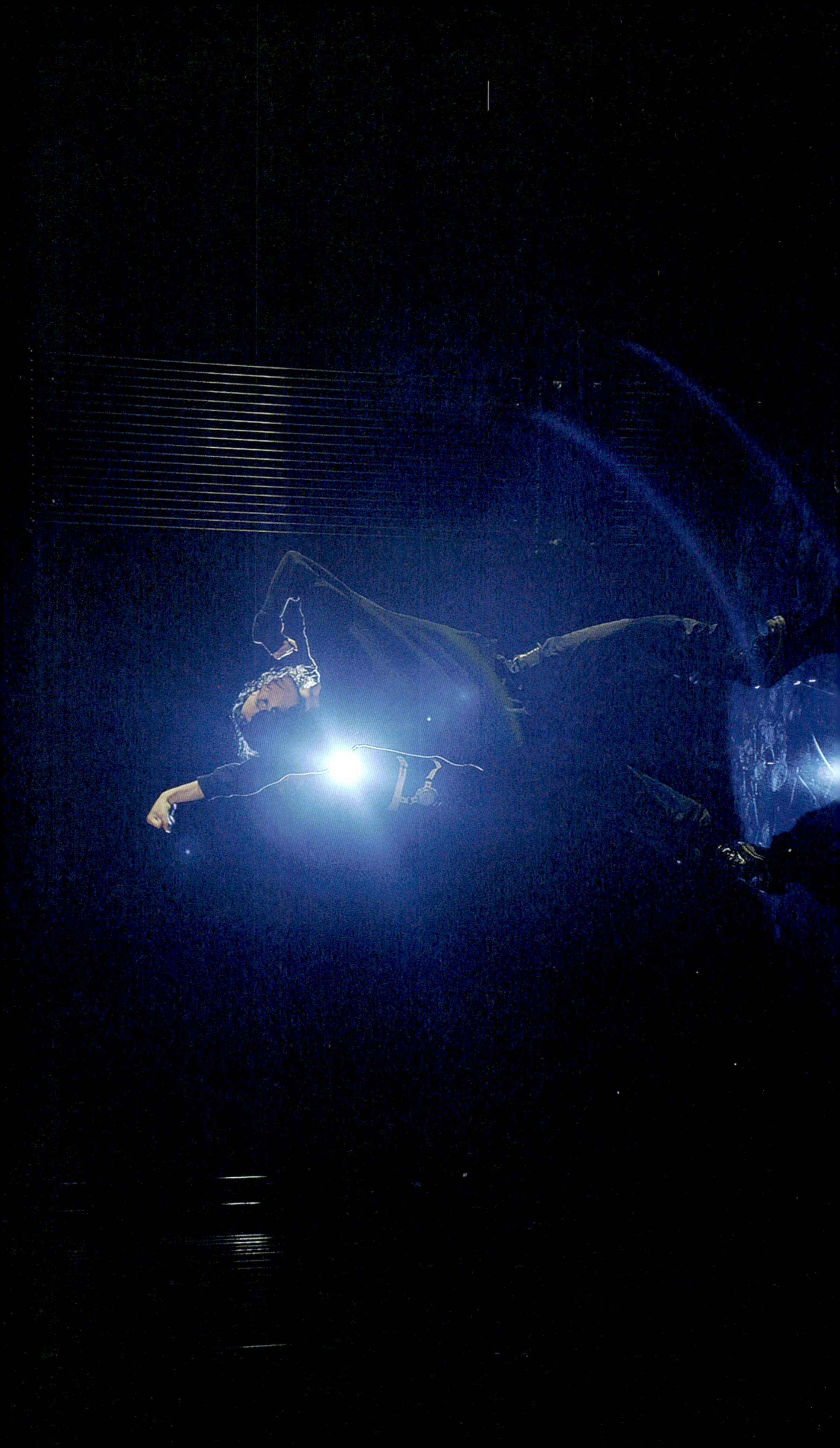

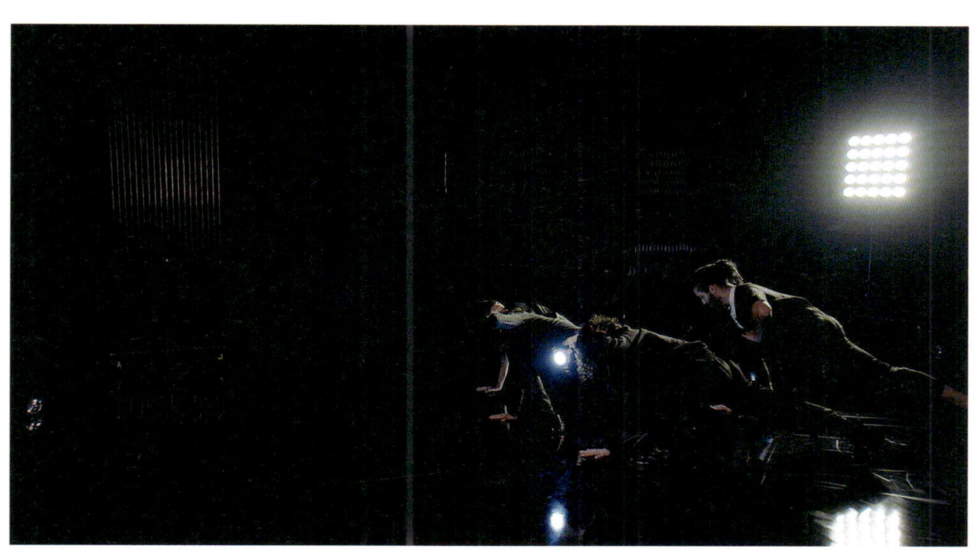

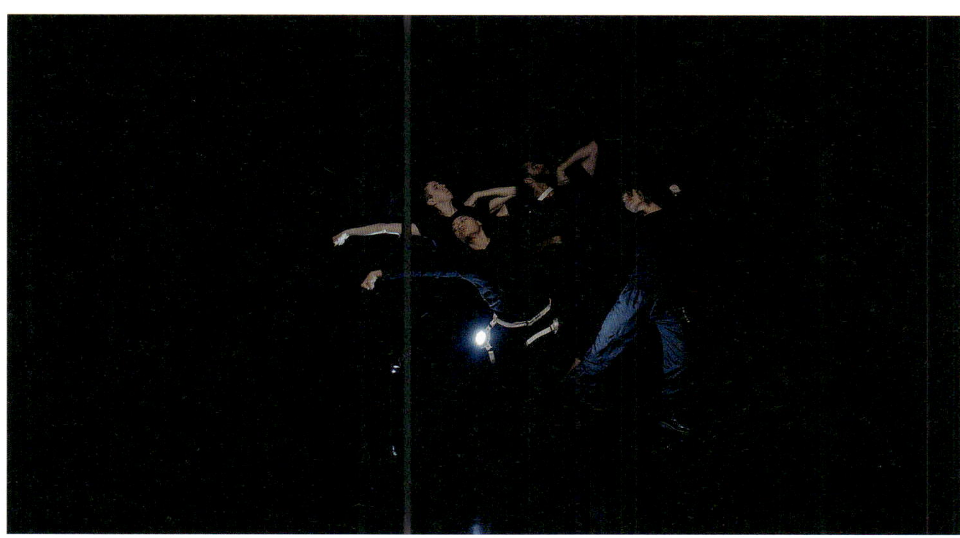

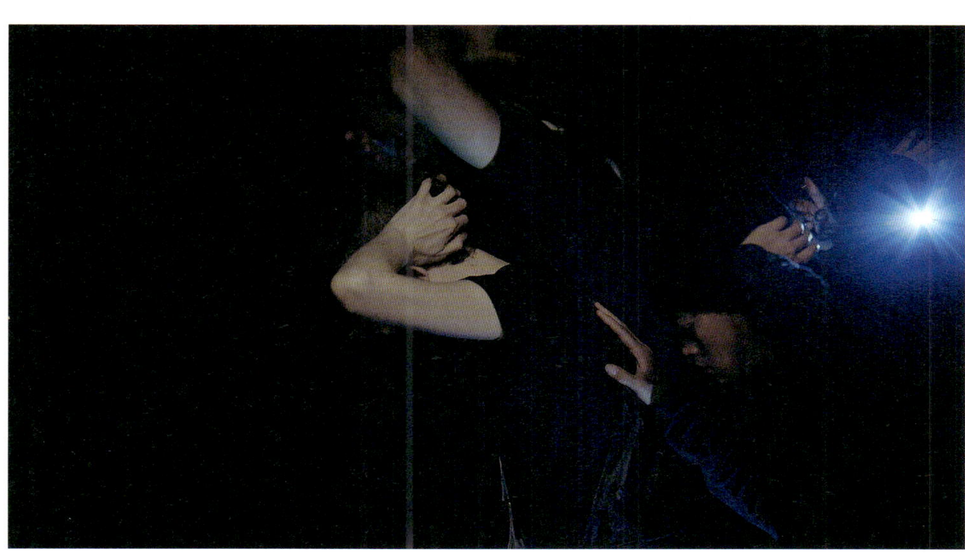

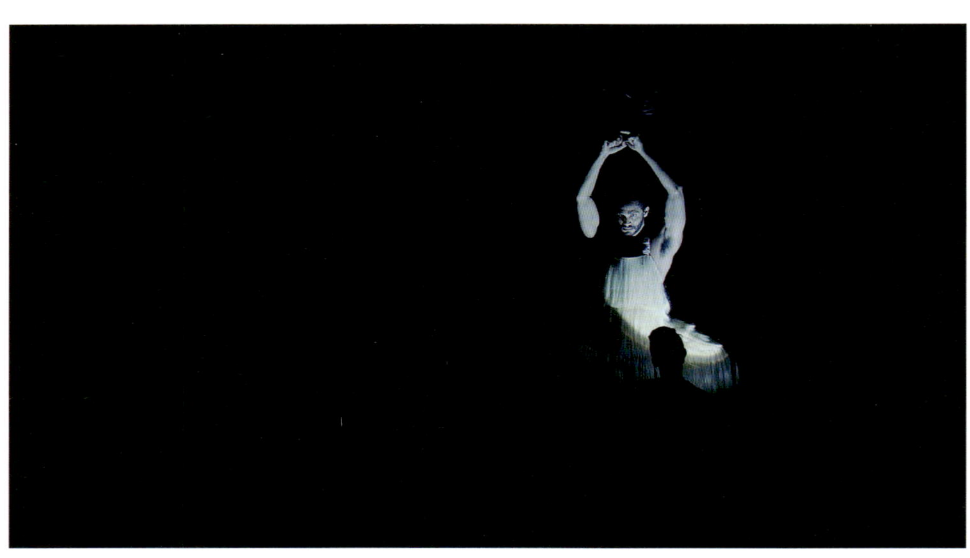

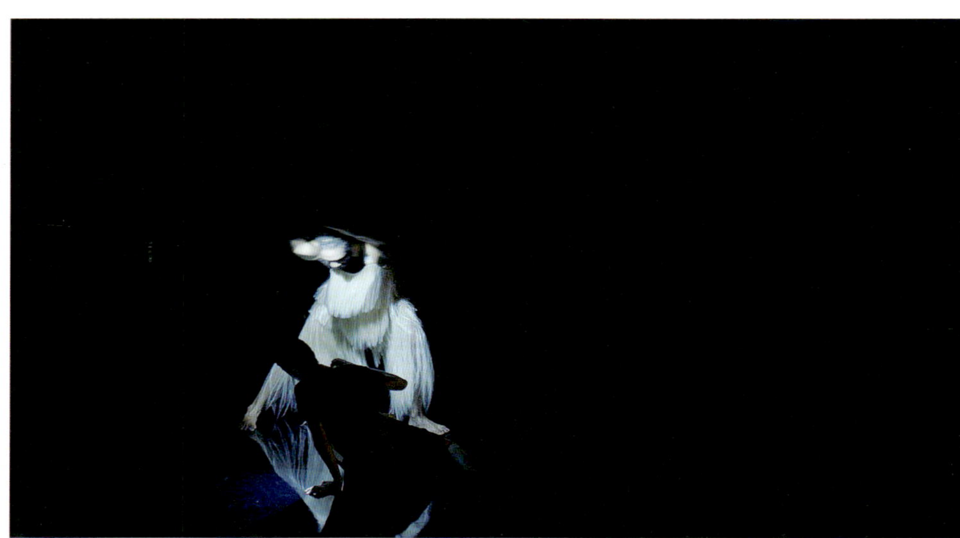

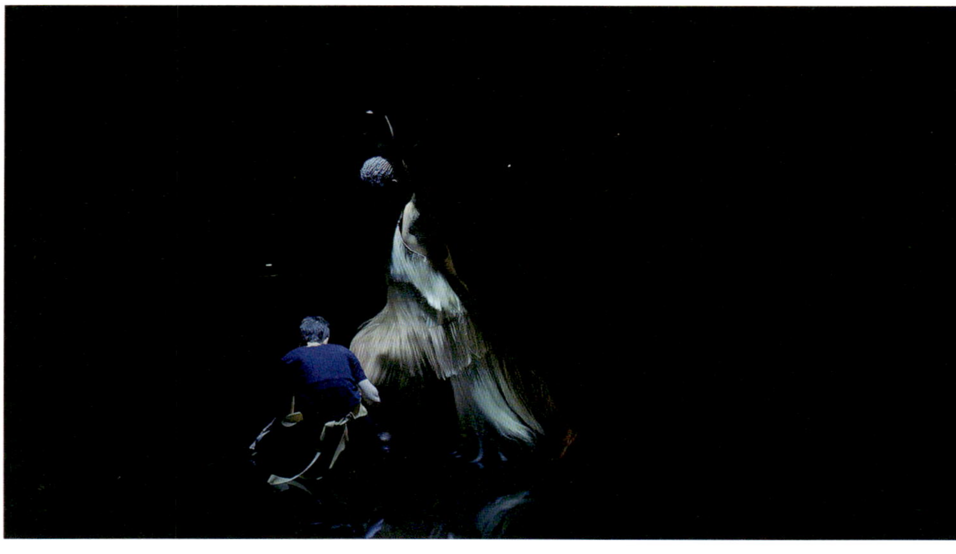

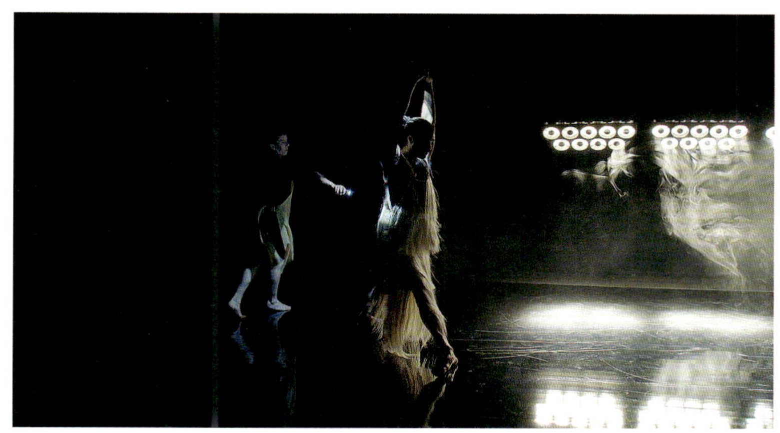

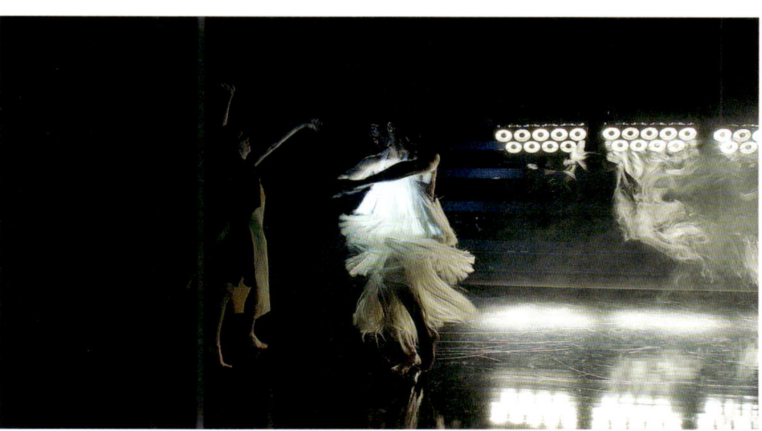

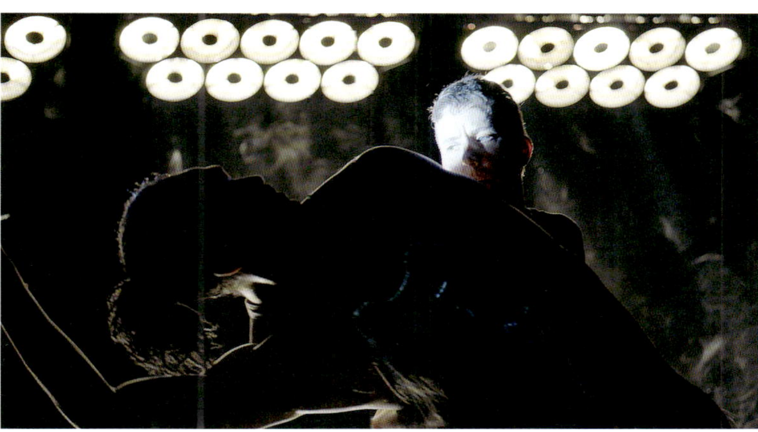

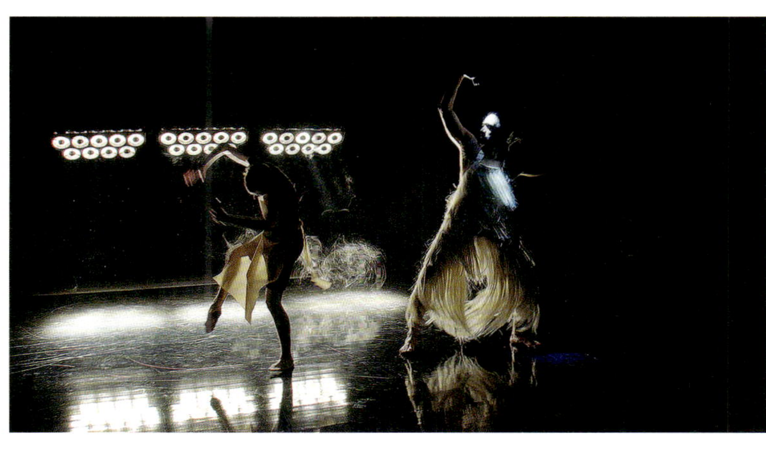

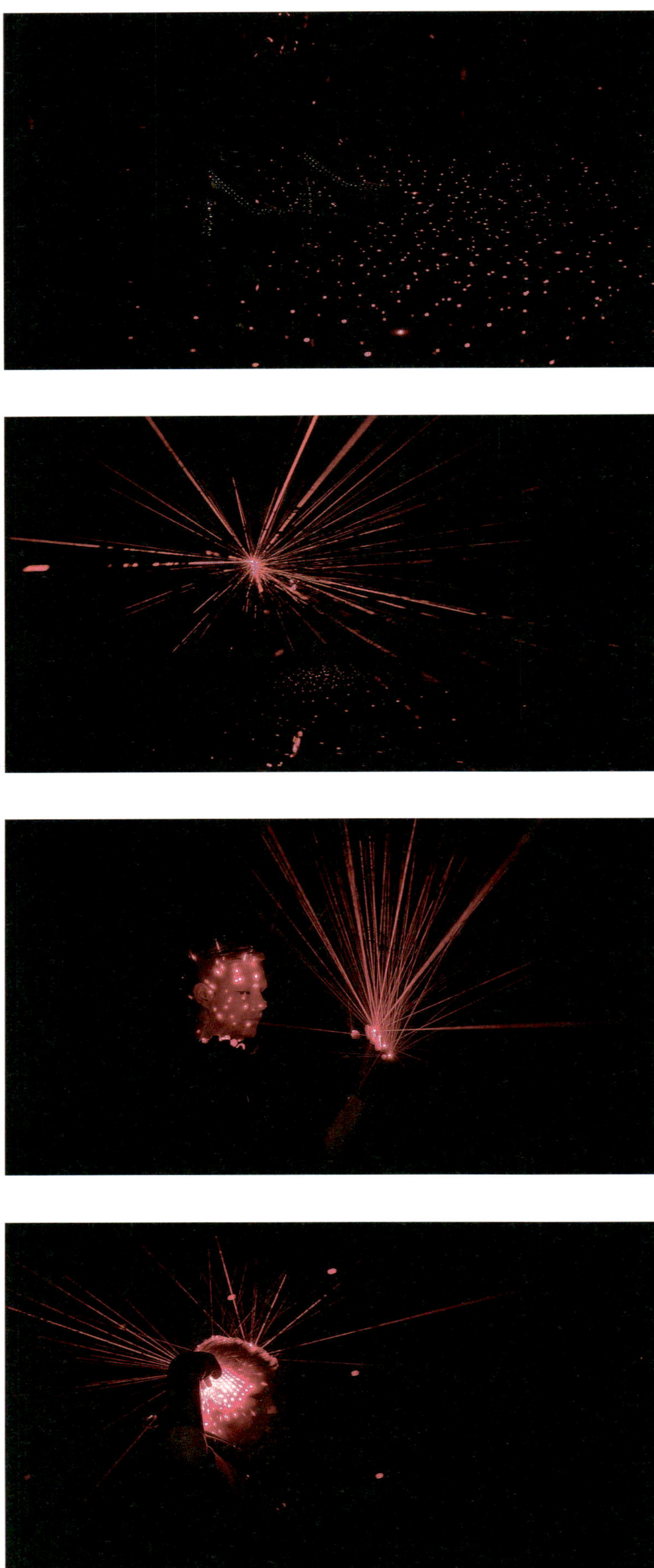

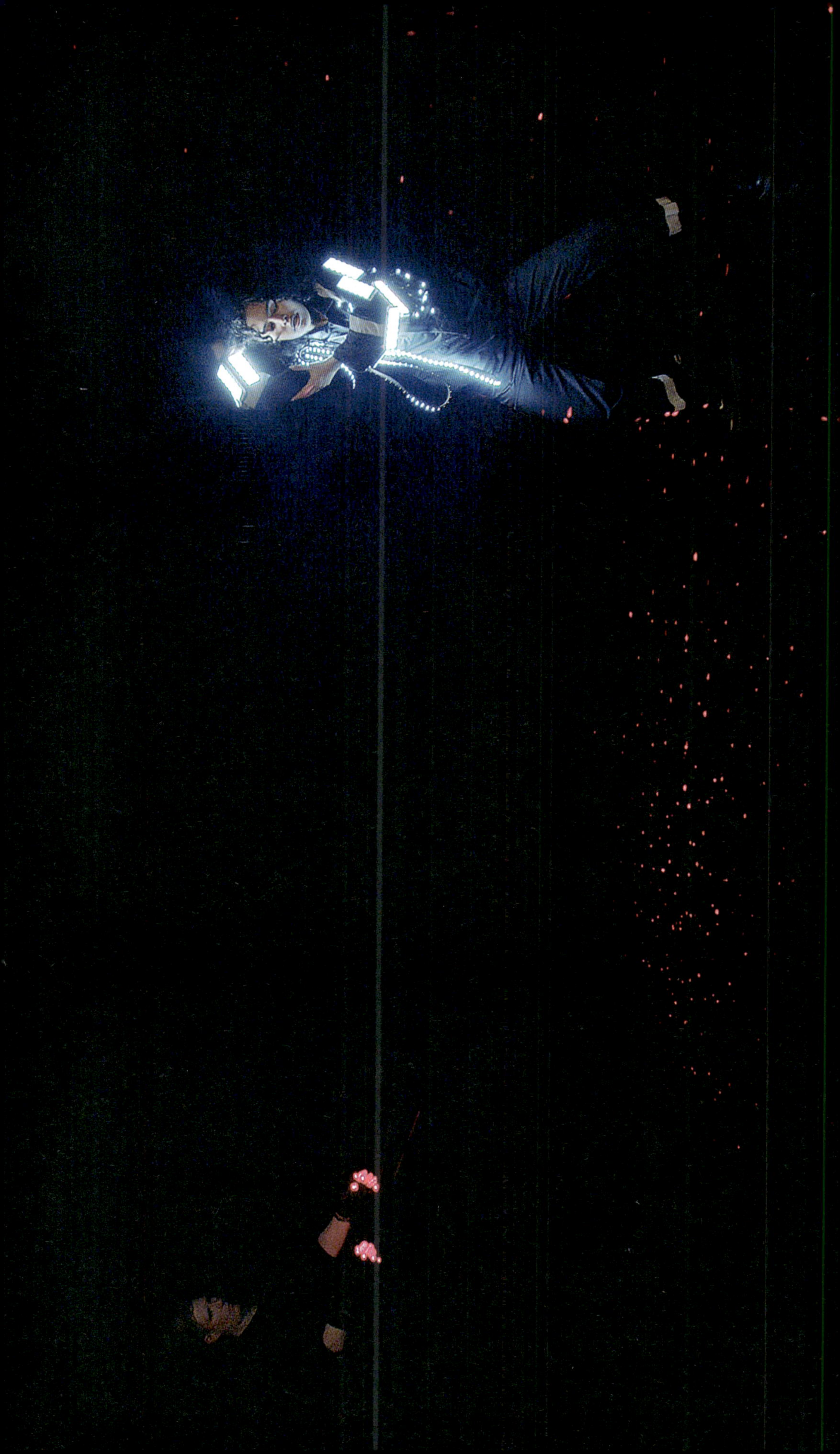

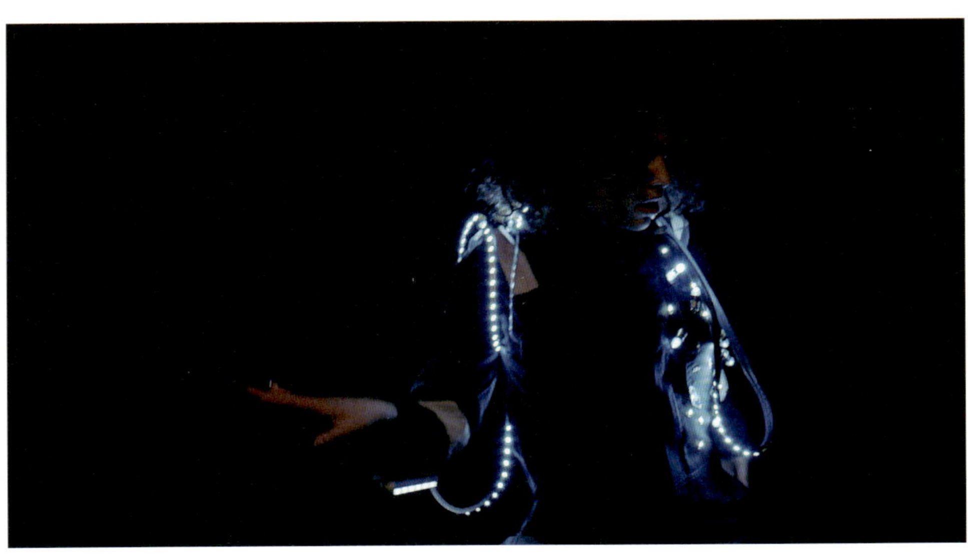

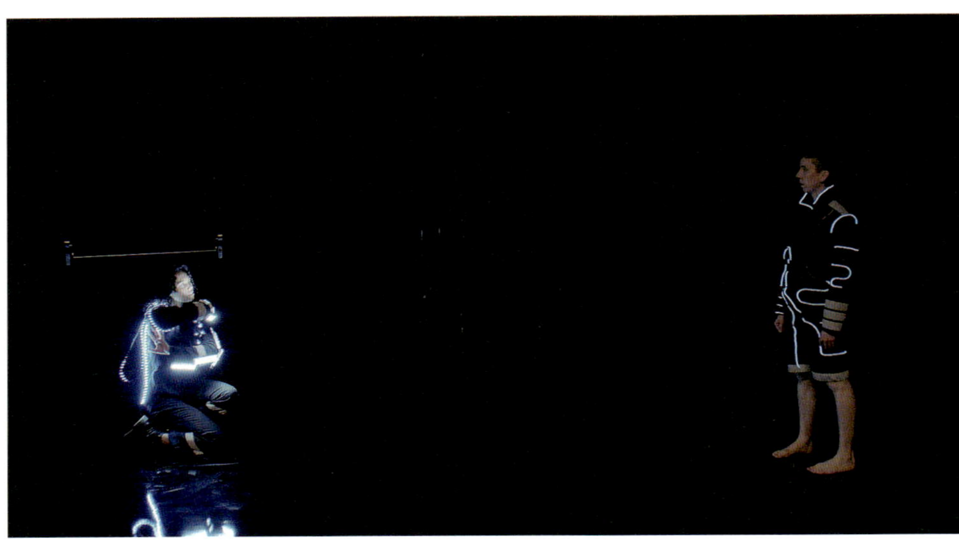

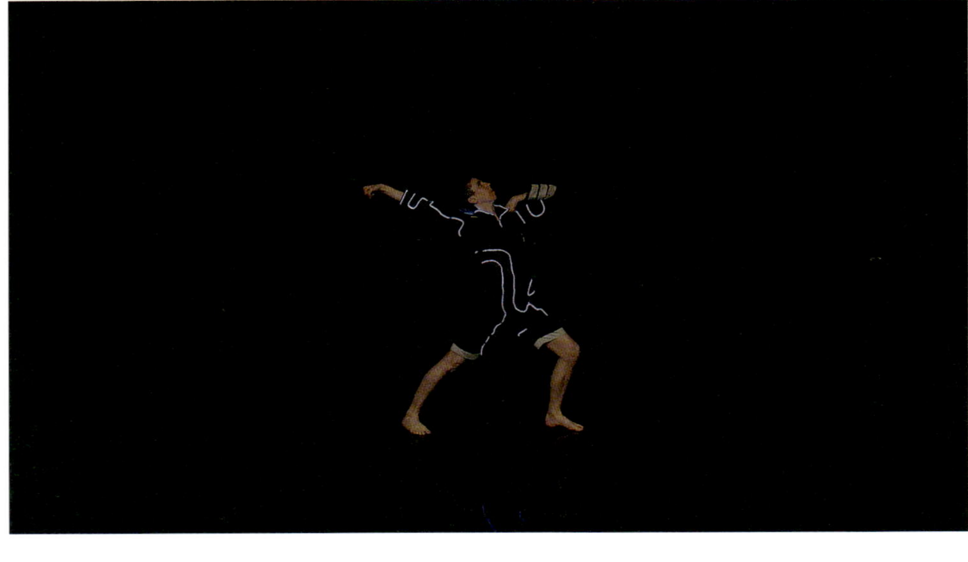

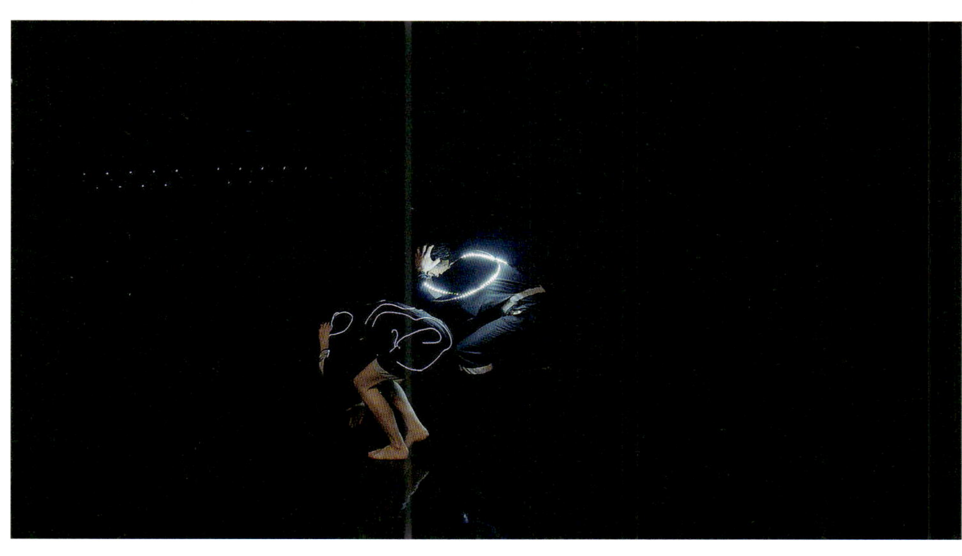

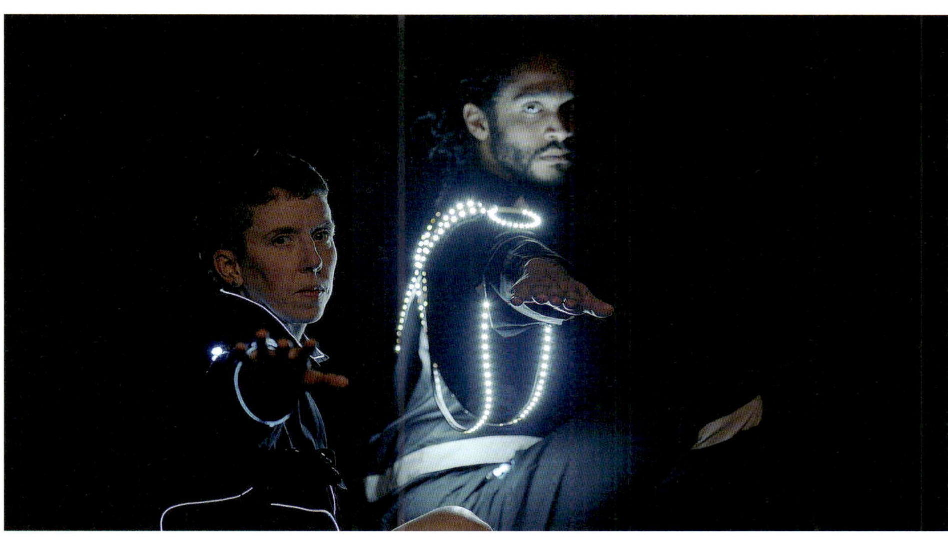

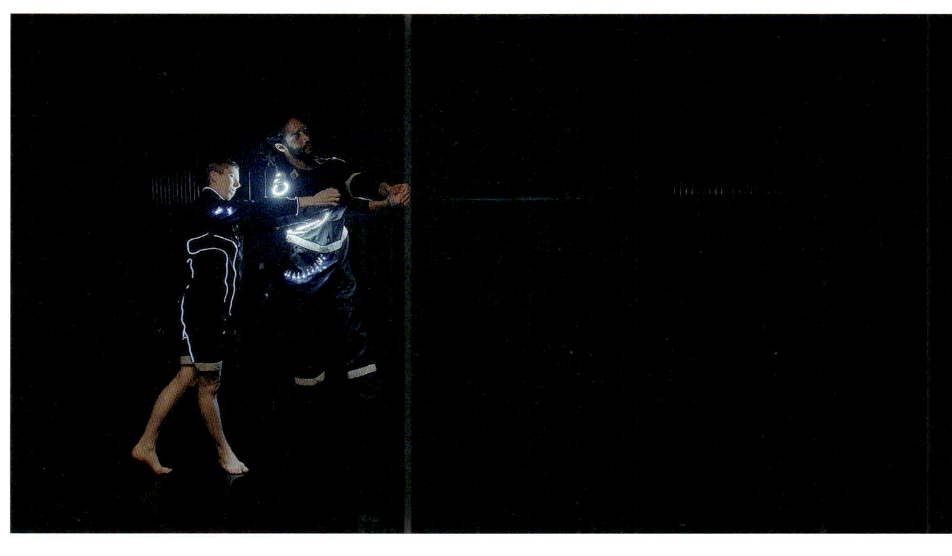

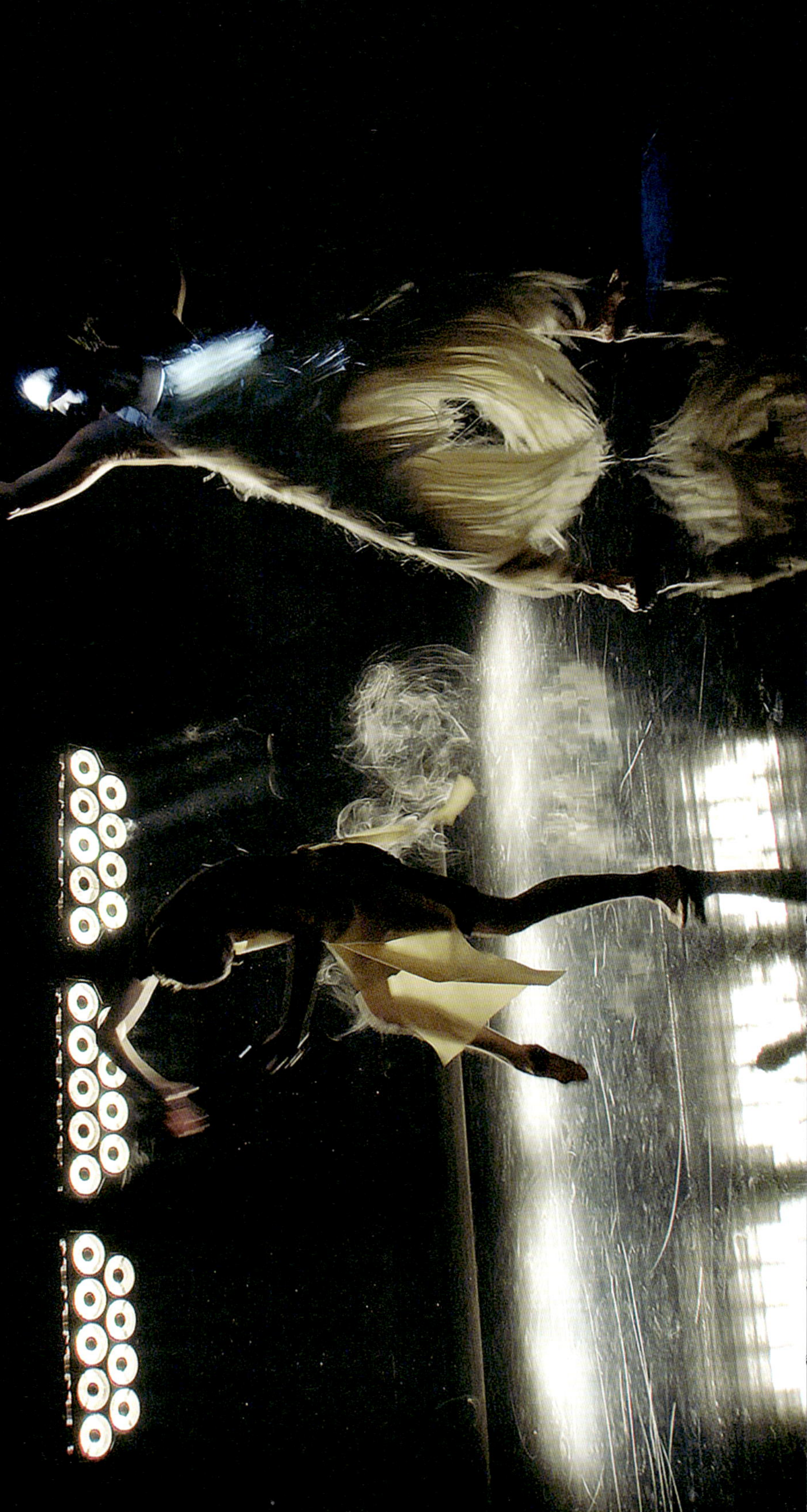

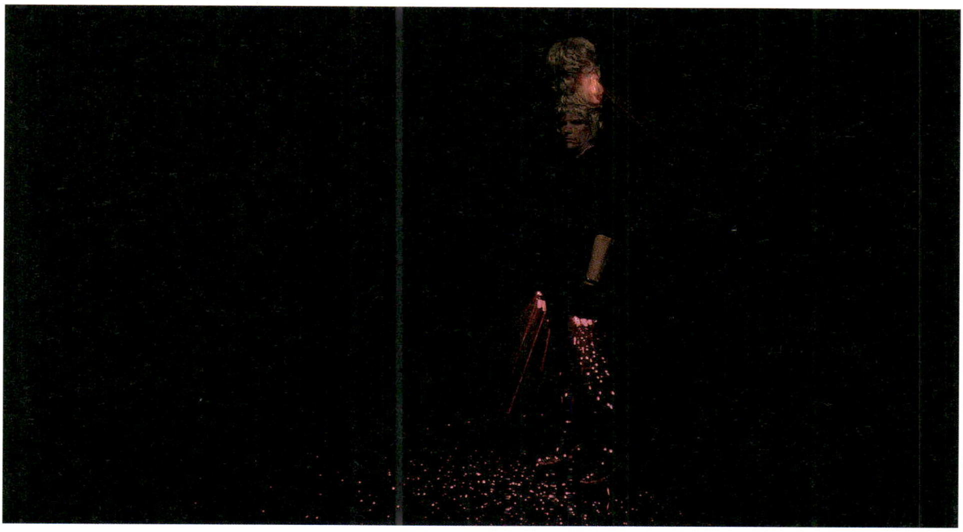

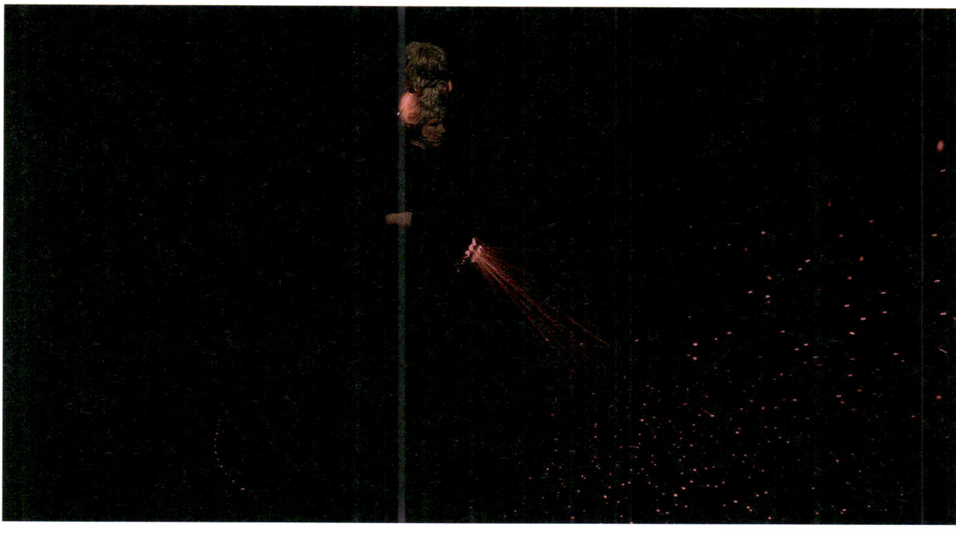

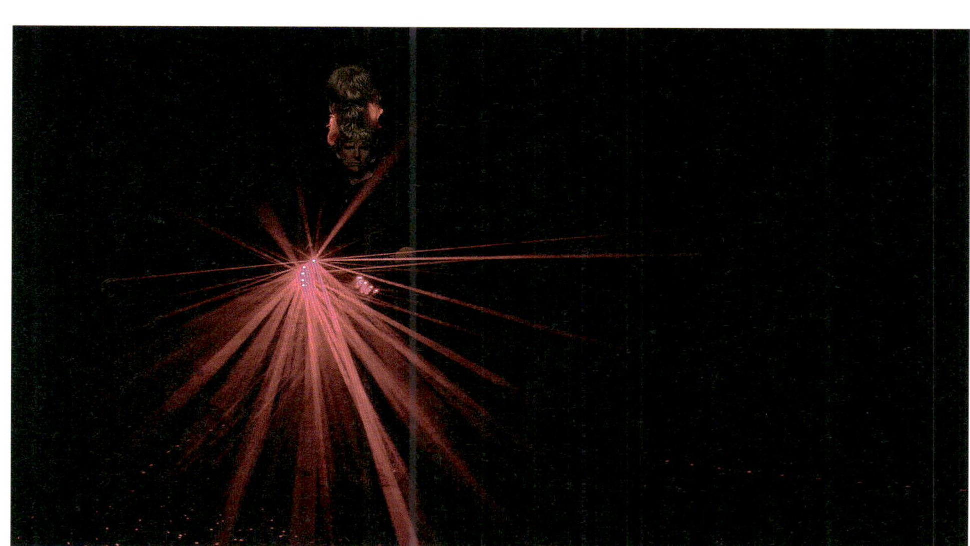

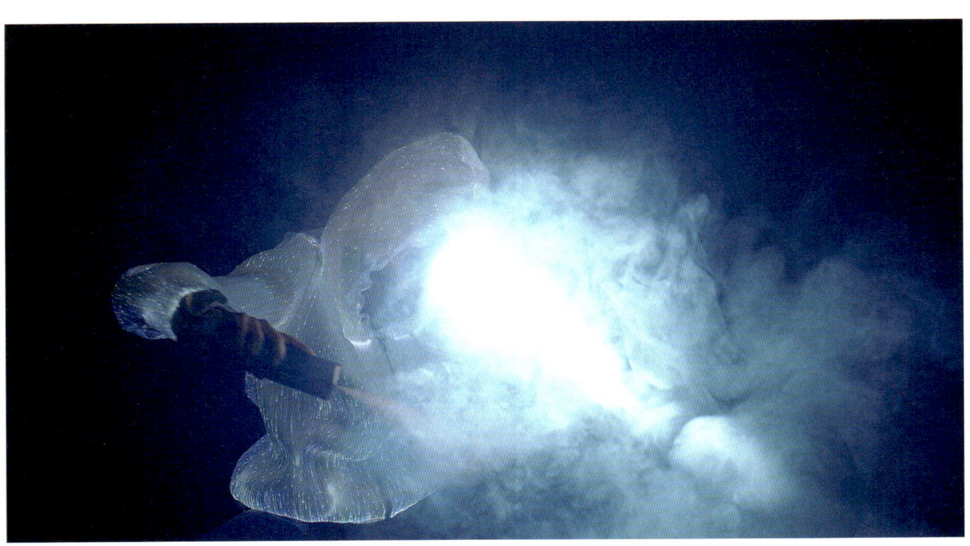

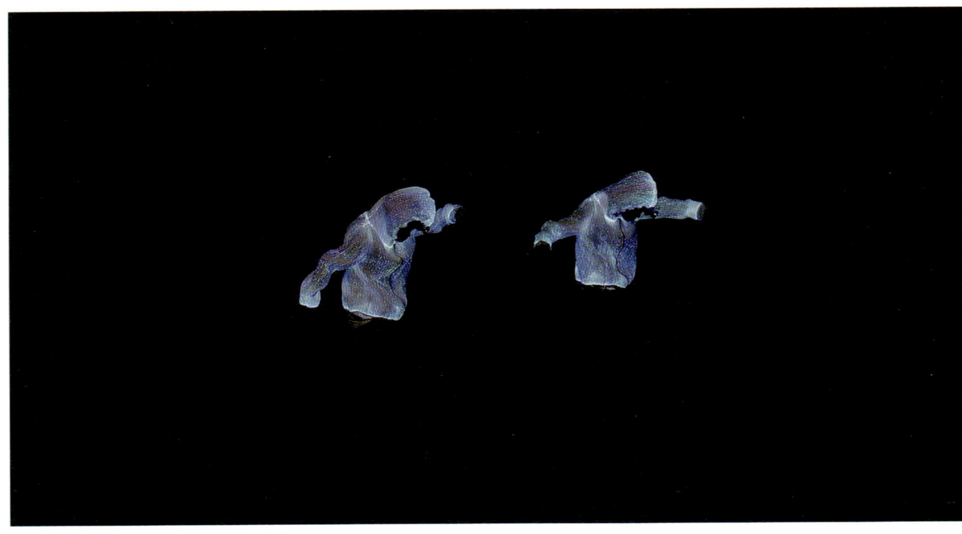

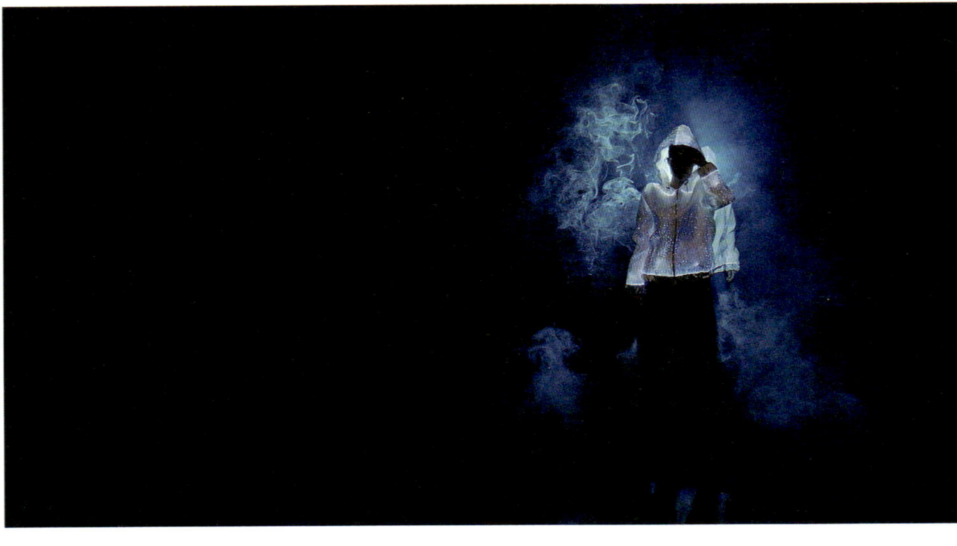

Pauline Boudry and Renate Lorenz's two-channel film installation *Les Gayrillères* (2022) opens in total darkness accompanied by rustling and clomping sounds and then tiny specks of moving light begin to animate the screen. Beams and flickers of light gradually provide glimpses of bodies and eventually we see figures moving in the dark.

The title *Les Gayrillères* draws inspiration from Monique Wittig's *Les Guérillères* (1969), a novel written against the backdrop of May 1968, which imagines that *elles* (the feminine plural pronoun in French) have waged a war against *ils* (masculine plural) and the patriarchal order, replacing it with a new lesbian-feminist society. Wittig mirrors this with an assault on literary and linguistic traditions, destabilising language, deconstructing and reconstructing words and the fixity of meaning. *Guérillères* is, for example, an invented word that paradoxically suggests both warriors and healers. Combining Wittig's title with the word gay, Boudry and Lorenz further open signification to slippage, fluidity and multiplicity.

In *Les Gayrillères*, the gay guerrillas are embodied by a diverse group of six dancers (Harry Alexander, Julie Cunningham, Werner Hirsch, Nach, Joy Alpuerto Ritter and Aaliyah Thanisha) who occupy a nocturnal space, a club or a clandestine underground meeting place. Dancing solo or in duets or quartets, they appear predominantly dressed in black, sometime with lights strapped to white harnesses. Other costumes are more elaborate: a fluorescent latex apron, a dress made from platinum-blonde wigs, a black playsuit with electroluminescent piping, fibre optic hoodies, strings of LED beads, laser beam gloves and other glowing accessories. The choreography, which builds on each dancer's background, is drawn from a mixture of ballet, dancehall, hip hop, contemporary dance and drag performance. The dancers' movements shift from upright to moving low to the ground and are illuminated primarily by light sources attached to their costumes, along with a few UV stage lights. One of the dancers uses an aerosolised spray to create a smoke screen, which masks their presence.

Each performer experiments with varying levels of visibility and invisibility, transparency and opacity. Guerrillas and LGBTQIA+ communities share a need disguise their identities in certain situations, while the latter also desires a greater degree of visibility. The concept of opacity was developed as an anti-colonialist stance by the French Caribbean writer and philosopher Édouard Glissant. In *Poetics of Relations* (1990), Glissant observes the limitations of transparency and argues for 'the right to opacity' as a poetics and politics of difference that refuse to reduce and classify the Other within the terms of dominant cultures.

The soundtrack in *Les Gayrillères* oscillates between the sounds made by the performers and four music tracks. While the dancers' movements are at times difficult to discern in low lighting, they are palpable through sound. A krumping solo, an energetic and exaggerated style of street dance, for example, combines sound created by rapid arm motions and vigorous foot stomps that produce noise from the dancer's costume with an instrumental track by Tragic Selector. Ivo Dimchev's song 'Overrated' is the accompaniment to four dancers whose bodies move in unison to the melancholic music. By contrast, Anohni's cover of Nina Simone's 'Be My Husband' plays alongside two short solos and a duet by dancers wearing red and blue electroluminescent costumes, underscoring the different possible meanings and emotional undertones of the song. Fittingly, the latter two tracks are torch songs that keep the flame burning for unrequited love.

*Les Gayrillères* is installed in a room fitted with the same reflective dance flooring that was used in shooting the film. The glossy surface reflects the light from the film, which is projected on a wall and presented in parallel on an ambient LED curtain at a lower resolution. Occasionally, the dance floor is activated by live dancers who spontaneously appear while the film is playing in the gallery. But it also beckons the visitor to break out a few dance moves of their own.

Lydia Yee

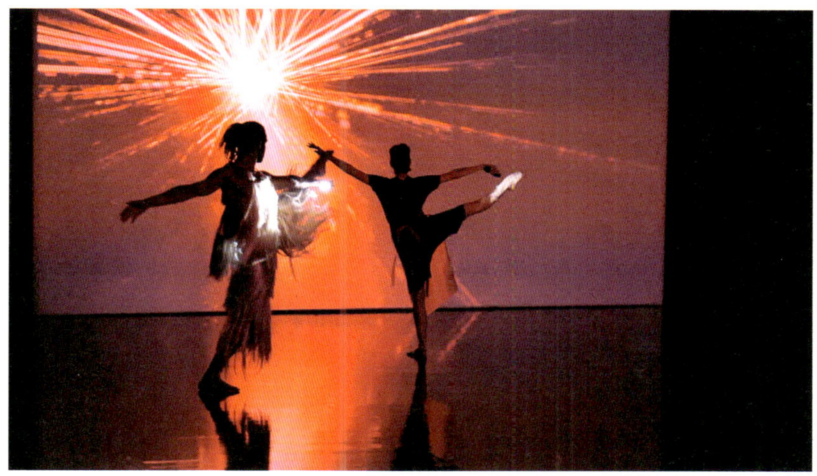

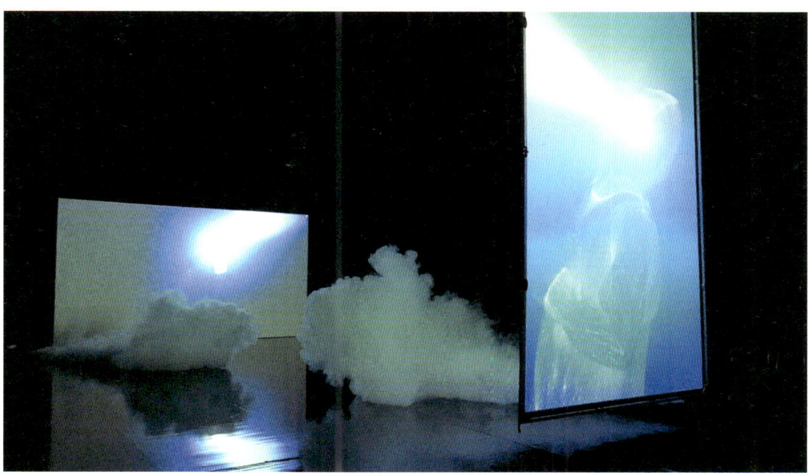

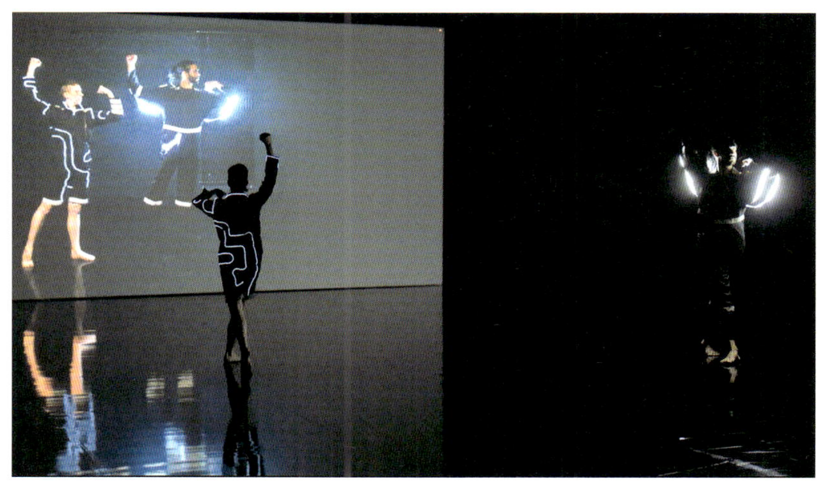

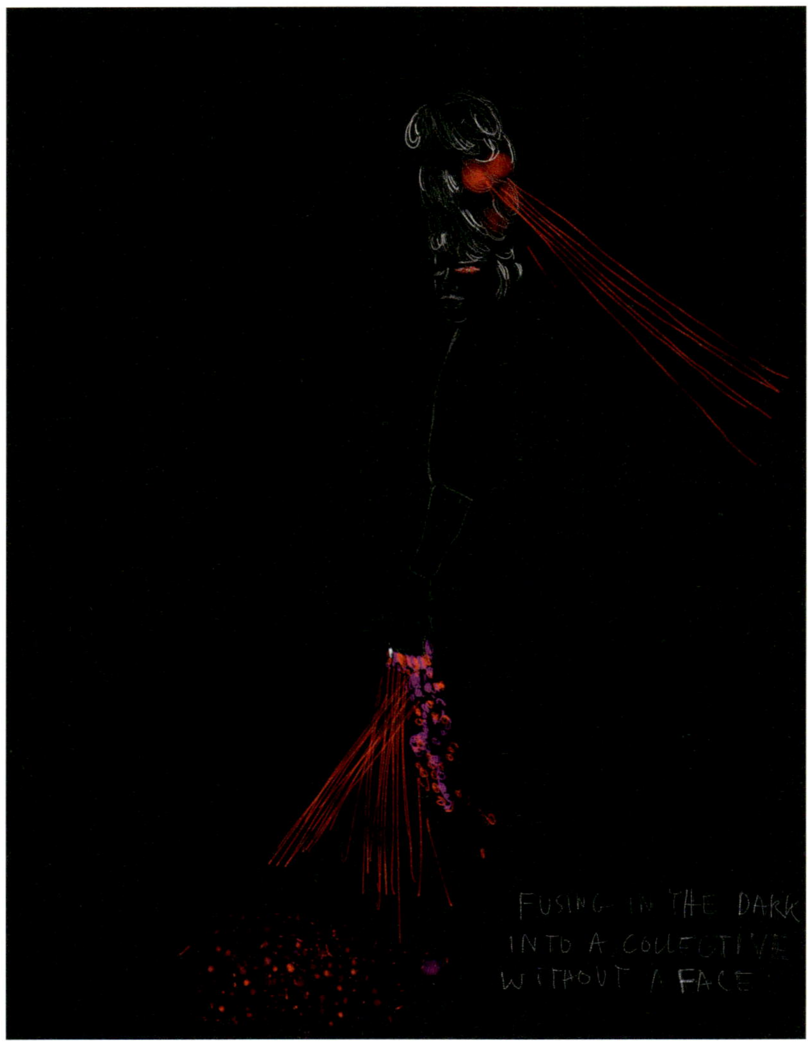

FUSING IN THE DARK
INTO A COLLECTIVE
WITHOUT A FACE

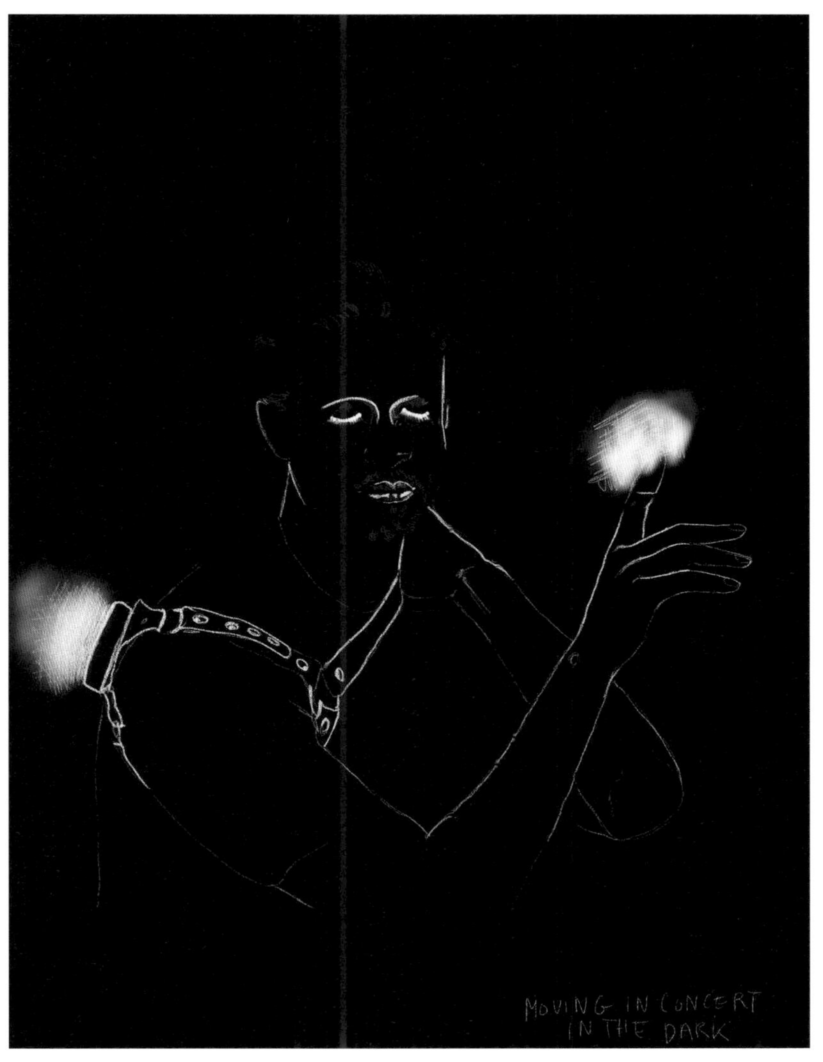
MOVING IN CONCERT
IN THE DARK

# Eglė Budvytytė
in collaboration with
Marija Olšauskaitė
and Julija Steponaitytė
*Songs from the Compost:
mutating bodies,
imploding stars*, 2020

HD video, colour, sound;
29 minutes

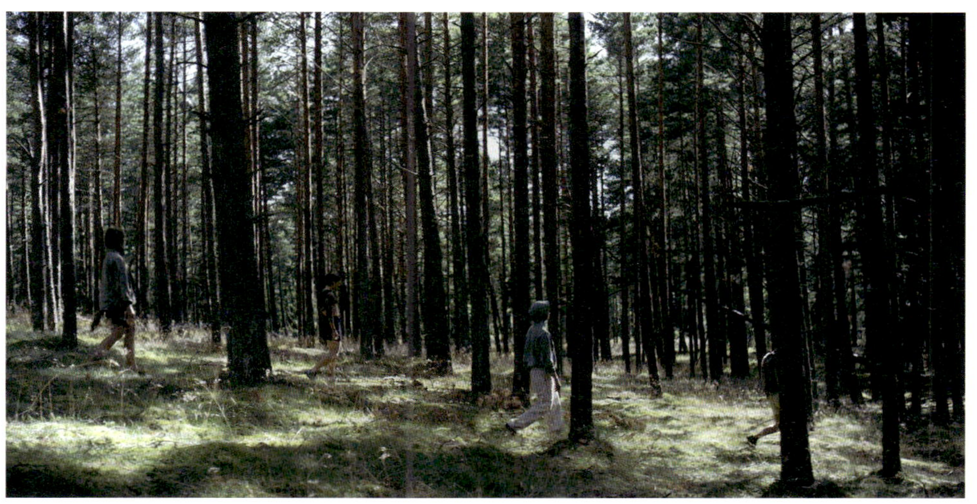

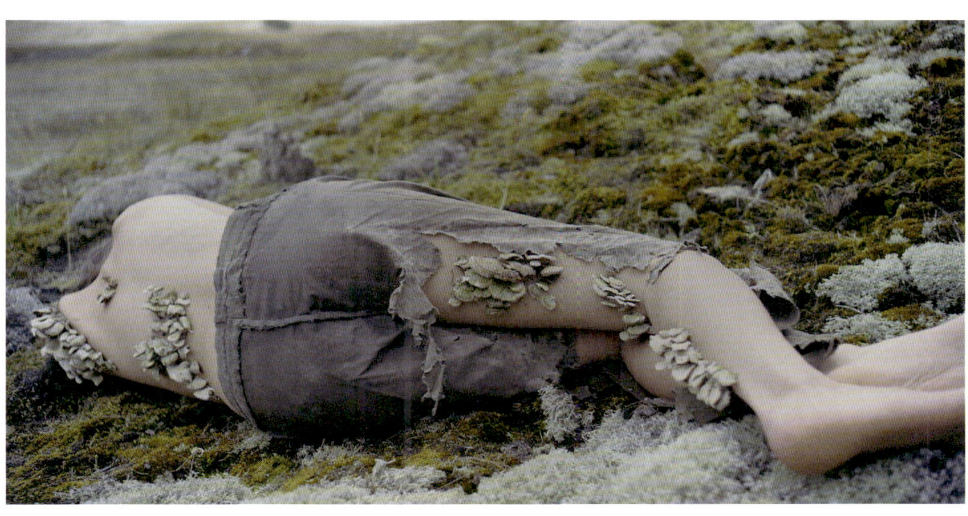

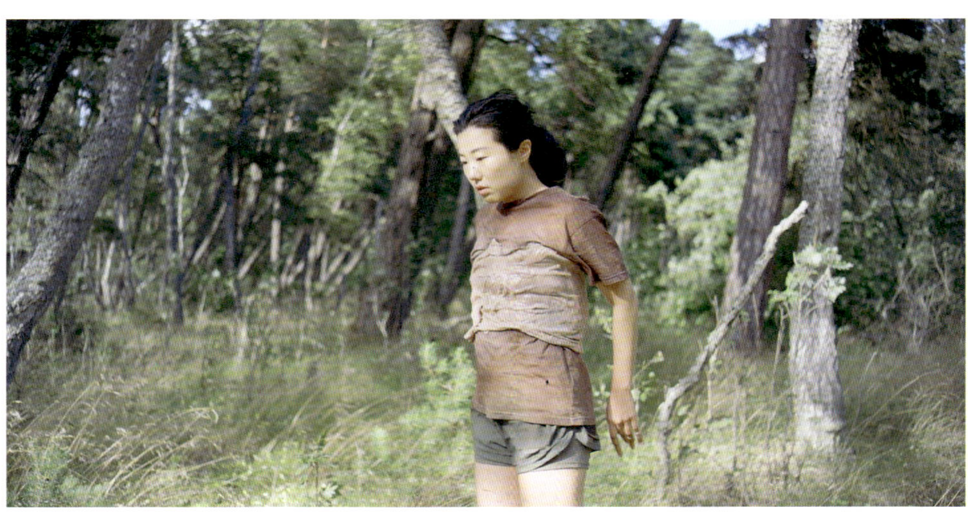

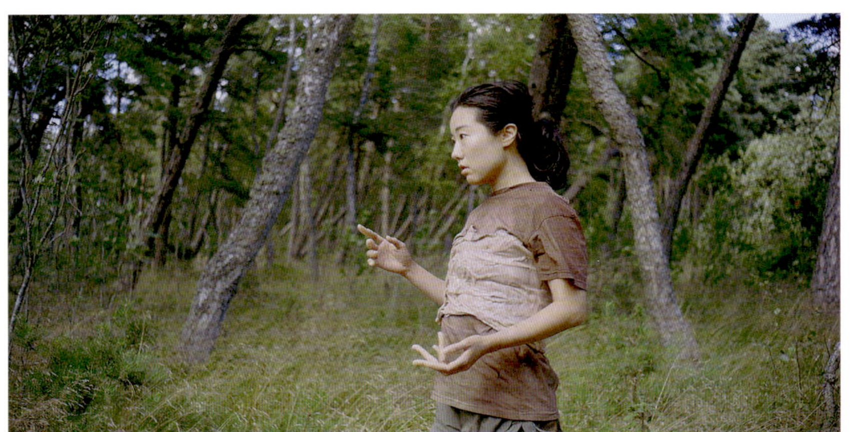
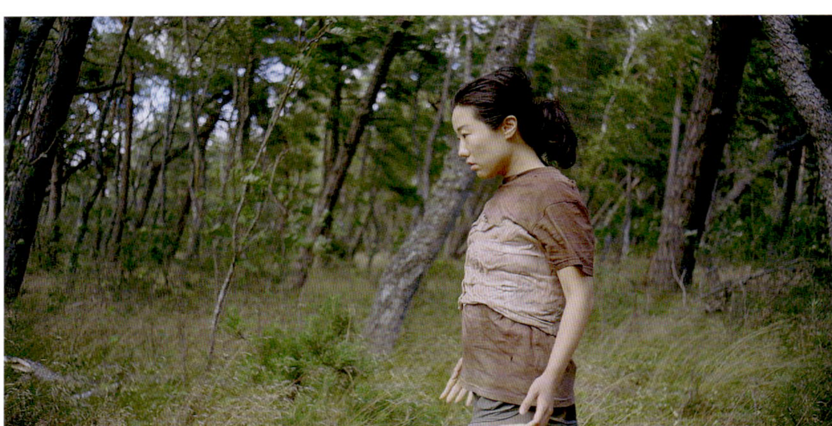
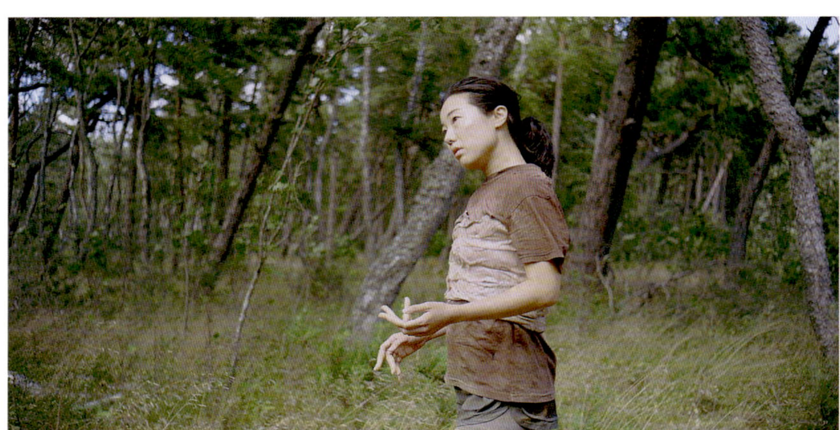
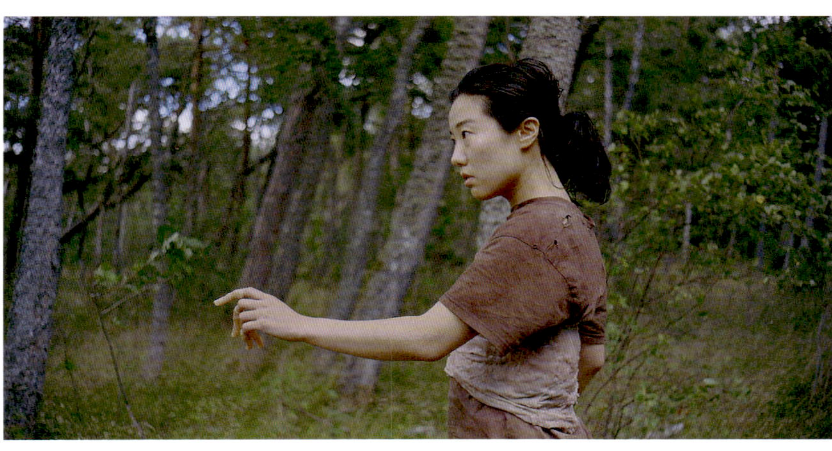

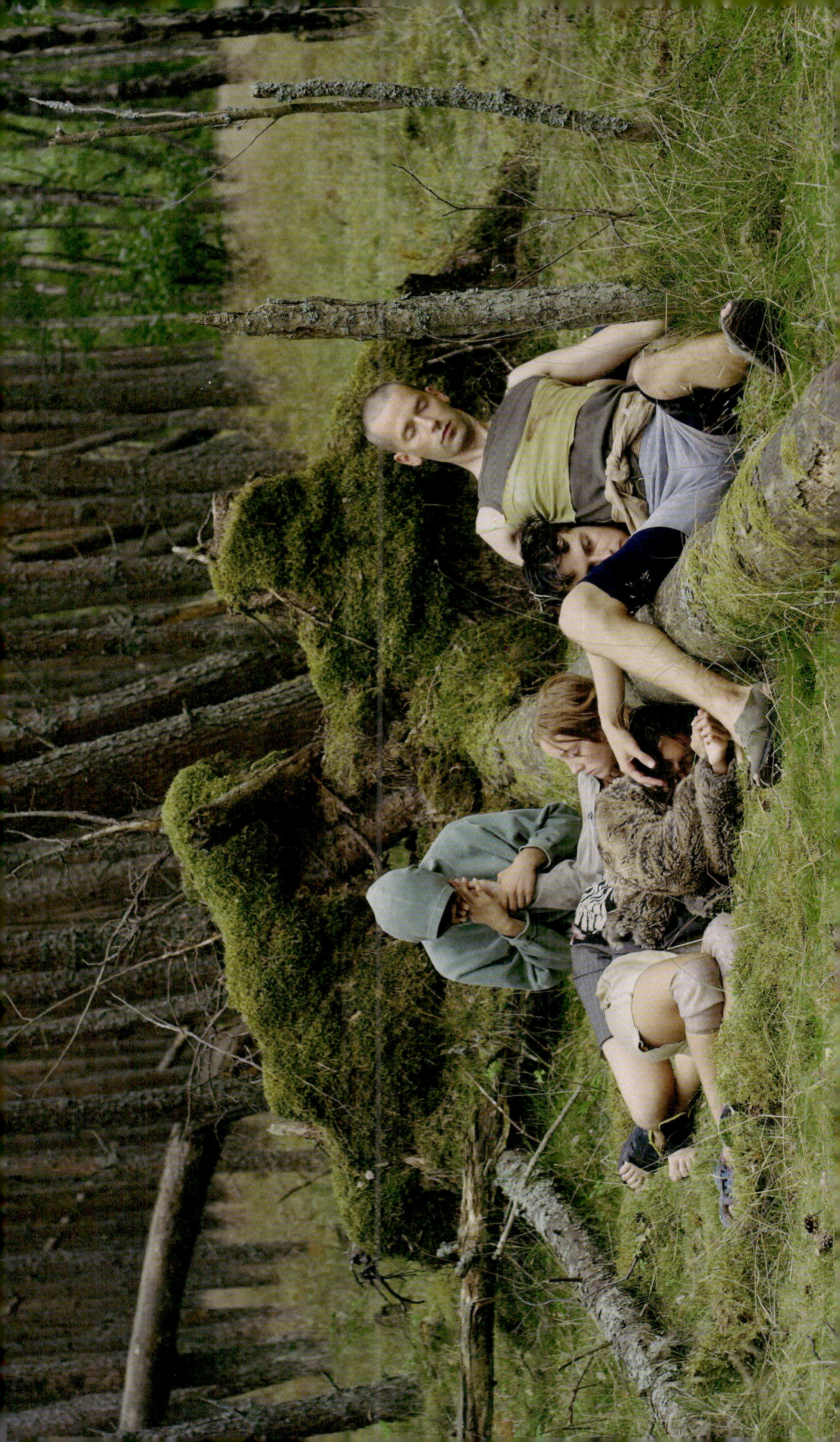

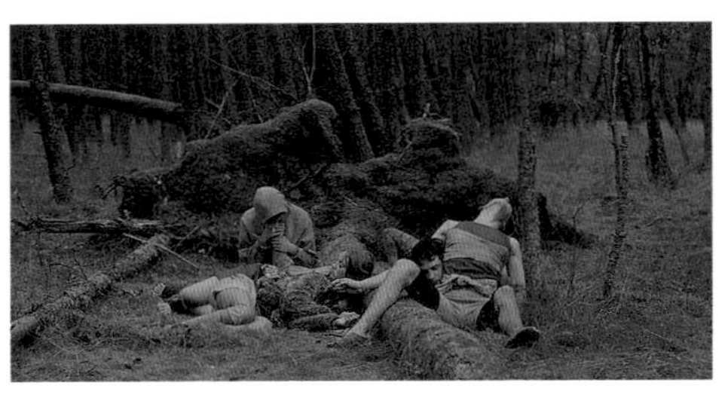
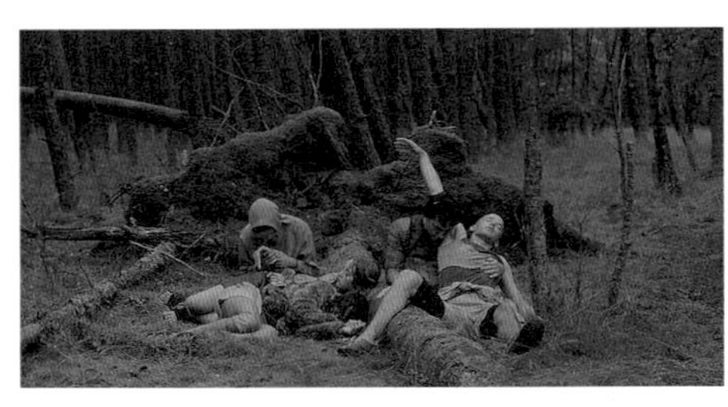
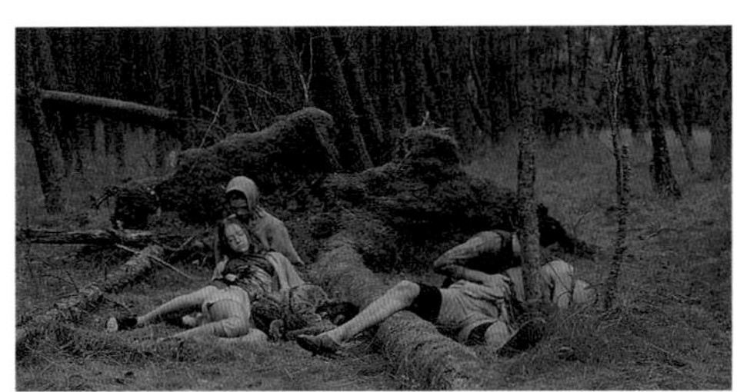
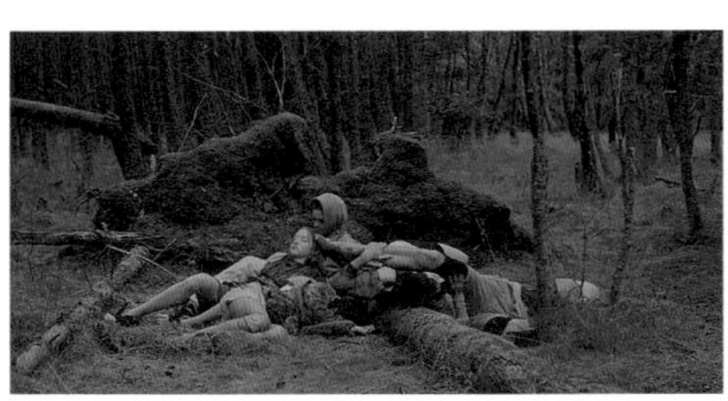
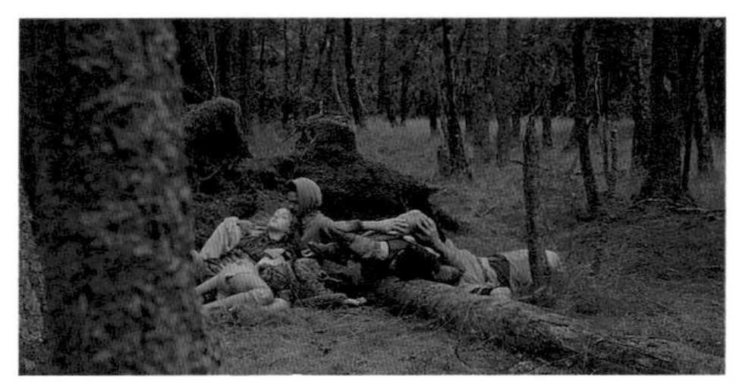
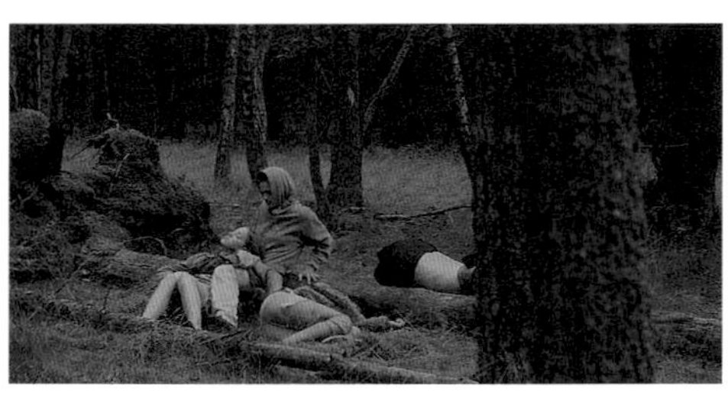
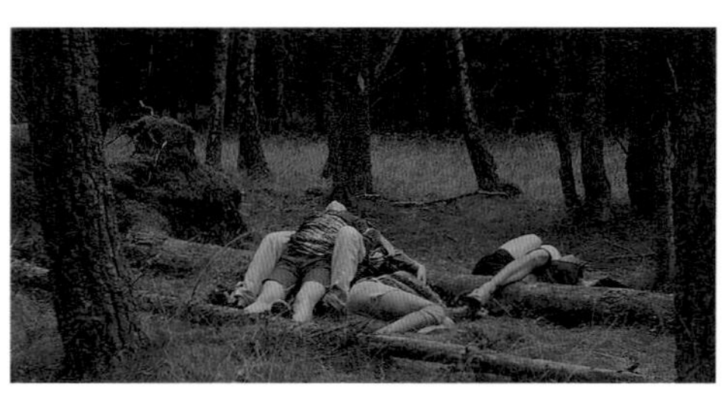
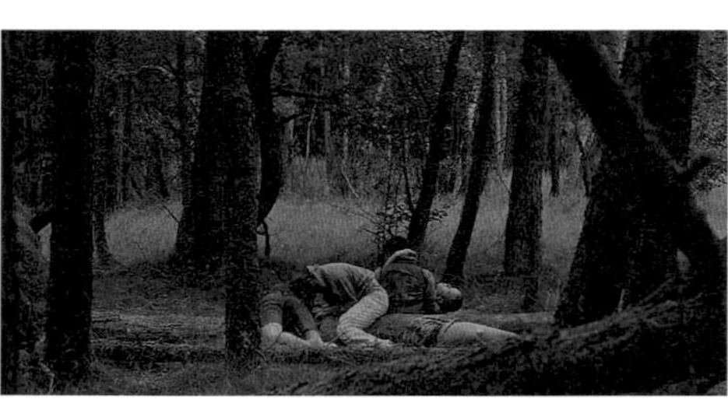

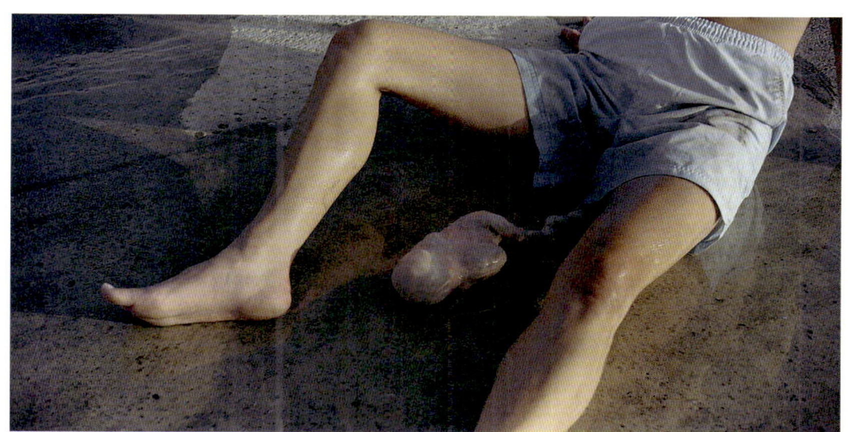

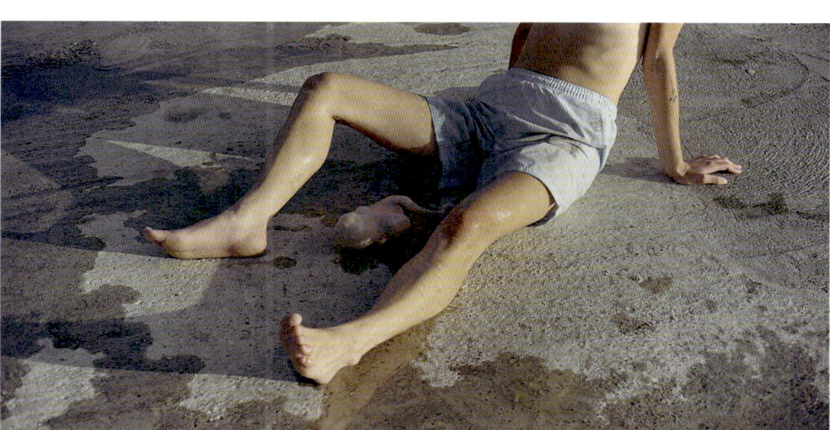

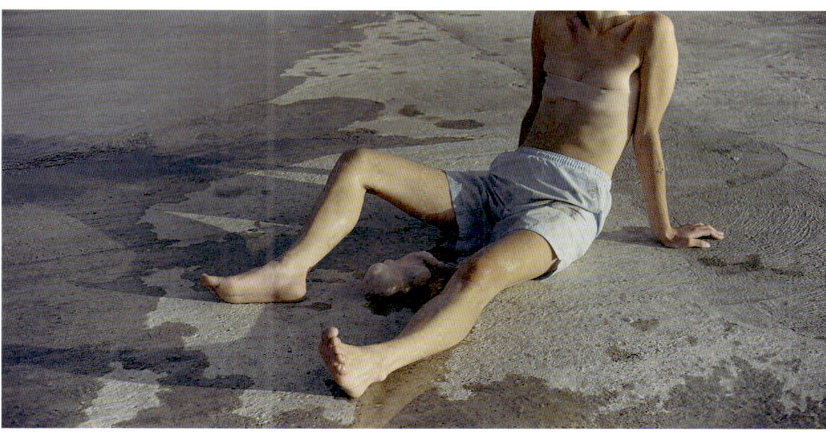

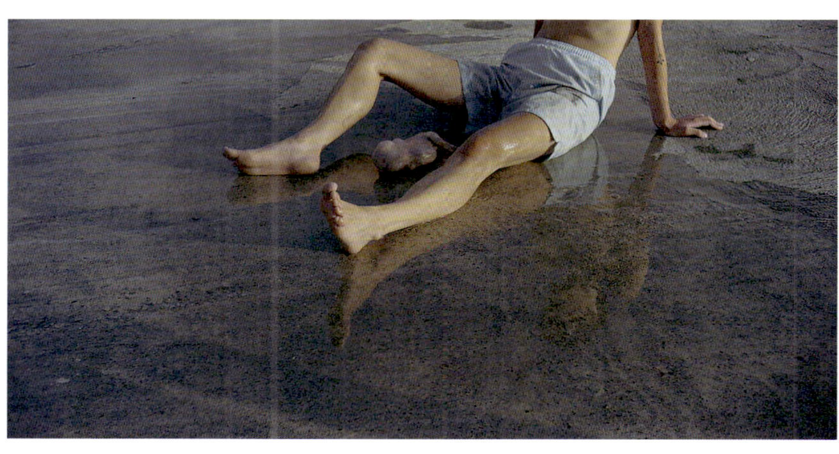

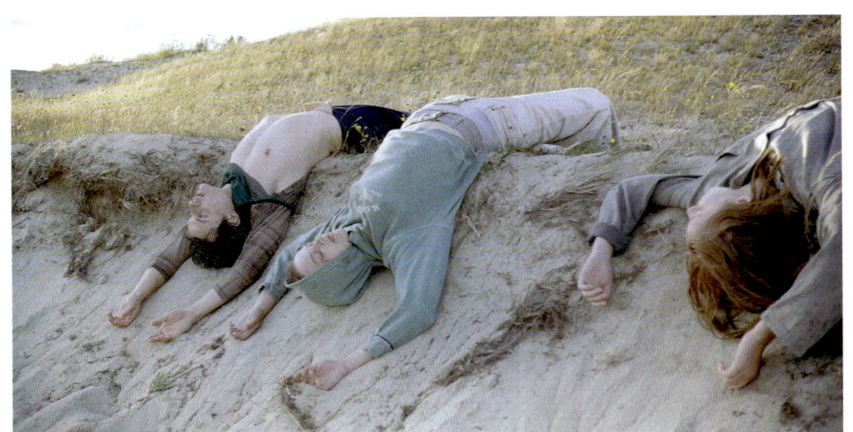

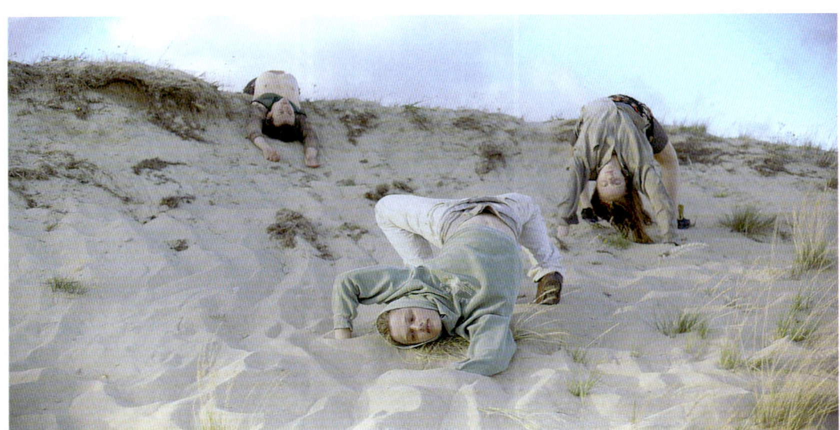

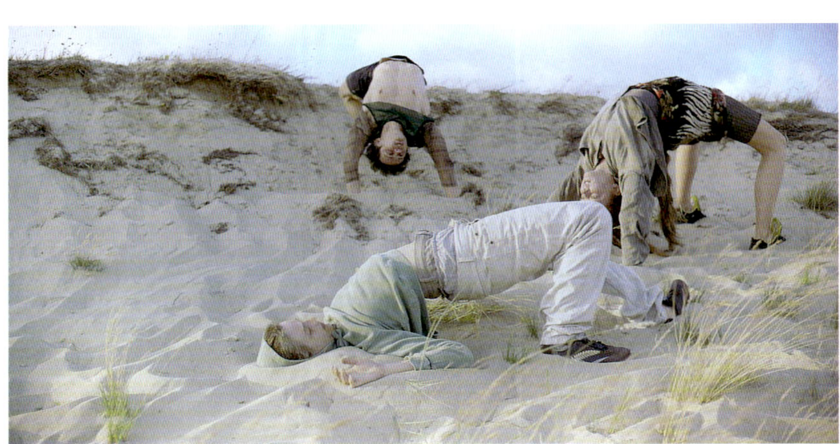

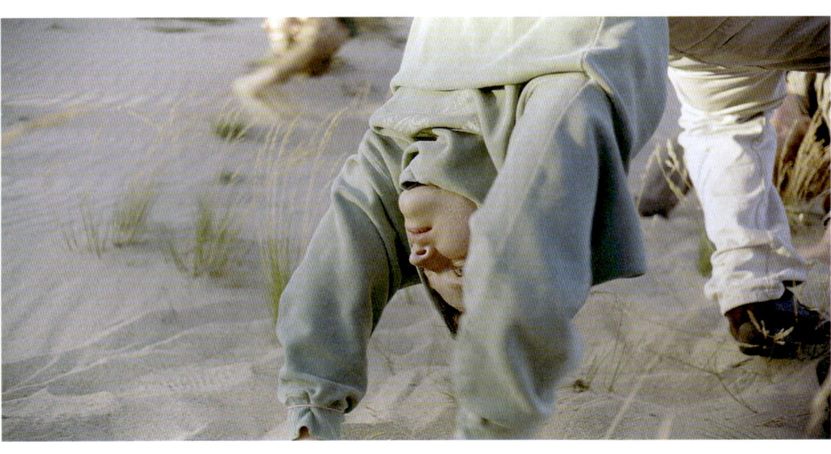

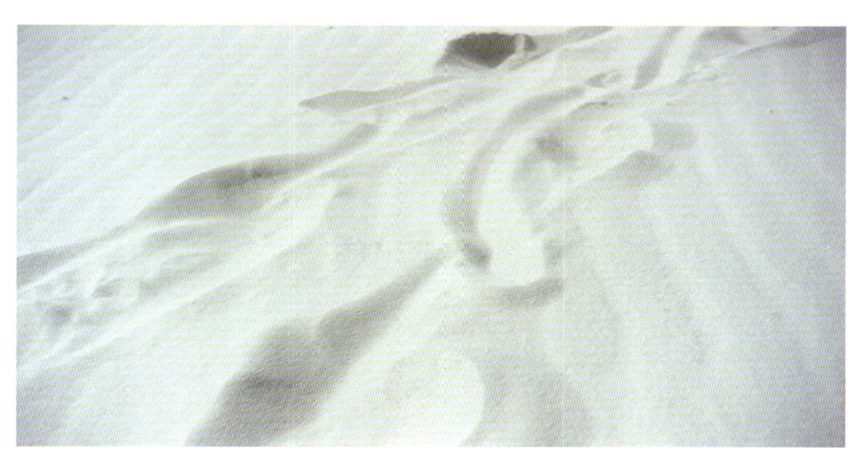

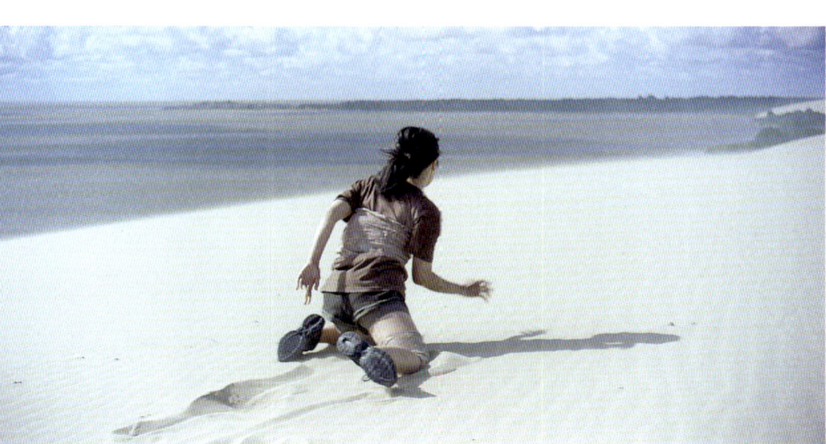

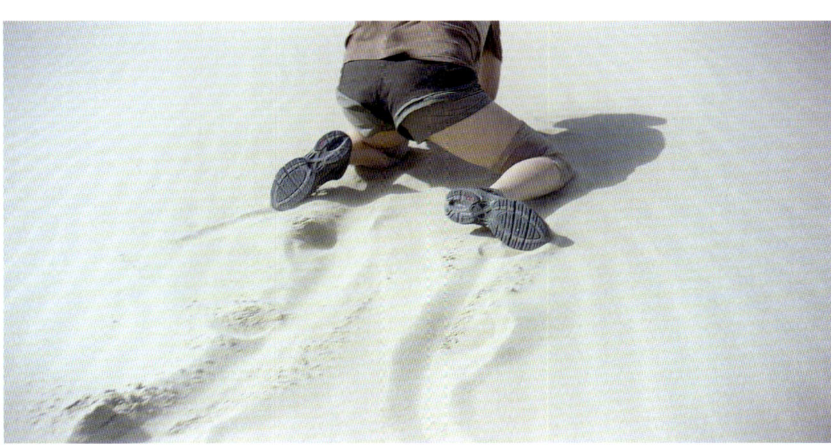

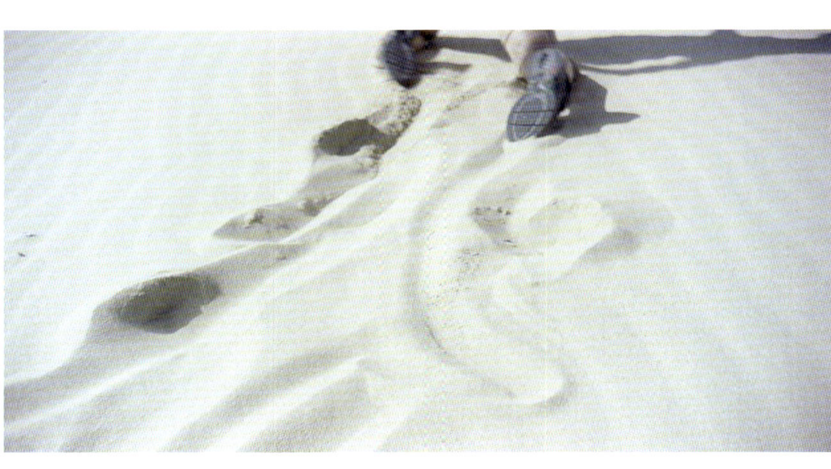

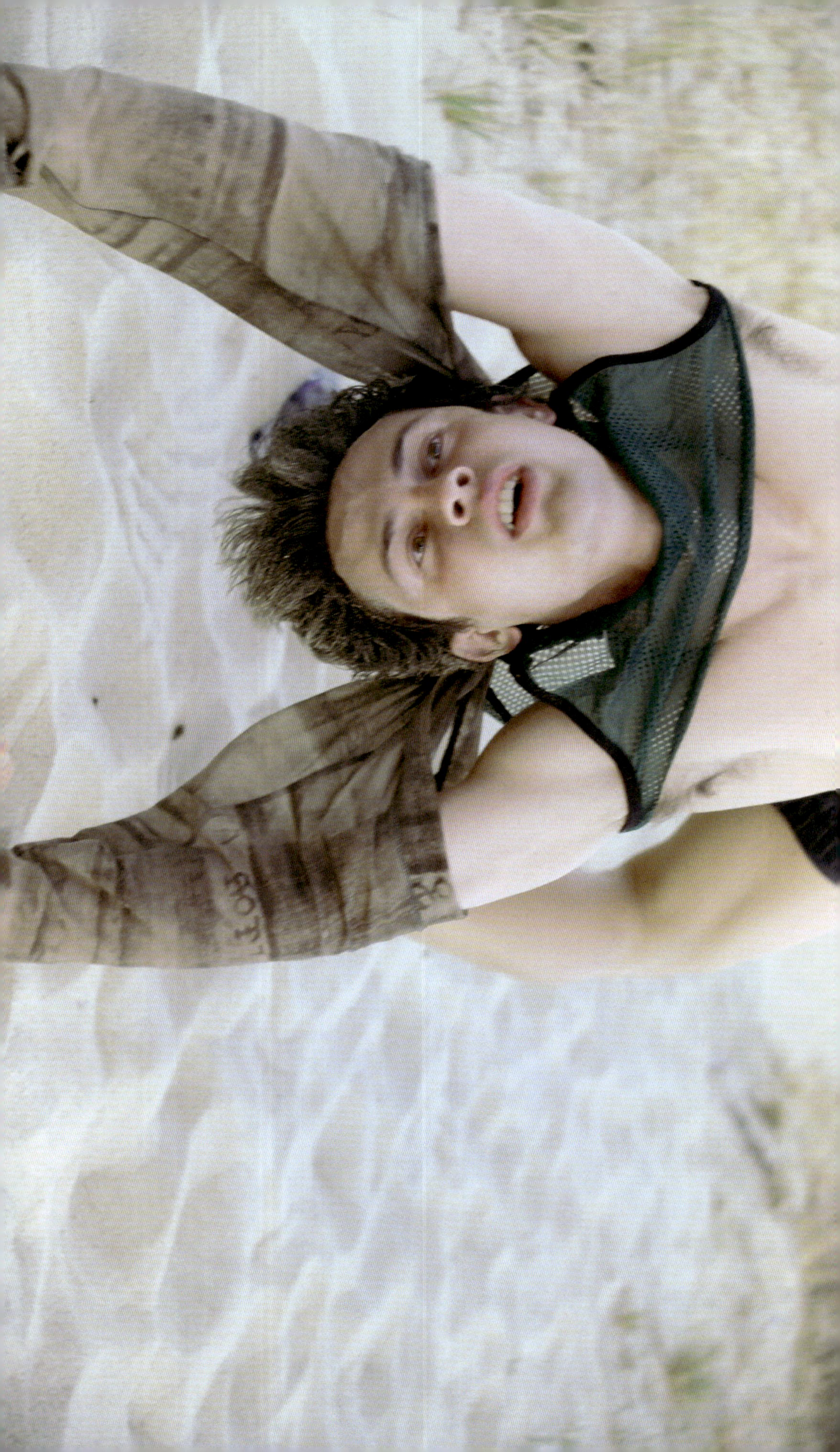

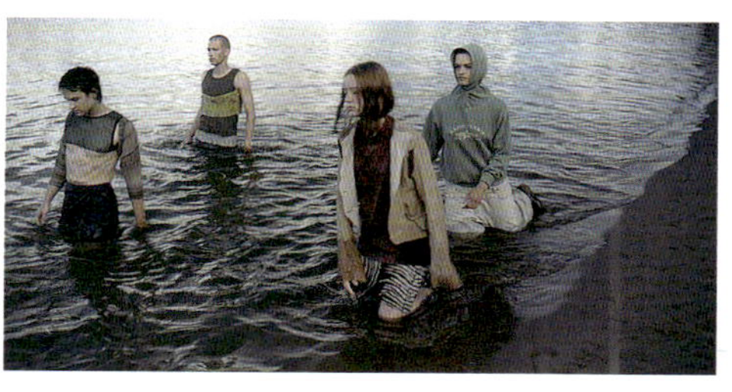
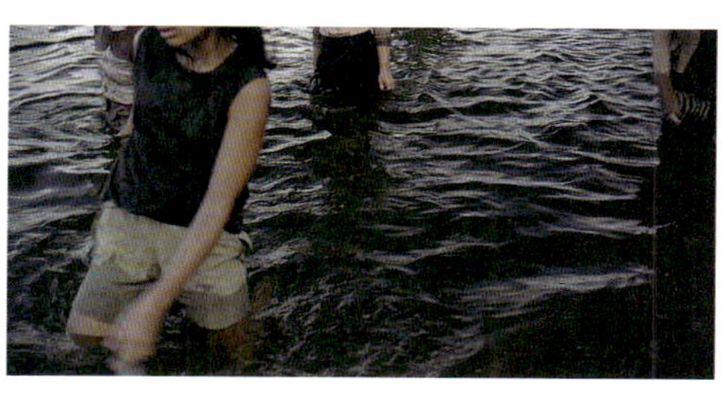
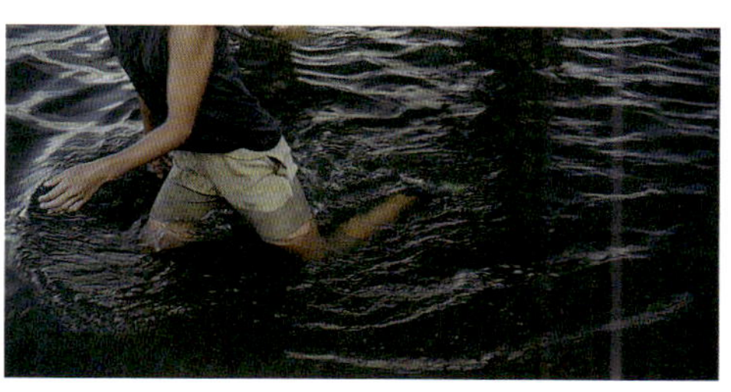
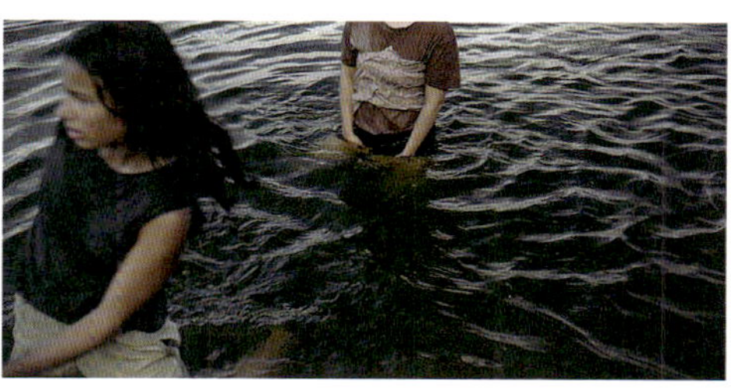
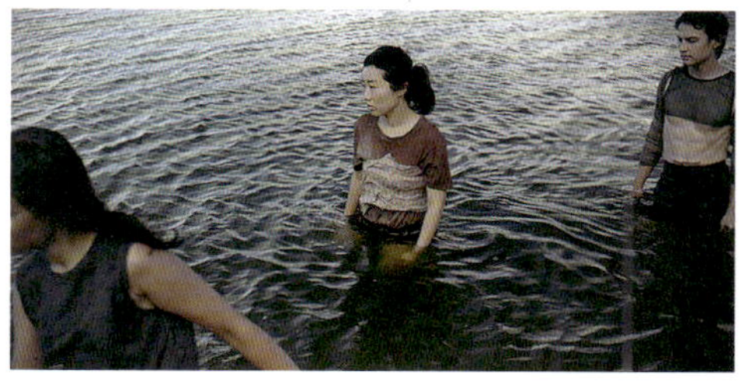
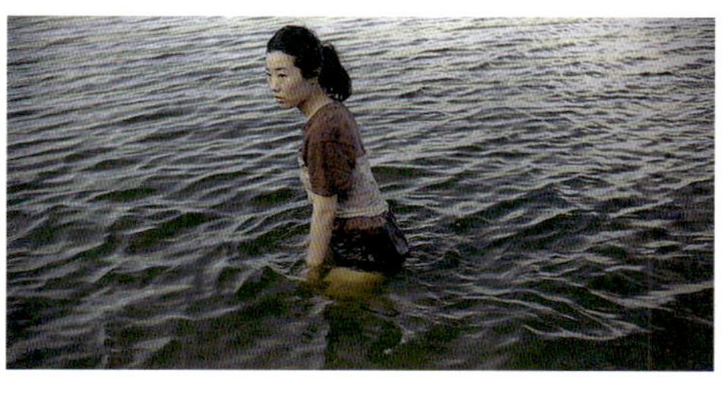
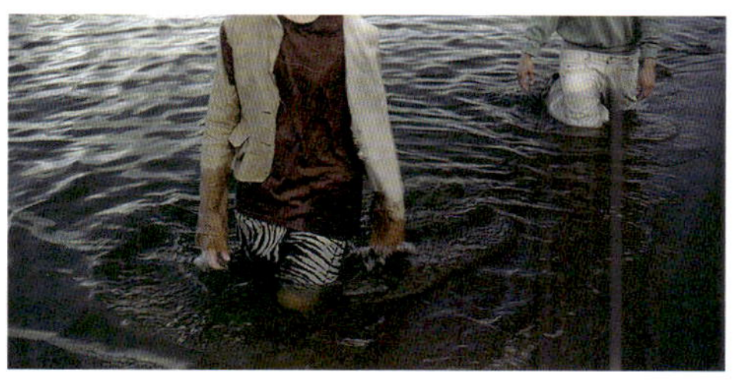
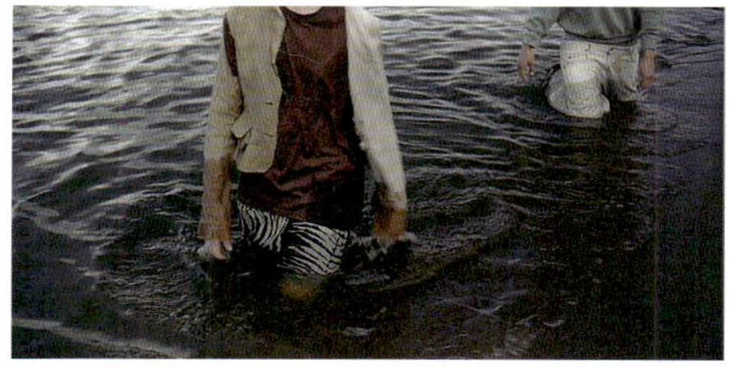

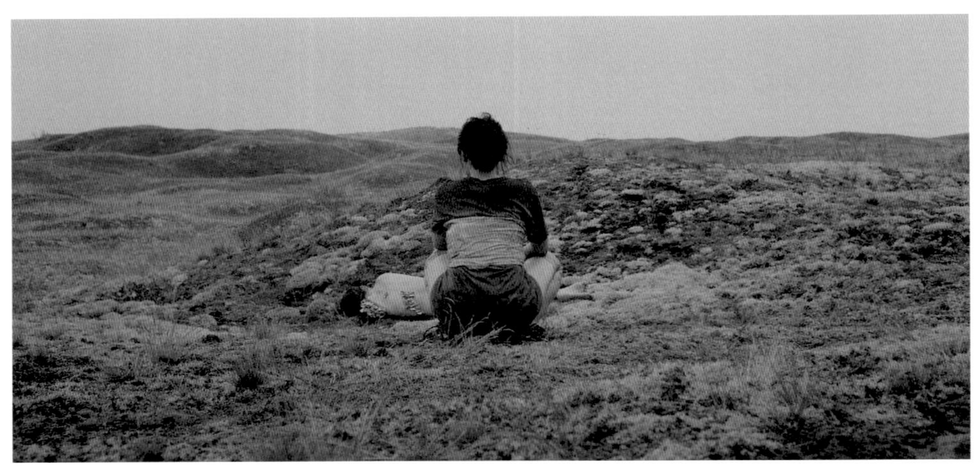

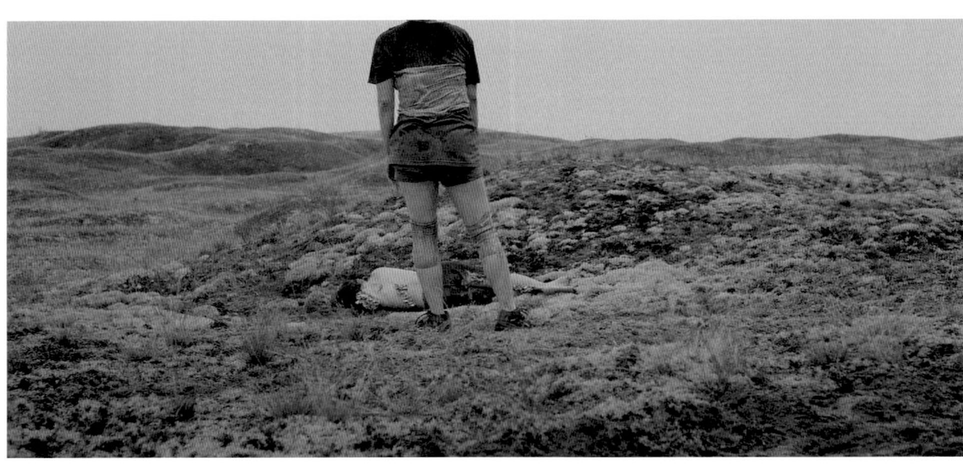

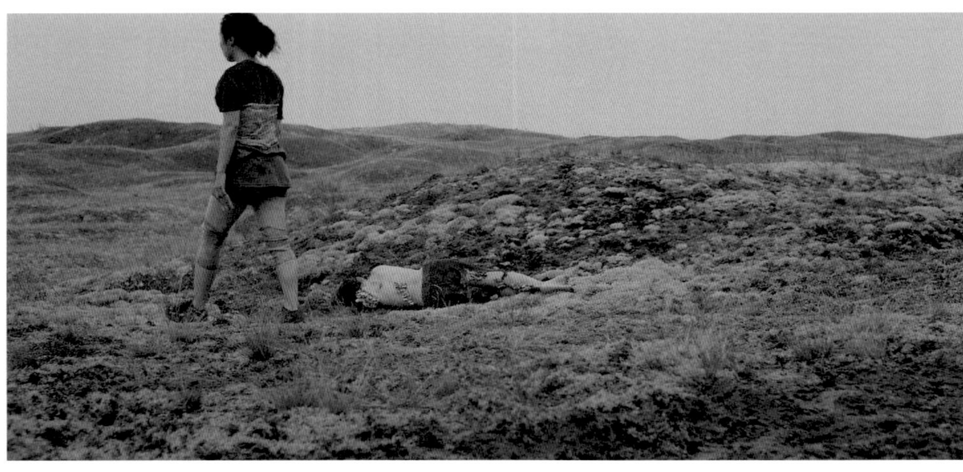

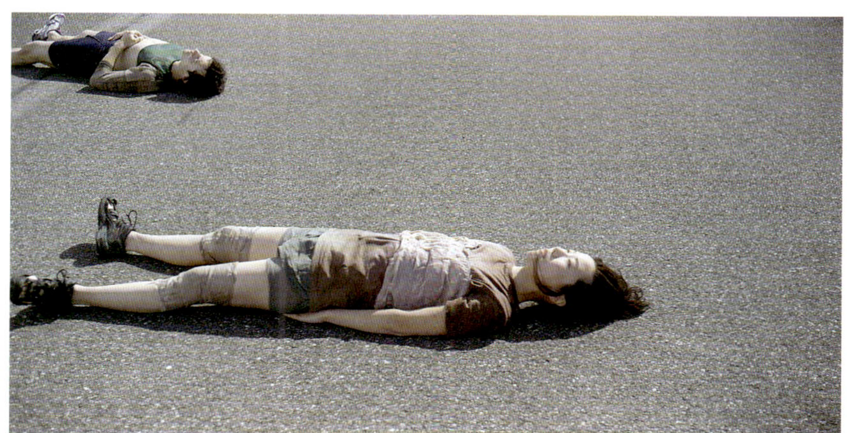
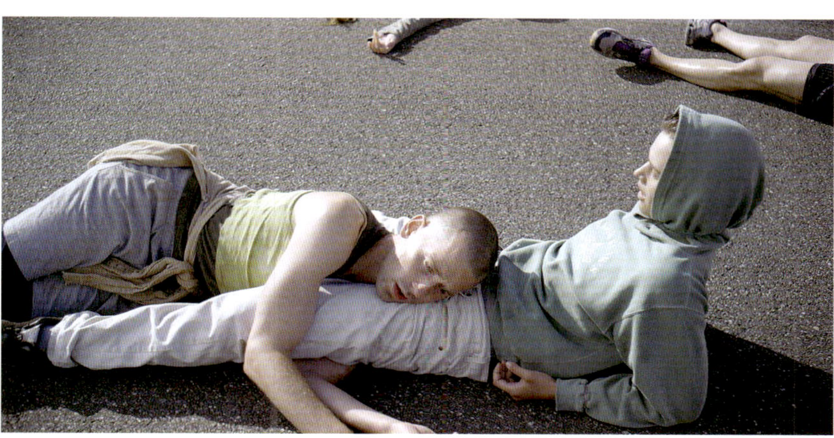
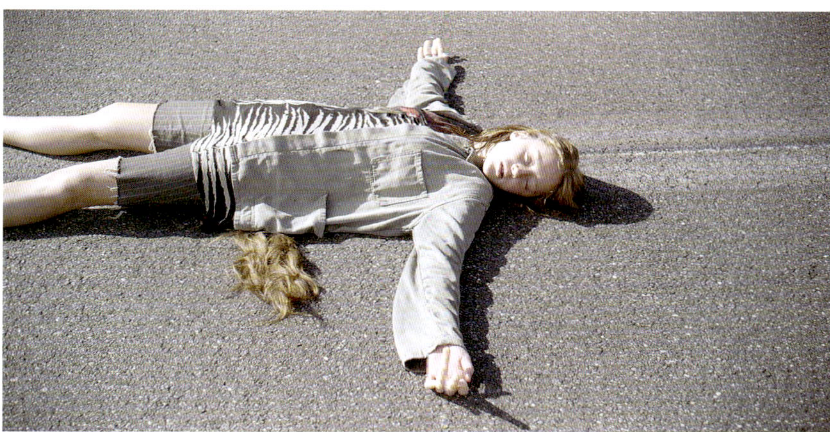
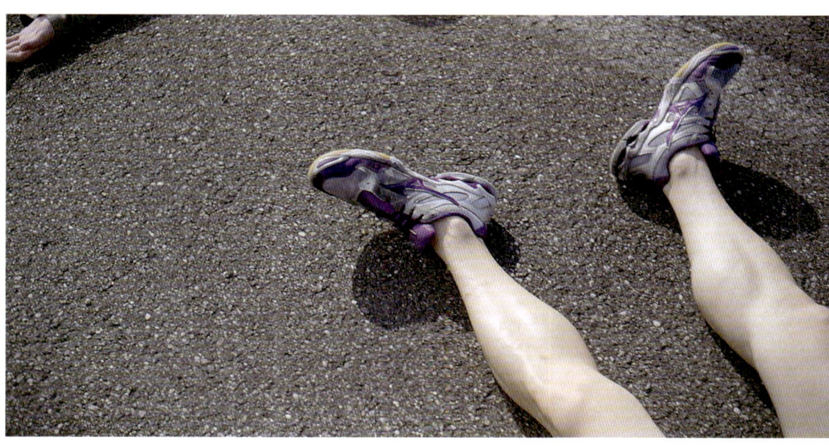

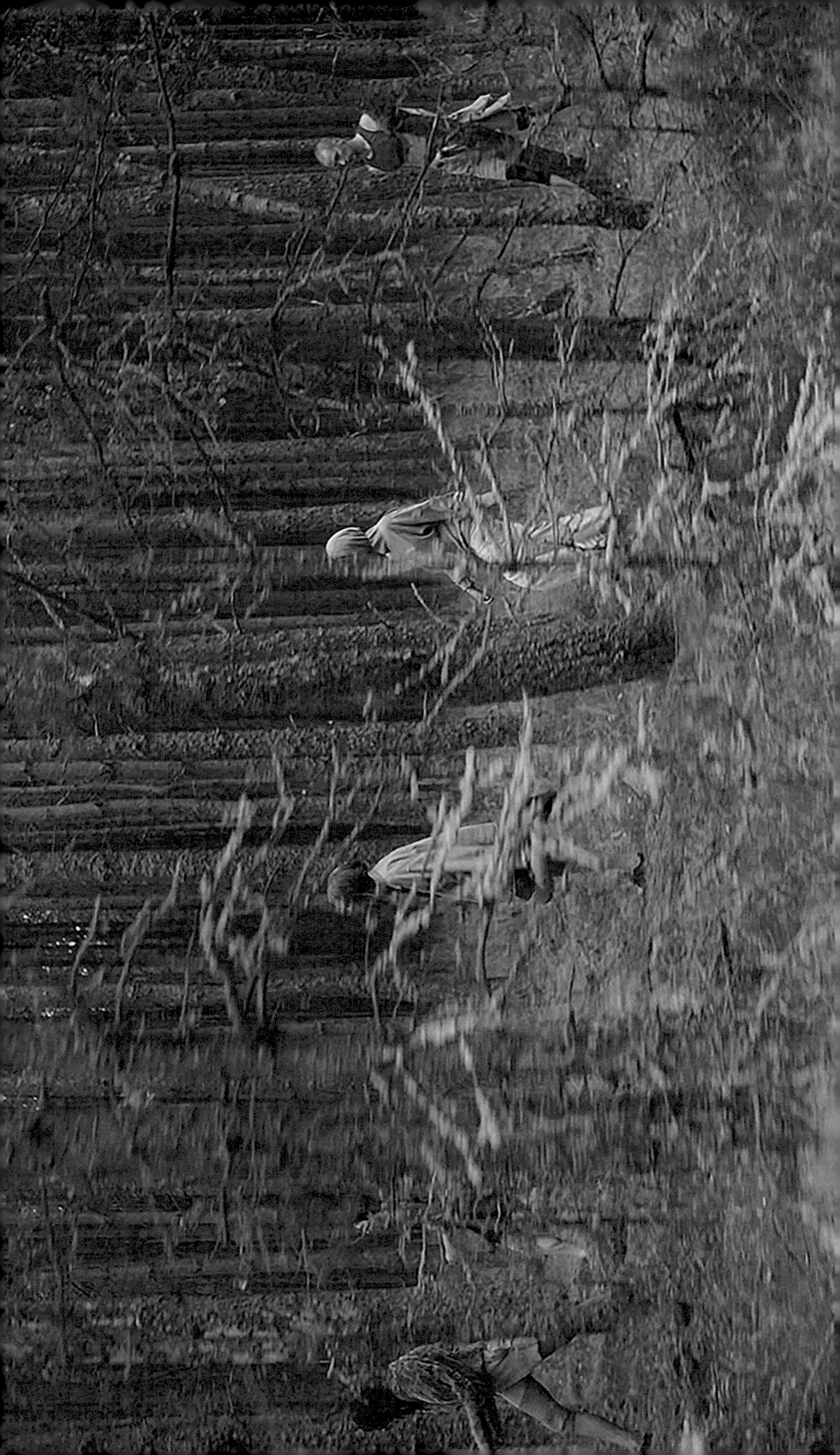

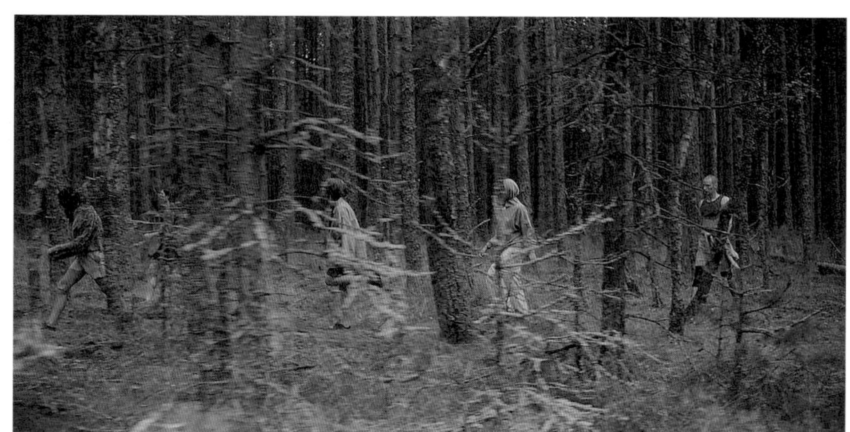

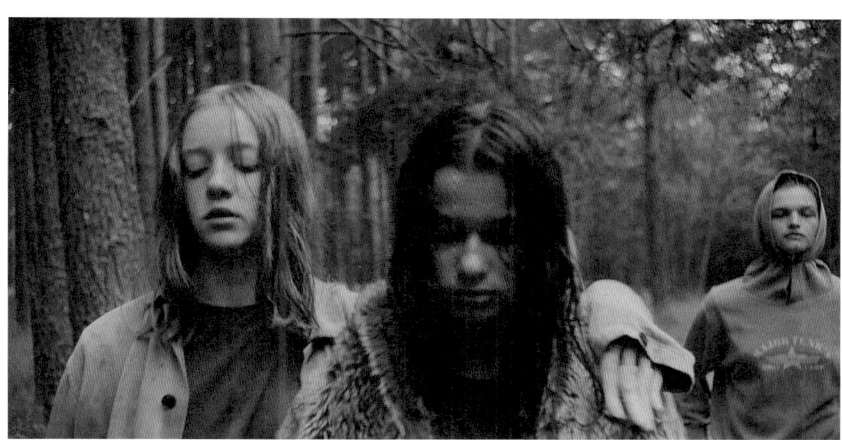

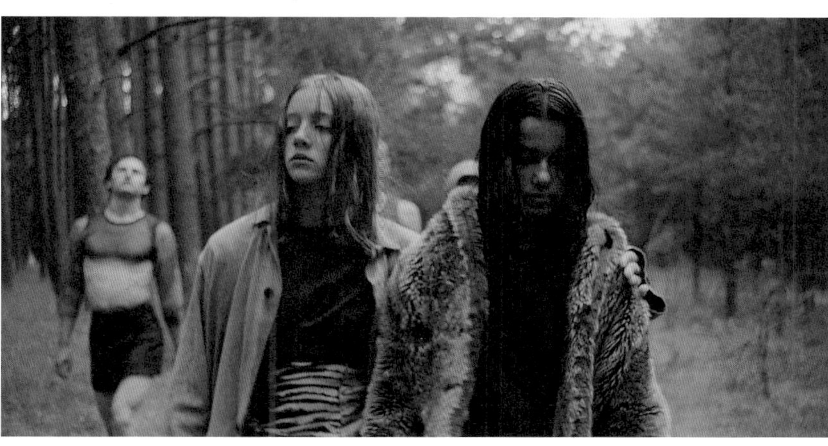

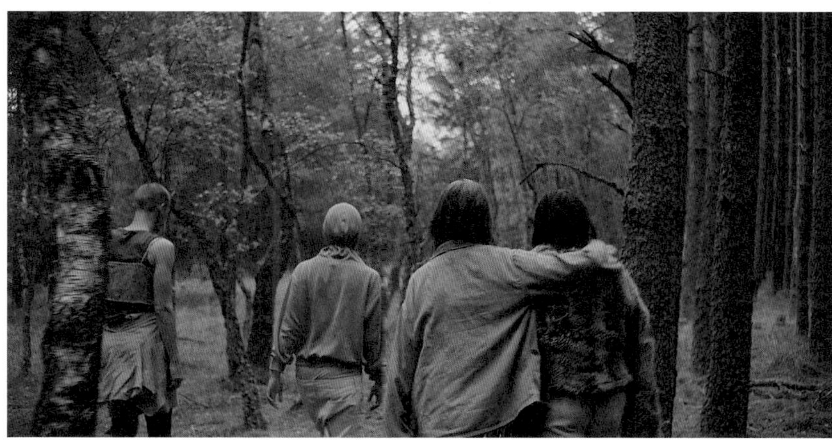

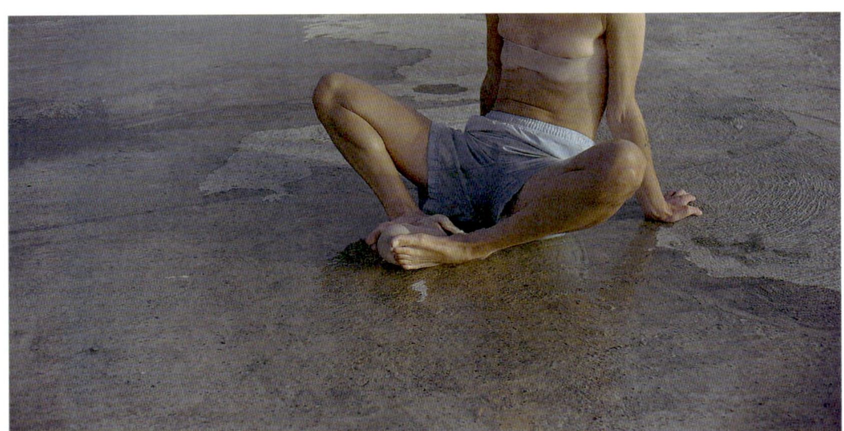
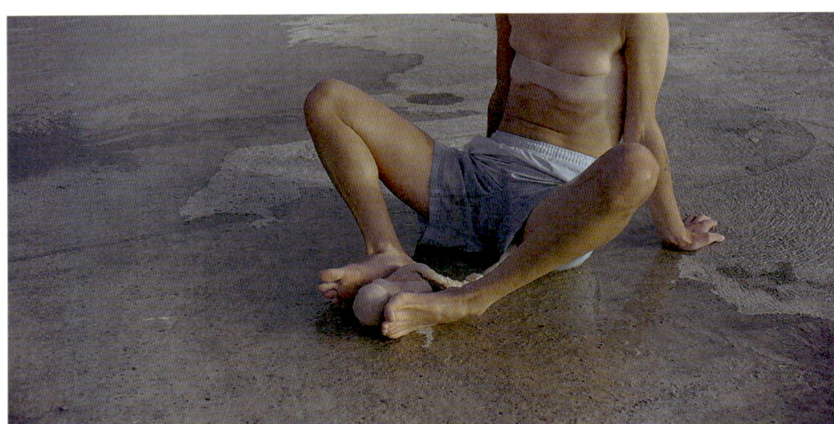
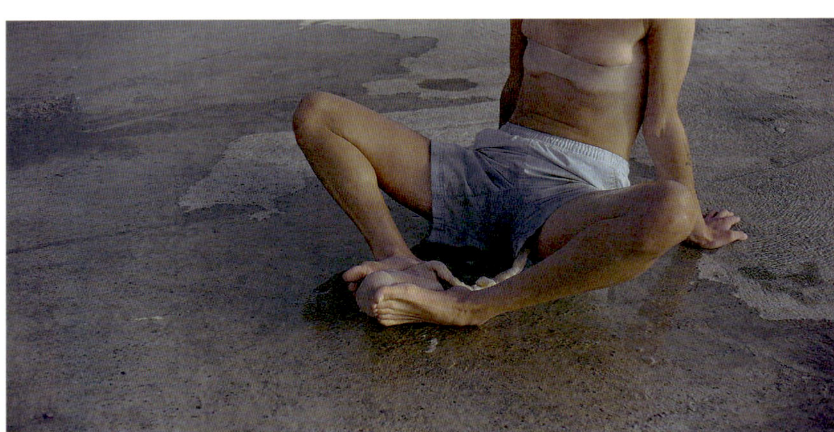
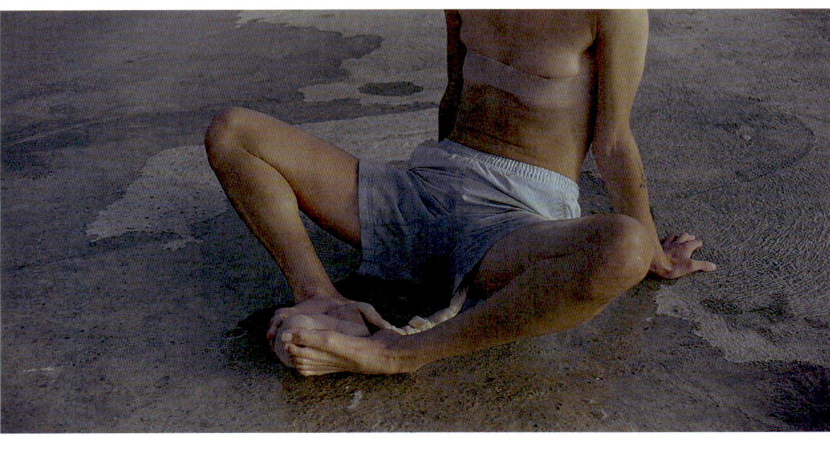

Lithuanian artist Eglė Budvytytė works across music, film, poetry and performance to explore the power of collectivity, vulnerability and permeability between bodies and the environments that they inhabit. *Songs from the Compost: mutating bodies, imploding stars* was made during a residency in Lithuania. Shot in the lichen forest of Nida and the sand dunes of the Curonian Spit, a 98-kilometre-long thin, curved strip that separates the Curonian Lagoon from the Baltic Sea, the film follows six performers as they move through their surroundings alone and alongside each other. Budvytytė worked with a local cast and crew; some of the performers are teenagers from a nearby ballet school, while others are young contemporary dance professionals based in the area.

The opening scene shows four cast members dressed in earth-toned garments as they walk through the lofty pine trees in the distance, then cuts to a lone figure lying motionless on the mossy forest floor, wearing ripped clothing with lichen growing along their bare legs, back and shoulder blades; they appear to morph into the ground below, which is echoed by the lyrics of the soundtrack, 'I am a border line between stone and animal intelligence…I will gently guide you through a process of becoming a stone, becoming slow, becoming a stone.'

While there is no dialogue in the film, Budvytytė speaks of the performativity and tangibility of language, and the potential of words when sung to become a continuation of the body. The score is of central importance, drawing on evolutionary biologist Lynn Margulis' endosymbiotic theory which contests that different types of bacteria form more complicated single organisms through symbiogenesis – becoming by living together. The lyrics also reference the speculative science fiction writing of Octavia E. Butler, and her exploration of the symbiotic relationships between human and nonhuman organisms in order to disrupt anthropocentric hierarchy. Discussing the soundtrack, in which Budvytytė's voice is processed through a vocoder, she says, 'these songs hum not so much about death itself as about the fluid line between life and decay and rotting processes that are particularly evident in forest life.'[1] This notion of entropy is further explored in the scene where a group of five figures lie intertwined on the damp earth with their eyes closed. The camera circles around them as they writhe slowly over the fallen moss-covered tree trunks; their movements feel familiar, rather than drawing on the formal vocabulary of dance. This scene is derived from a body-oriented practice, in which the idea is for one person to touch and manipulate the body of another with the intention of providing care, helping relax the other's muscles in a similar way to how a tree trunk releases itself into the moss. The performers wear brown-, green- and cream-coloured hoodies, netted vests, shirts and shorts which are ripped and bound around their chests and knees. The costumes were created by Budvytytė's collaborators Marija Olšauskaitė and Julija Steponaitytė to offer worn-out clothing as a desirable aesthetic, as a riposte to fast fashion. Olšauskaitė purchased second-hand fabric and clothing and buried the material underground for several weeks, after adding banana peel and vegetable scraps to absorb the underground colour and heighten mineral exchange. In the ground, the fabrics were eaten by micro-organisms, an indicator of healthy soil. The accompanying soundtrack suggests 'how about decay, rotting, decomposing as technologies for non-linear time' and assures the viewer that 'bacteria will take care of you.'

The scenes that follow take place on the beach and feature bodies in acts of physical exertion. Three of the figures move over and across the dunes in crab poses, collapsing under their own weight into the sand and pulling themselves back up again. The horizontality of the figures at various points throughout the film is notable in suggesting interdependence between bodies and landscape and challenging human-centrism. In the next scene, performed and choreographed by Mami Kang, she is pictured with a bandaged chest, her movements jolted, dragging herself along the shoreline on her knees, without placing her arms on the sand. The lyrics speak of 'swimming together in a deep time', 'crossing geological formations' and 'millions of years of mineral solitude'. This notion of geological time links the stones of the forest to the grains of sand on the beach, formed from rocks broken down from weathering and erosion over millions of years, some transported thousands of miles down rivers and streams, slowly decomposing along the way.

Grace Storey

1.  Aistė Marija Stankevičiūtė, 'I have no desire to slip out of this skin, but rather to leap into it entirely. A conversation with Eglė Budvytytė' (9 November 2020), https://echogonewrong.com/i-have-no-desire-to-slip-out-of-this-skin-but-rather-to-leap-into-it-entirely-a-conversation-with-egle-budvytyte/

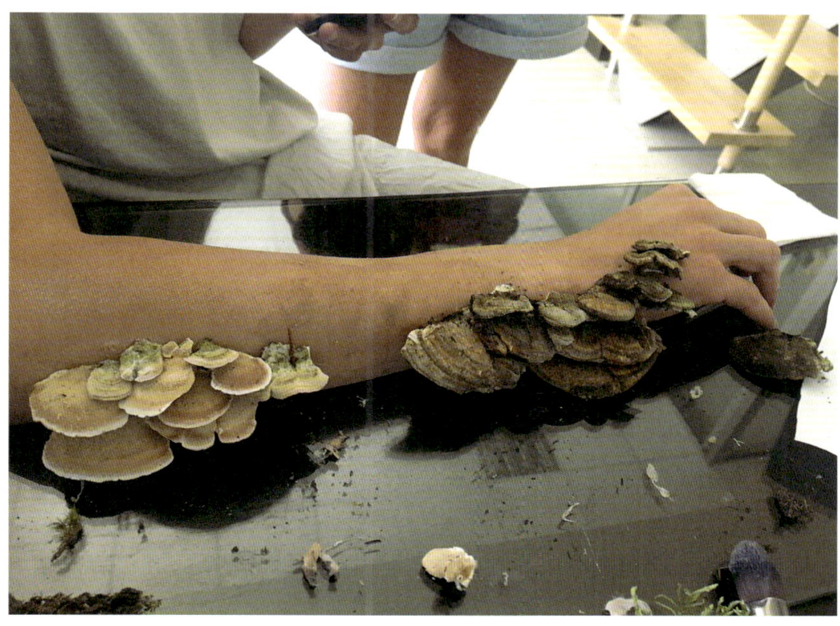

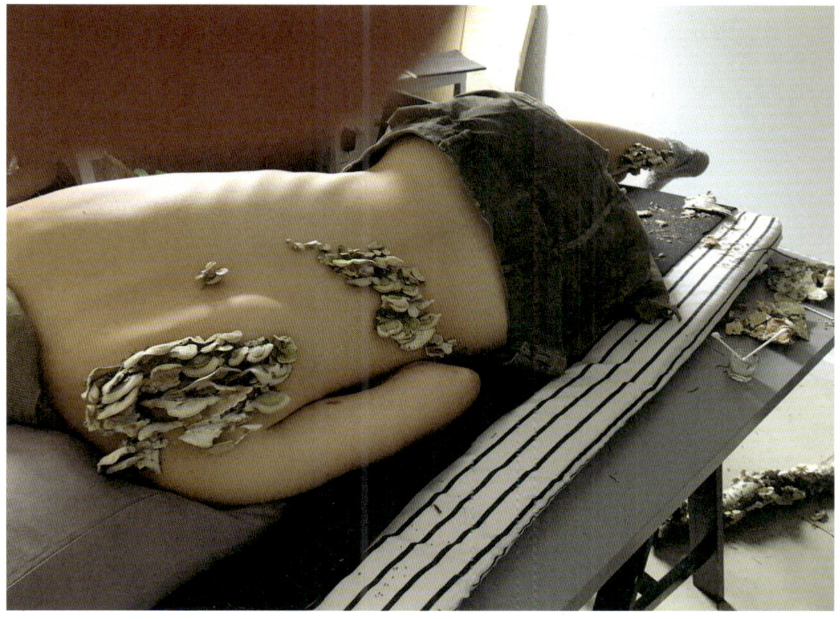

we have never been pure
we have never been clean

      we have never been pure
      we have never been clean

hello,

I am a cyborg
    a symbiosis
        a non binary alien
            after gender abolition
                my name is medusa

hello,

      I am a portal

I am a border line
between stone and
animal intelligence

I will gently guide you
through a process of becoming a stone


becoming slow
becoming a stone

      grave stone
      tender stone

sinking like the stone
into the bottom
of the ocean
into the bottom
of the ocean

      floating like a stone
        floating like a stone

I am an agent of a deep time
sustained attention
I am a child of medusa
I will guide you through the process of
mineralisation

    baby i'm your stone
    baby i'm your stone

a shift in perception

      a crack in the rock
      a crack in the narrative
      a crack in the history
      a crack in the scull
      a crack in the geological time
      a crack in the stone
      a crack in my bone

learning from the stone community
learning from the stone community
implementing stone values
swimming together in a deep time
sustained attention
crossing geological formations
millions of years of mineral solitude

I am not your resource
baby, I am your stone

    I am a shell
    I am a ghost
    I am a host

    I am being hosted
    I am a host hosting
    I am being hosted

    I am a shell
    I am a shell
    I am a ghost
    I am a host

I am being hosted
I am a host hosting
I am being hosted
I am a host hosting

                I am a shell
                I am a ghost
                I am a host

I am hosting snakes on my head
I am hosting bugs in my gut

        I am being hosted
        I am a host hosting
        I am being hosted
        I am a host hosting

I am a shell
I am a ghost
I am a host

I am hosting snakes on my head
I am hosting bugs in my gut

# Éric Minh Cuong Castaing

*Form(s) of Life, –*
*ÉLISE*, 2021,
HD video, colour, sound;
7:39 minutes

*Form(s) of Life –*
*KAMAL*, 2021,
HD video, colour, sound;
5:58 minutes

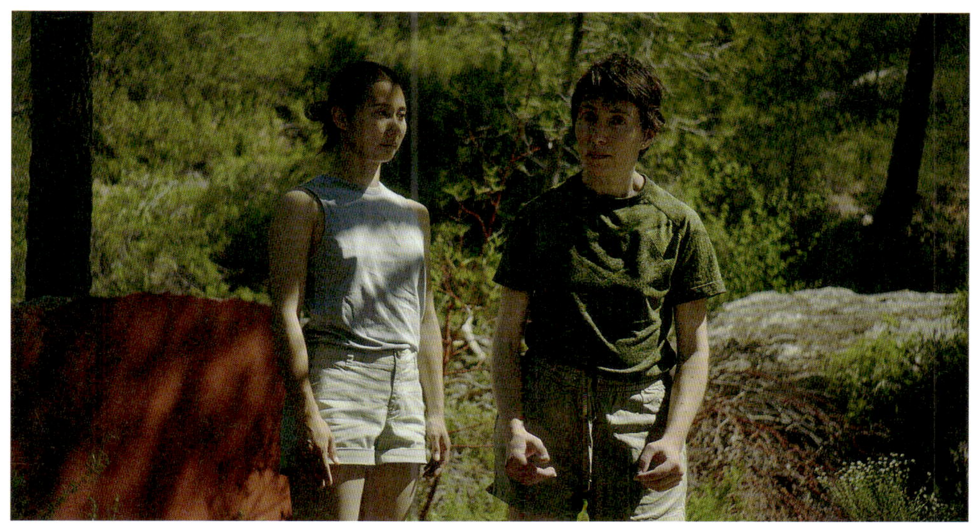

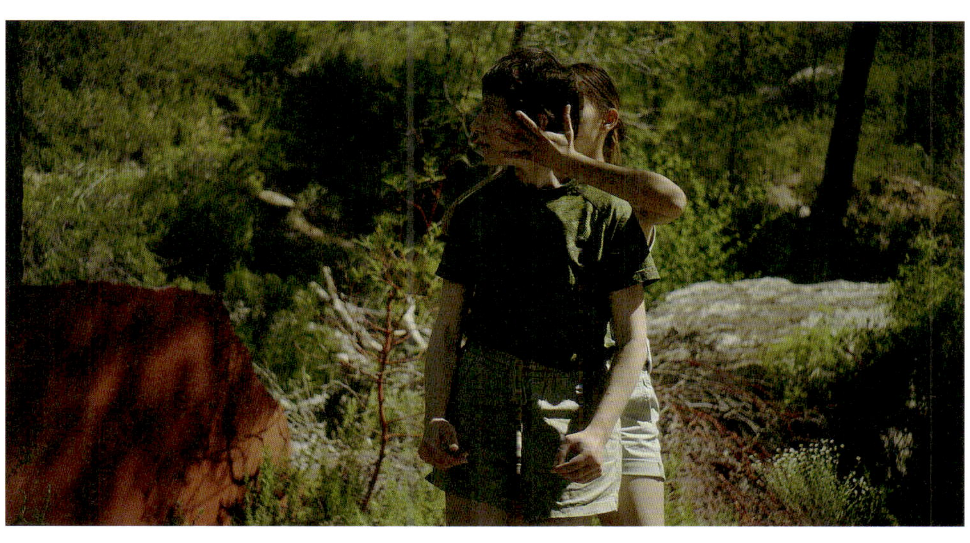

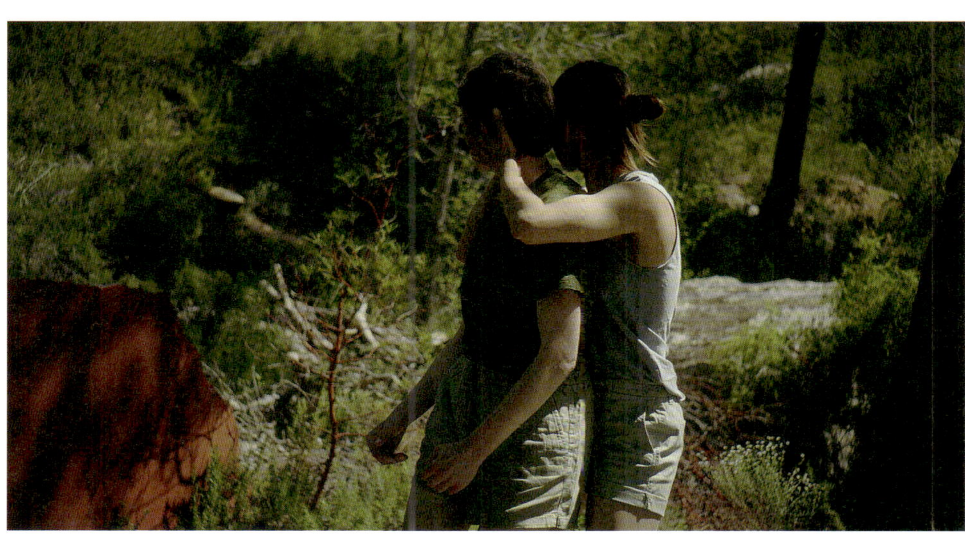

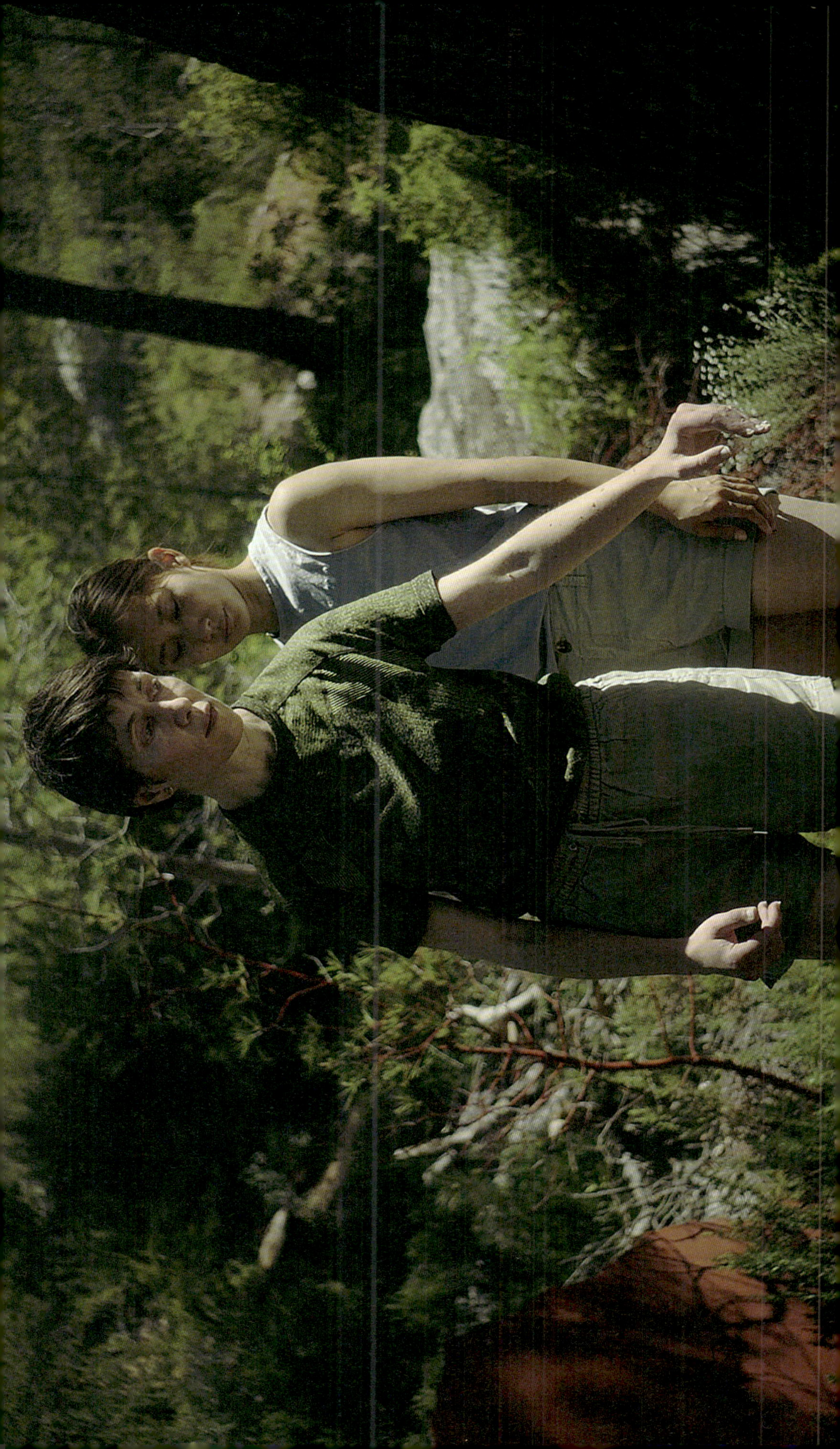

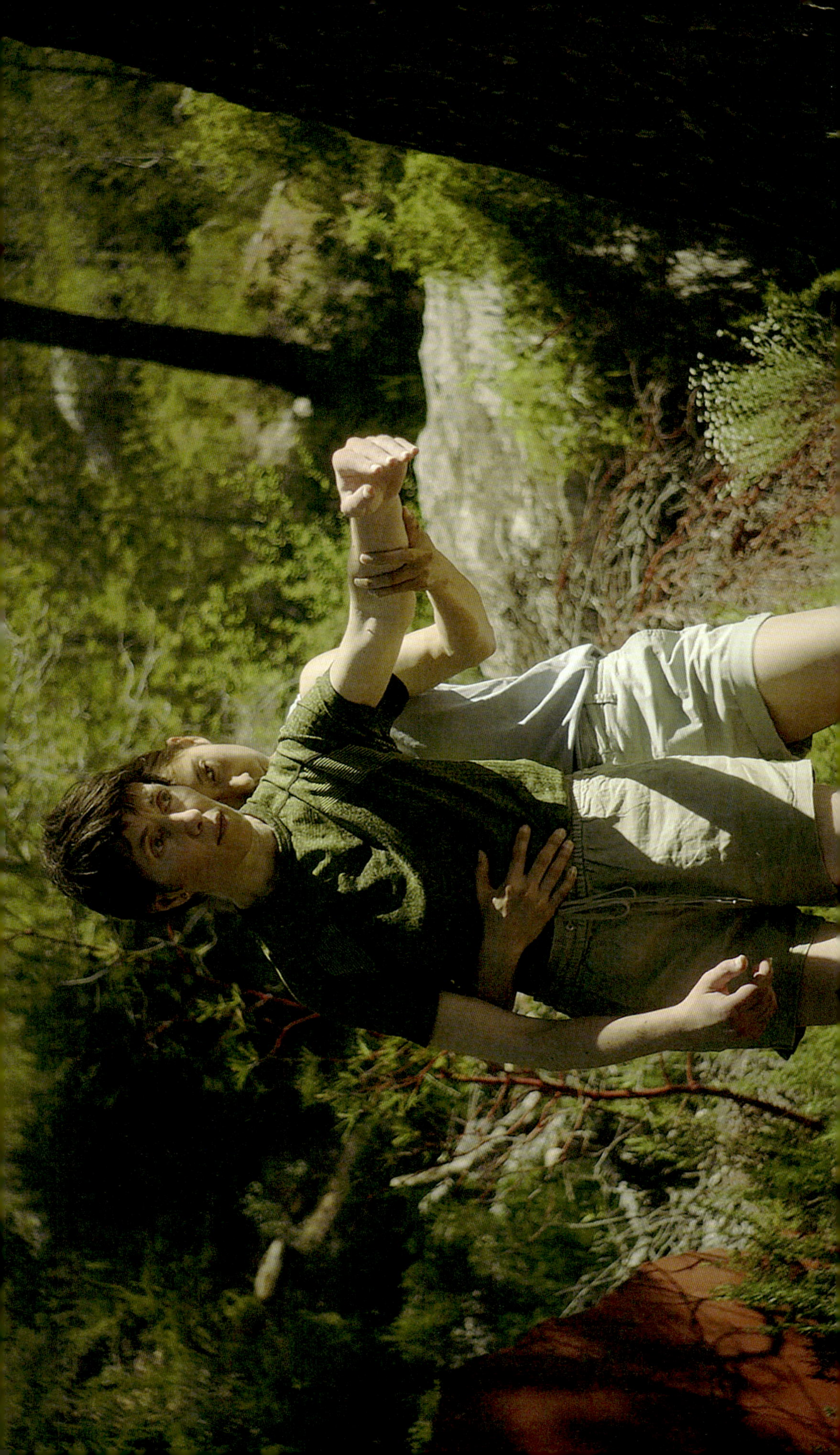

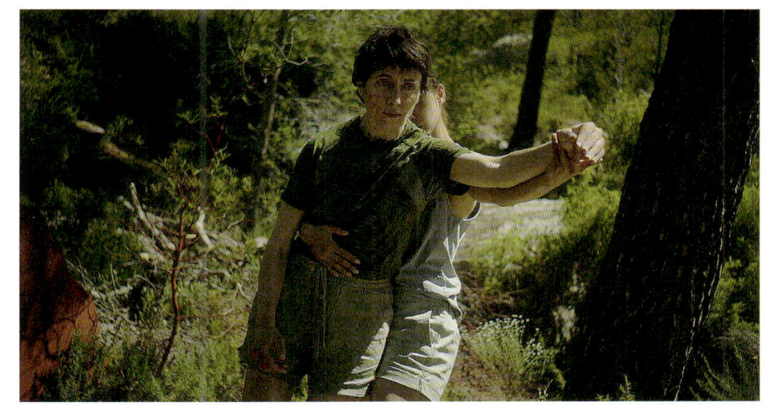

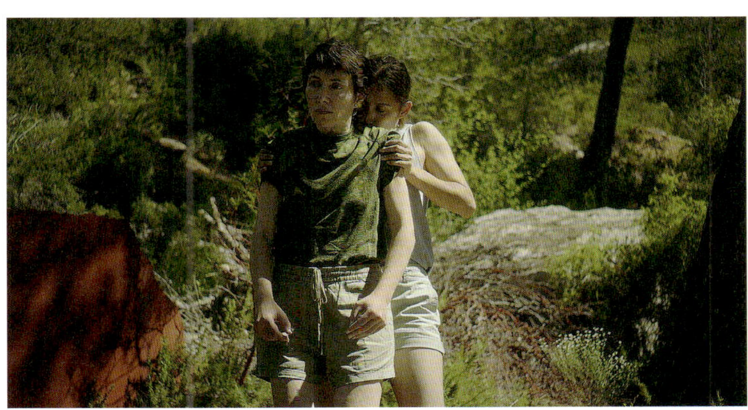

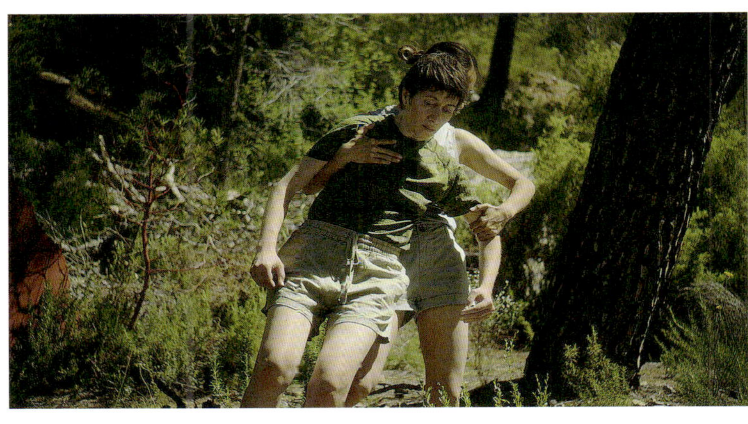

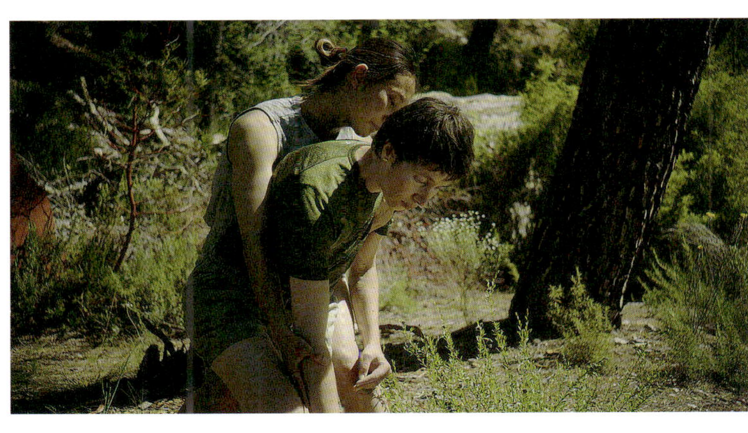

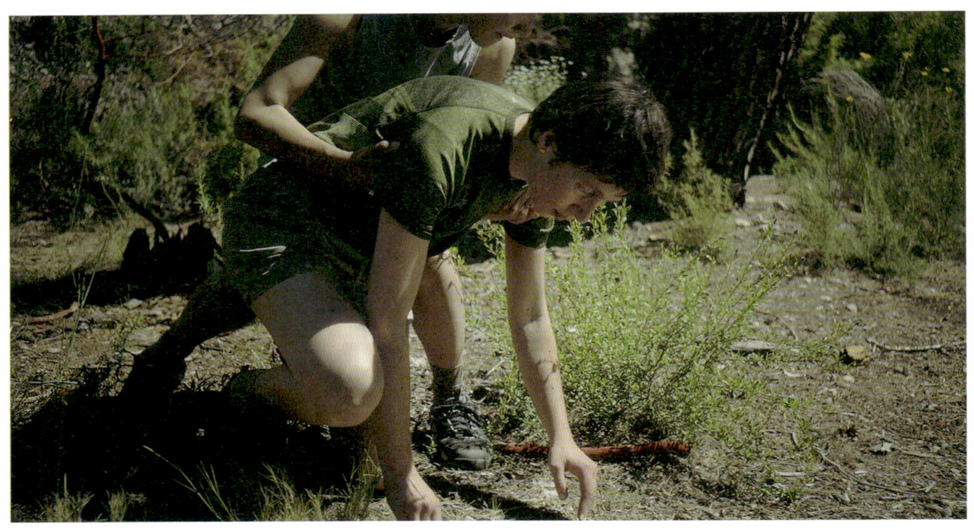

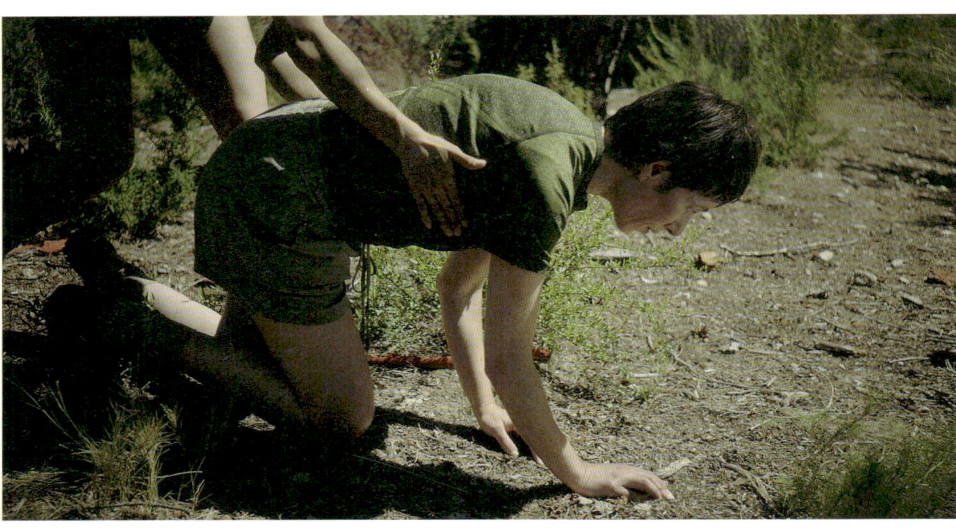

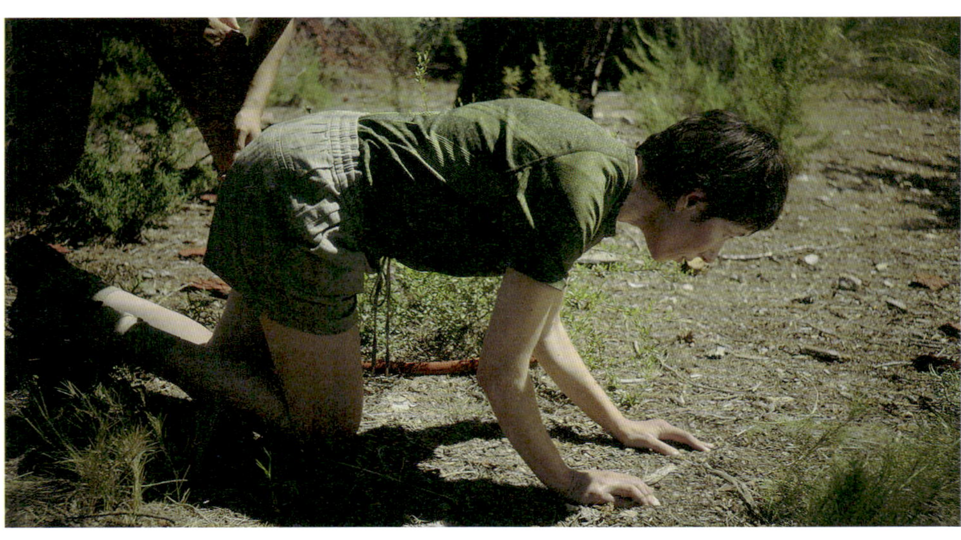

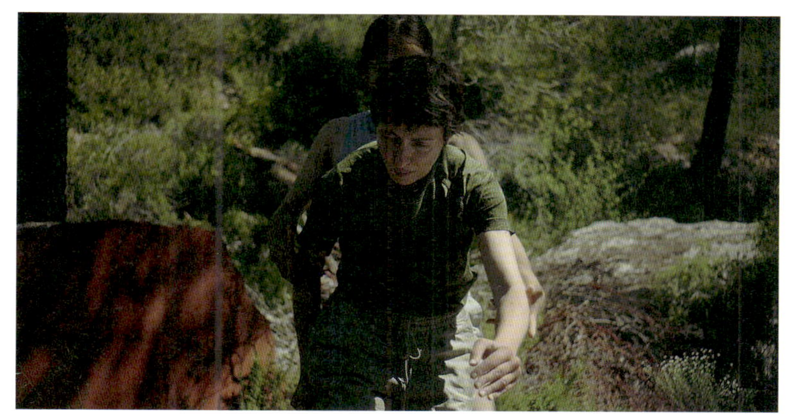

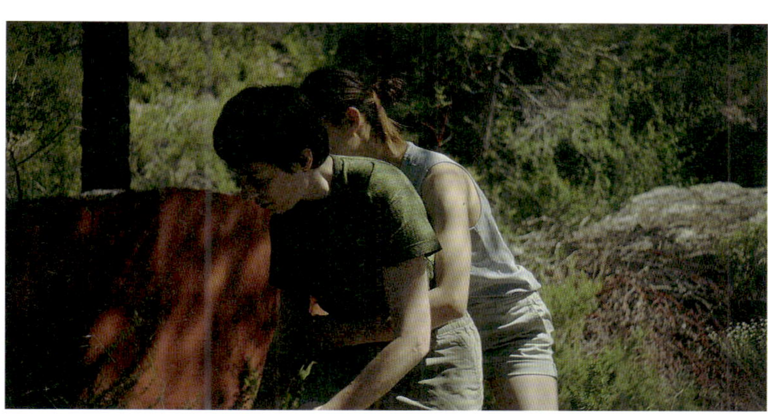

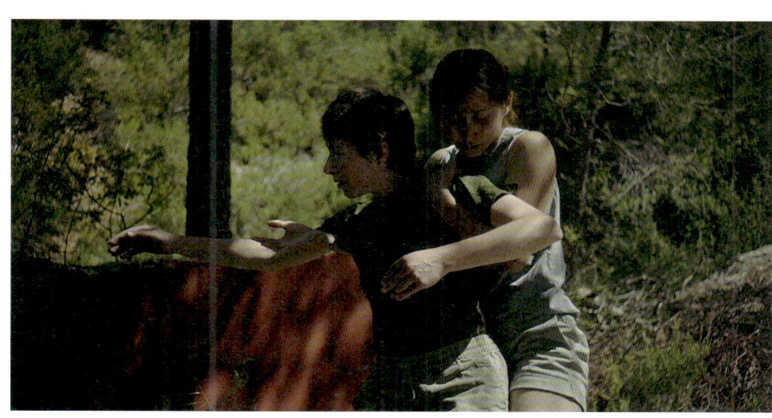

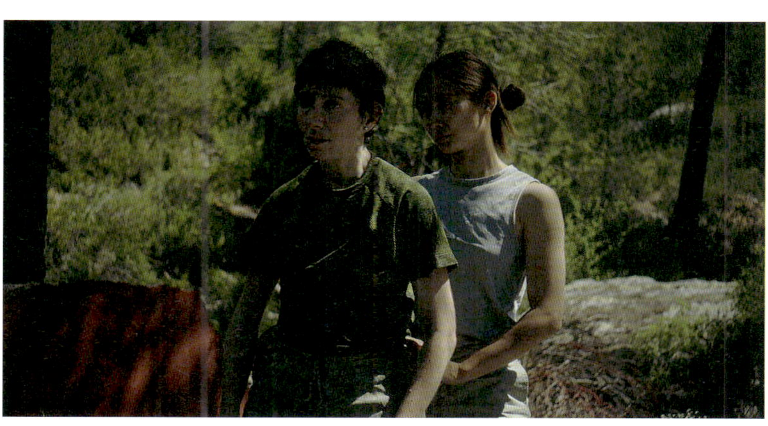

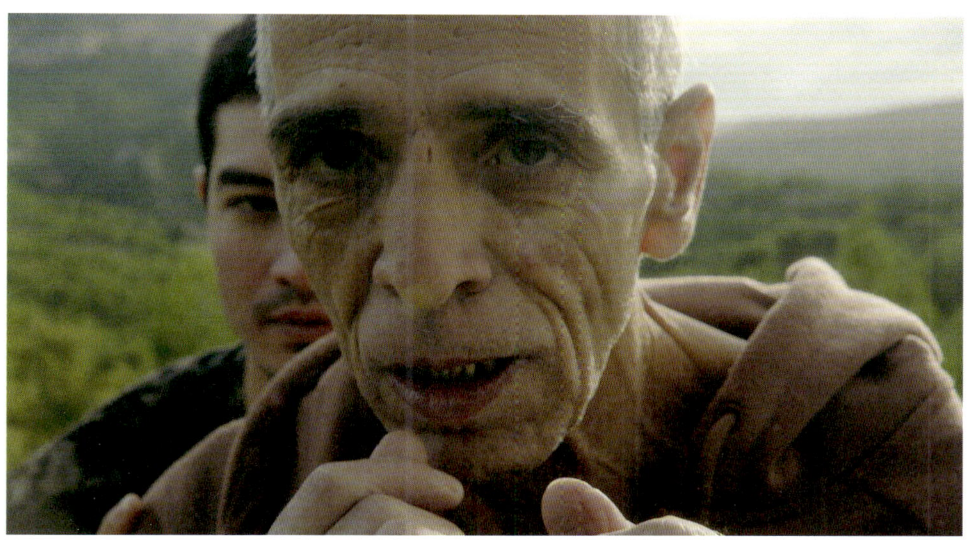

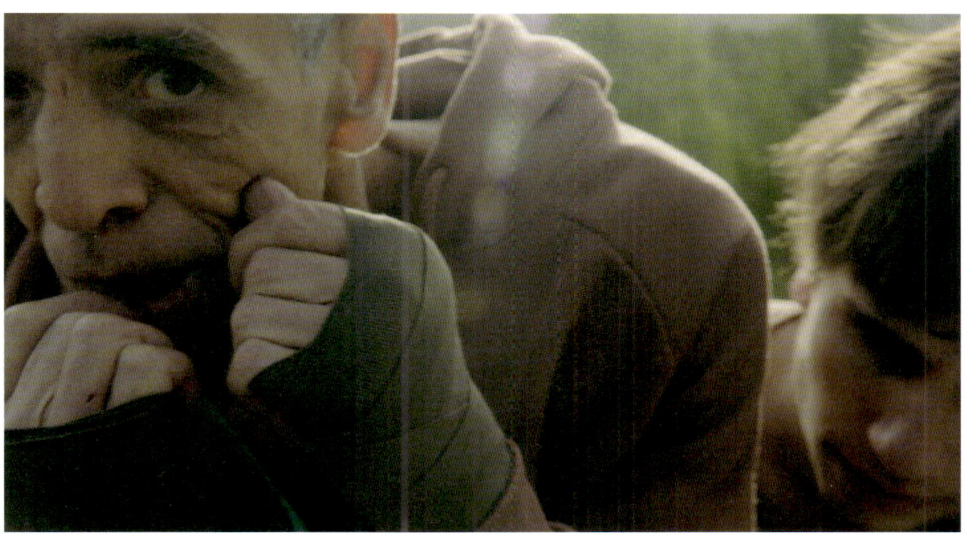

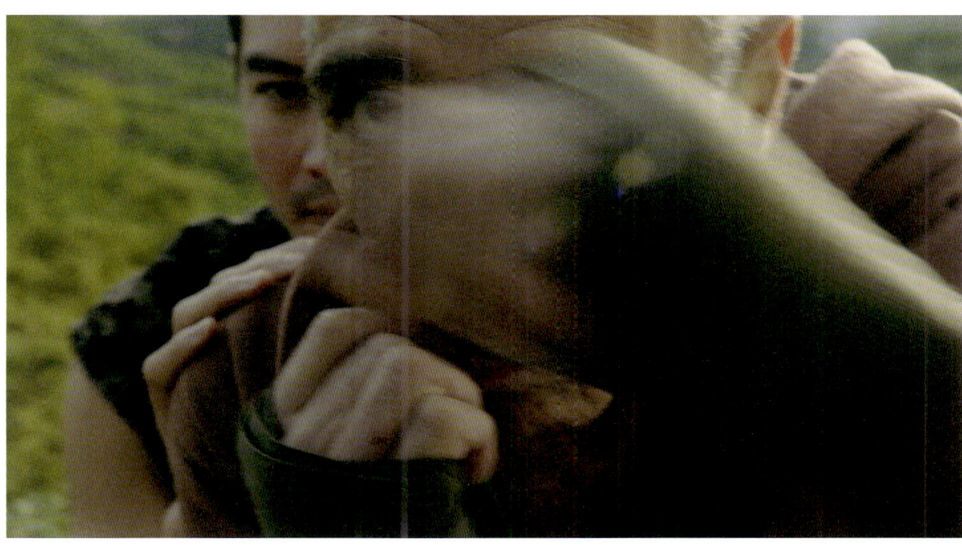

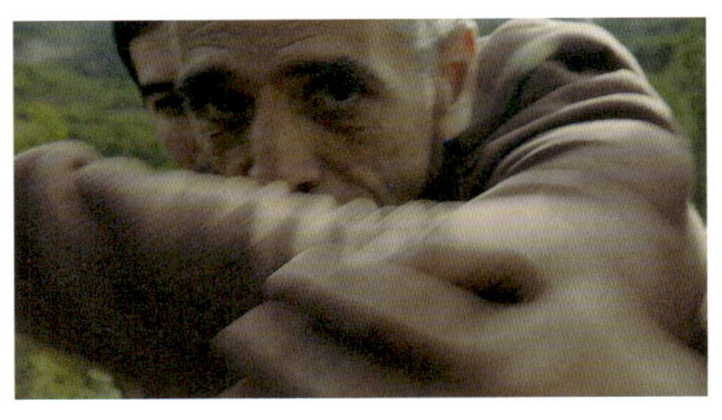
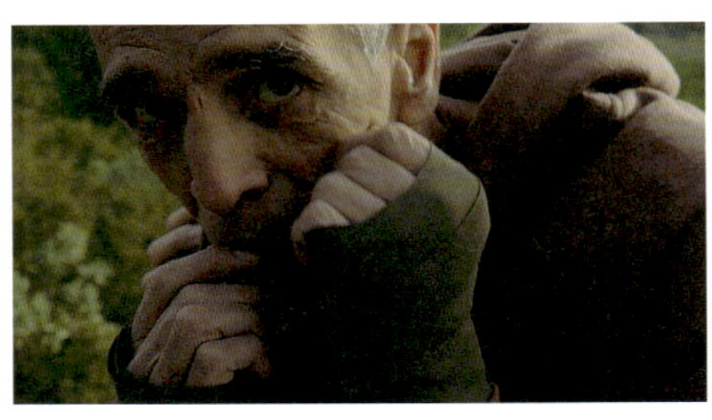
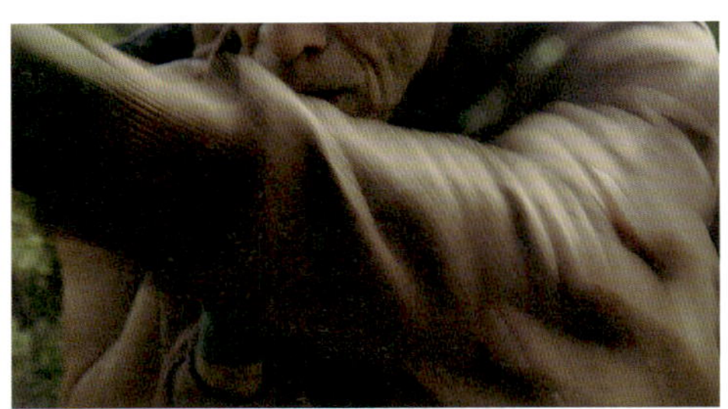
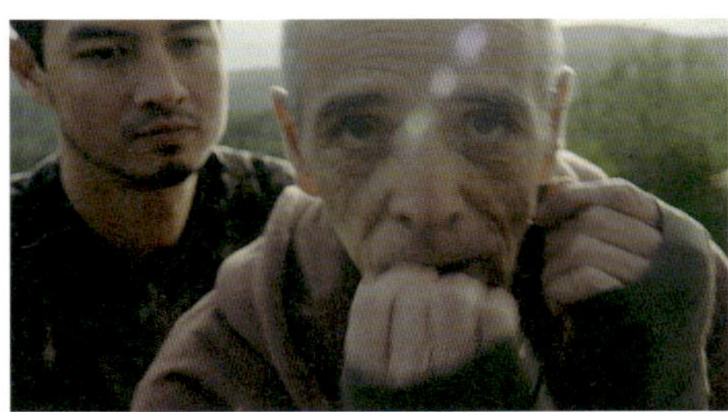
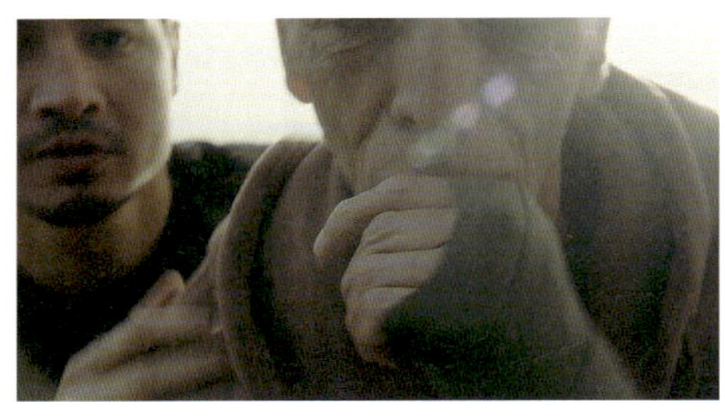
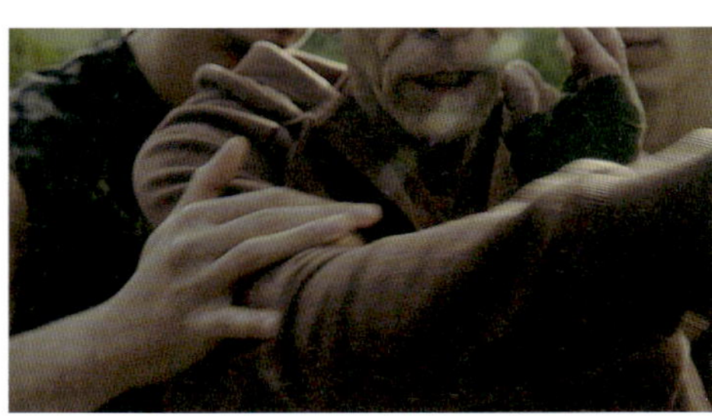
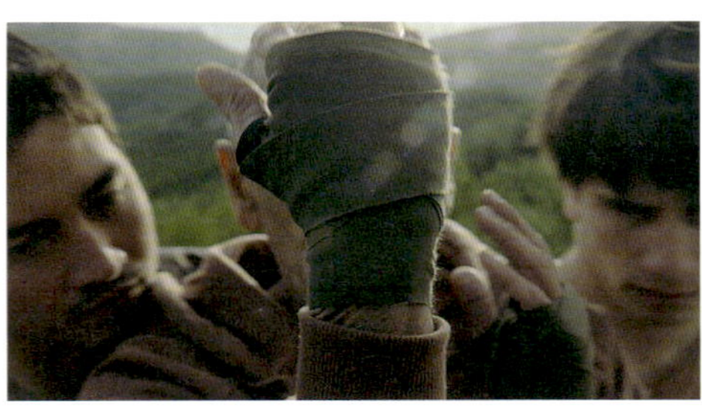
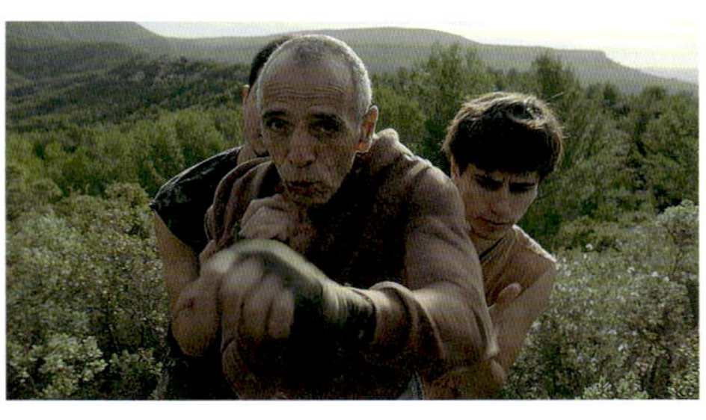

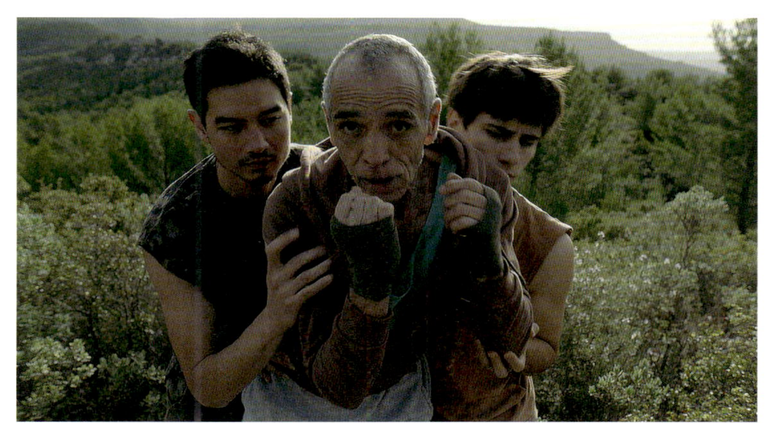

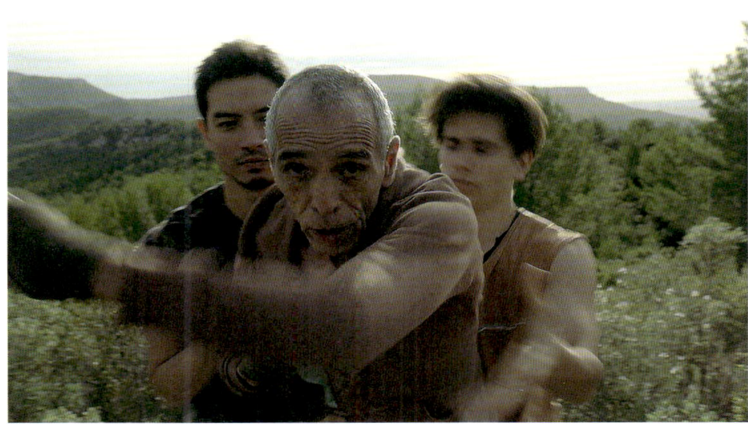

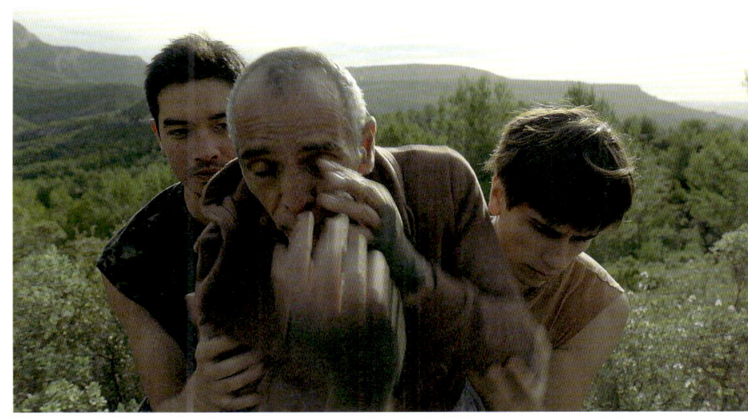

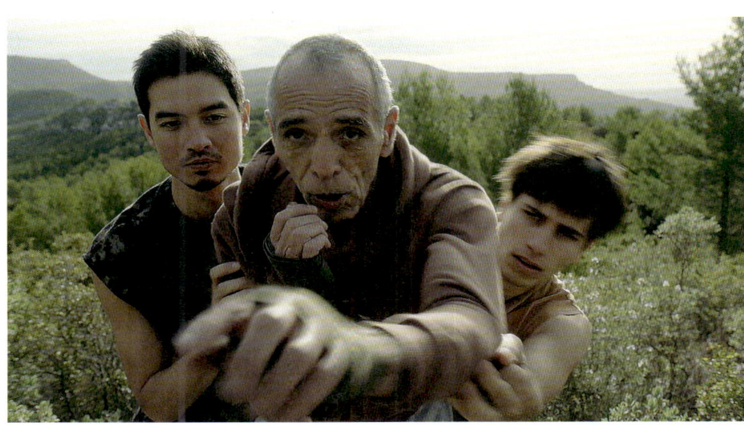

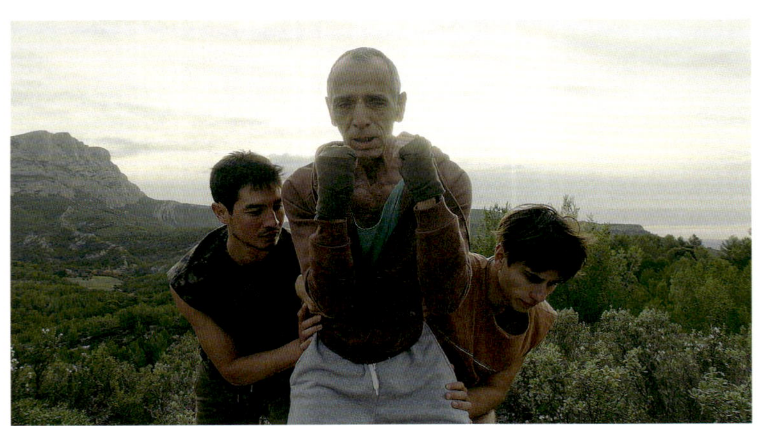

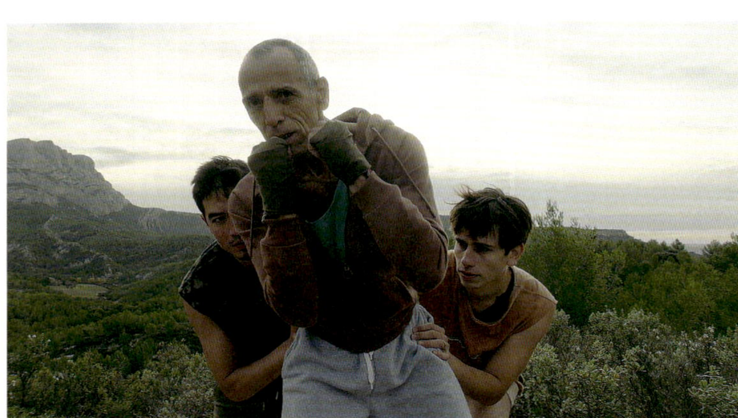

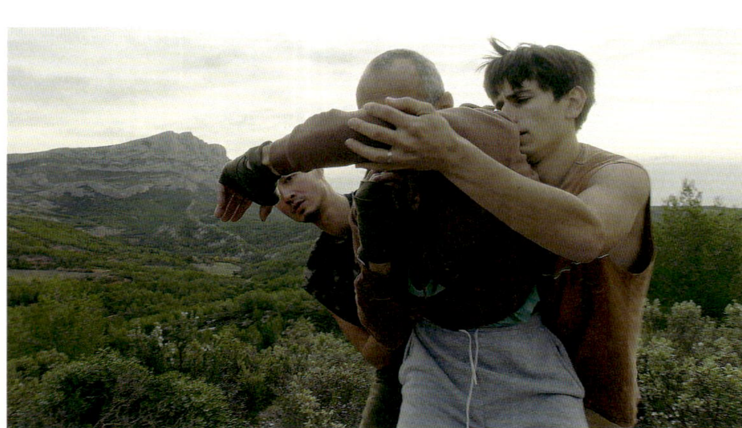

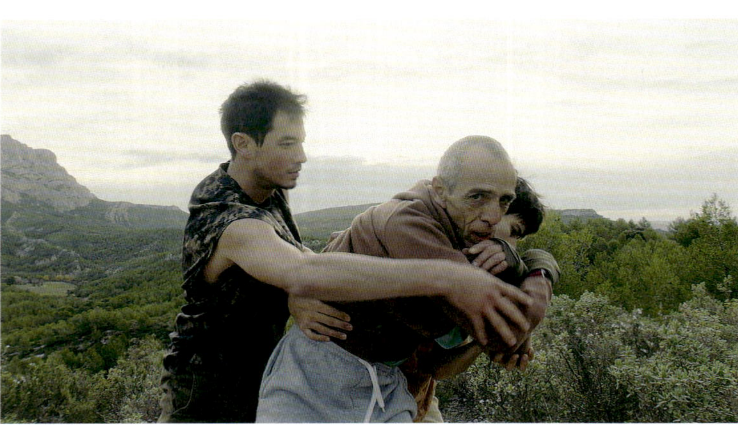

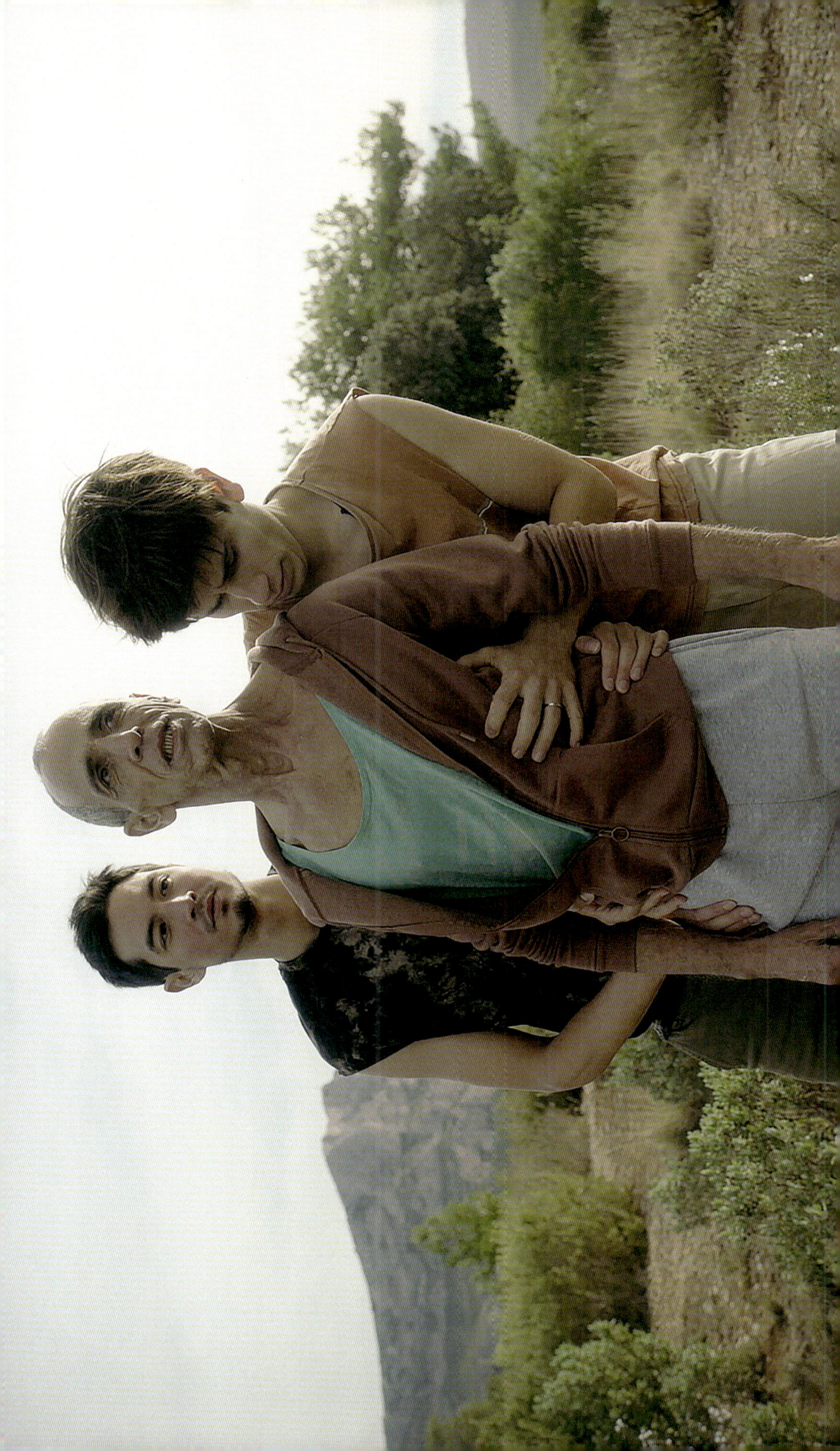

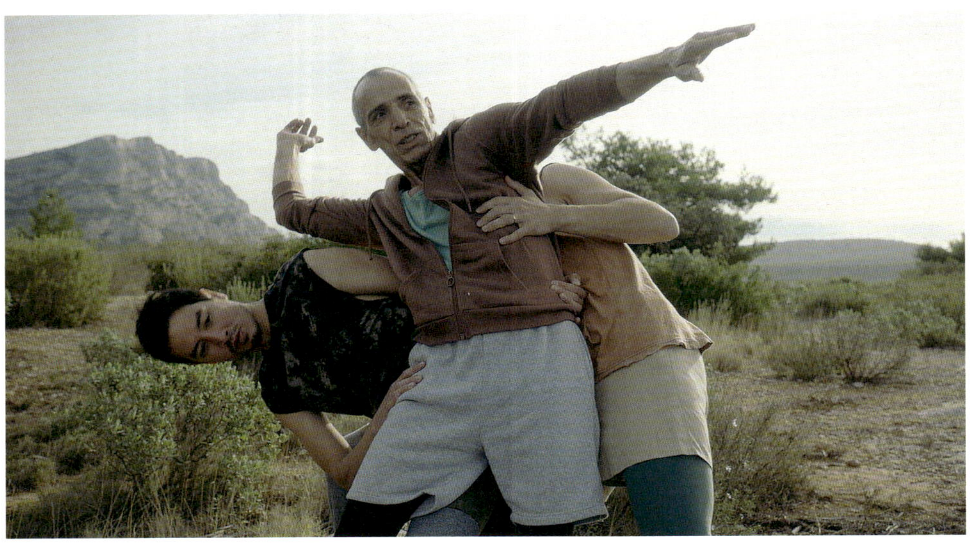

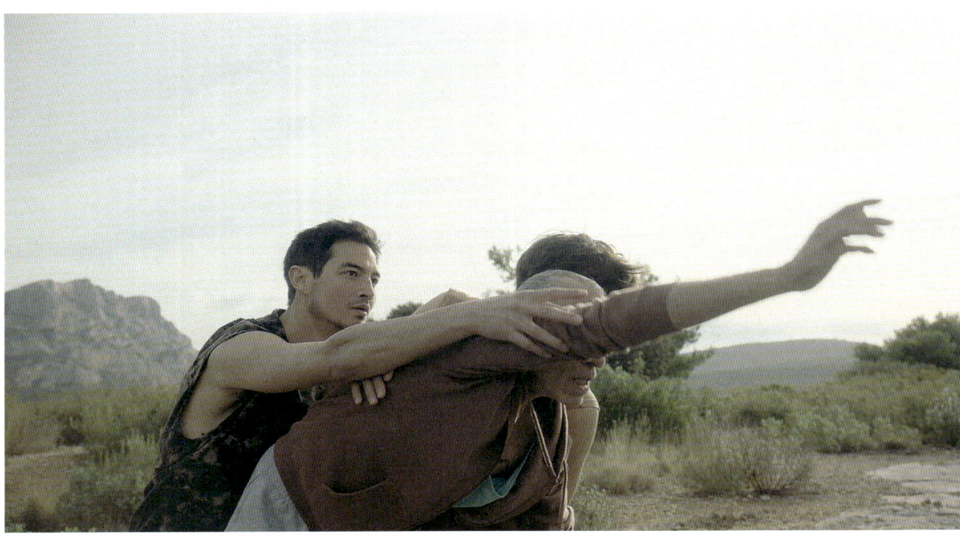

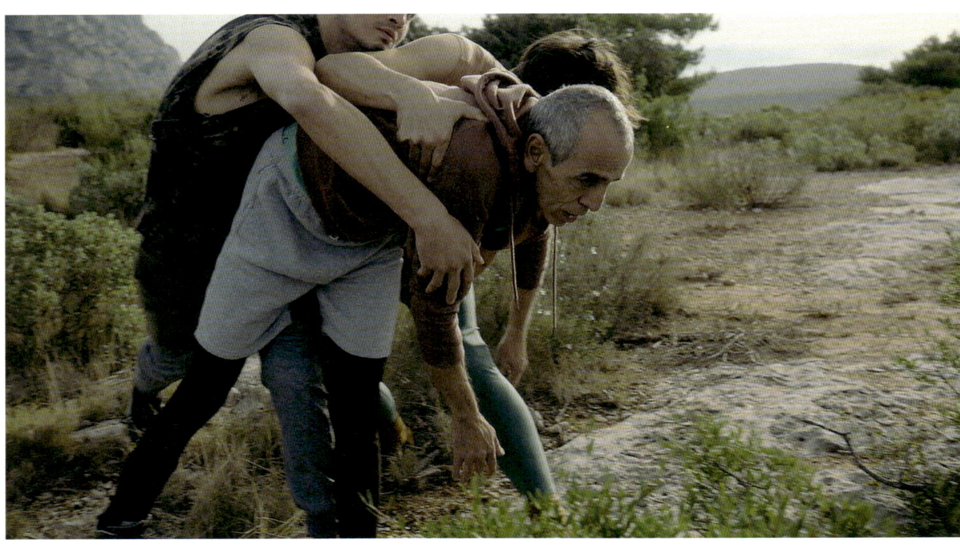

Éric Minh Cuong Castaing is an artist and choreographer whose works explore human interaction and the representation and perception of bodies. He describes his research projects as in socius, partnering with institutions to devise workshops which offer new ways of dancing for people with affected mobility. In 2007, he founded the dance company Shonen, who produce shows, installations, performances and films, and from 2016–19 he was associate artist at the Ballet National de Marseille.

*Form(s) of Life* is a project comprising seven short films ranging from four to eight minutes long, made in 2021 in collaboration with residents of La Maison de Gardanne, a palliative care centre in the South of France established in 1994 for patients with degenerative illnesses. The centre, known for its pioneering approach which places importance on all aspects of the individual and the relationship between caregivers and patients, offers a programme of activities and communal living based on respect and solidarity.

For the project, which Castaing describes as being 'at the crossroads of caregiving and choreography', he organised workshops along with a co-choreographer and a small group of dancers from Shonen to help patients with muscular and motor deficiencies regain some of their former movement. They devised choreographic sequences adapted to the bodies of each individual, enabling them to connect with and reinhabit their former movements and develop unique gestures, which demonstrate the adaptive power of bodies.

The films were shot at the care centre and outdoors at Calanques National Park, in the outskirts of Marseille. 'Moving Bodies, Moving Images' features two videos filmed in the park, using the landscape as a stage. The project was made during the height of the COVID-19 pandemic, and the expansive surroundings, which the residents would not otherwise have had the opportunity to visit, offer choreographic possibilities and relief, as the patients are liberated from the confines and associations of the clinical environment. The temperature, the wind and the sounds of nature, from birdsong to the rustling of leaves in the trees, stimulate their senses and movements.

One film features Kamal Messelleka, a former professional boxer who suffered a stroke. It opens with a close-up shot of him inhaling and exhaling slowly, his clenched fists held close to his chest, with the luscious forest in the distance behind him. He is supported by two dancers, who he taught how to box during the earlier workshop. They stand behind each of Messelleka's shoulders with their eyes downcast in concentration as they focus on his body and react to his shifting weight. Messelleka begins to move from side to side, jabbing and making left and right hooks as the dancers hold his arms and shoulders. He grunts as he exerts himself and his movements become quicker as he rediscovers his former gestures and sequences of movement from thirty years ago, making uppercuts and wide hooks.

Another film features Élise Argaud, a former professional dancer with Parkinson's disease. Argaud's movements have a slowness to them and her body is stiff as a result of her neurological condition, meaning her gestures are not automatic and every movement requires intense concentration. As the film opens, Argaud is pictured wearing a green T-shirt and shorts, standing poised with her arms by her side and looking straight ahead, rather than directly at the camera. A dancer stands behind Argaud, adapting to her pace and helping intuit her movements as she turns her head to the right and back again and extends her left arm. Moving tentatively, but with purpose, she lowers herself to the ground on all fours, supported by the dancer. She tells her, 'I am trying to extend my left leg', before gradually extending her left leg and right arm, then being guided back up to a standing position.

In both films, the dancers help augment the bodies of the patients by acting as interpreters and prostheses. There is a sense that the people both in front of the camera and behind it are in motion and involved in the performance. The camera work by cinematographer Victor Zébo follows the movements of the performers closely, enabling the viewer to observe each stage of the sequence, capturing the experience of fragility, non-verbal communication and the importance of gestures to connect and communicate with others.

Grace Storey

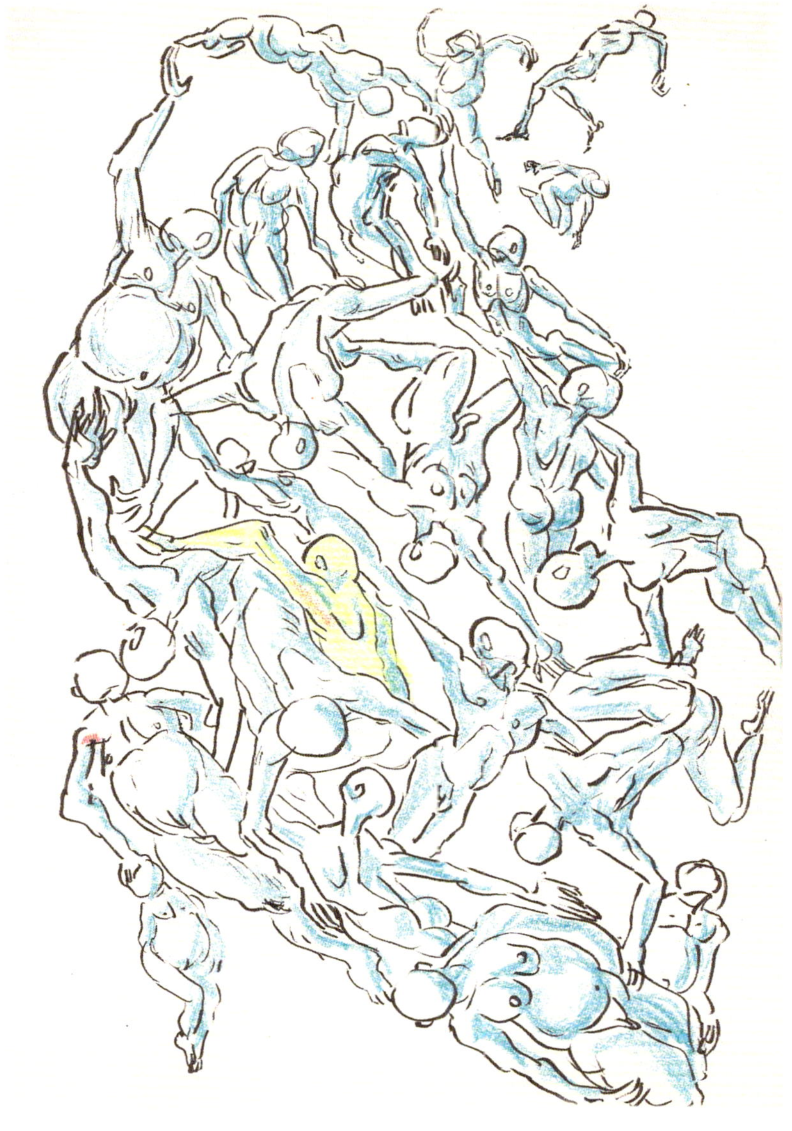

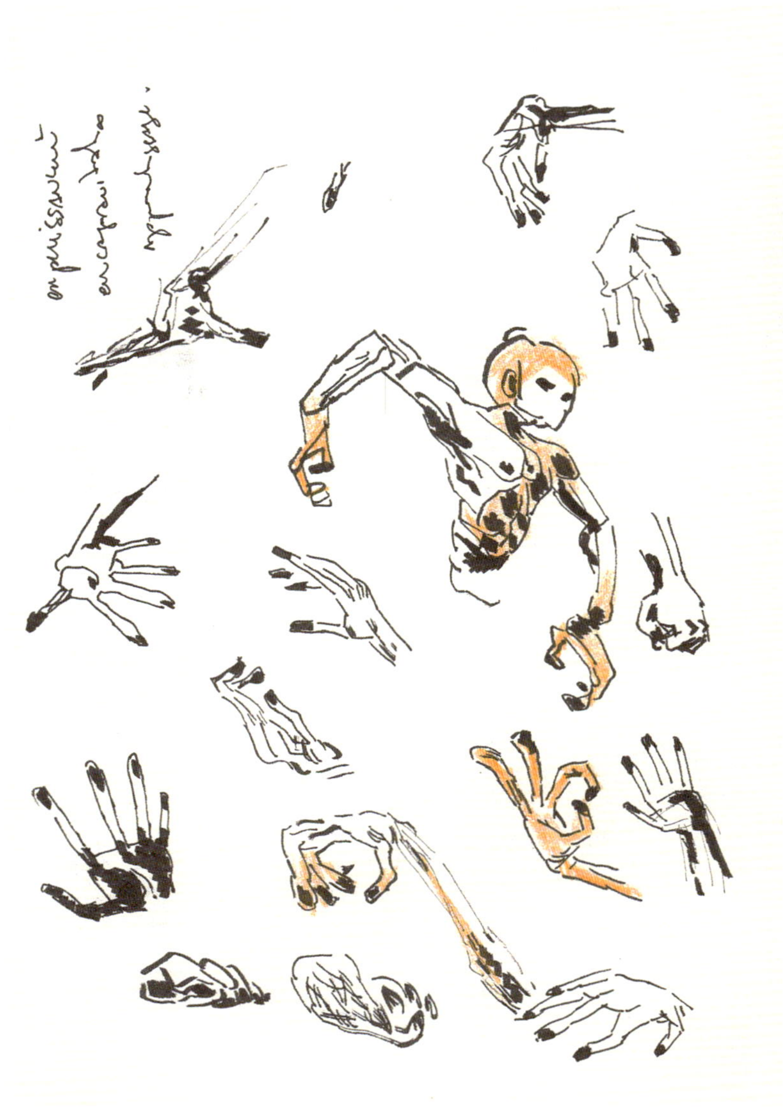

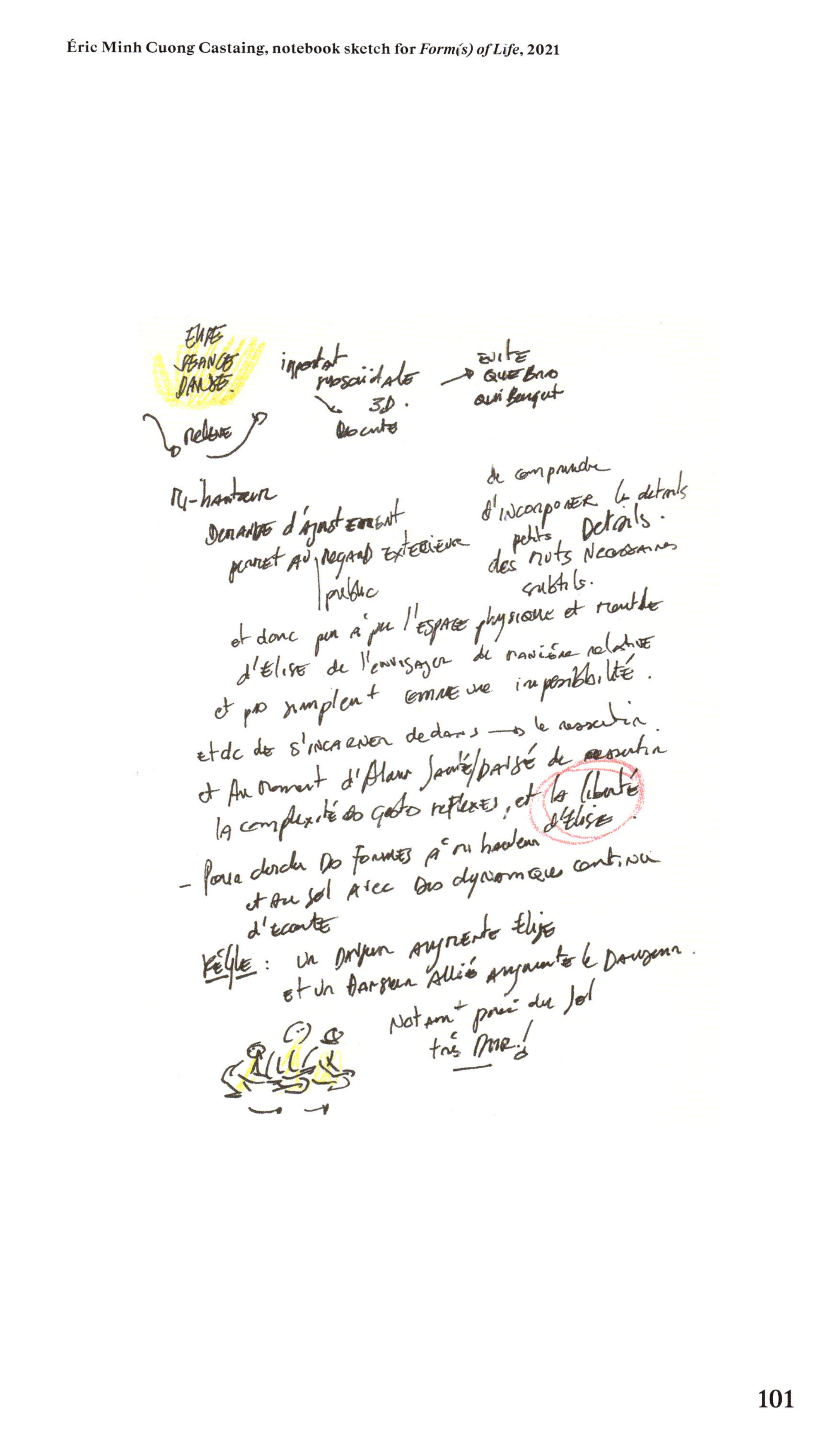

**Alia Farid**
*At the Time of the Ebb*, 2019

**HD video, colour, sound;
15:43 minutes**

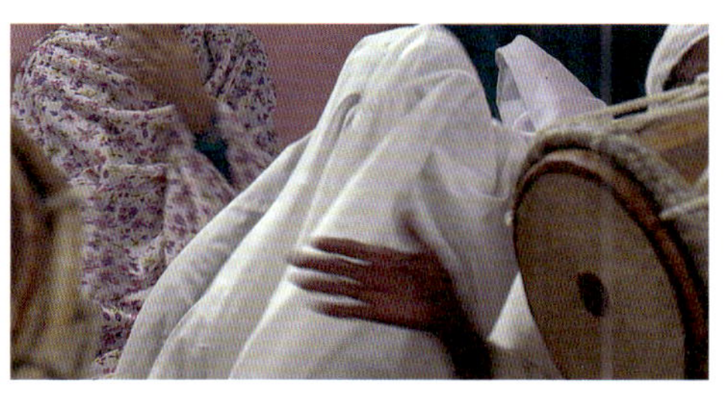
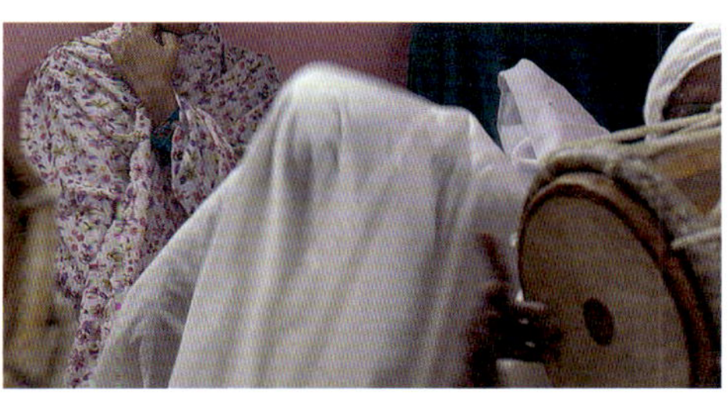
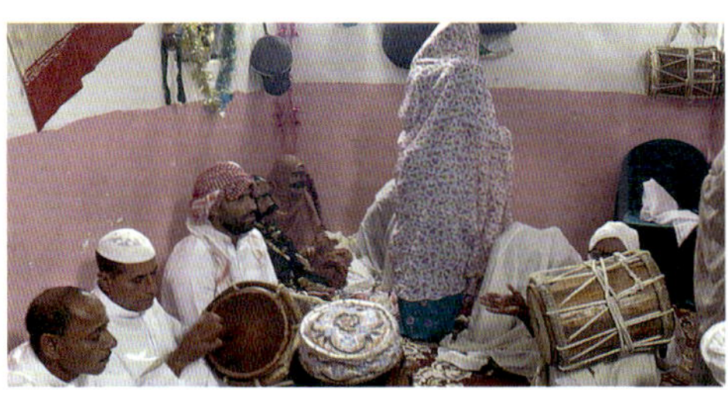
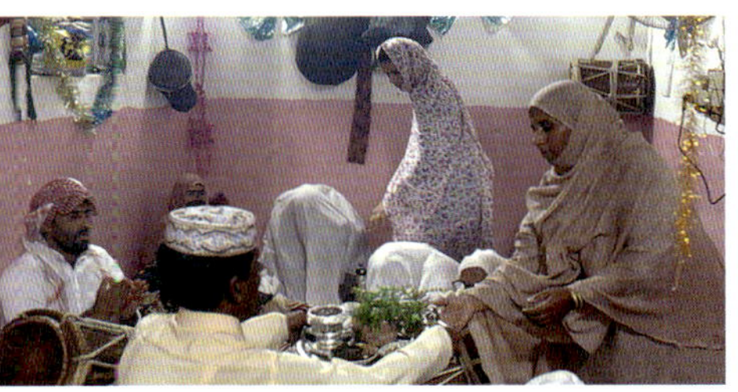
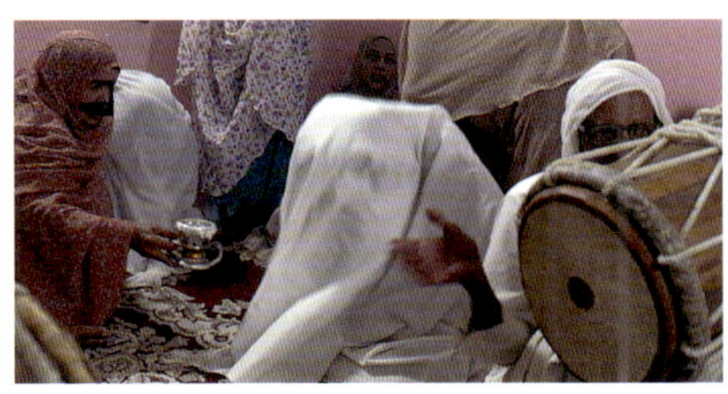
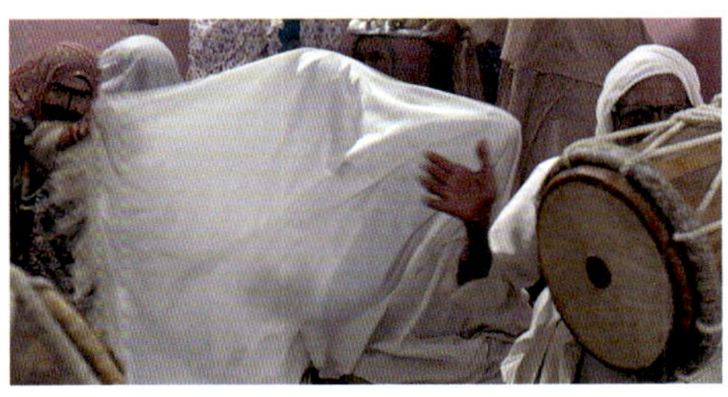
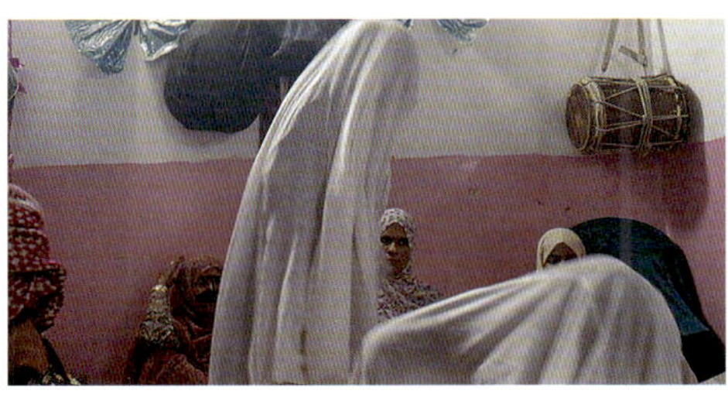
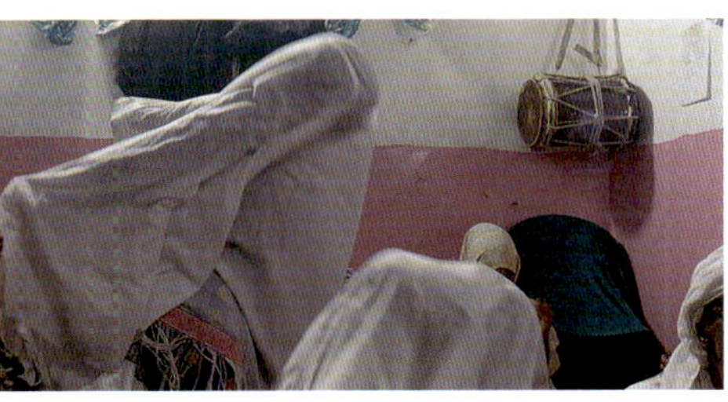

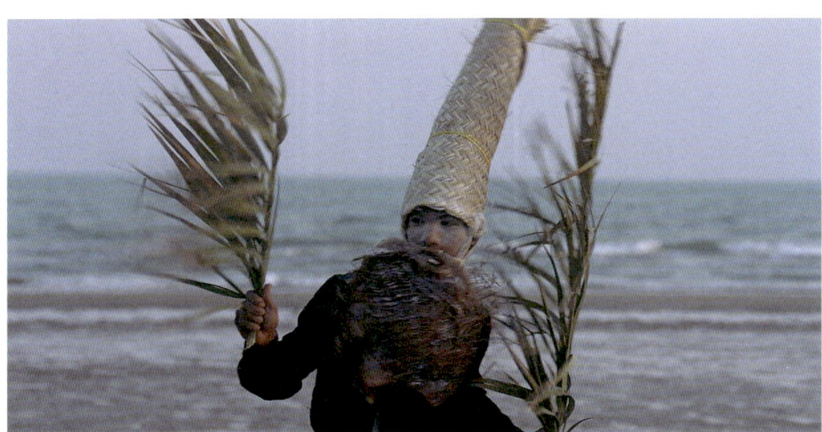

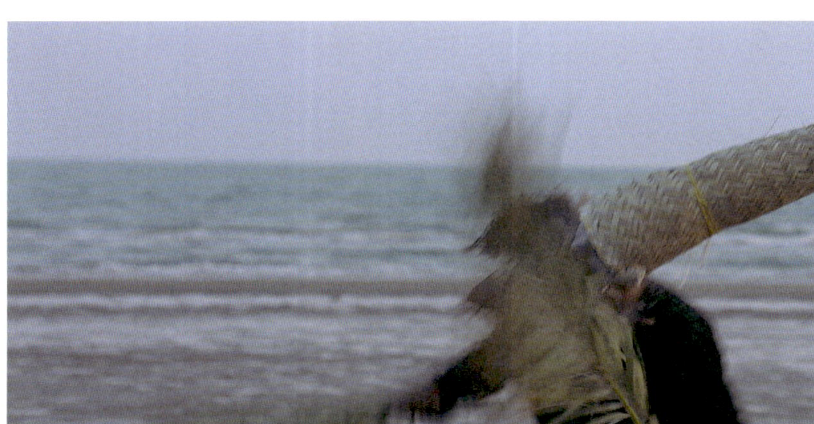

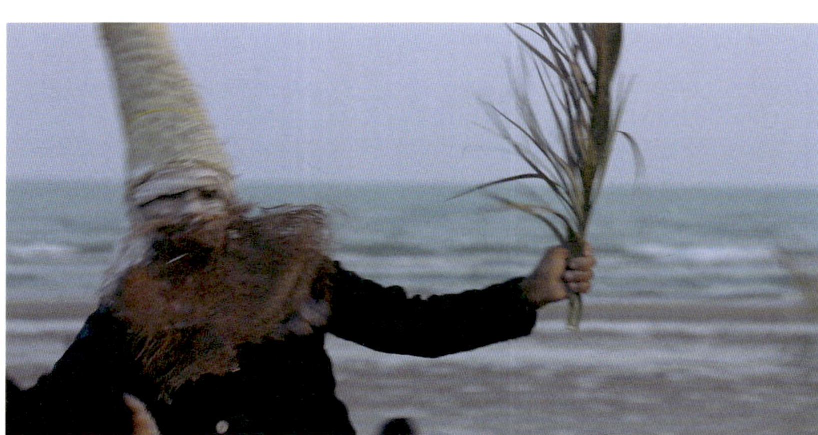

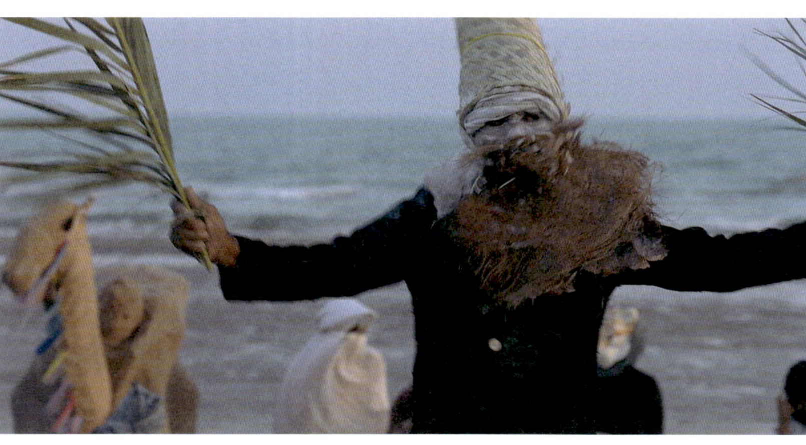

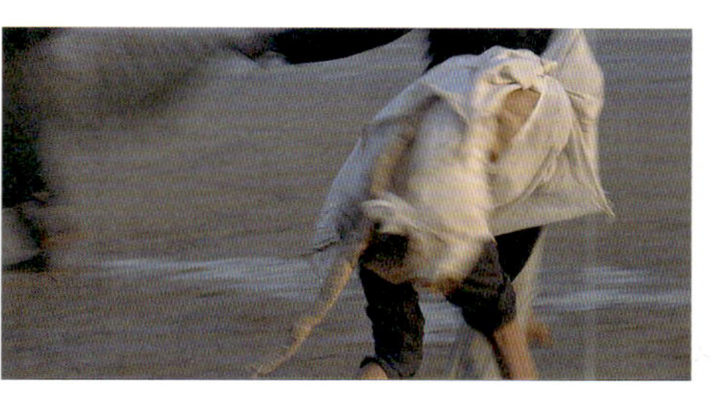 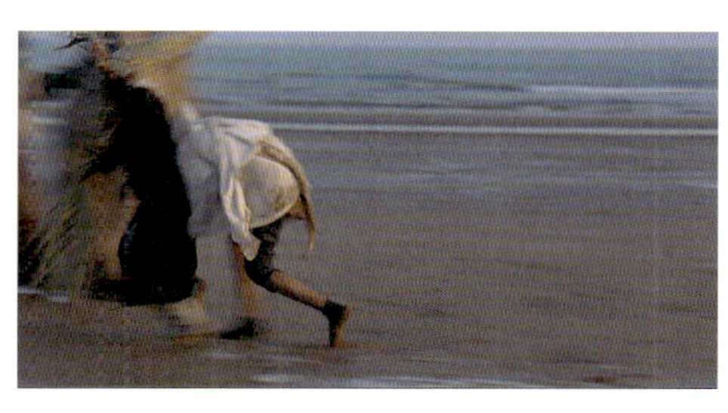

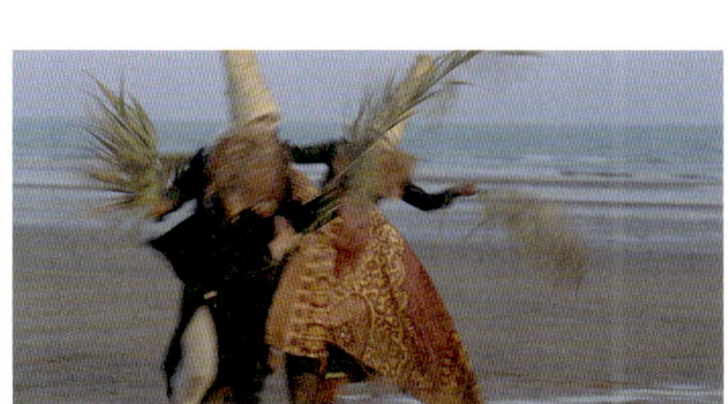 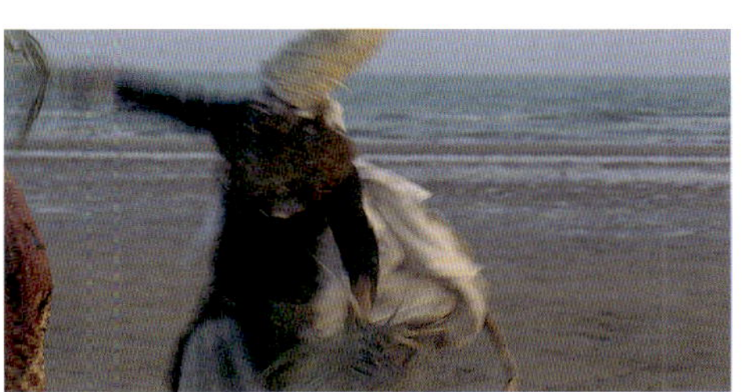

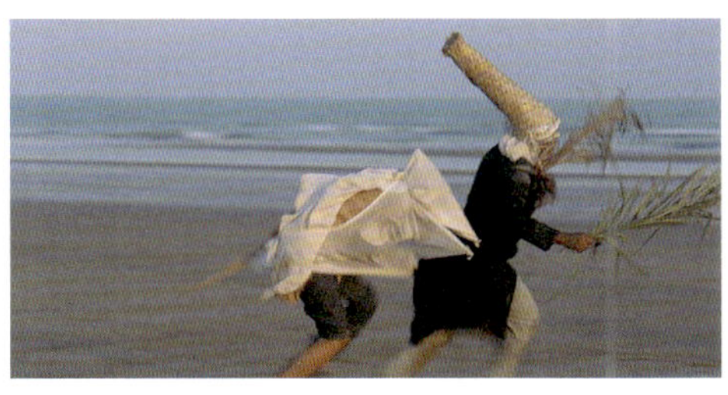 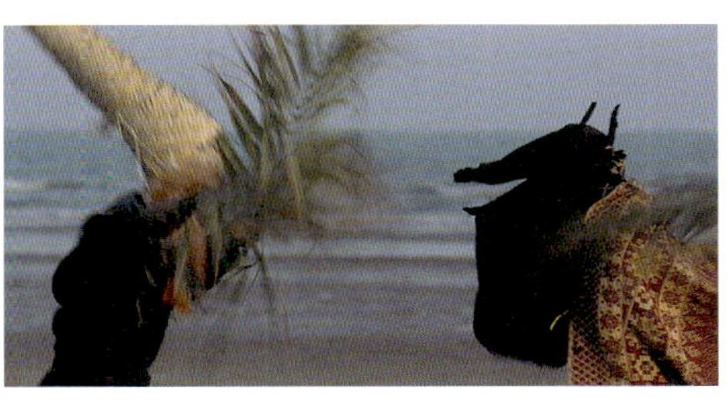

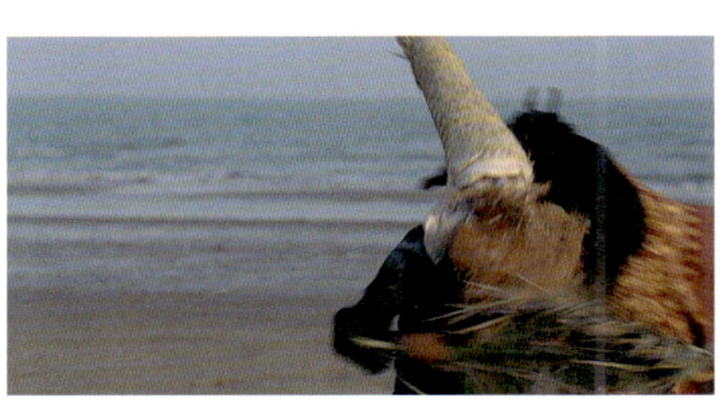 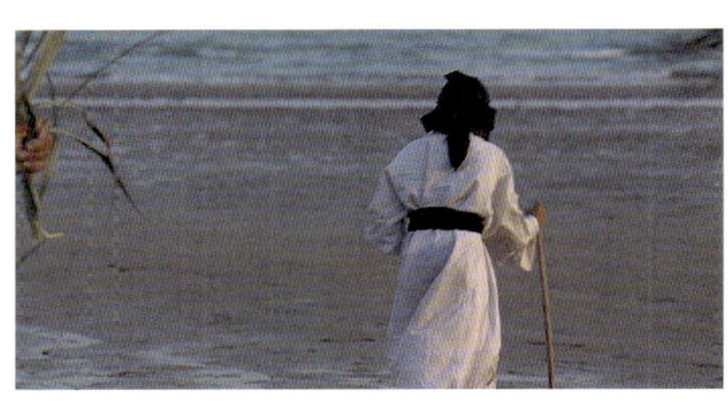

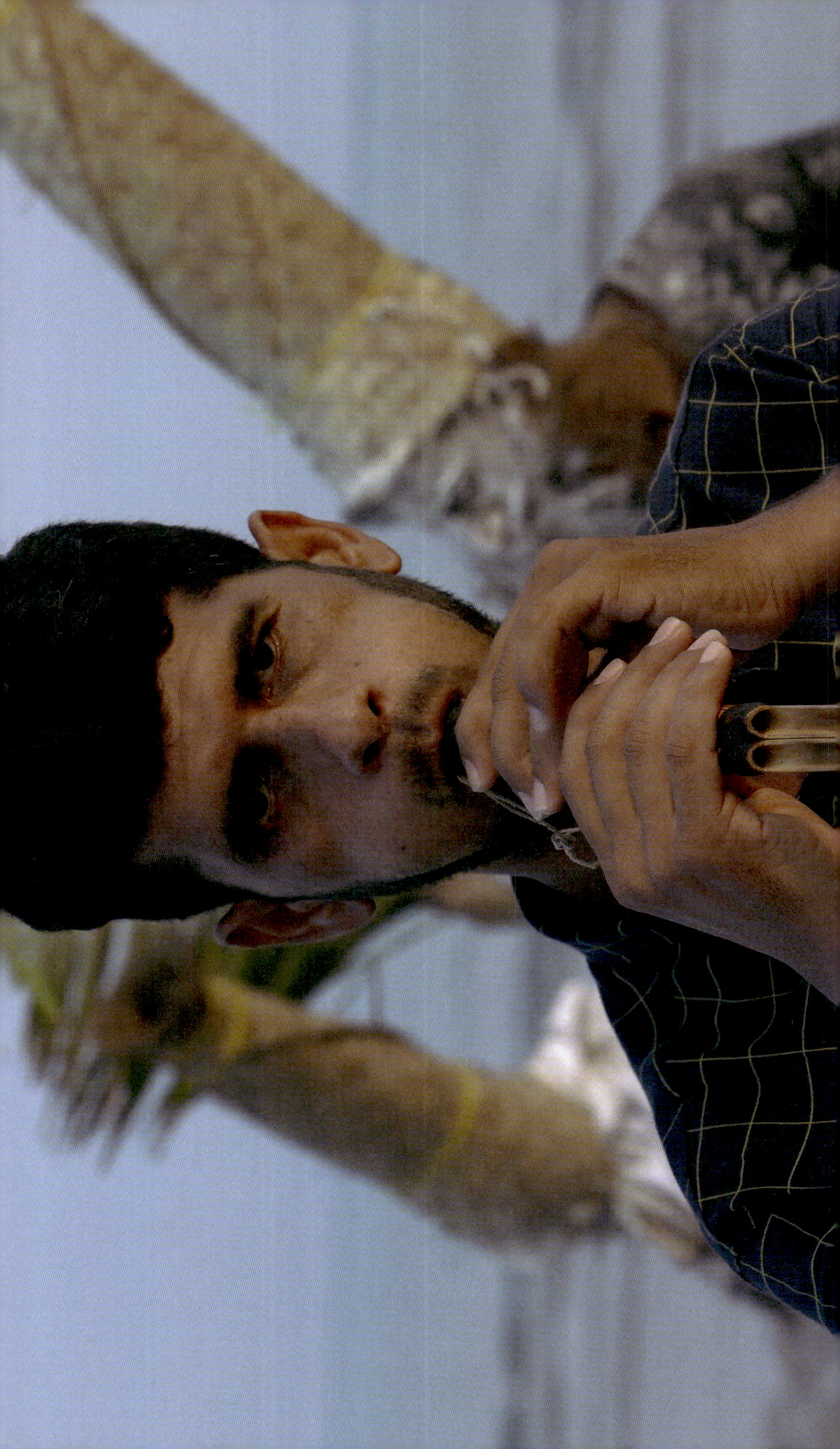

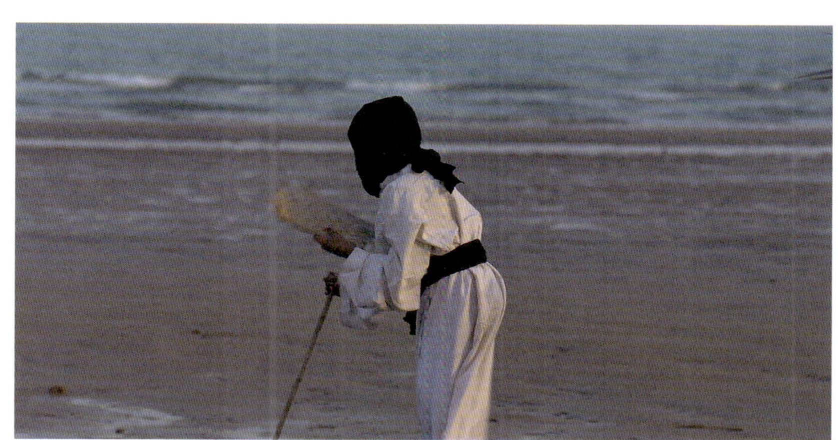
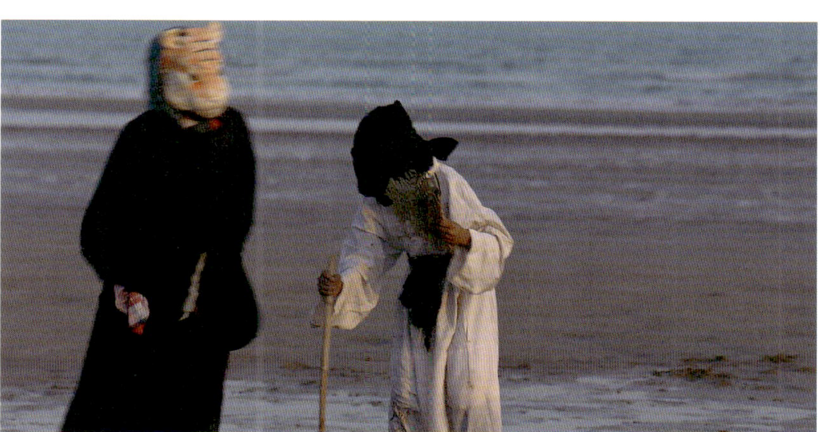
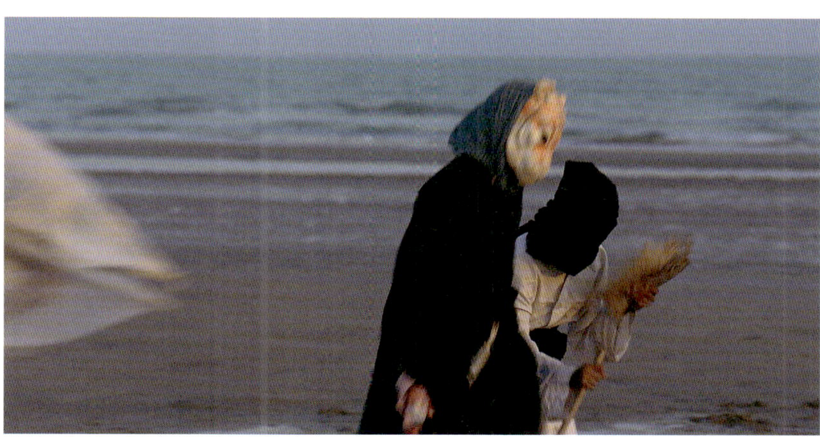
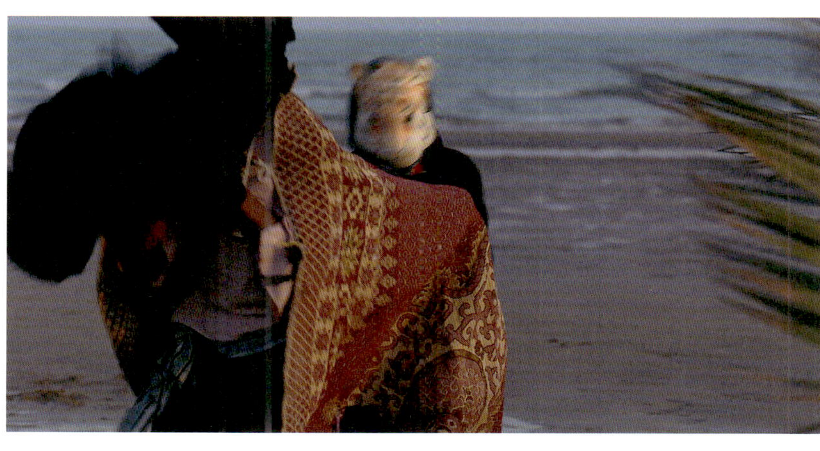

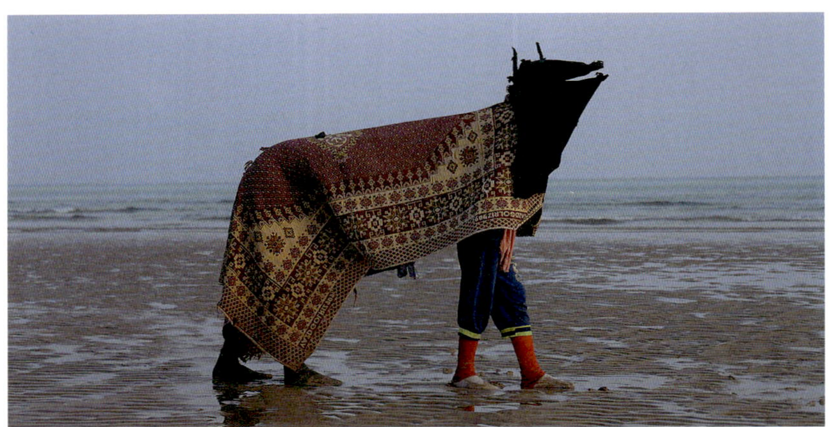
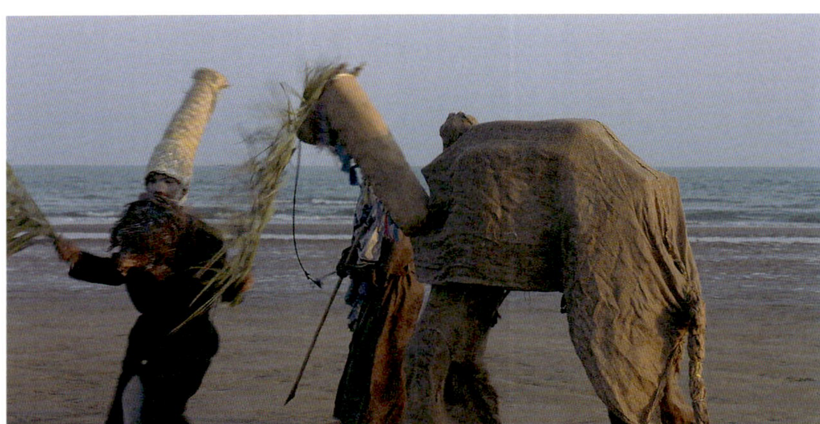
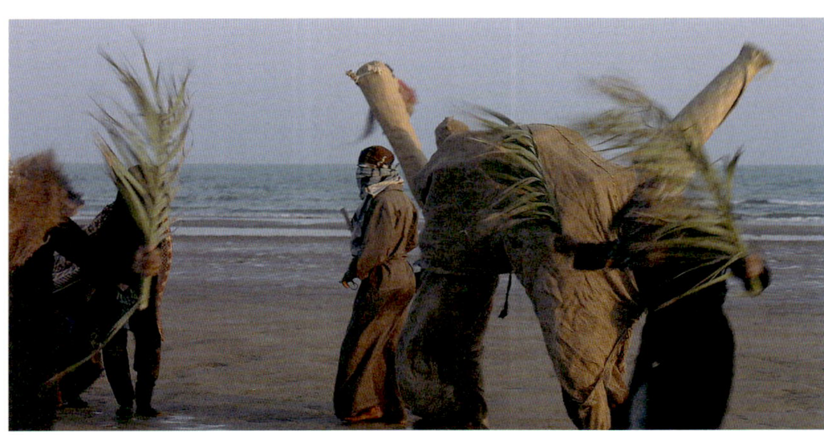
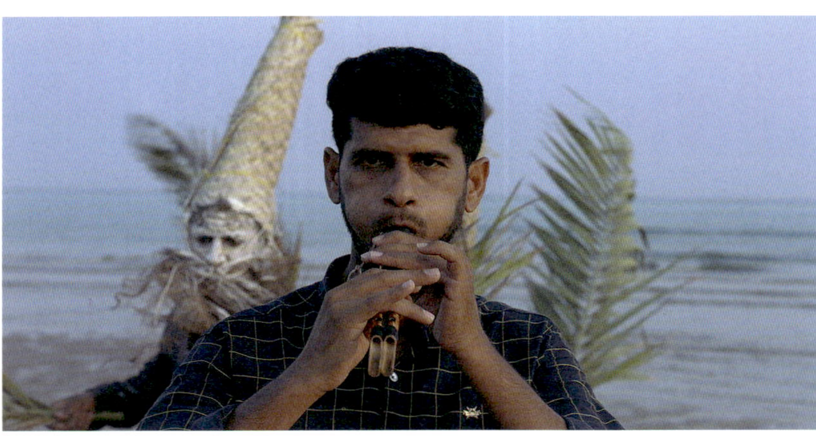

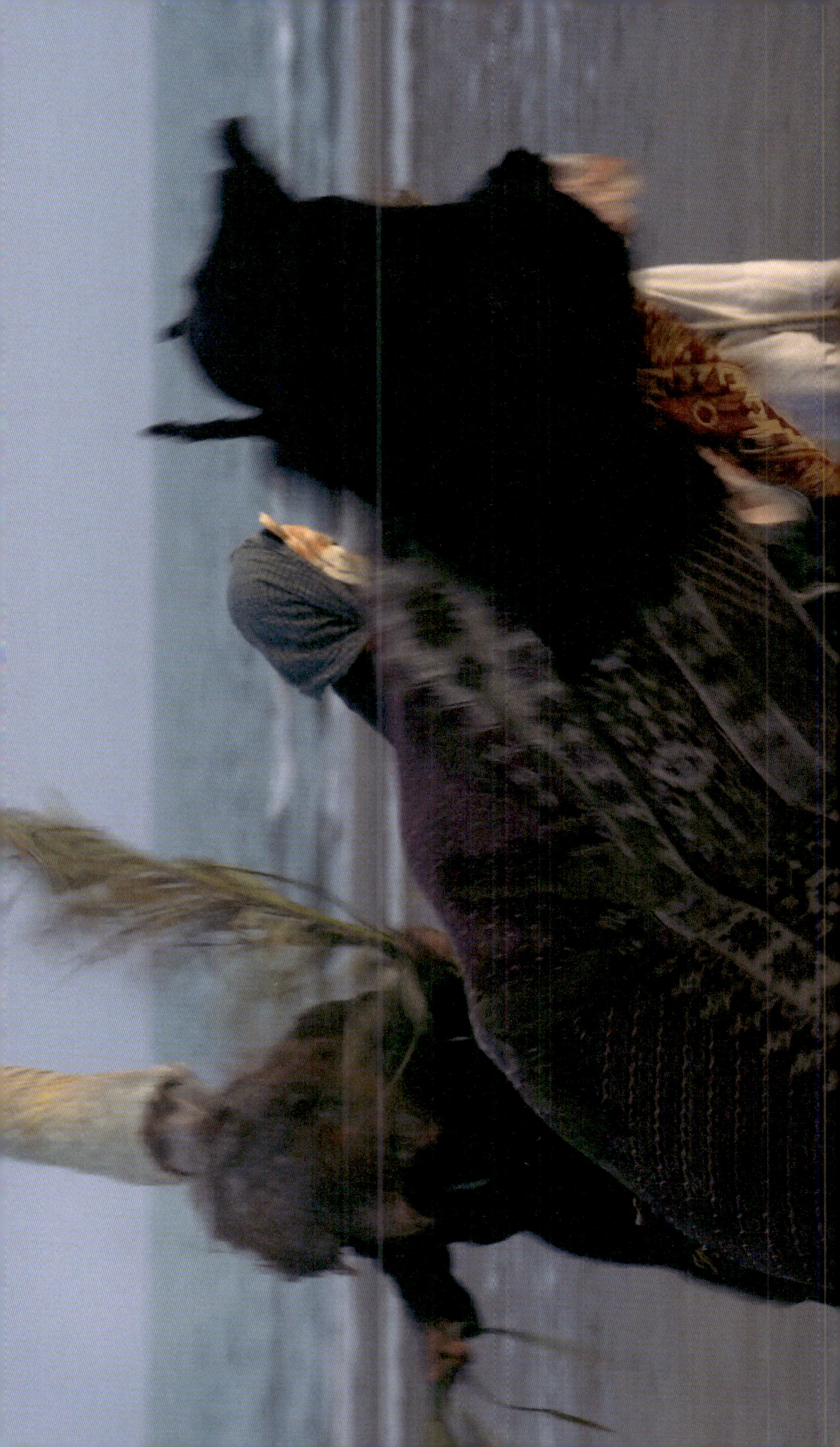

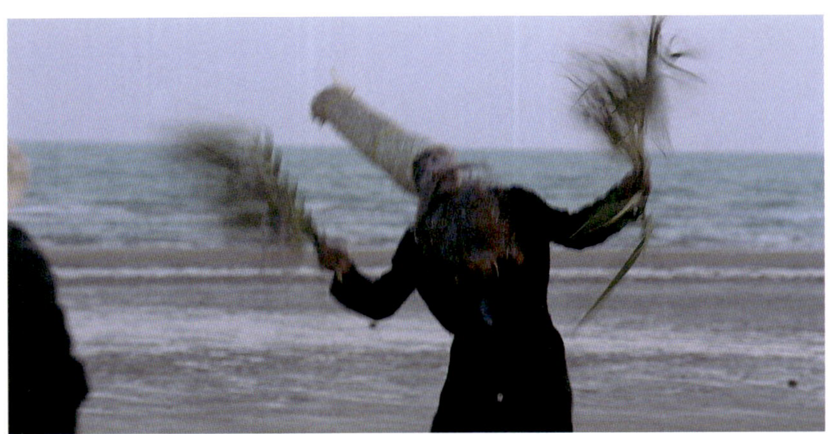

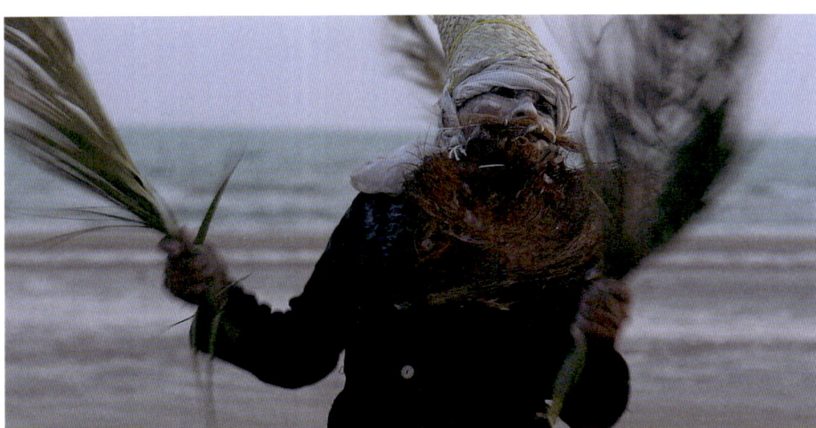

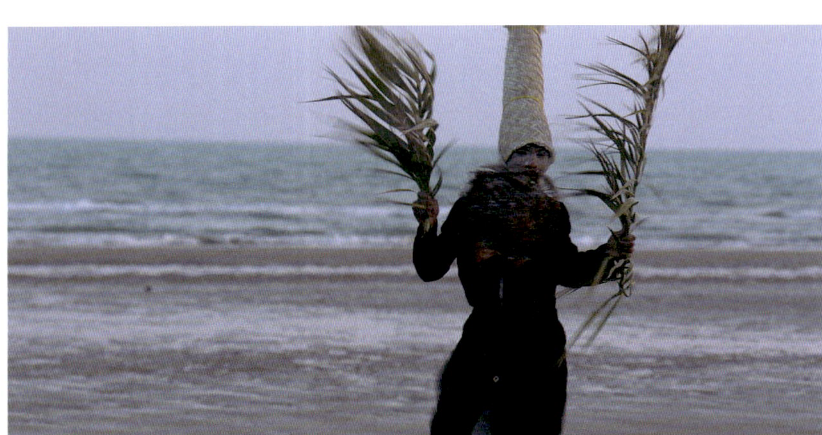

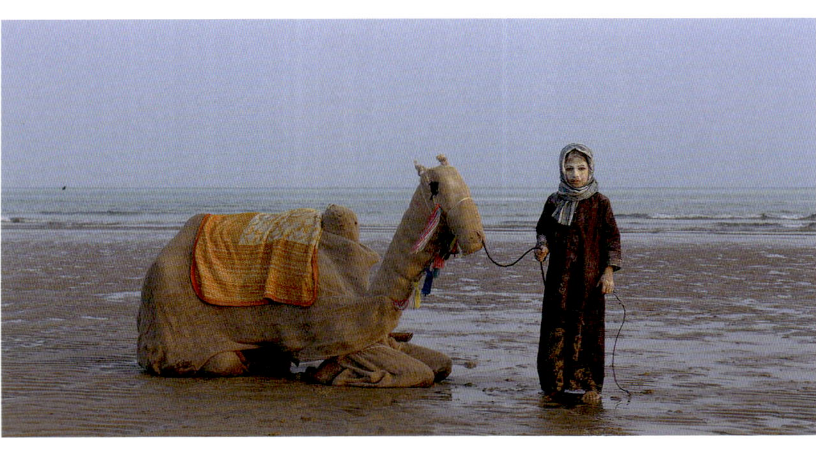

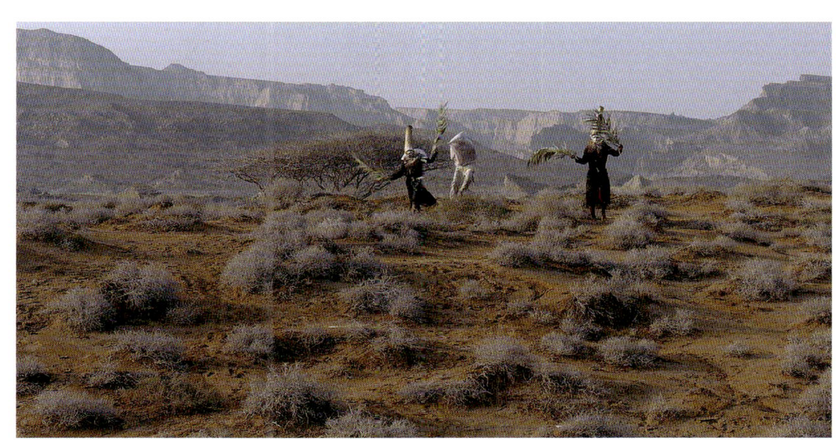

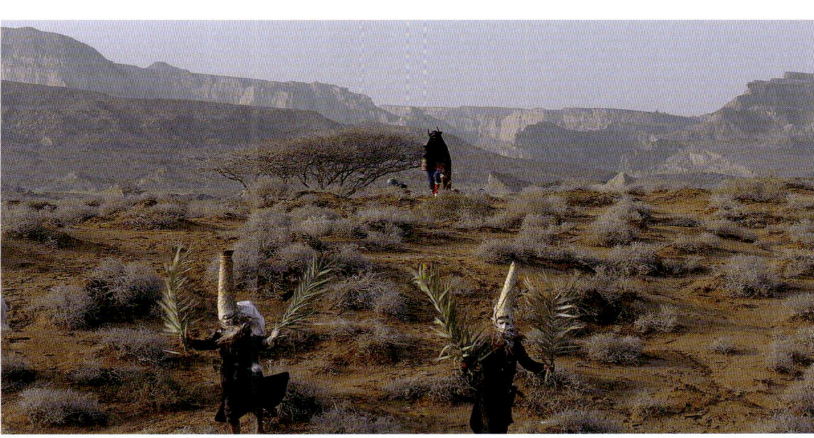

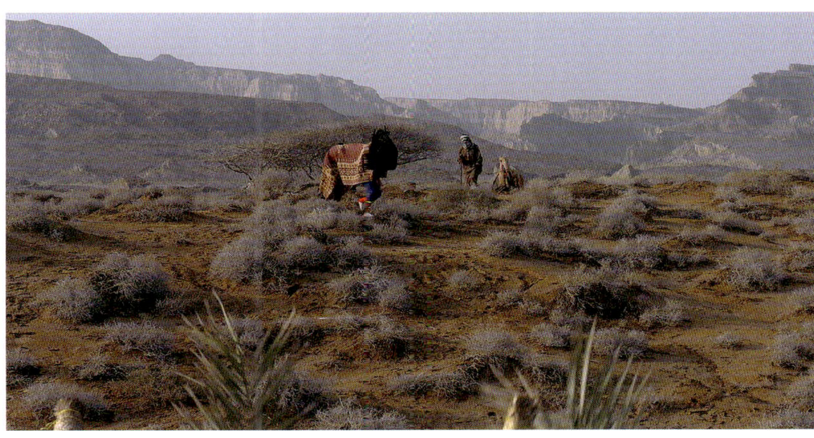

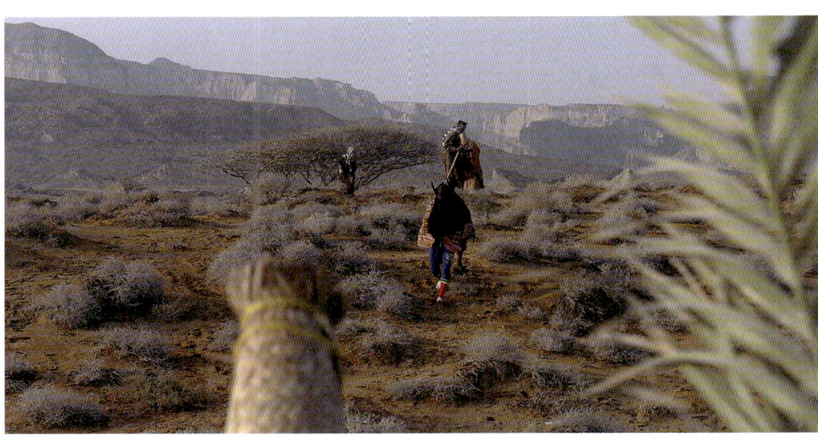

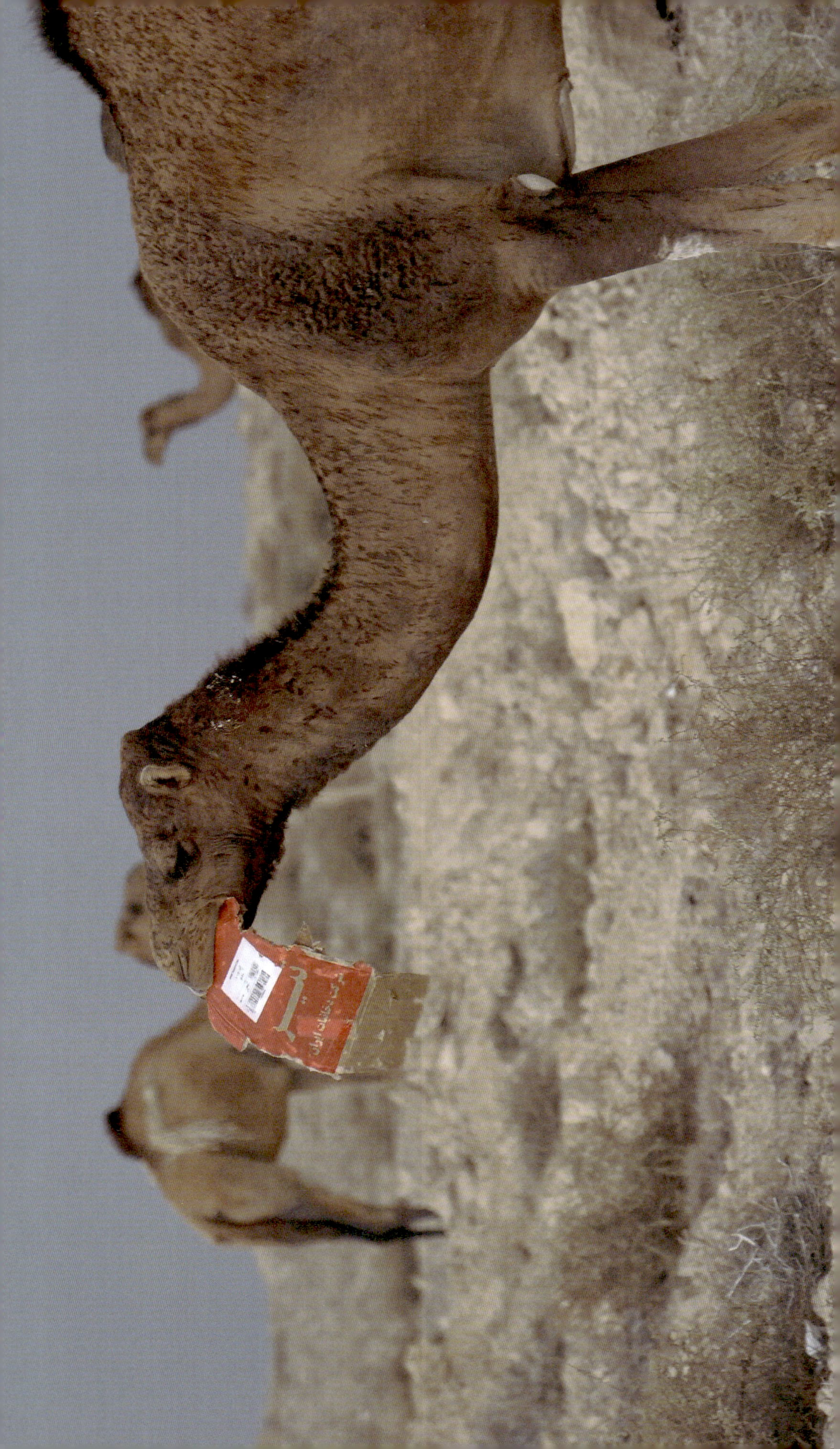

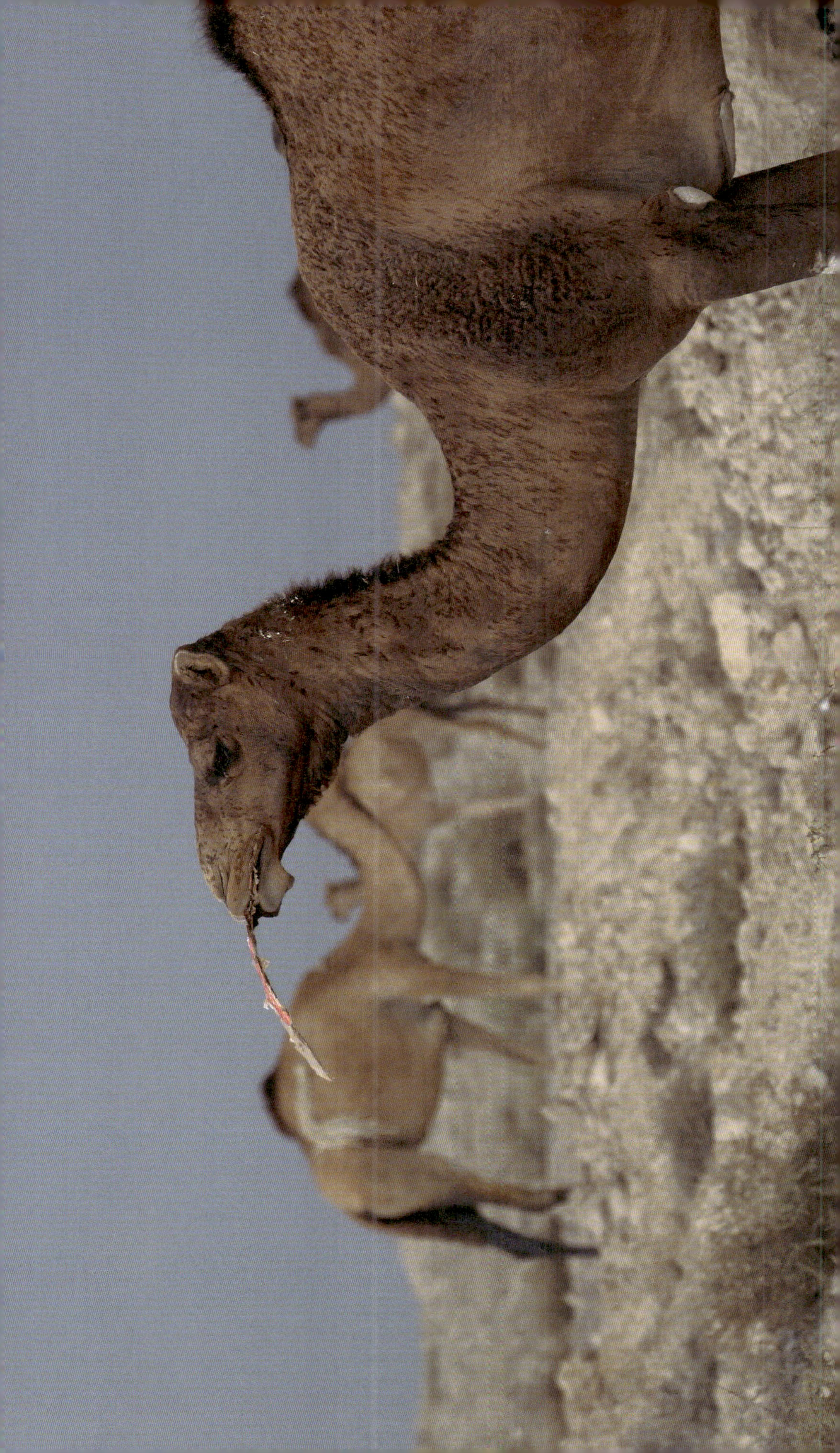

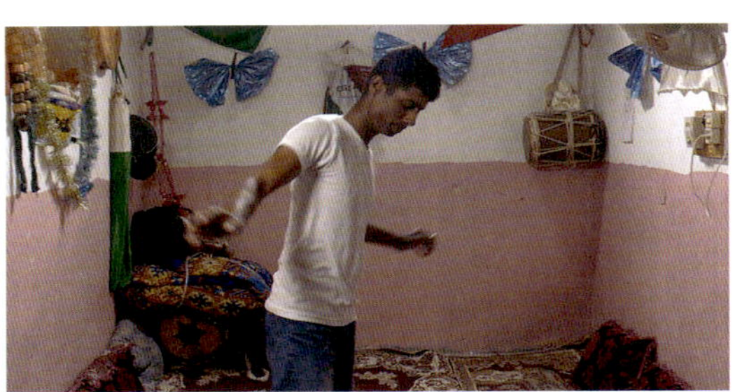

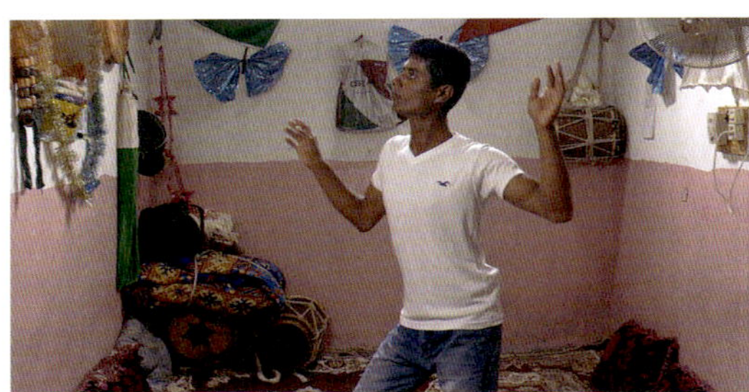

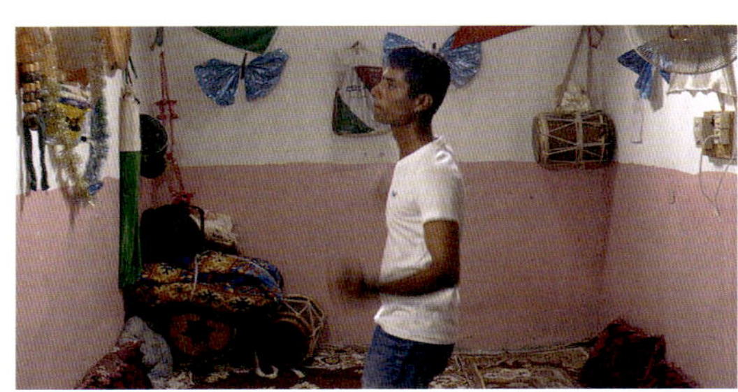

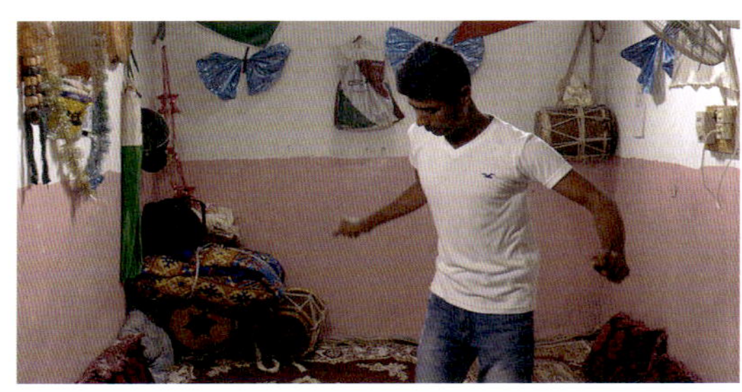

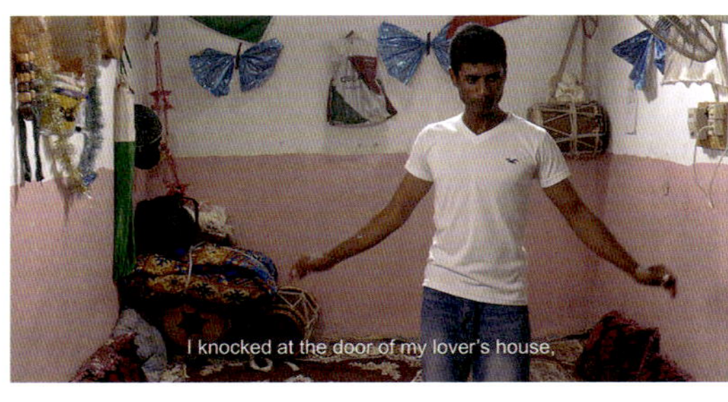
I knocked at the door of my lover's house,

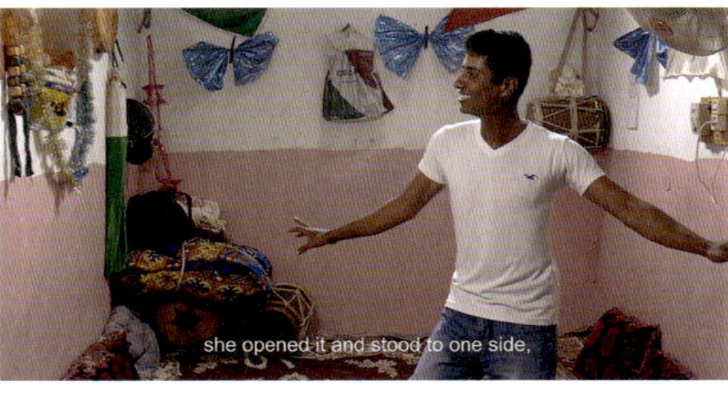
she opened it and stood to one side,

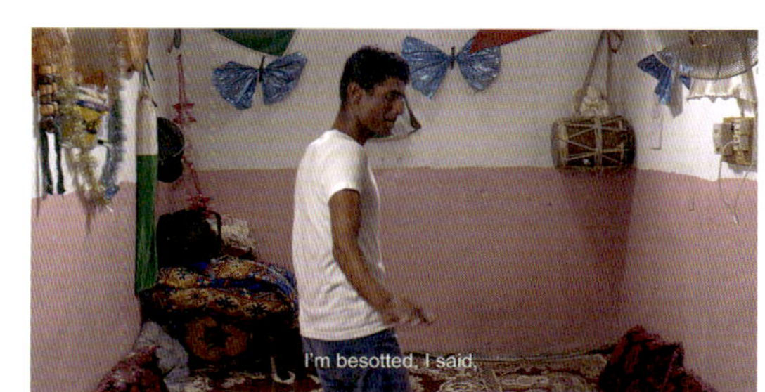
I'm besotted, I said,

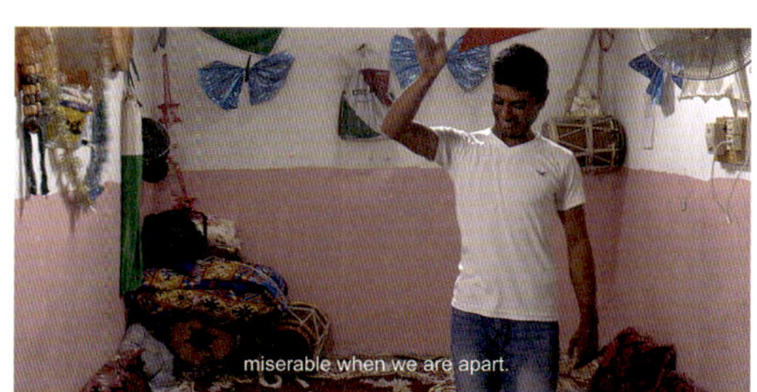
miserable when we are apart.

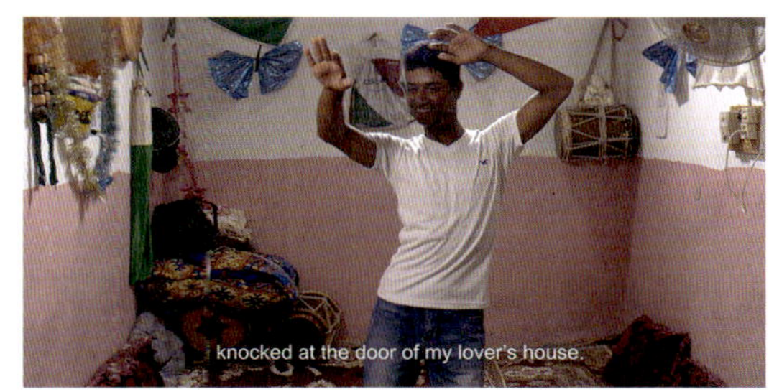
knocked at the door of my lover's house.

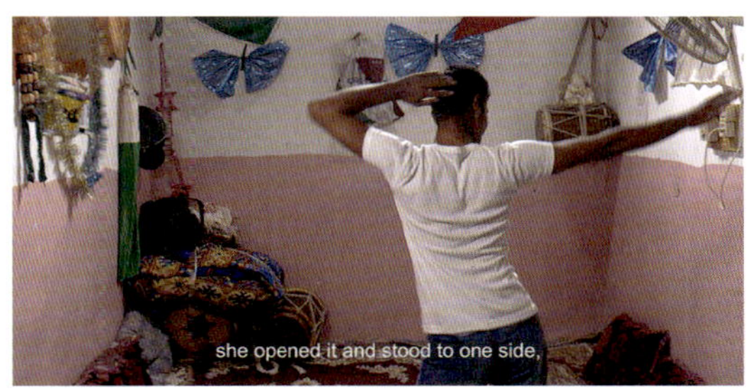
she opened it and stood to one side,

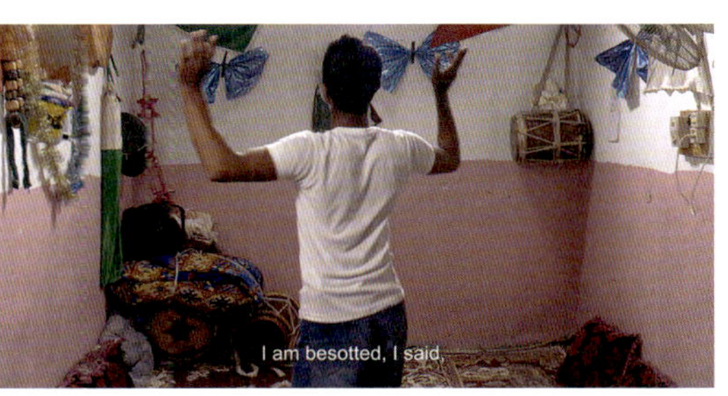
I am besotted, I said,

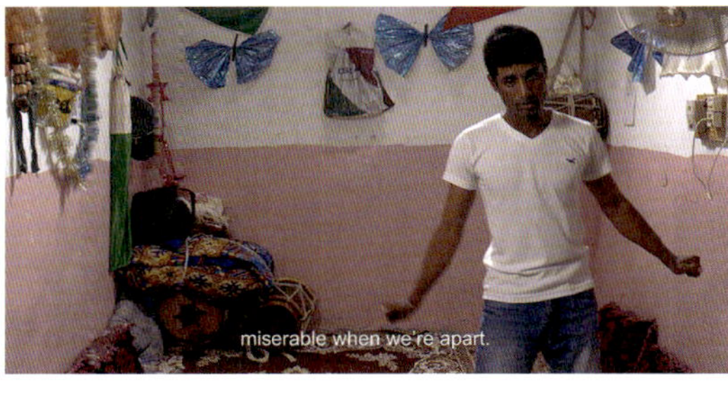
miserable when we're apart.

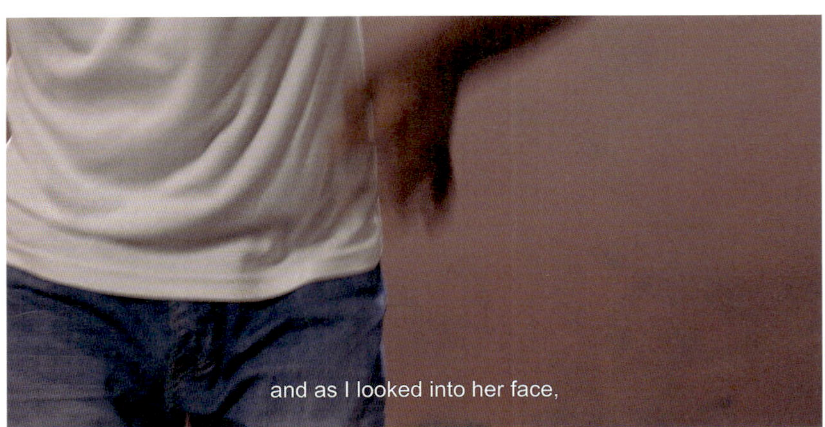

and as I looked into her face,


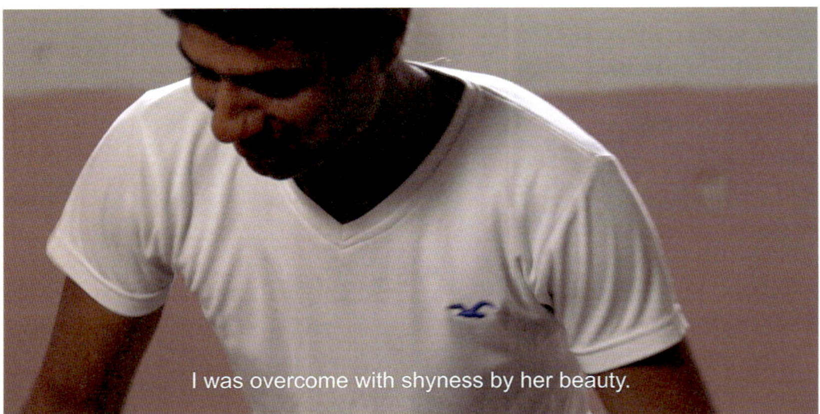

I was overcome with shyness by her beauty.


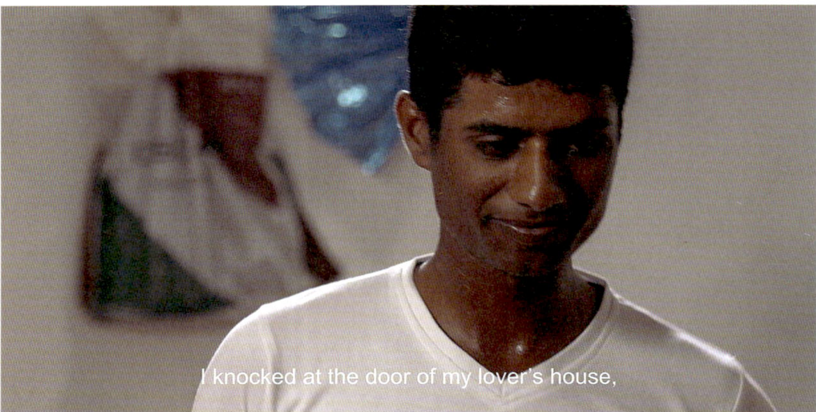

I knocked at the door of my lover's house,


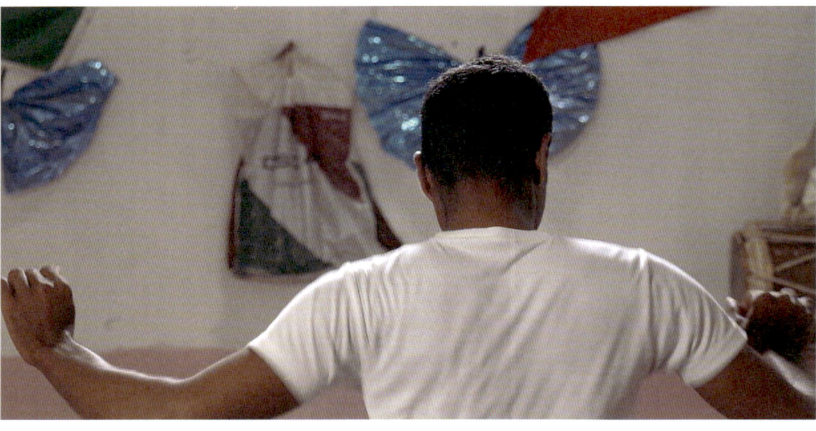

Working in film, sculpture and installation, Alia Farid aims to give visibility to narratives obscured by the dominant discourse. Her work is concerned with migration, national identity and colonial histories of the Global South, in particular in Kuwait and Puerto Rico, where Farid is from. *At the Time of the Ebb* was commissioned by Sharjah Art Foundation for the Sharjah Biennial 14: 'Leaving the Echo Chamber' (2019). Farid travelled 100 nautical kilometres from Kuwait to Qeshm Island, the large arrow-shaped Iranian island in the Strait of Hormuz, the strategic passage for the global oil trade in the Persian Gulf.

Encompassing music, dance and performance, the film traces the island's inhabitants as they celebrate Nowruz Sayadeen (Fishermen's New Year), an annual festival held on the summer solstice to mark the beginning of the fishing season, whereby villagers stay on land and refrain from consuming anything from the sea, to give thanks for nature's abundance. The performance draws upon local customs and surviving festival traditions. In an interview with curator Claire Tancons, Farid speaks of her interest in 'making visible the porosity between lands, identities, cultures. Not in a nostalgic way, but rather in thinking about the vernacular and the past as a way forward.'[1]

The sixteen-minute film unfolds across four chapters, guided by Farid's encounters on the island. In the conversation with Tancons, she says 'I didn't have a script or strict idea of what I was there to film. I was interested in learning and being shown, and with that, remembering.' A horizon line links the distinct sections, shifting from a domestic interior towards the sea, up to the mountains and back indoors. The first chapter takes place inside a carpeted room with tall ceilings from which decorations and djembe drums are suspended. The walls are painted pink up to shoulder height and a group of figures are seated around the edge of the room. Some of them drum, chant and clap, while the others, draped in thin material, move from side to side, rocking their heads and bodies alone or in tandem with the music in a trance-like state.

The second chapter begins at dawn on the beach, looking out to the Arabian Gulf. Two dancers, or *shushis*, figures who represent the ungovernable self, stand on the sand wearing tall hats made of woven palm leaves and holding fronds in their hands.

They move to the music in a stylised manner and begin to lead a cast of performers dressed in makeshift animal costumes including a horse, who wears a black fabric mask and carpet on its back, a lion, who represents the sun and a camel with its herder and plastic-mask tiger.

At the end of the scene, the *shushis* are filmed walking across the vast, mountainous landscape as they lead the cast over the shrubland towards the camera. The landscape takes on a dominant role in this panoramic vista, and in the third chapter, Farid shows Qeshm as an eco-tourism destination and alludes to the impacts of urbanisation upon the landscape. The camera focuses on a herd of camels on the rocky ground, and one is pictured chewing on a scrap of discarded packaging.

The final chapter takes place inside a pink room similar to the one in the first scene, with decorations and percussive instruments also suspended from the ceiling. A young local man named Farzad Draye, who Farid met by chance while working on the film when she was buying a watermelon, is captured dressed in a white T-shirt and jeans, smiling broadly and shimmying in a circle while mouthing the lyrics to the accompanying song, which speaks of an exchange between a man and his lover. Farid was initially surprised by Draye's desire to be involved in the film, but she 'later understood that dancing for guests was a form of hospitality, and remembered it was also something practiced in the Gulf before the advent of oil and modernity.' This chapter brings the film full circle, reflecting Farid's continued exploration of the resurgence of the past within the present.

Grace Storey

---

1.  Claire Tancons, 'Conversation with Alia Farid', *Vdrome* (5 May 2020), https://www.vdrome.org/alia-farid/

Alia Farid, production still from *At the Time of the Ebb*, 2019, print on Hahnemüle Photo Rag Baryta paper, 40 × 60 cm

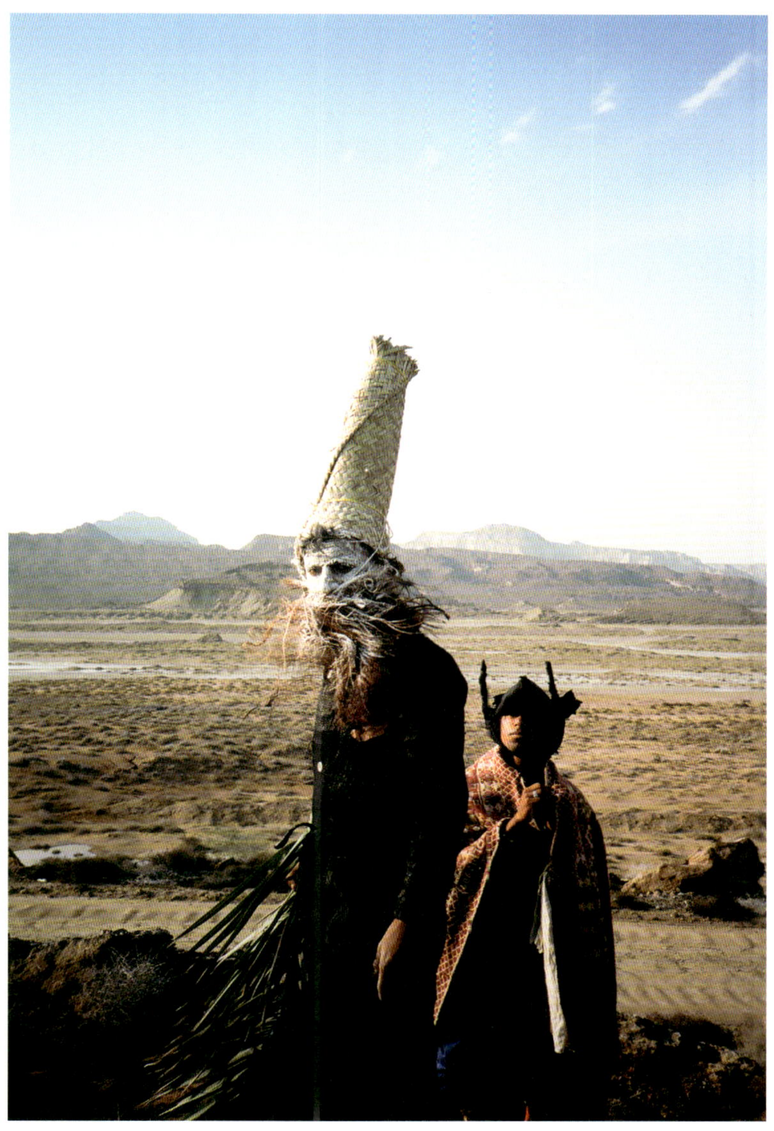

**Hetain Patel**
*Trinity*, 2021

**HD video, colour, sound;
23 minutes**

[ Mum speaking Gujarati ]
I first learned of it in the v llage, from Mother.

She told me that the souls of our ancestors

lie sleeping in women's bodies...

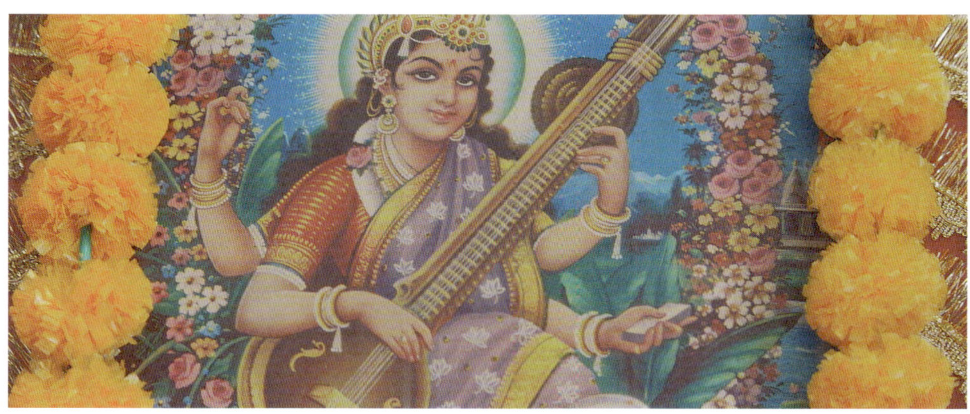

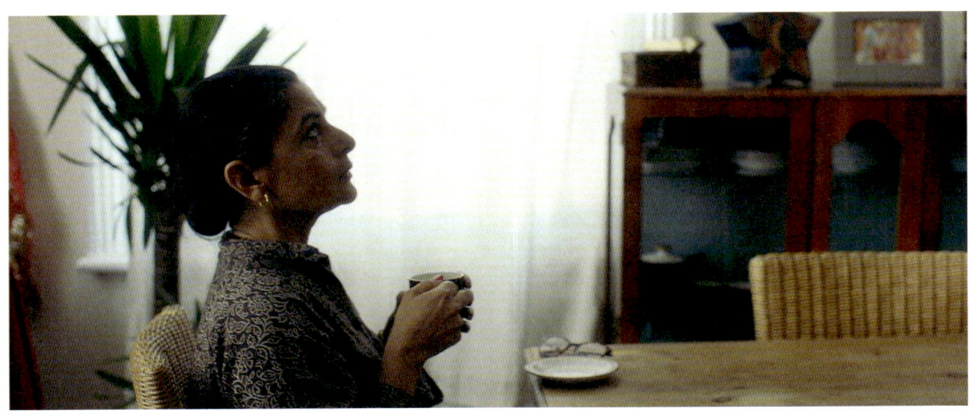
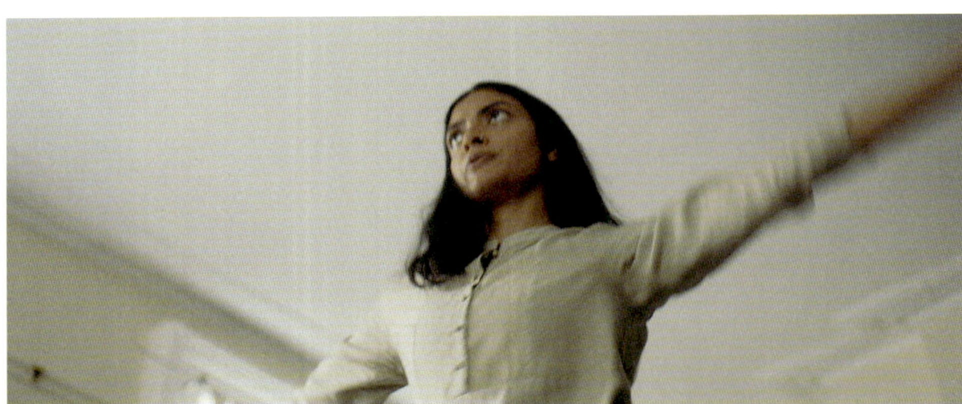
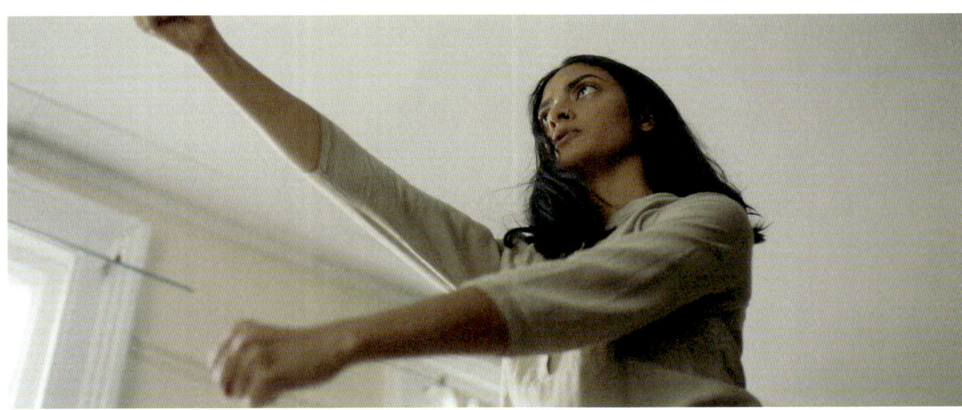
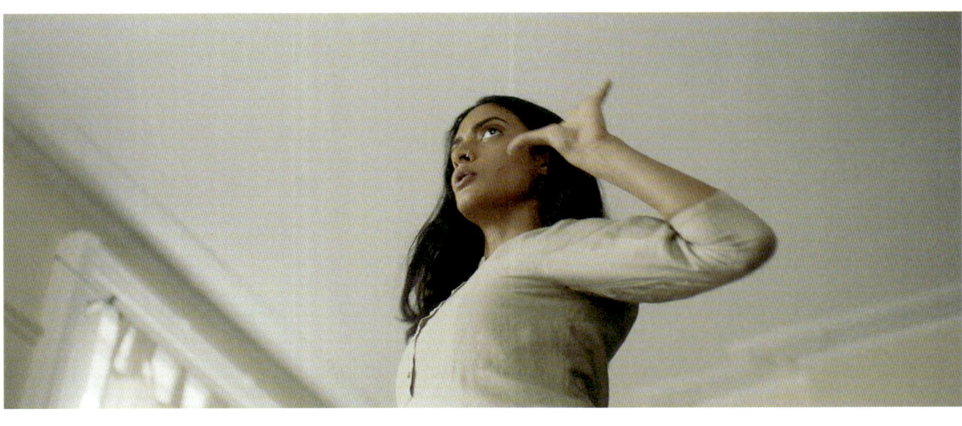

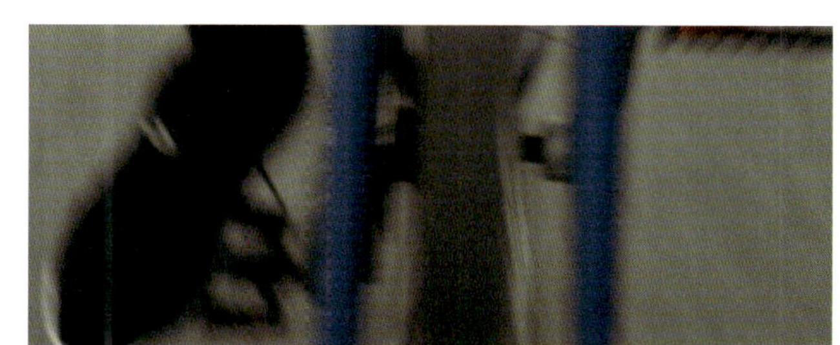

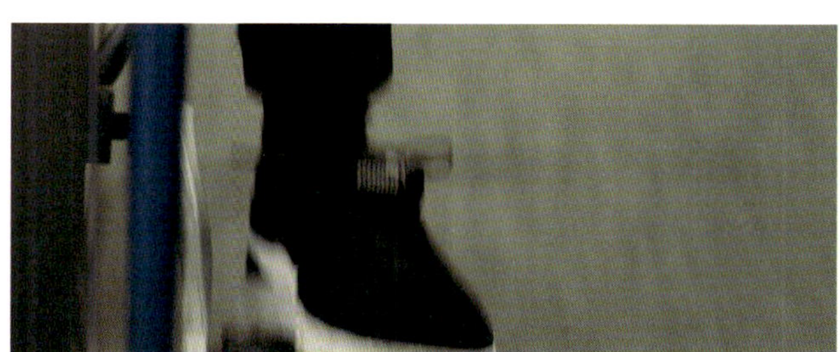

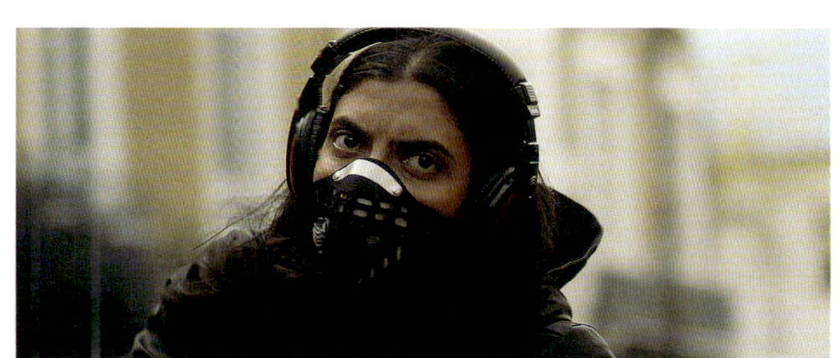

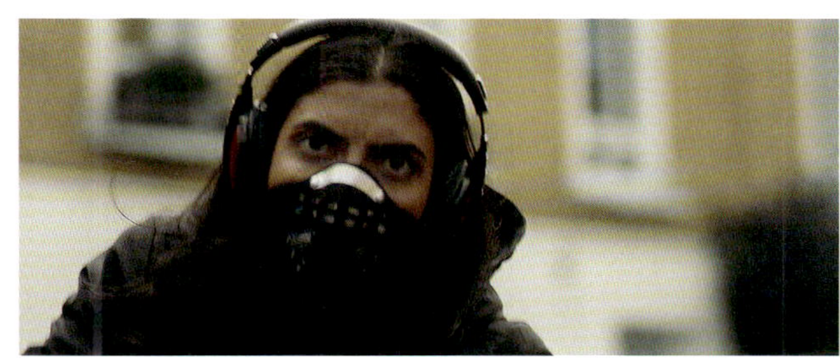

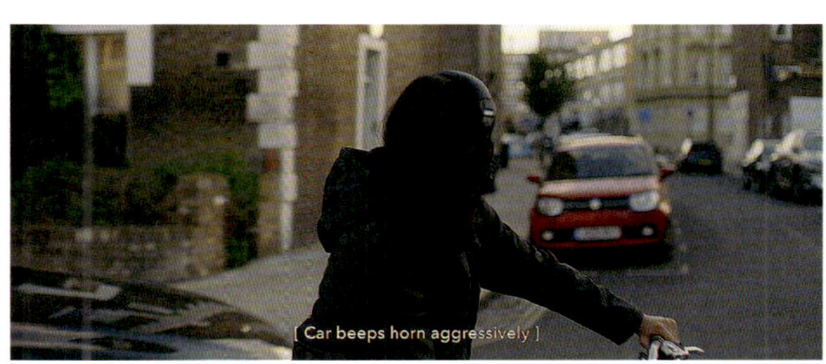
[ Car beeps horn aggressively ]

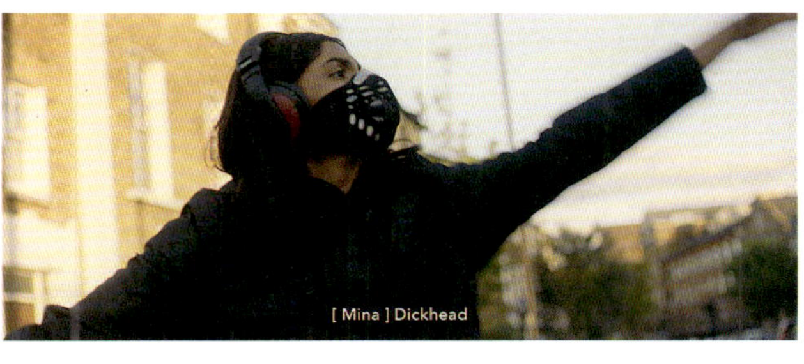
[ Mina ] Dickhead

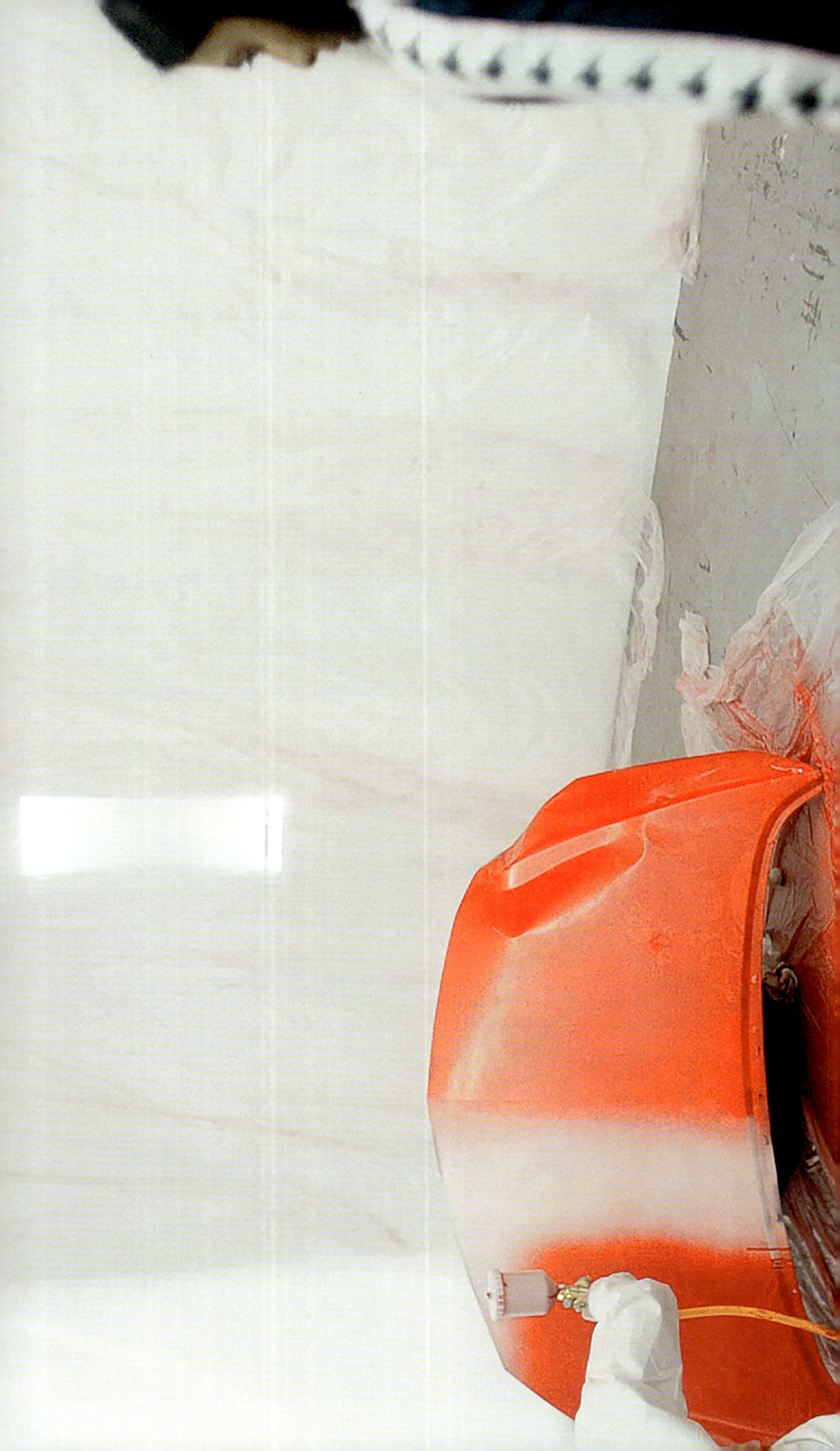

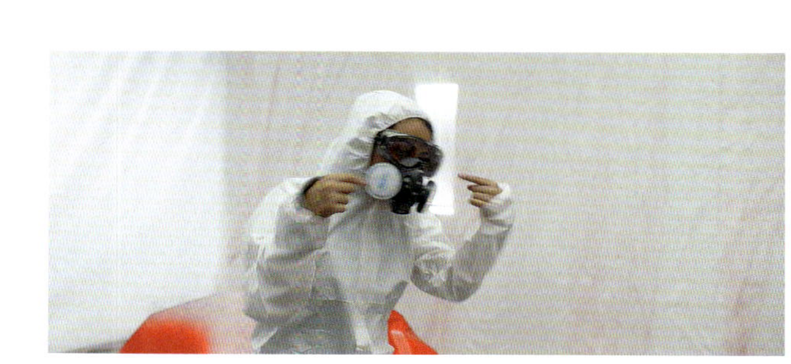

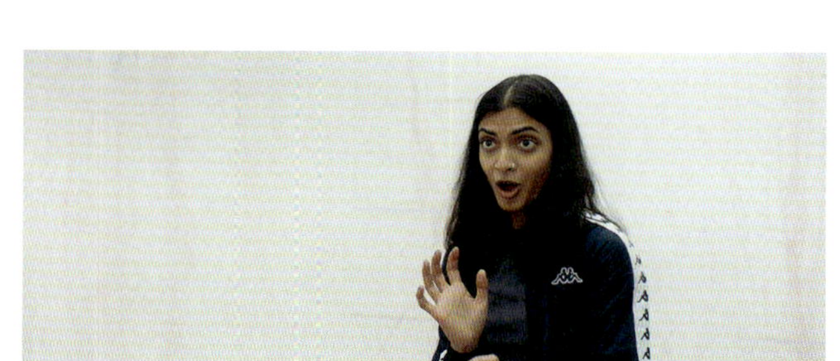

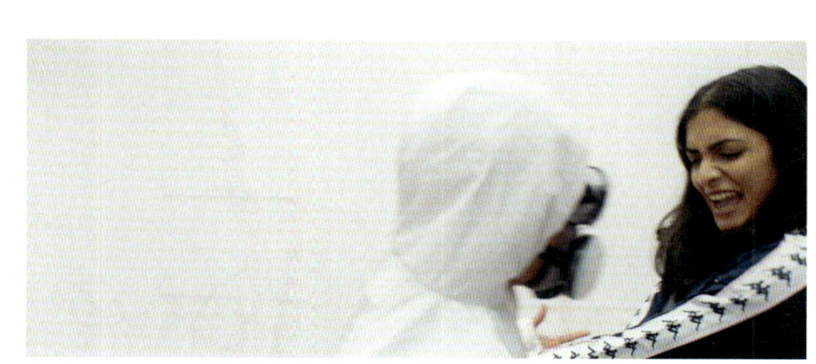

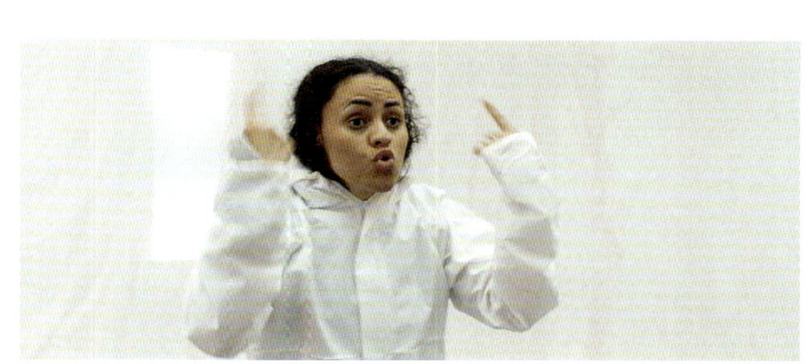

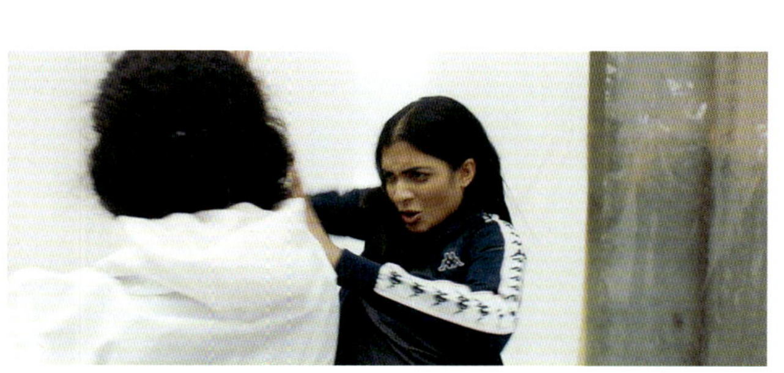

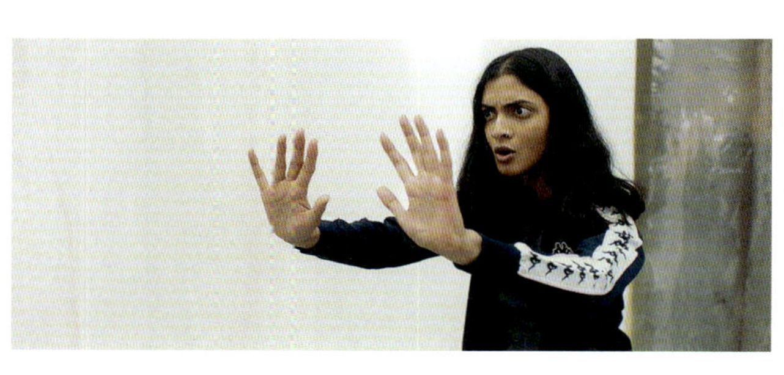

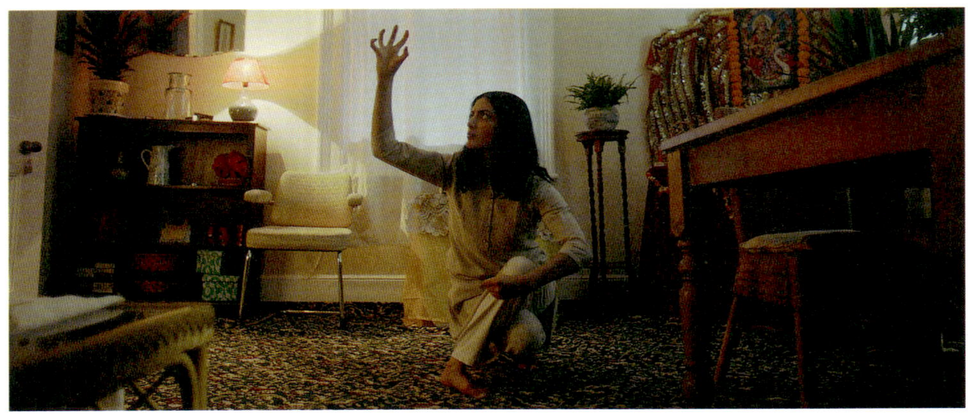

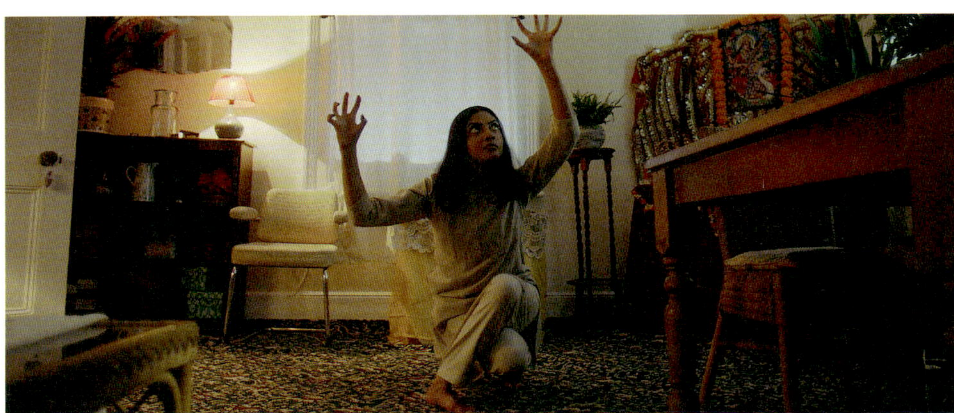

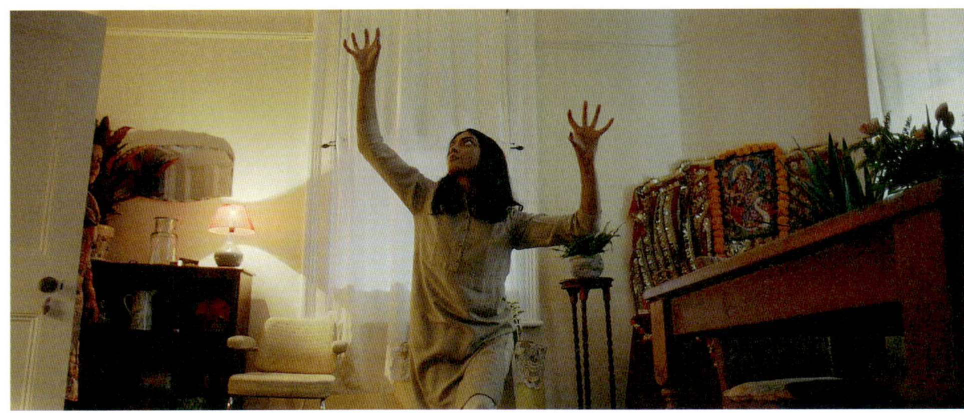

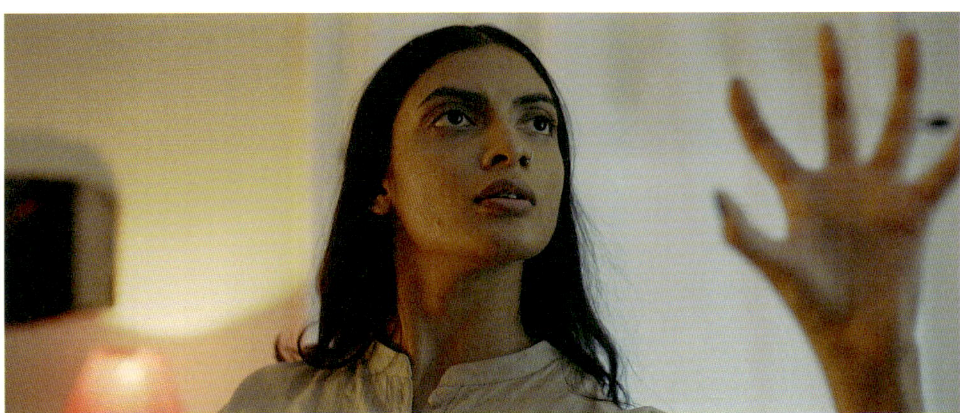

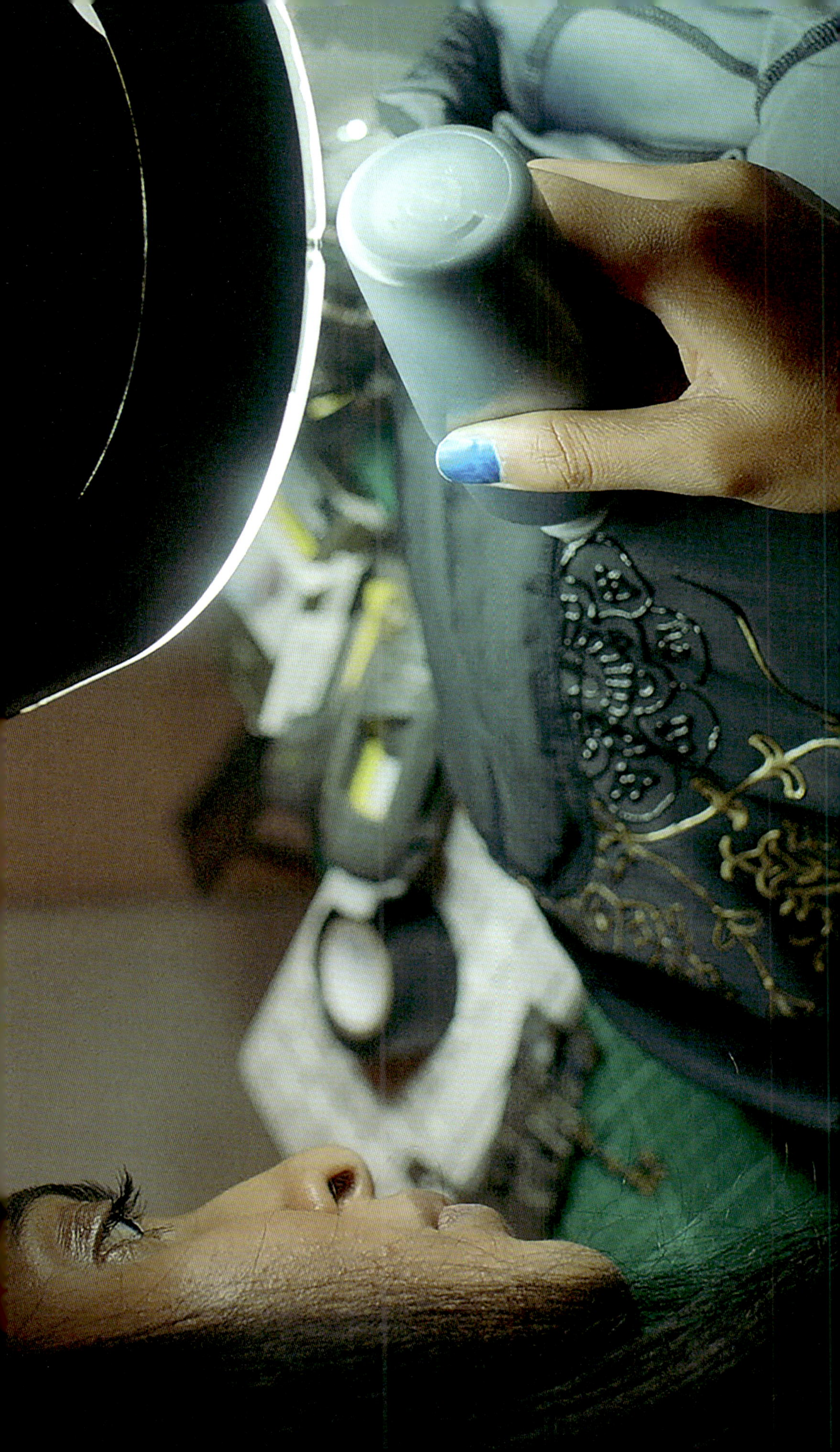

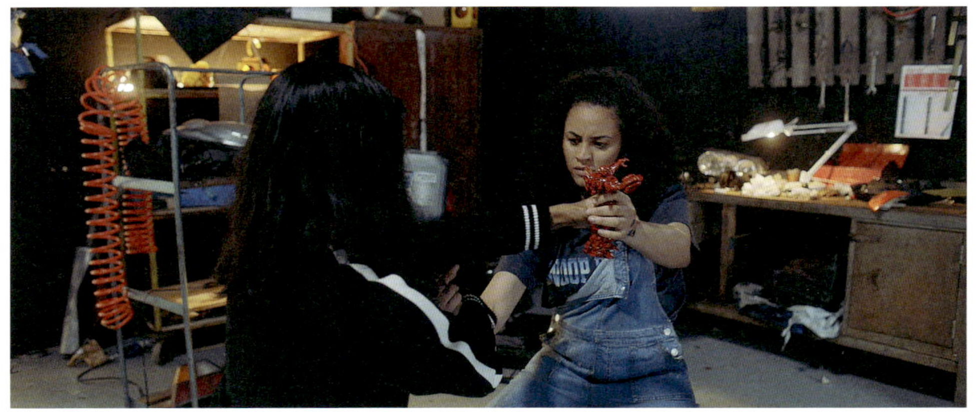

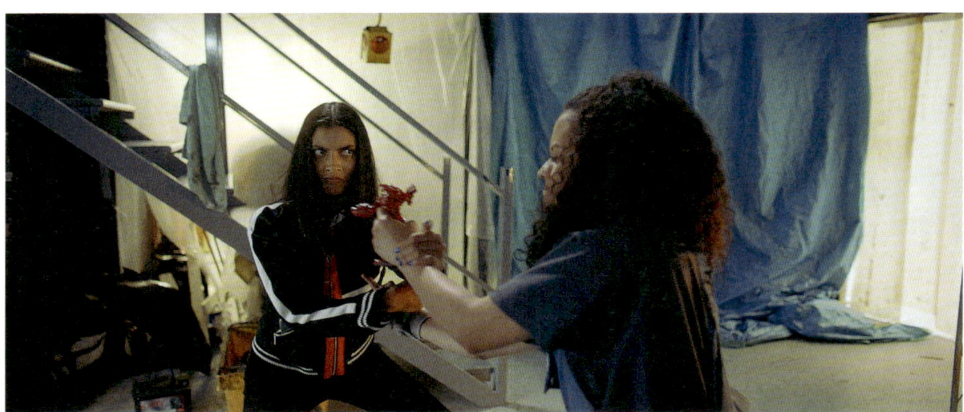

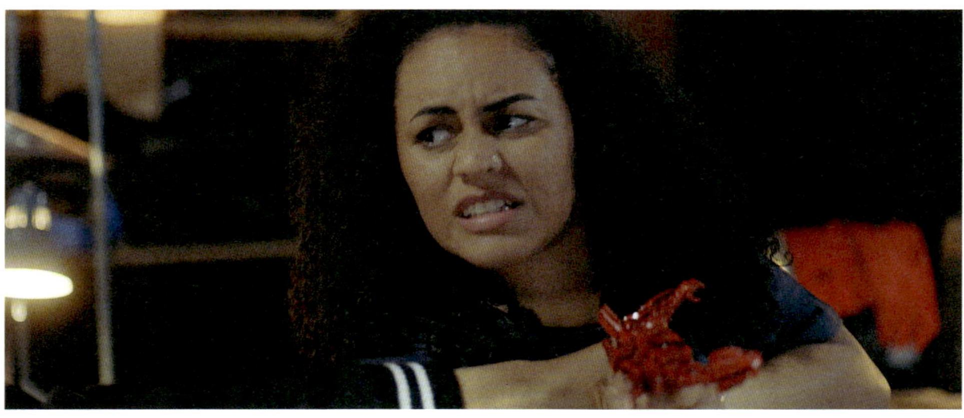

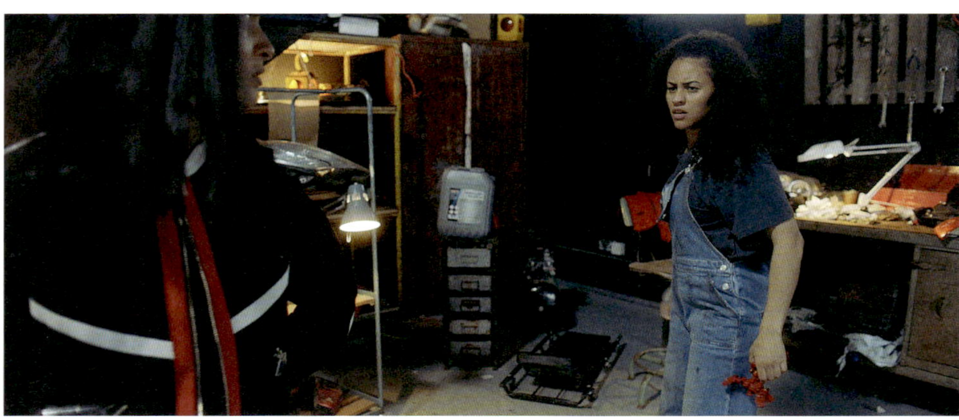

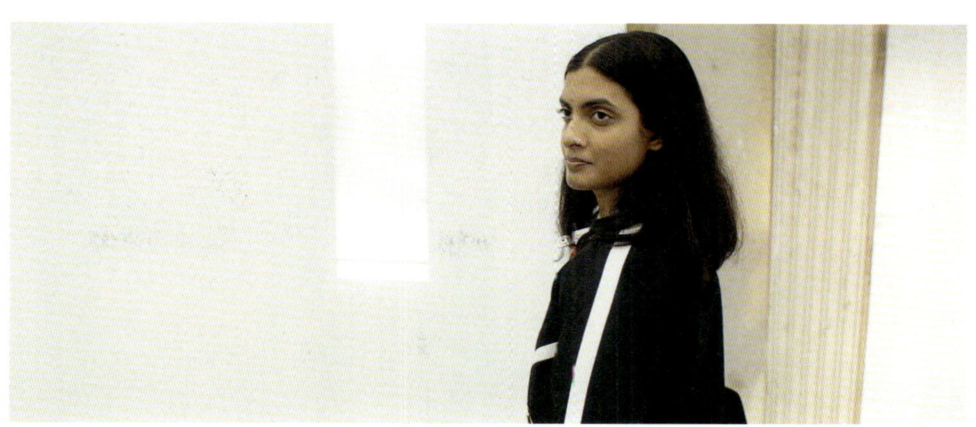

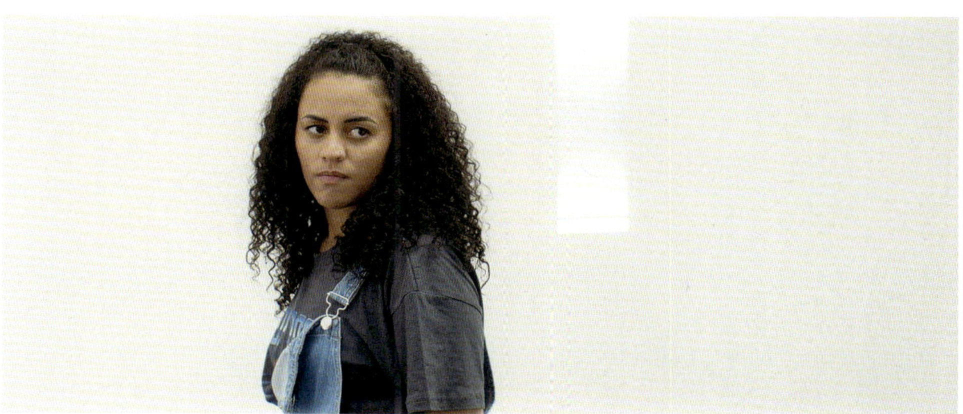

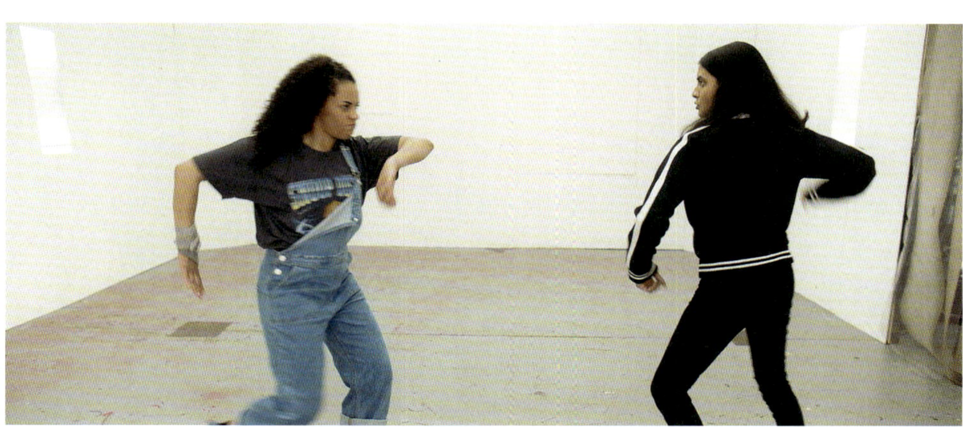

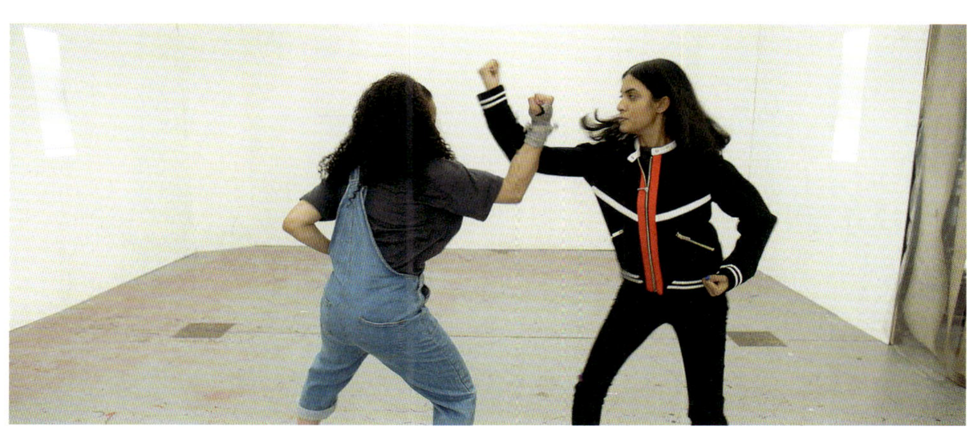

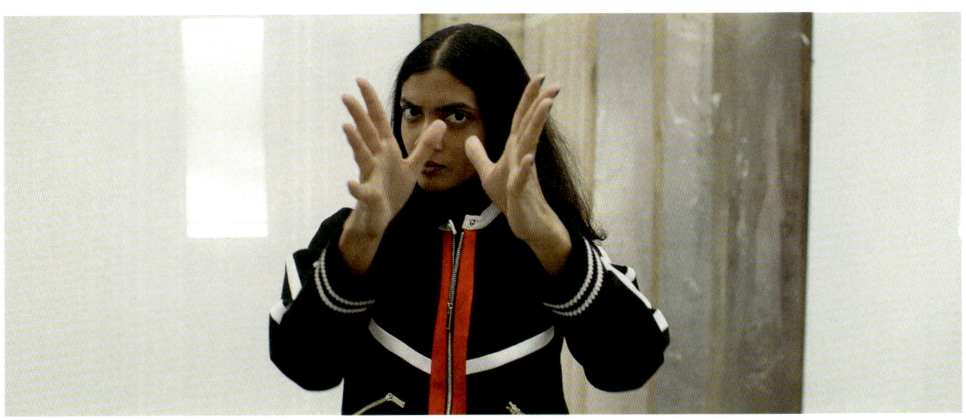

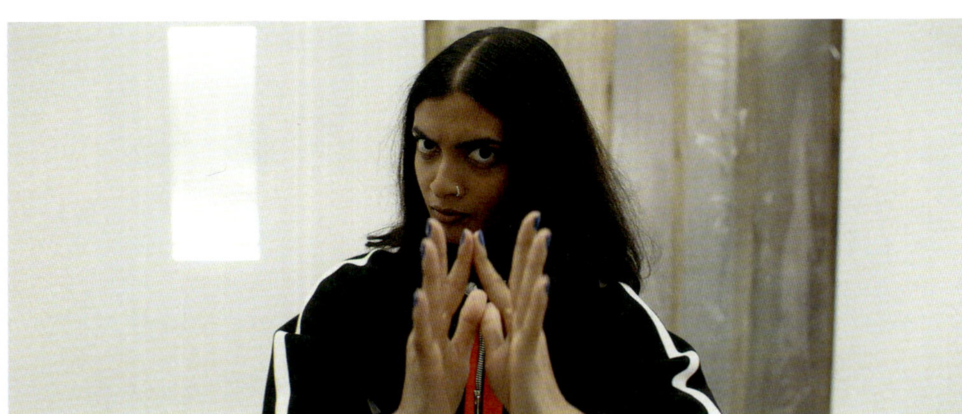

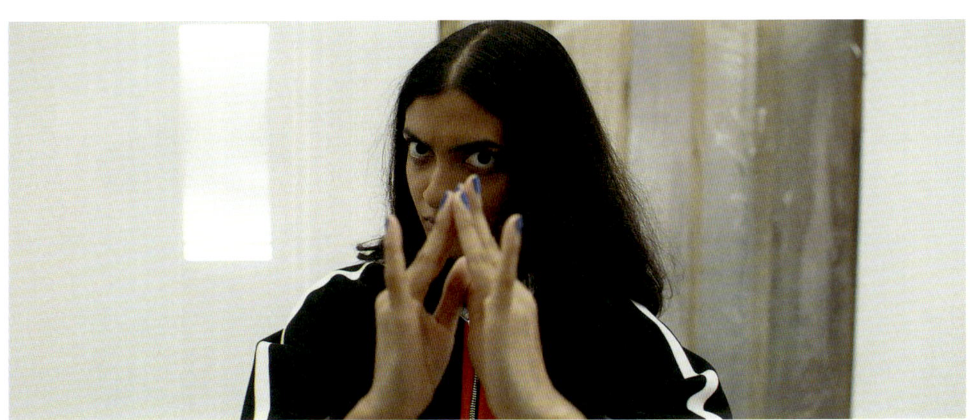

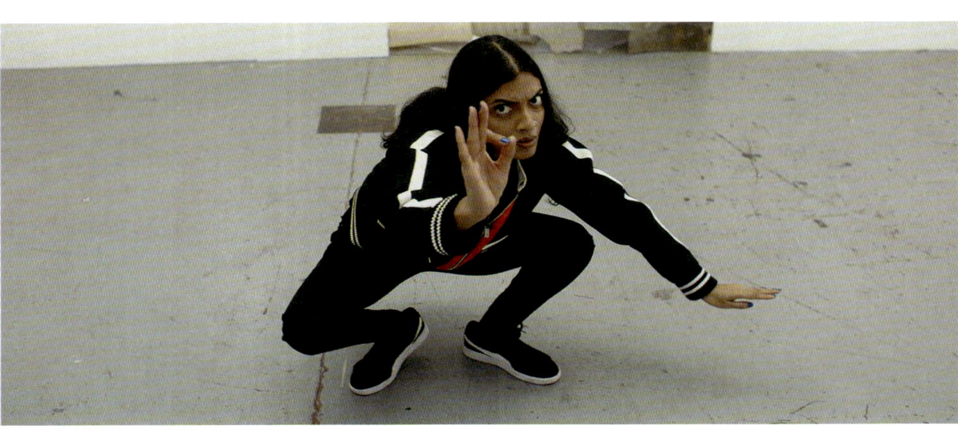

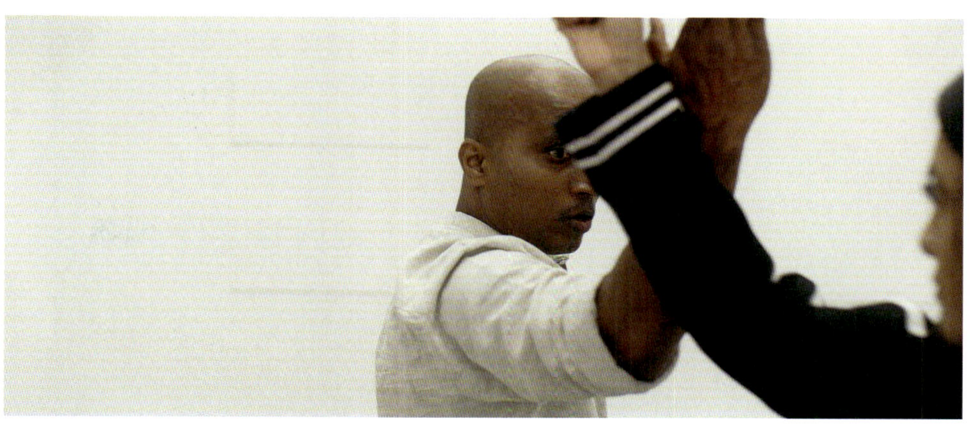

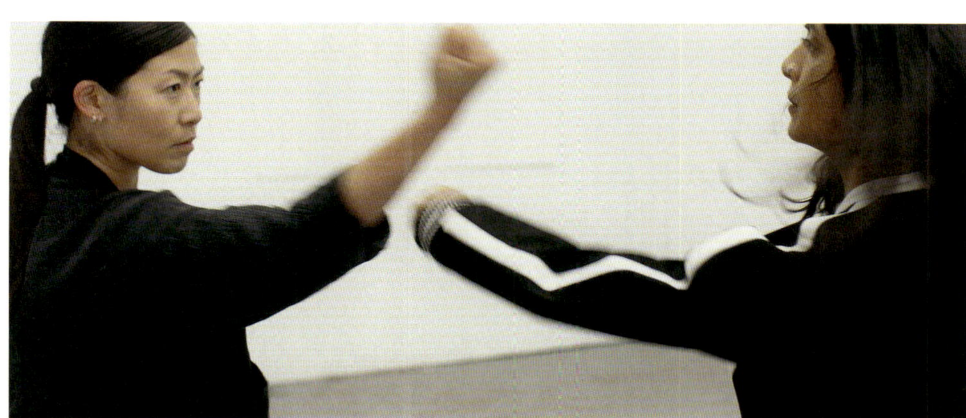

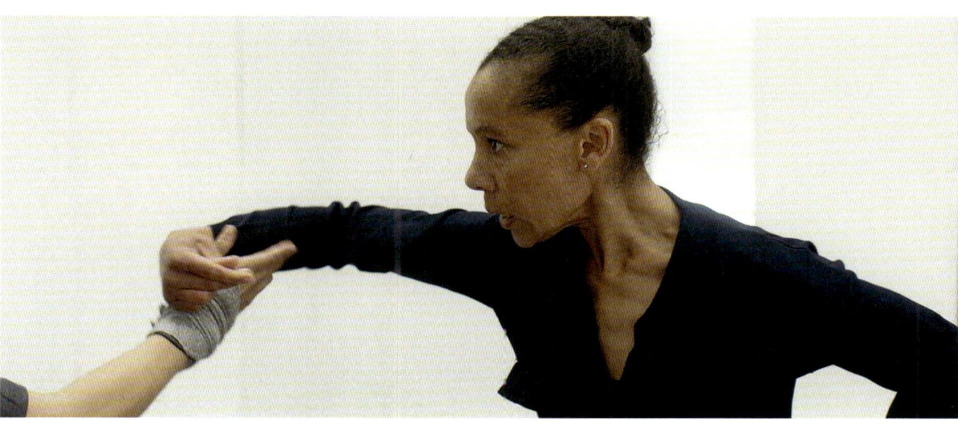

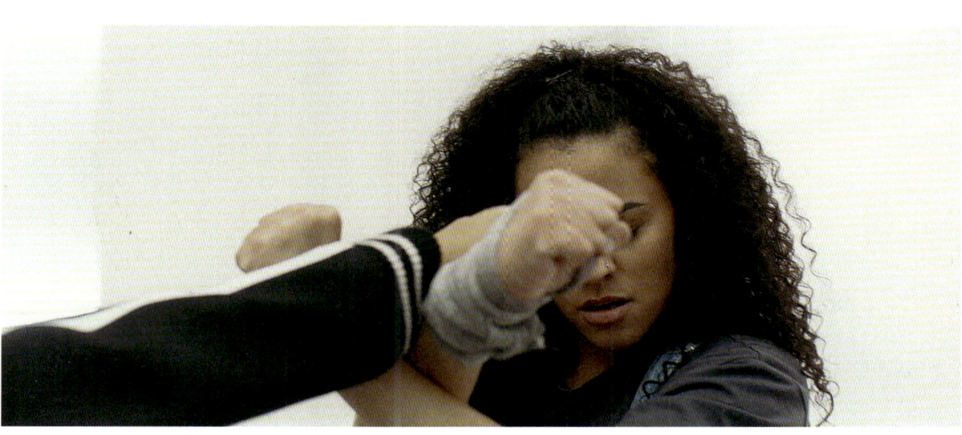

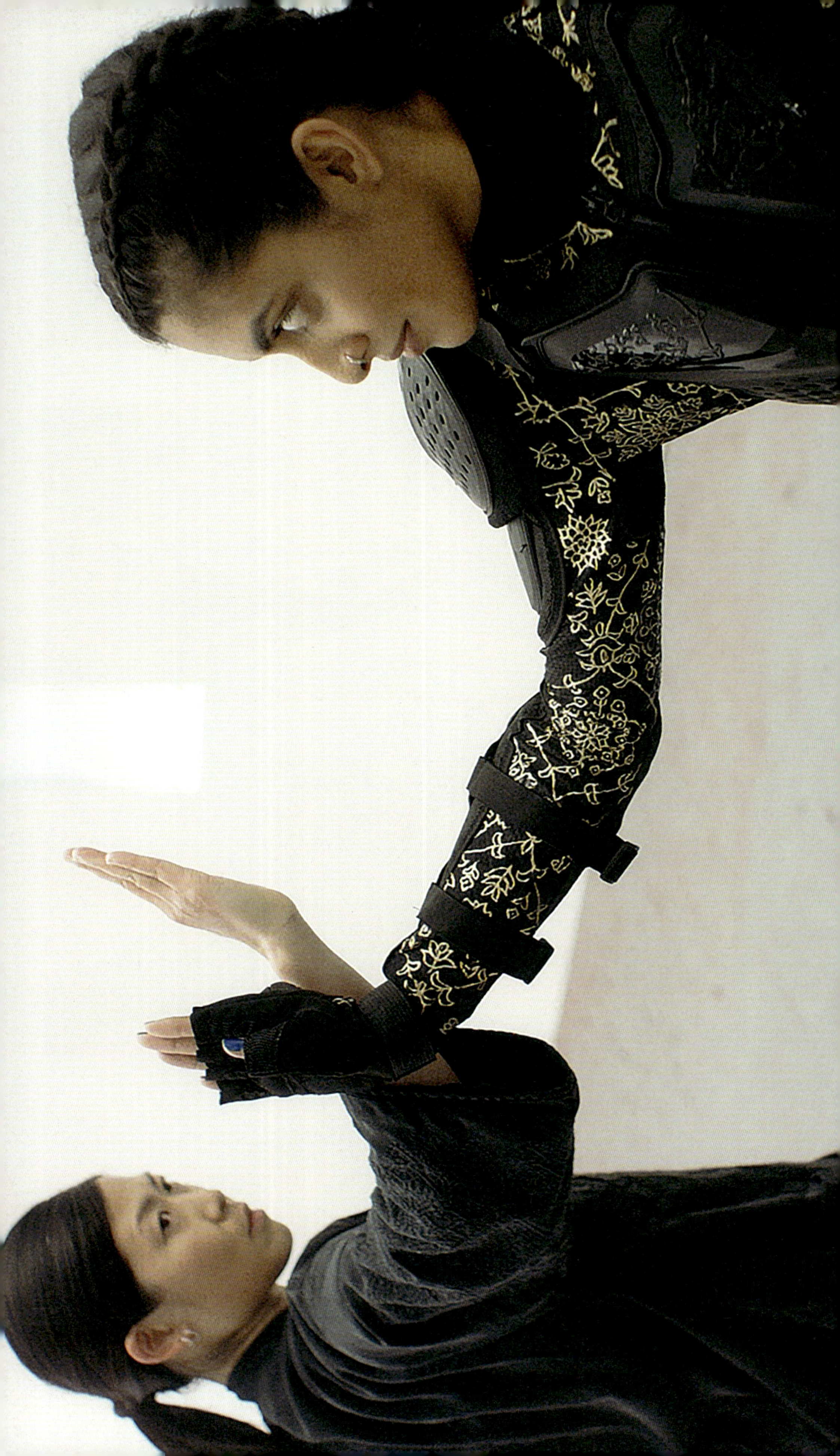

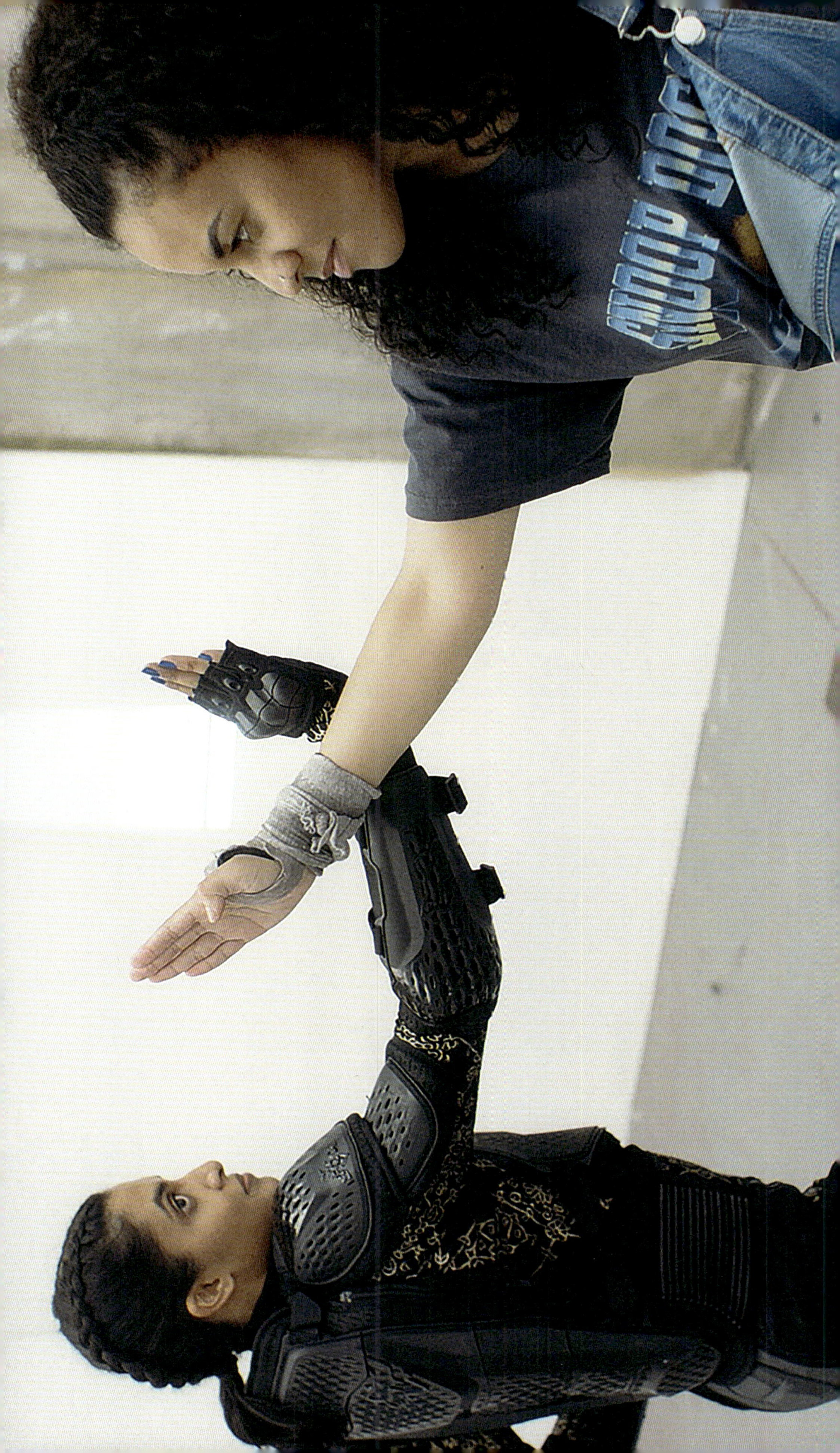

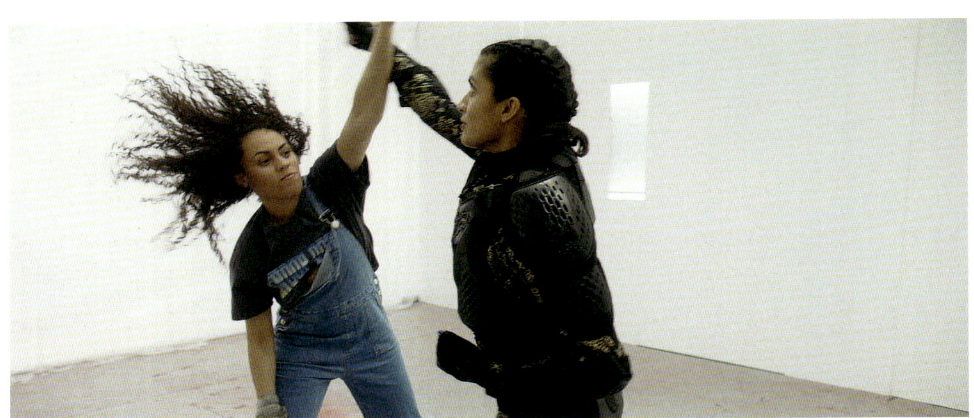

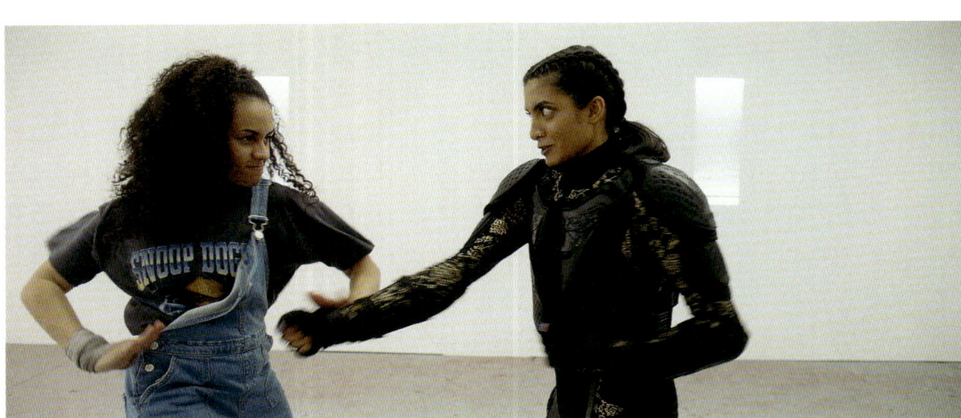

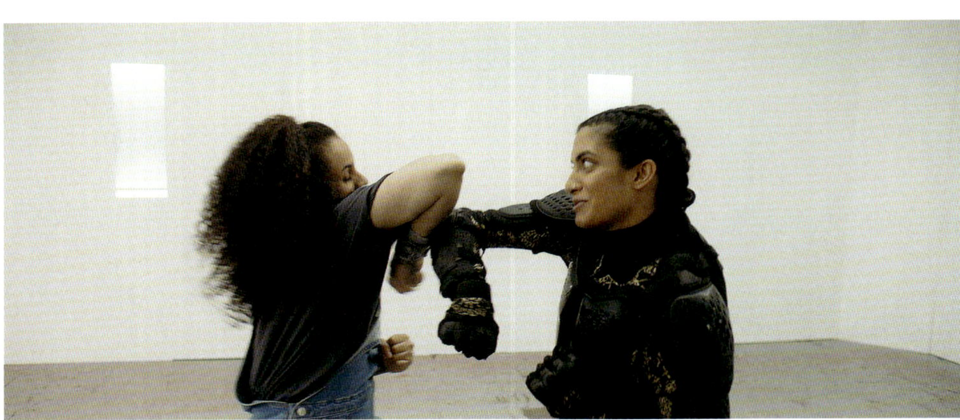

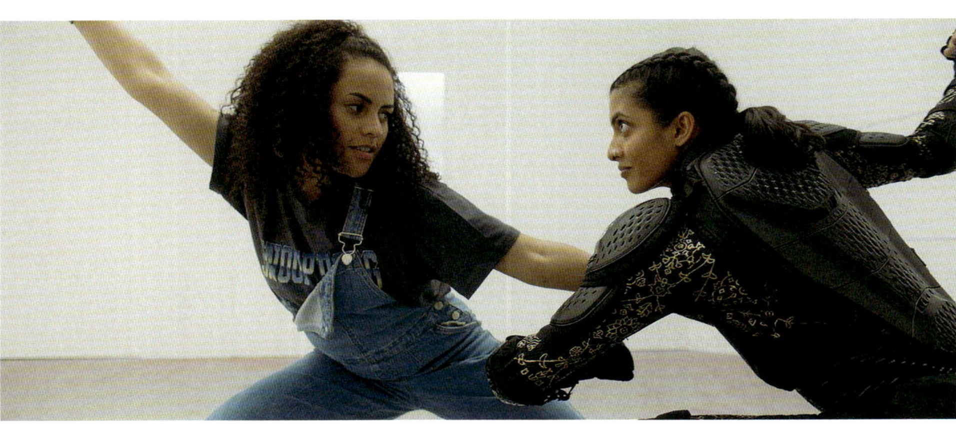

The camera zooms in on the intimate details of a domestic space: a colourful home shrine including representations of the Hindu deities Saraswati, goddess of education, creativity and music, and Ganesha, the symbol of wisdom and understanding revered as the remover of obstacles, and a table with a photograph of an elegant older woman in a gold arabesque frame. The protagonist of Hetain Patel's film *Trinity* (2021), Mina (played by the dancer Vidya Patel) is introduced onscreen by her footwork. The young British Indian woman is assiduously practicing a ceremonial rite on the dining room table under the watchful tutelage of her mother Samanya who gives her guidance in Gujarati. Wearing a plain cotton kurti and trousers, Mina, in bare feet, jumps, turns and stomps without upsetting her mother's teacup and saucer. Although her movements, which blend martial arts and classical Indian dance, are firm and nimble, they do not pass muster with her stern maternal tutor who sees the graceful mastery of the combat ceremony as crucial to her daughter's successful wedding match.

*Trinity* focuses on intergenerational and intercultural connection and conflict. When Samanya reveals that she has invited the GP doctor Roshan and his parents for tea, Mina responds in a sarcastic tone and sneaks away on her bicycle to avoid meeting her prospective match. Only when Mina focuses on training and is able to commune with her ancestors, a group of ethnically diverse figures who share the secret rites, are mother and daughter able to understand one another. Mina's story draws on Patel's own experience of isolation, growing up just outside of Manchester, in a place where, as he has described, they were the 'only brown family in town'. As a child, he found refuge in martial arts films, masked superheroes and action figures. Similarly, Mina keeps an altar-like display of her own deities, Transformers toys, in her bedroom. She dedicates much of her time to the meticulous work of creating her combat outfit, which has the impenetrable exterior of Batman's suit or motorcycle body armour but lovingly decorated with intricate patterns based on textiles from Patel's grandmother's home. Like his protagonist, Patel collects Transformers, incorporating them into a series of sculptures titled *Heavy Metal* (2018), and also spent months making a Spiderman costume by hand for his film *The Jump* (2015). Costumes, for Patel, confer special powers on their wearers and enable them to assume new identities beyond their everyday lives.

Mina again faces conflict when she intrudes on a young deaf woman, Amy (played by the deaf actress and dancer Raffie Julien) at work in a car body repair shop. After a failed attempt to communicate that results in a brief physical altercation, Mina flees, but returns a couple days later and manages to converse with Amy using voice recognition software. She asks for an estimate to repaint her bike the colour of her red Transformer, and the two bond over their shared interest in collecting these toys. The film culminates in an extended combat ceremony between Mina and Amy, weaving together martial arts, dance moves and sign language. Building on the dance style of each actor and the identity of their characters, Patel developed their movements in collaboration with fight choreographer Chirag Lukha and artist and writer Louise Stern.

With its style and storyline, *Trinity* blends elements from mainstream film genres such as martial arts, neo-noir and science fiction. *Trinity* is named after the female lead in Hollywood film *The Matrix* (1999), which references the Christian doctrine of the three figures of God. While working on the screenplay Patel also spent time looking at films such as Nicolas Winding Refn's action thriller *Drive* (2011) and Chad Stahelski's *John Wick* (2014) to imbue his night scenes with a darker neo-noir vibe. While stylistically aligned with Hollywood action movies, Patel flips the script, going back to the roots of classic Hong Kong martial arts cinema while also pointing towards a more hybrid and inclusive future for film. In the words of Samanya, 'when the language is found again it will spread. And bring about the beginning of the new world.'

Lydia Yee

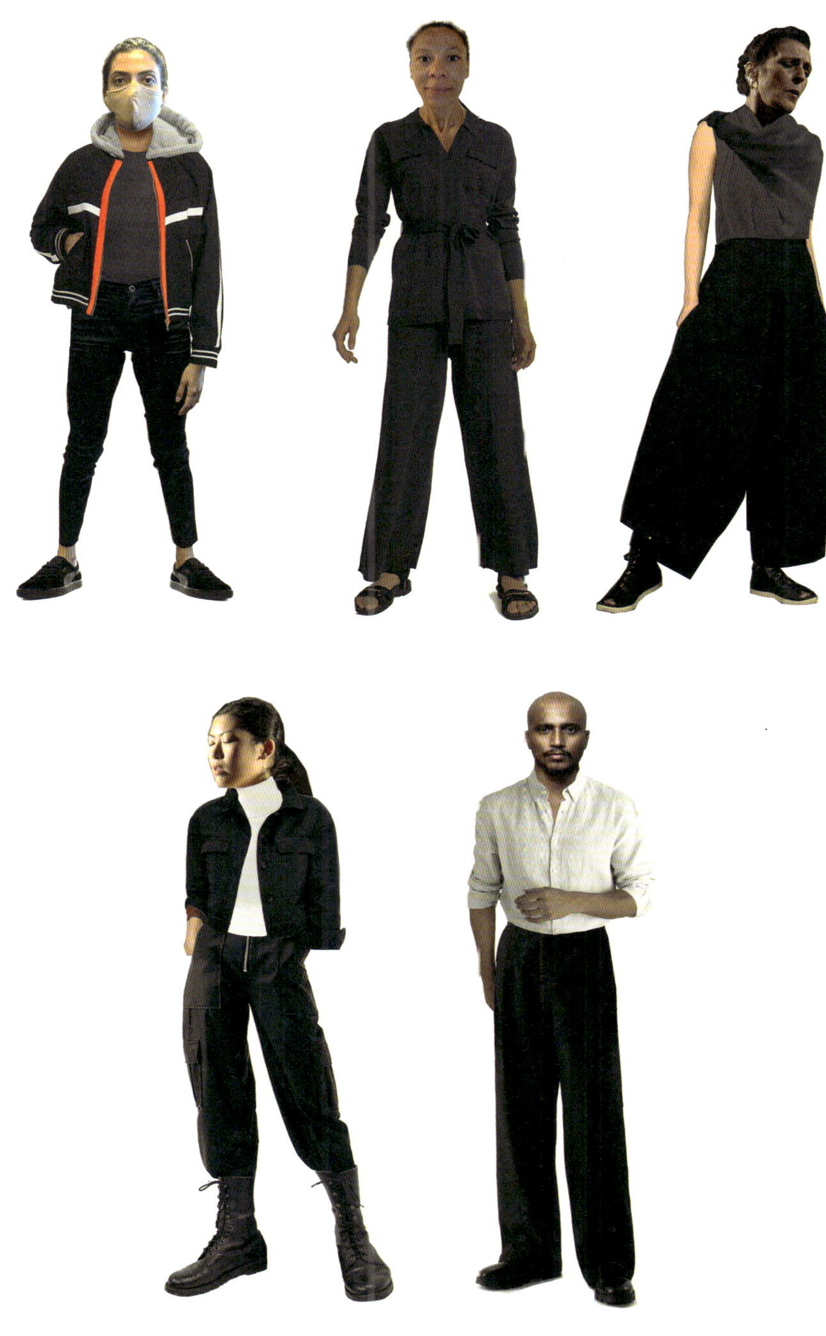

Top: Excerpt from design board for *Trinity* by costume designer Sarah Mercadé
Bottom and right: Excerpts from art boards for *Trinity* by production designer Bobbie Cousins

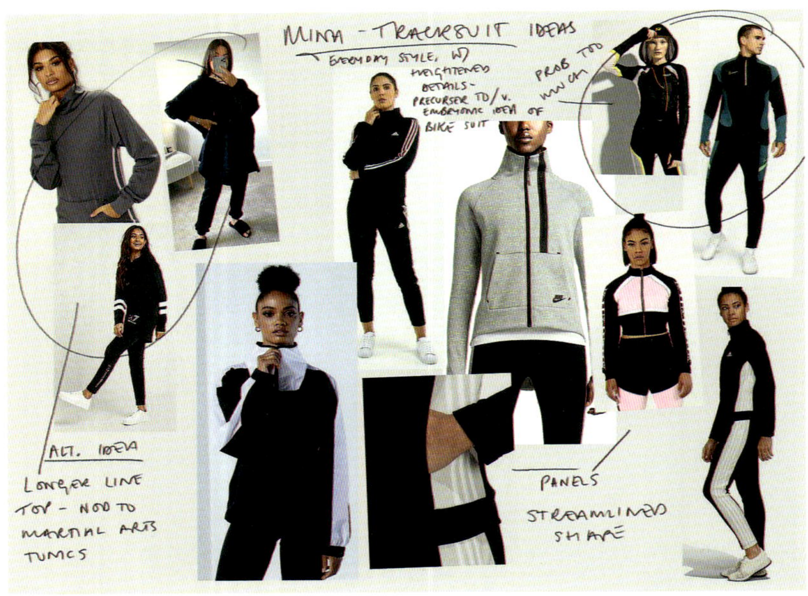

MINA - TRACKSUIT IDEAS
EVERYDAY STYLE, W/ HEIGHTENED DETAILS - PRECURSOR TO / V. EMBRYONIC IDEA OF BIKE SUIT
PROB TOO MW CM
ALT. IDEA
LONGER LINE TOP - NOD TO MARTIAL ARTS TUNICS
PANELS
STREAMLINED SHAPE

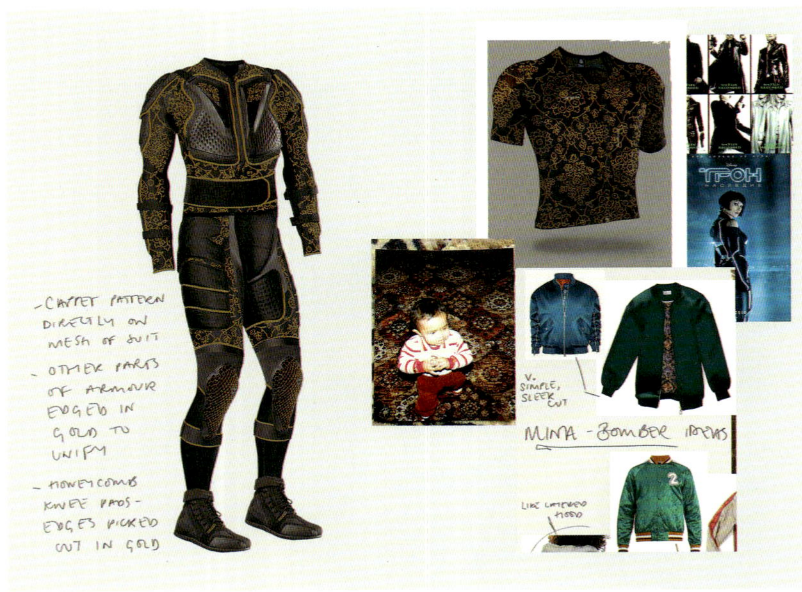

- CARPET PATTERN DIRECTLY ON MESH OF SUIT
- OTHER PARTS OF ARMOUR EDGED IN GOLD TO UNIFY
- HONEYCOMB KNEE PADS - EDGES PICKED OUT IN GOLD
V. SIMPLE, SLEEK CUT
MINA - BOMBER IDEAS
LIKE LAYERED HOOD

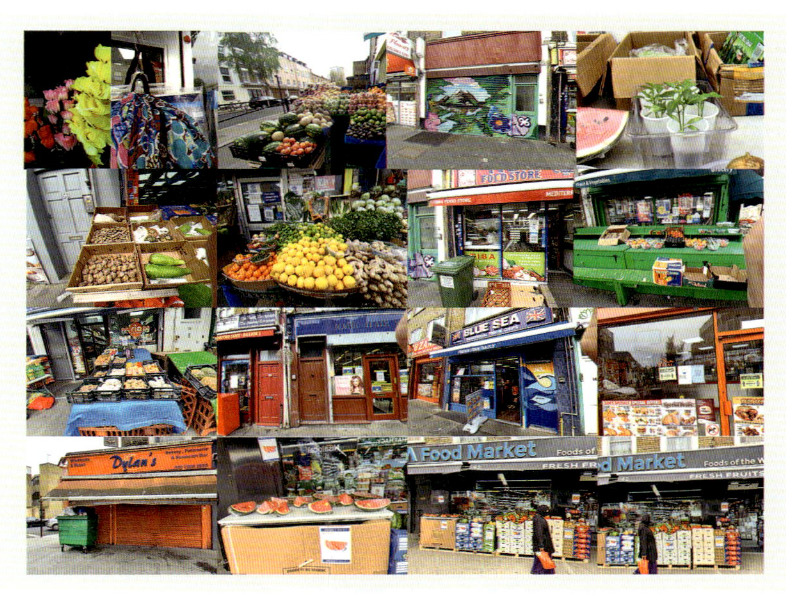

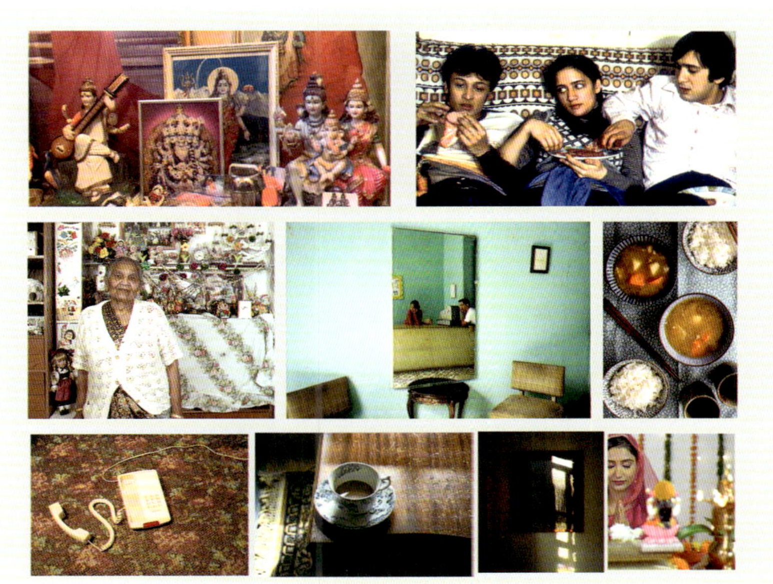

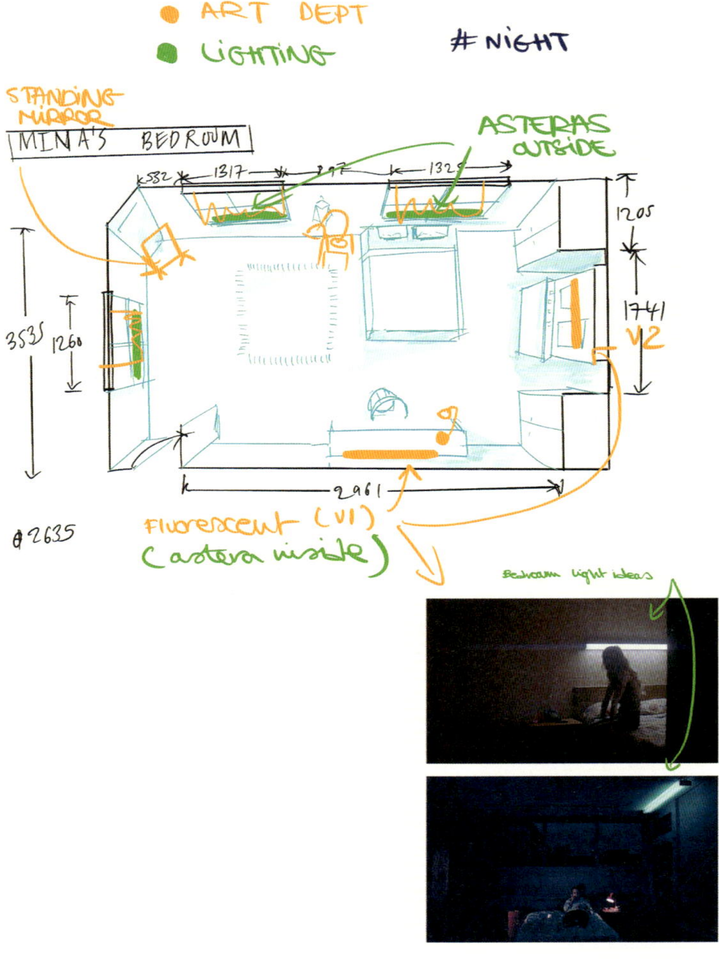
ART DEPT
LIGHTING
# NIGHT
STANDING MIRROR
MINA'S BEDROOM
ASTERAS OUTSIDE
582
1317
297
1325
1205
3535
1260
1741
V2
2635
2961
Fluorescent (V1)
(astera inside)
Bedroom light ideas

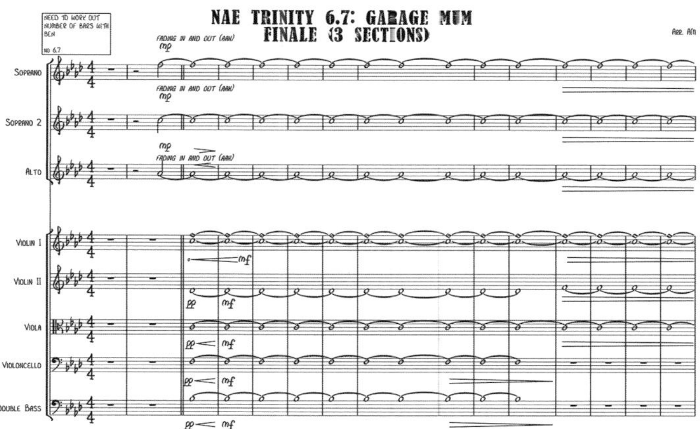
NEED TO WORK OUT
NUMBER OF BARS WITH
BEN
NO. 6.7
NAE TRINITY 6.7: GARAGE MUM
FINALE (3 SECTIONS)
ARR. AM
FADING IN AND OUT (AAH)
mp
Soprano
FADING IN AND OUT (AAH)
mp
Soprano 2
mp
FADING IN AND OUT (AAH)
Alto
Violin I
mf
Violin II
pp
mf
Viola
pp
mf
Violoncello
pp
mf
Double Bass
pp
mf

17
LONG PERCUSSION
ONLY SECTION
♩=80-100 (VARIABLE)
TACET
S.
A - SA - TYO, MA HAY  TEE__ POA BOO PA BA    MA SA - A    TAY TU LAY_ JA__  UN - DAR AN - DAR BAY
TACET
S.
A - SA - TYO, MA HAY  TEE__ POA BOO PA BA    MA SA - A    TAY TU LAY_ JA__  UN - DAR AN - DAR BAY
TACET
A.
A - SA - TYO, MA HAY  TEE__ POA BOO PA BA    MA SA - A    TAY TU LAY_ JA__  UN - DAR AN - DAR BAY
♩=80-100 (VARIABLE)
Vln. I
Vln. II
Vla.
Vc.
Db.
NAE TRINITY 6.7 GARAGE MUM FINALE

# Bárbara Wagner and Benjamin de Burca
*Faz Que Vai* (Set to Go), 2015

HD video, colour, sound;
12 minutes

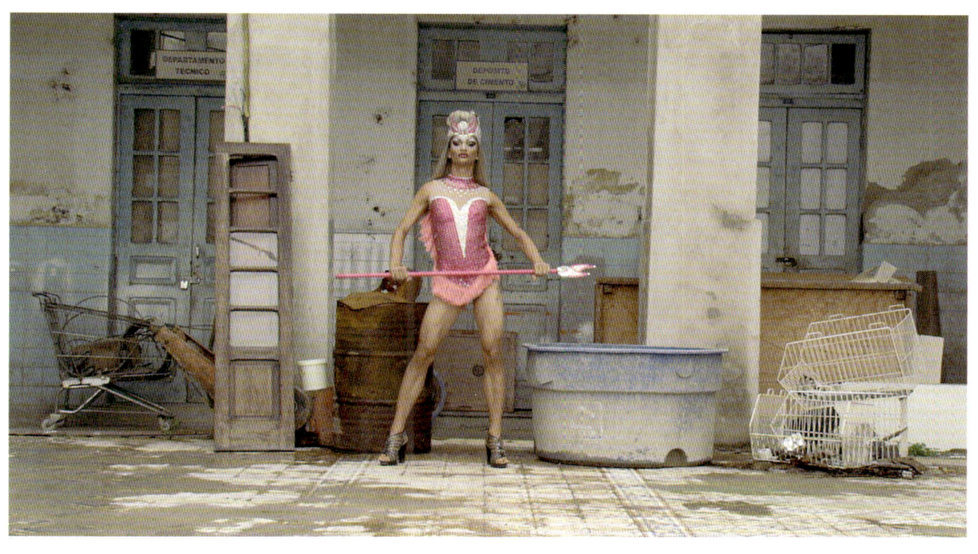

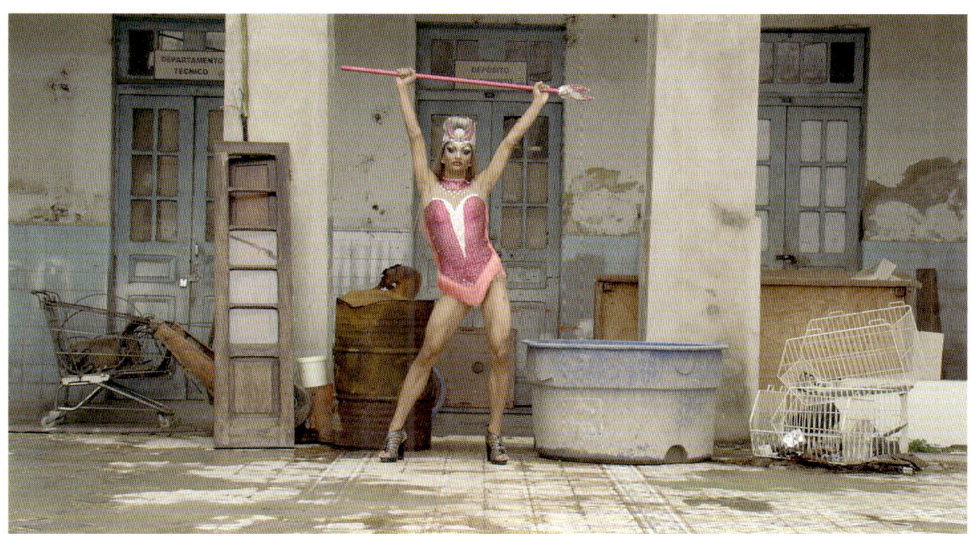

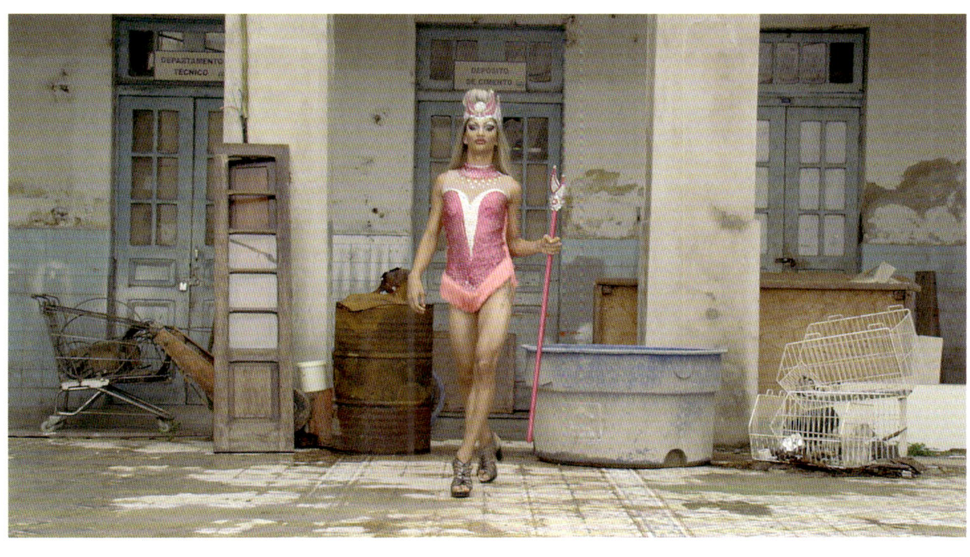

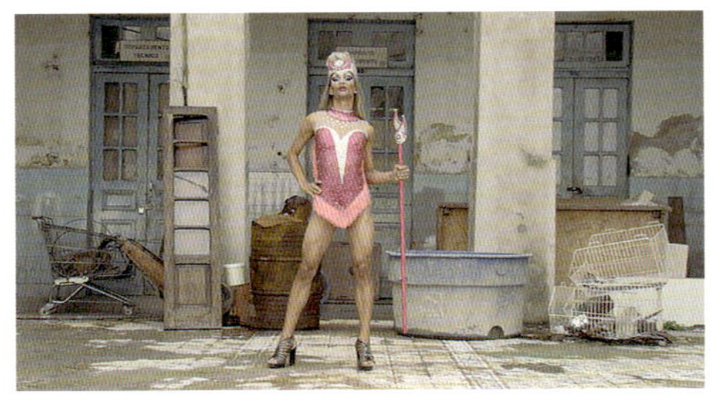
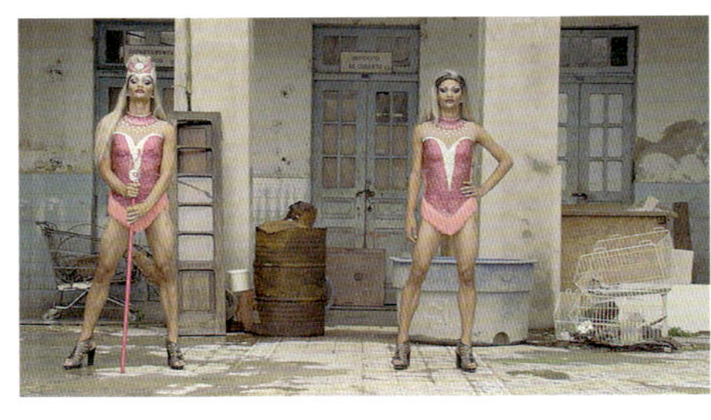
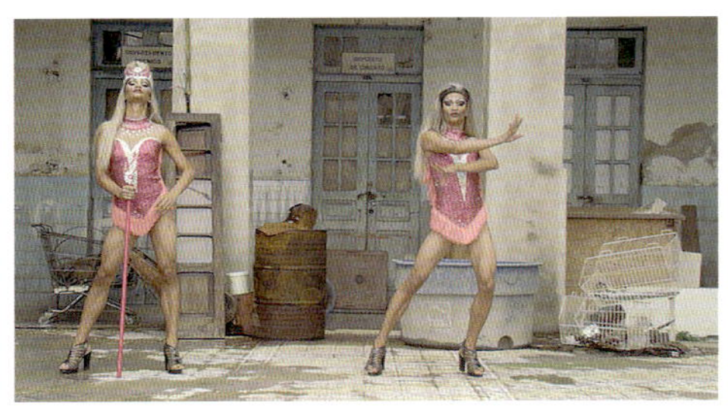
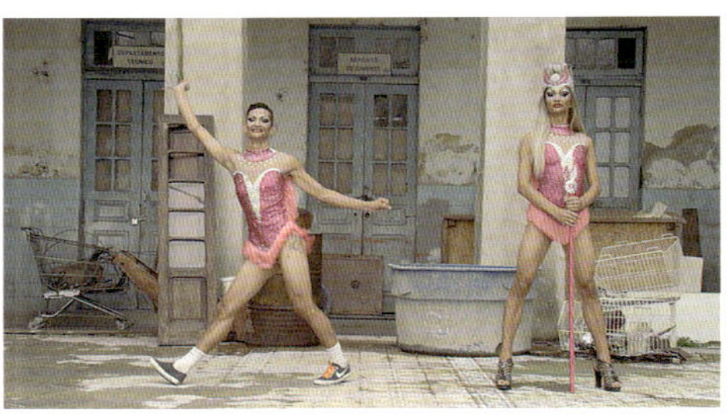
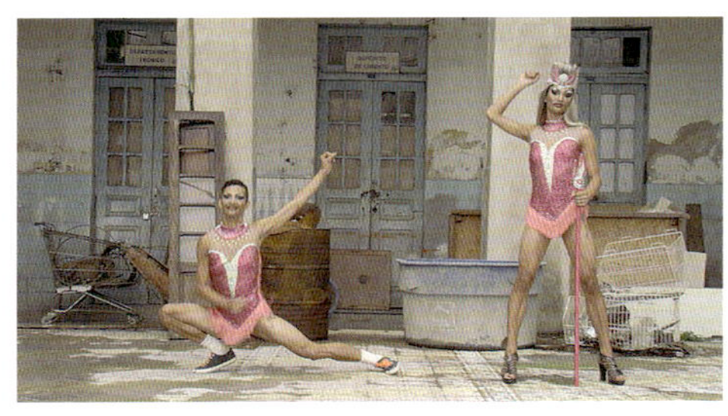
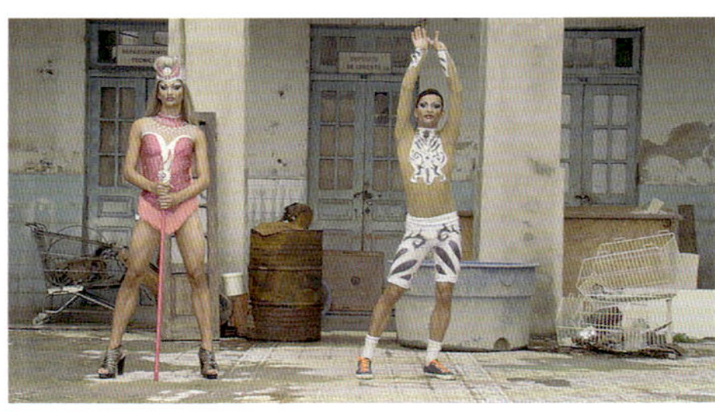
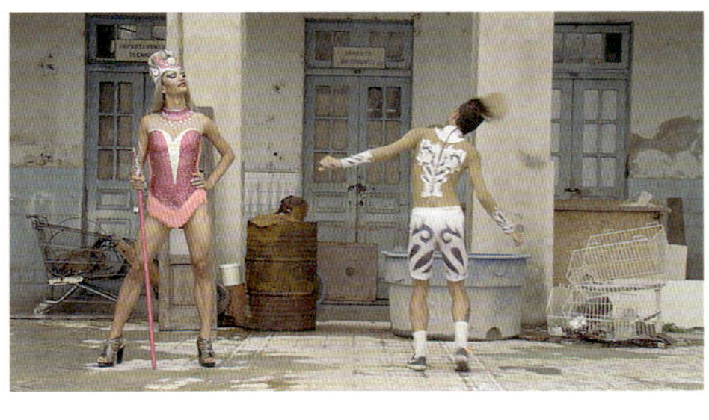
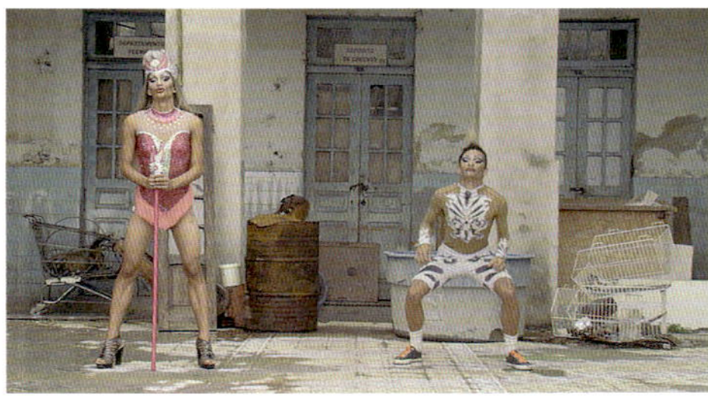

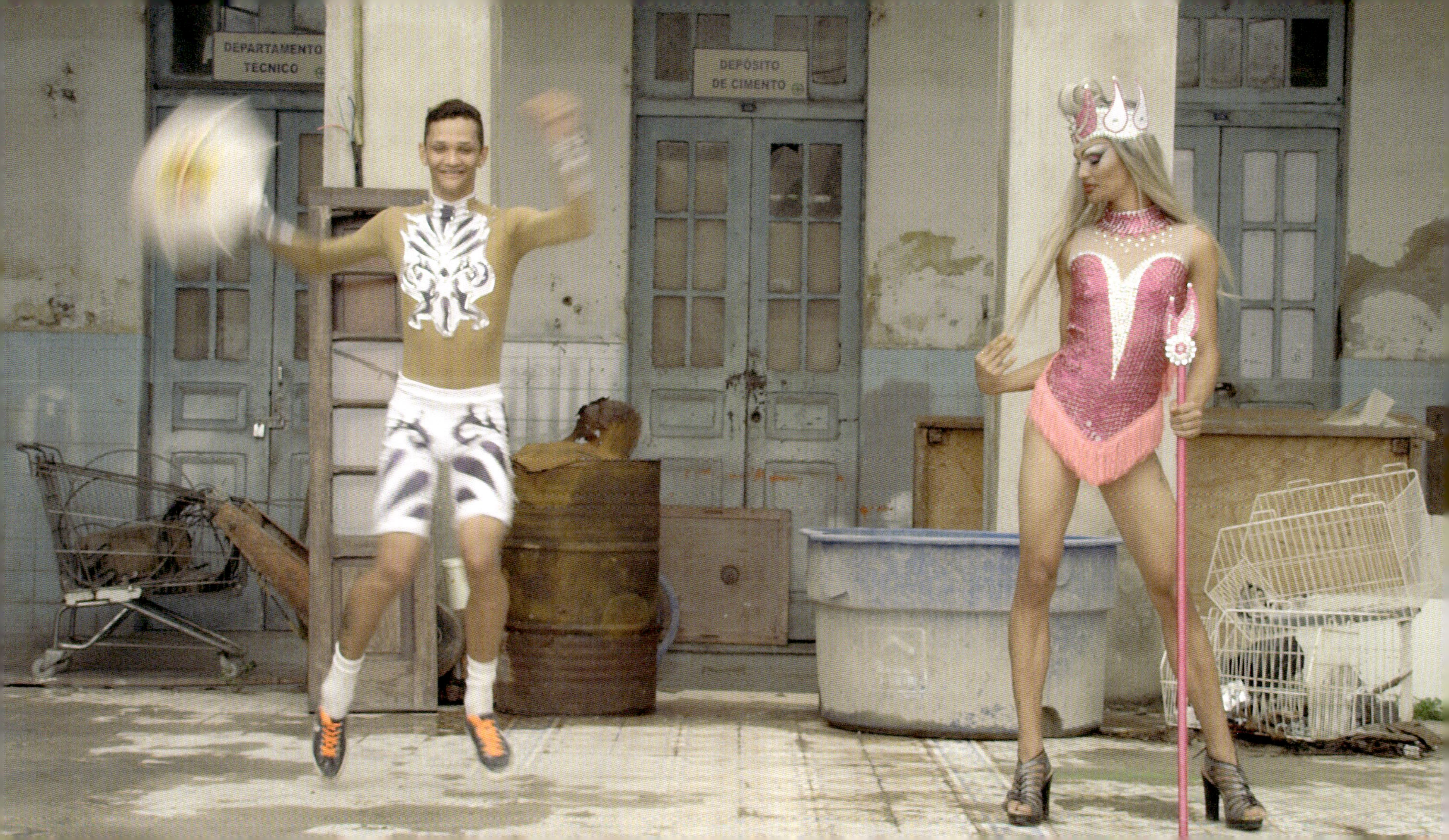

DEPARTAMENTO TÉCNICO
DEPÓSITO DE CIMENTO

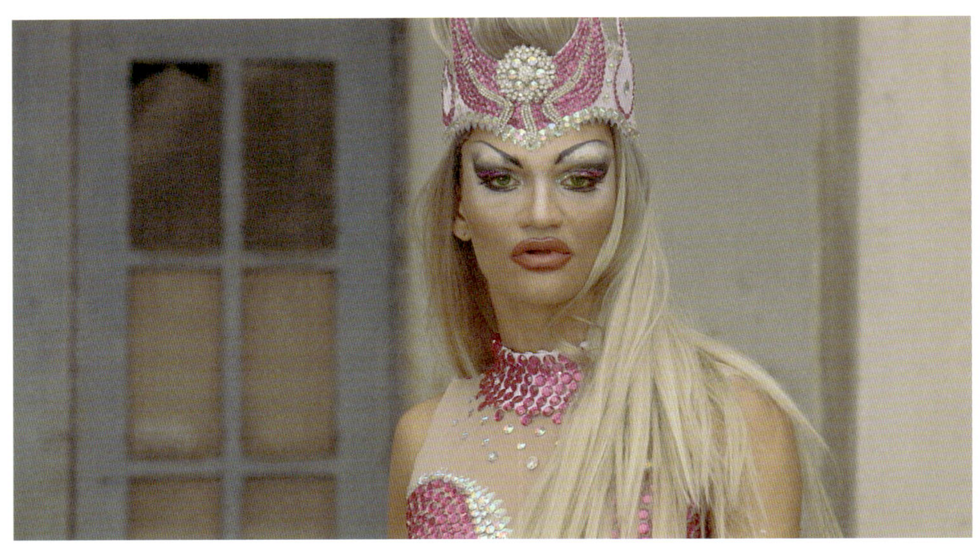

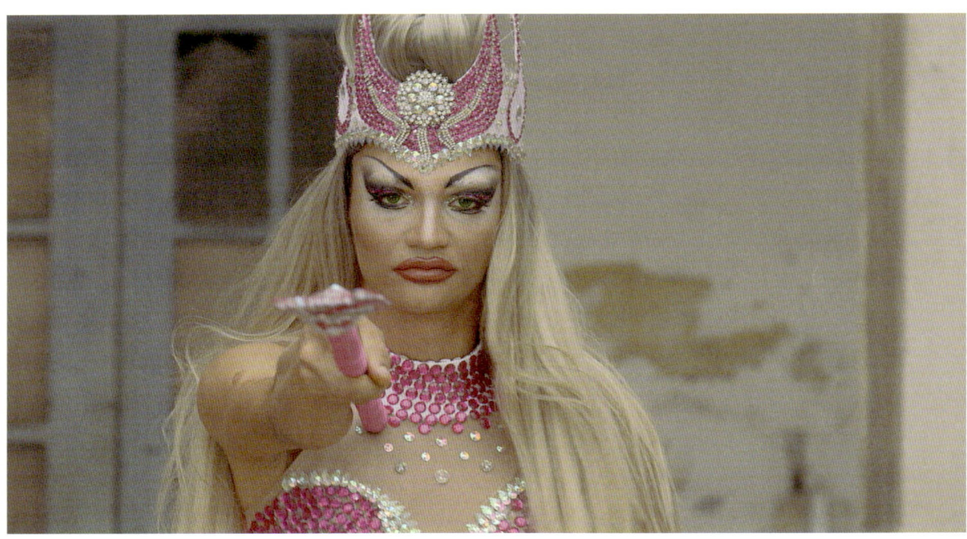

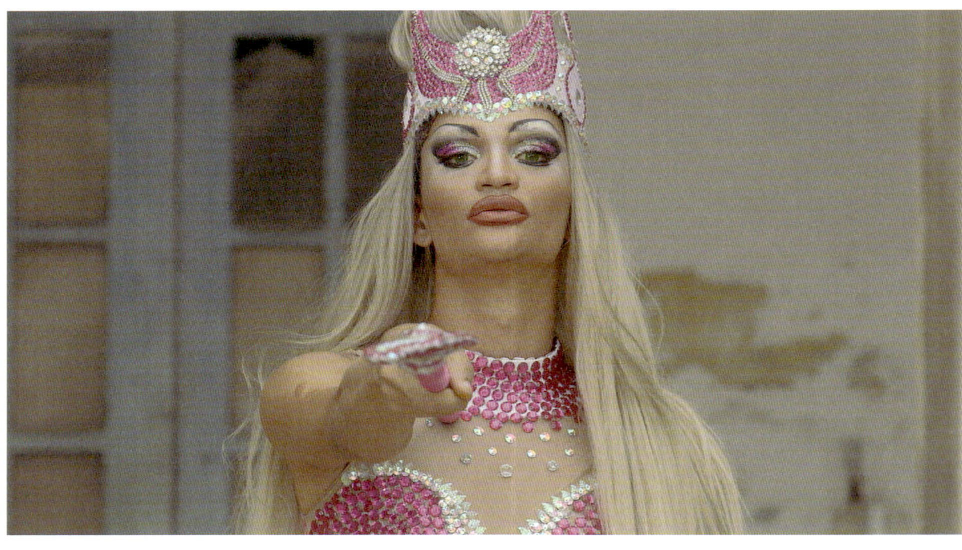

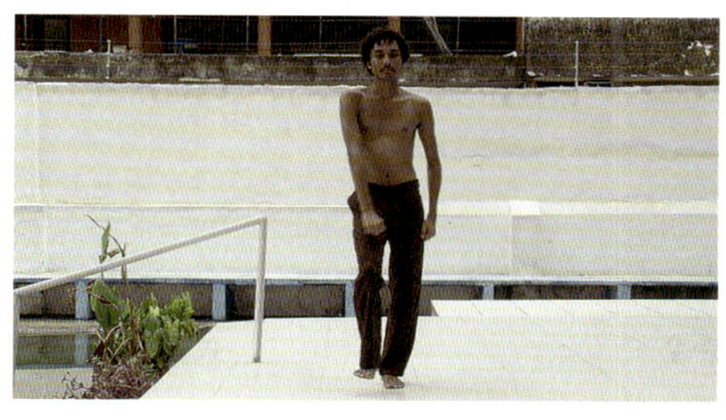
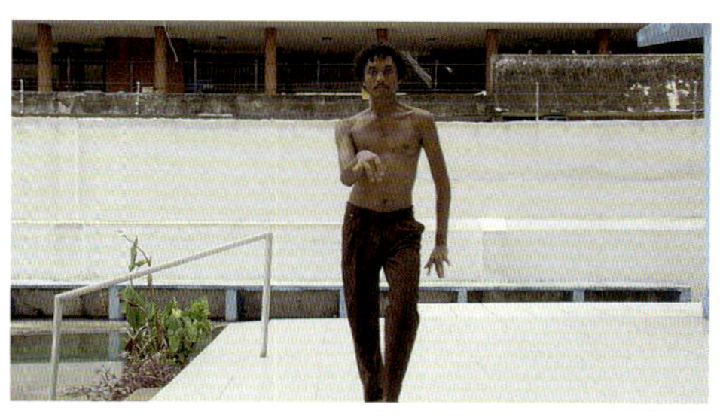
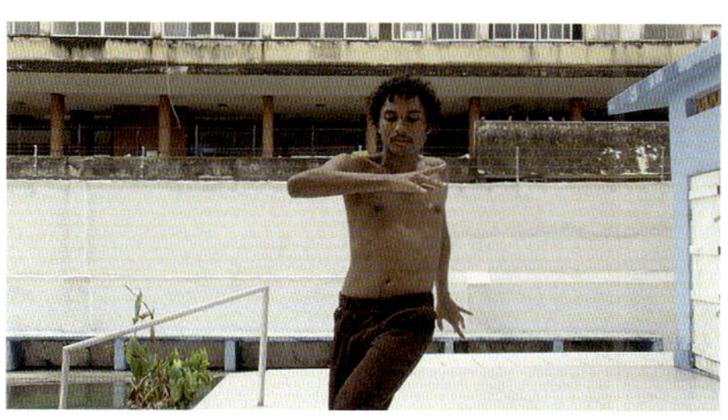
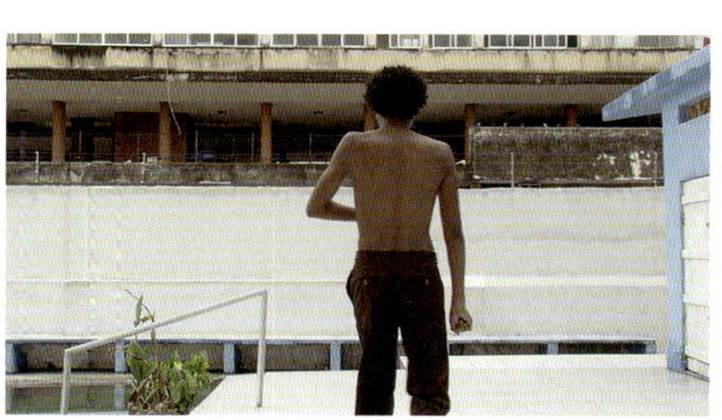
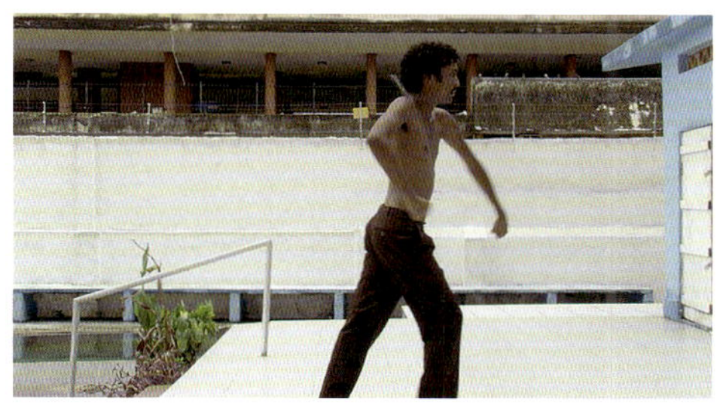
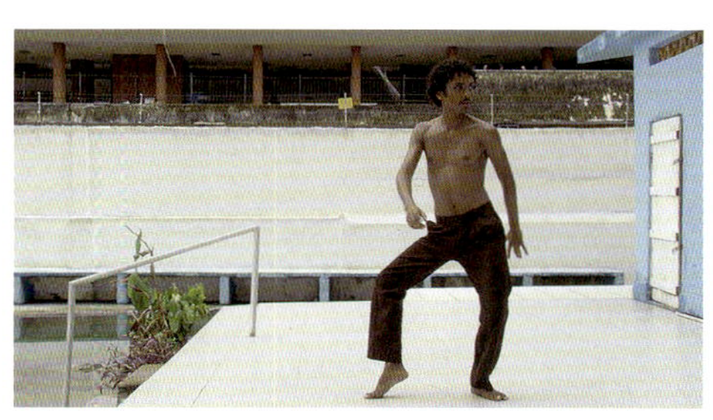
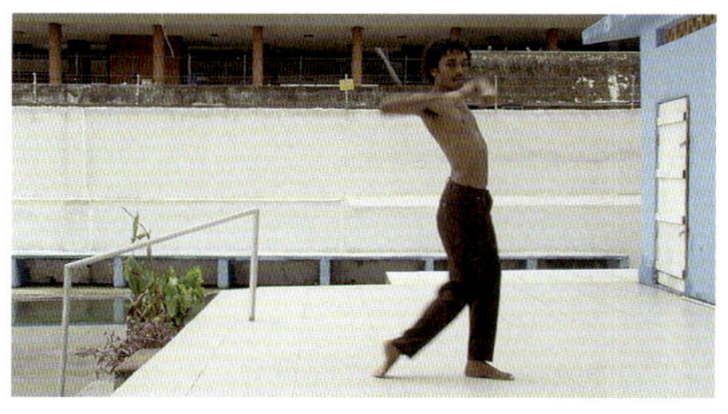
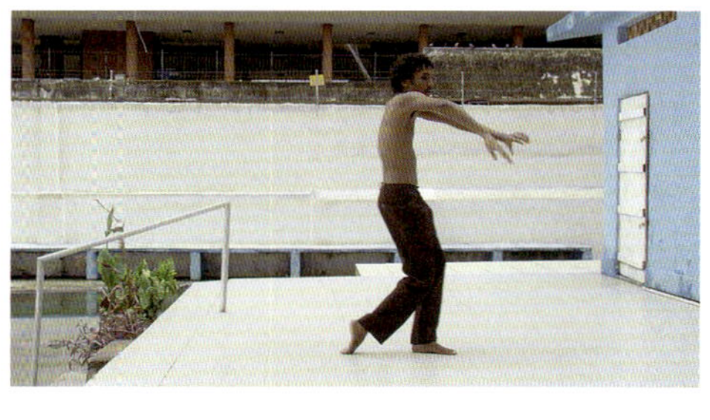

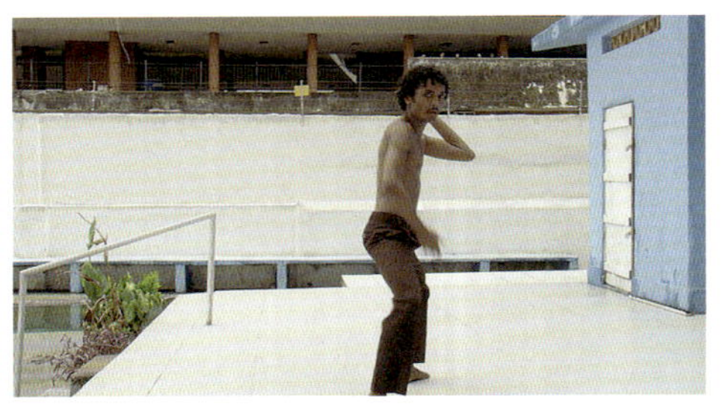
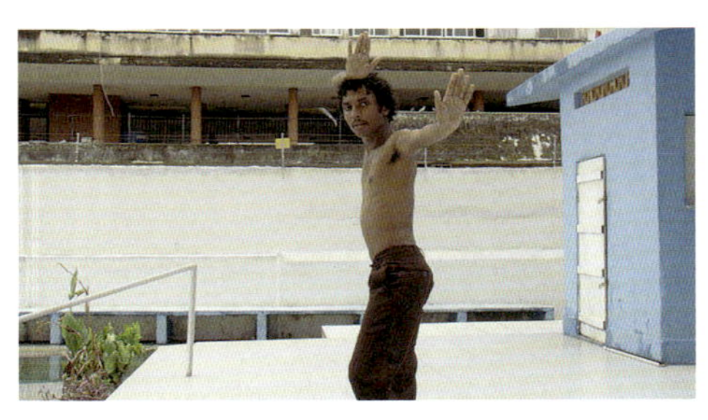
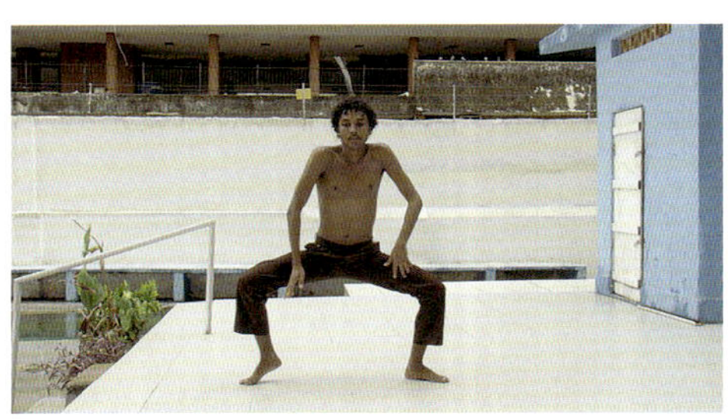
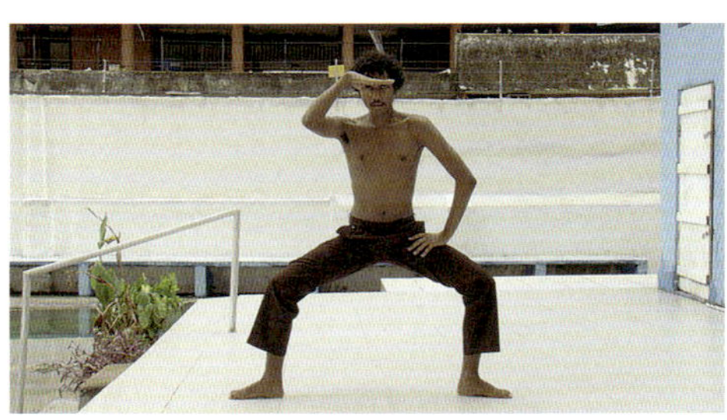
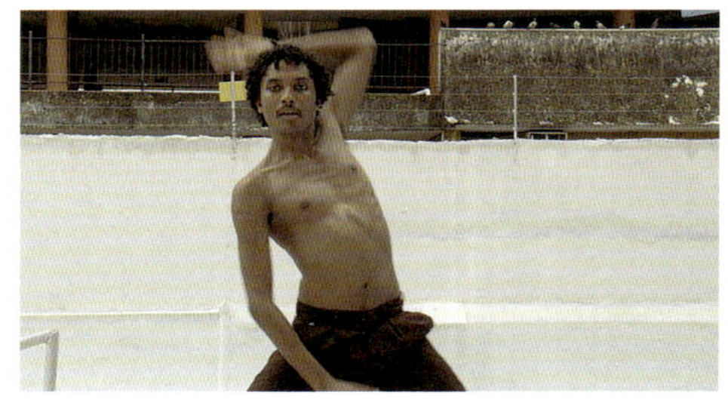
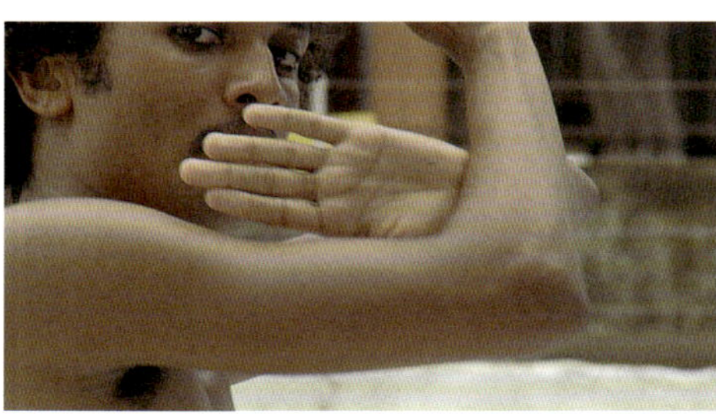
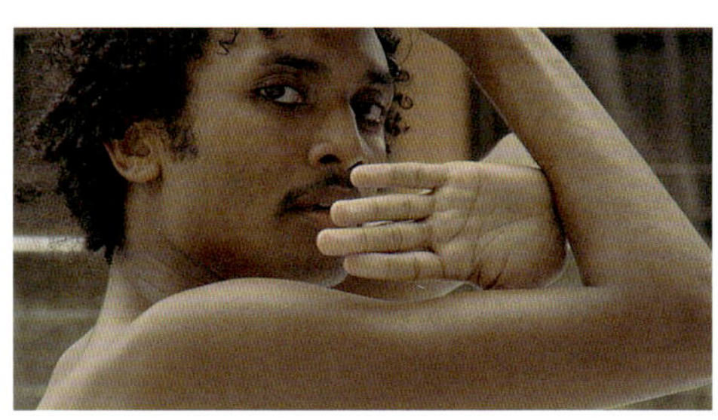
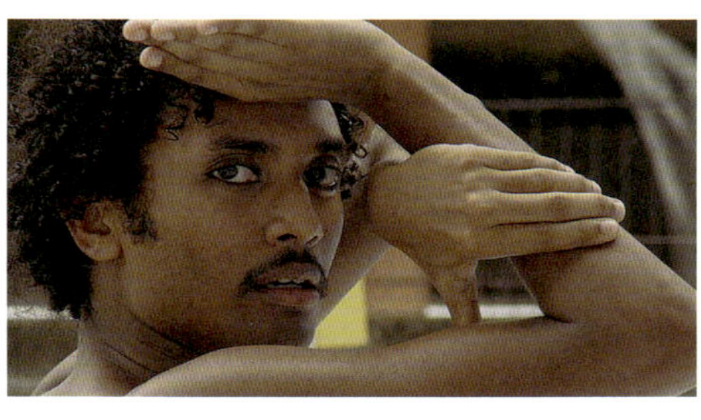

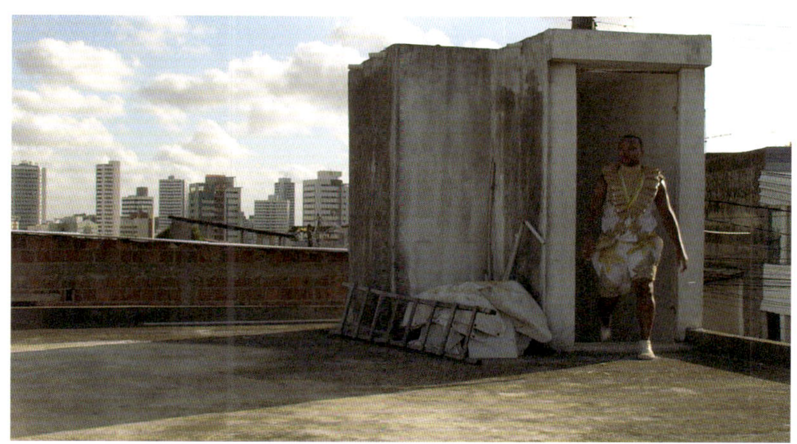
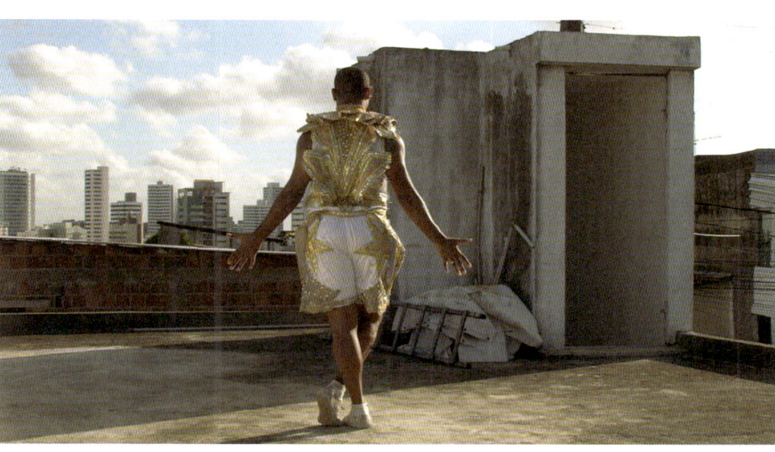
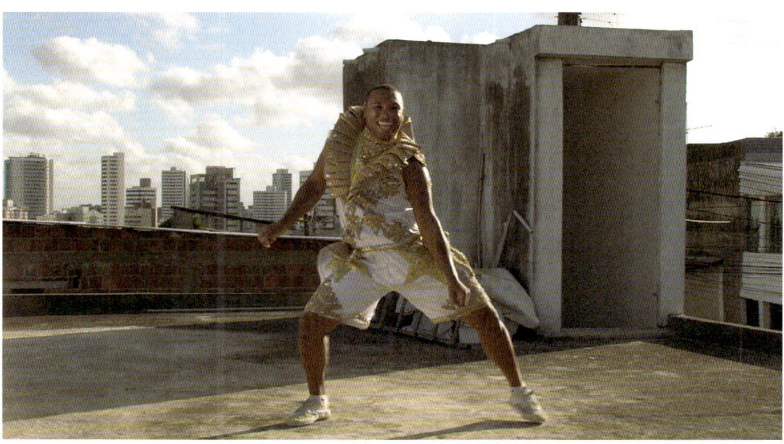
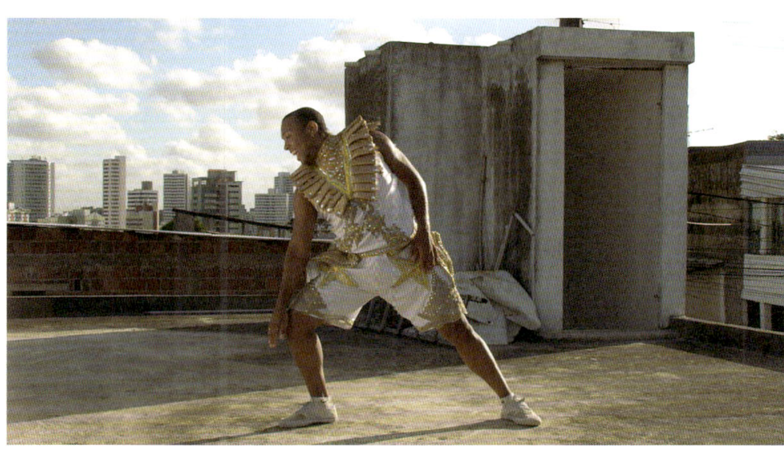

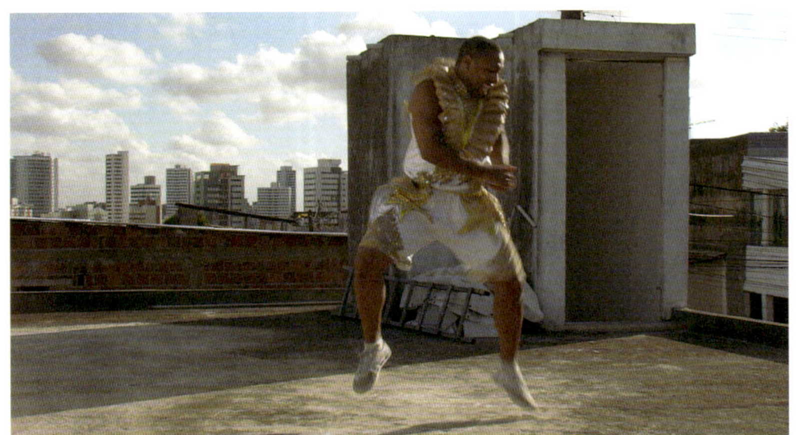

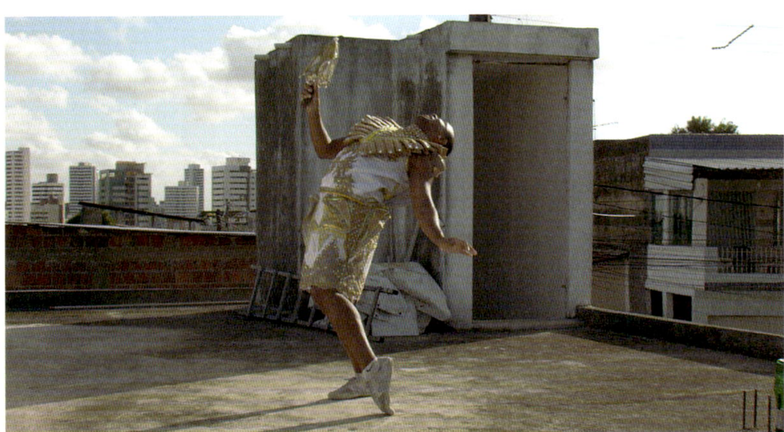

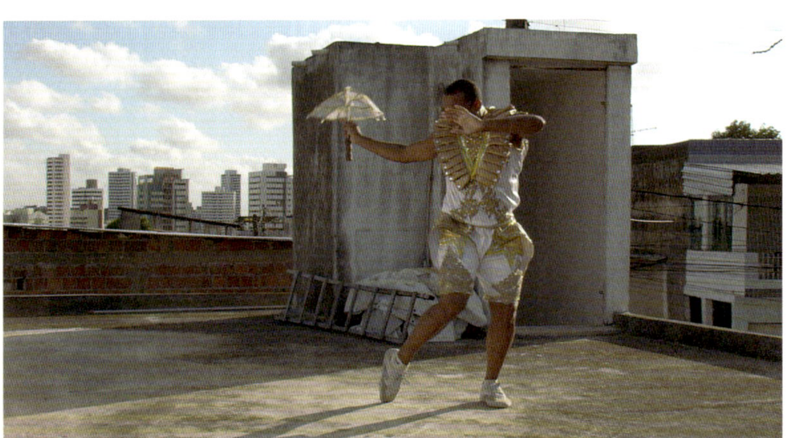

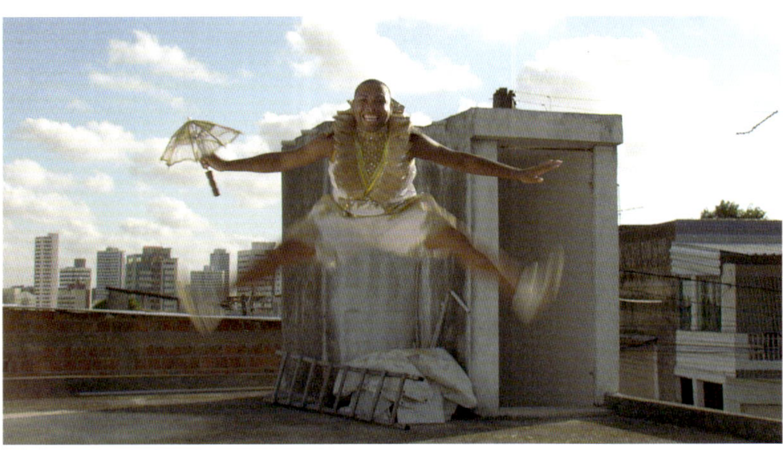

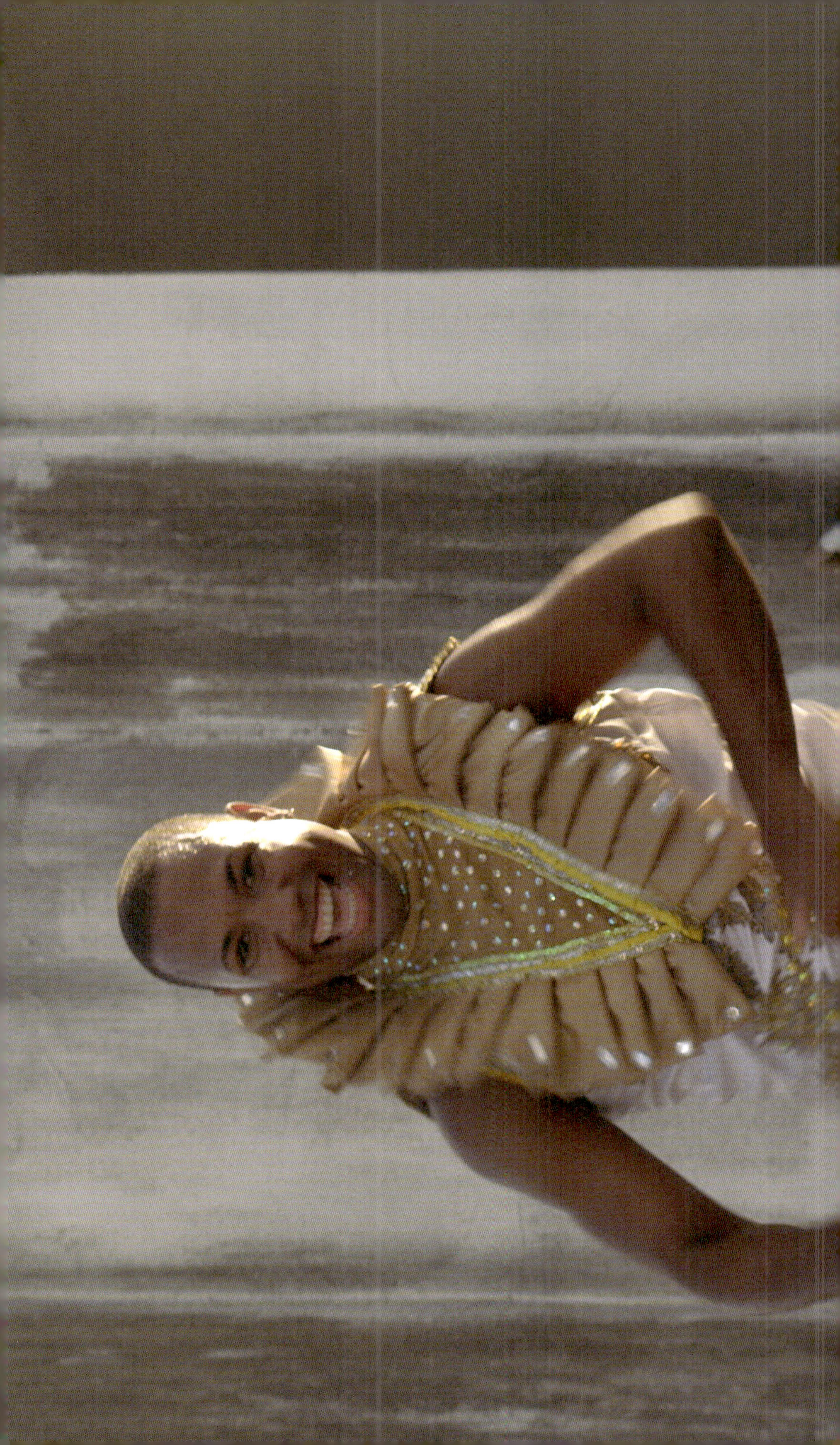

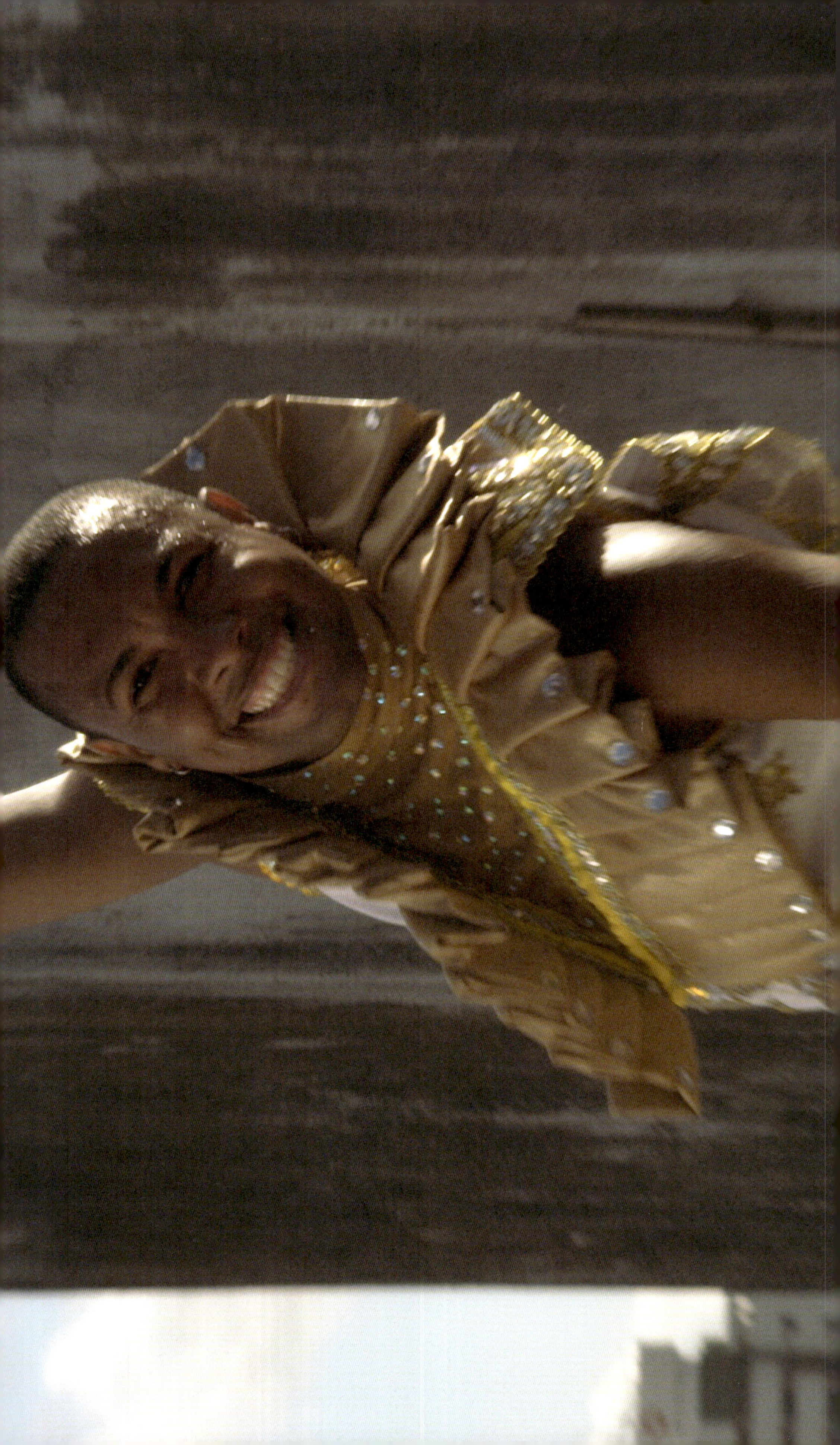

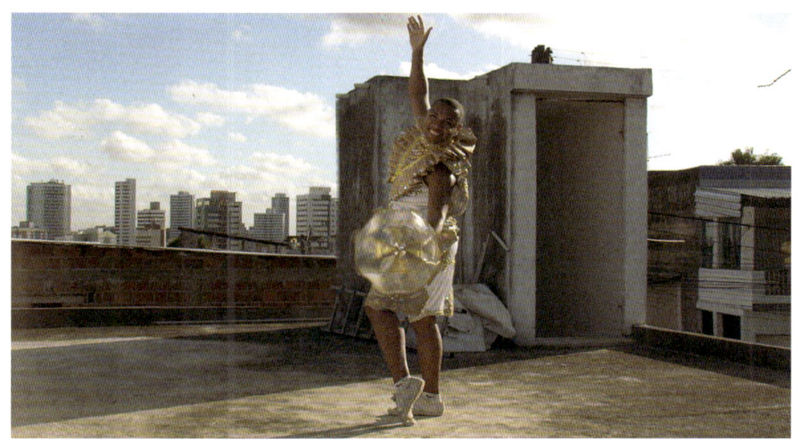

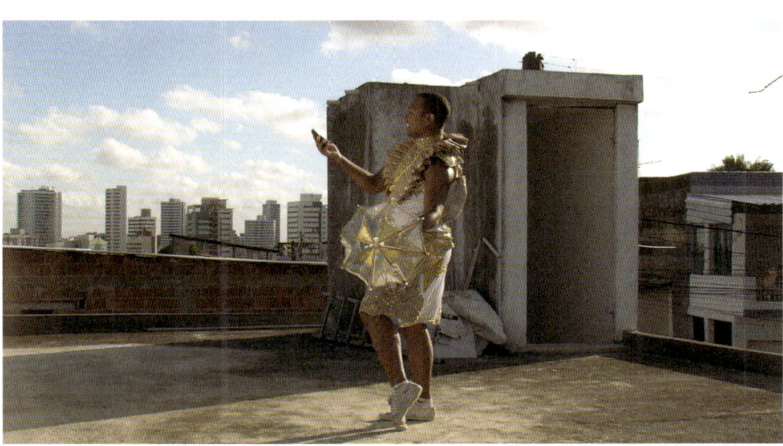

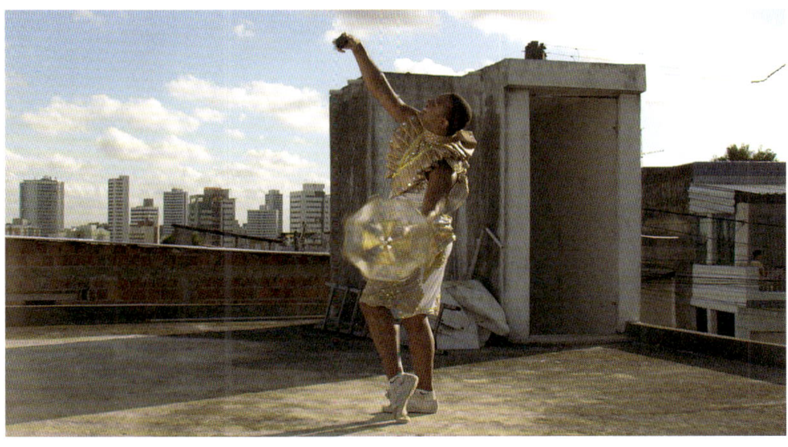

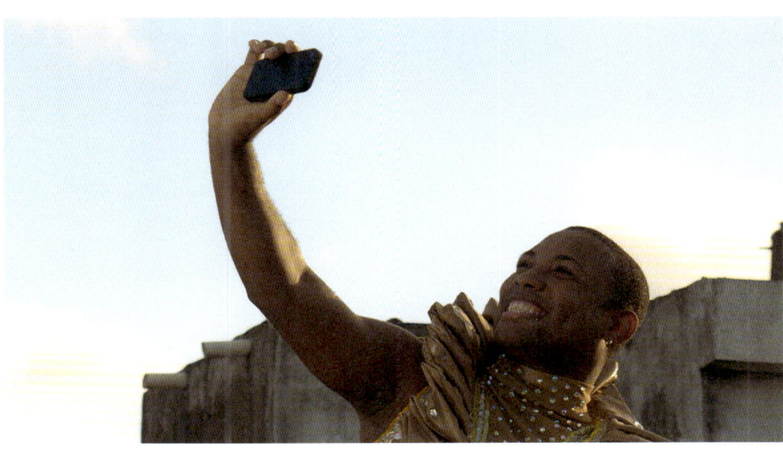

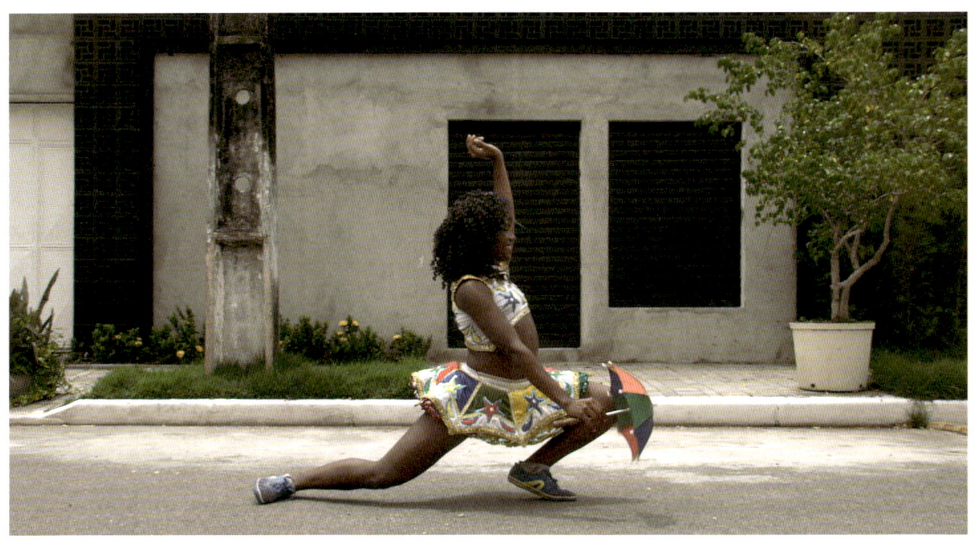

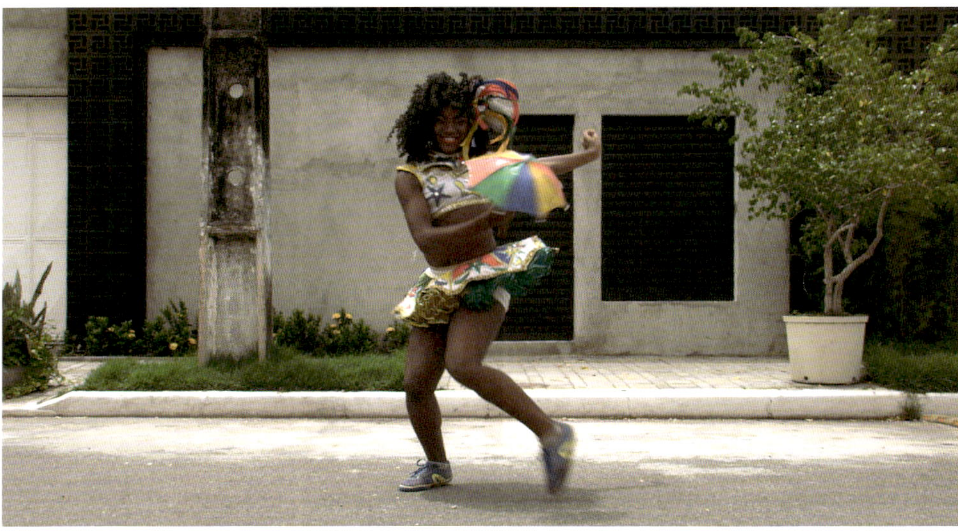

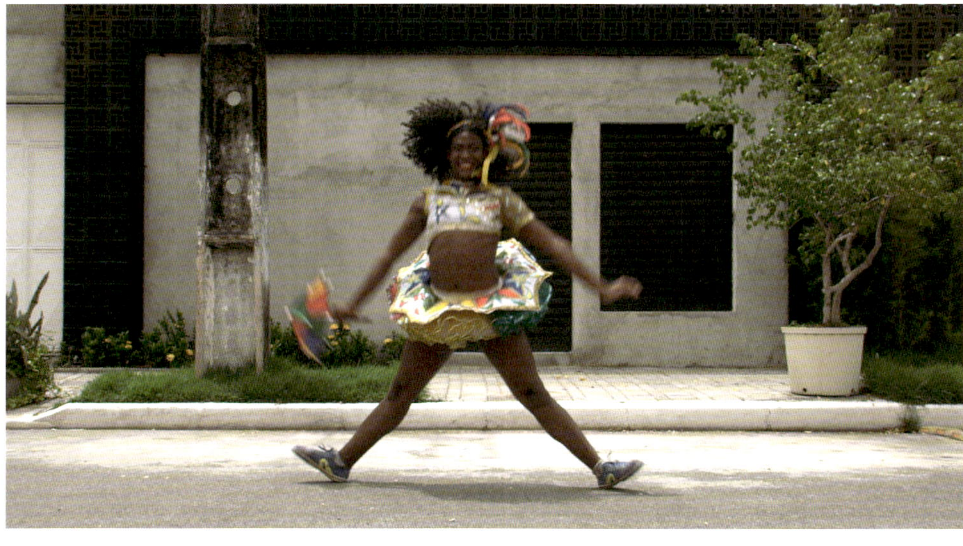

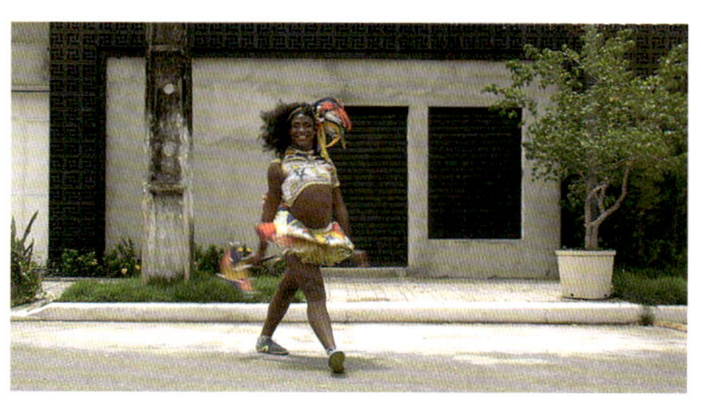
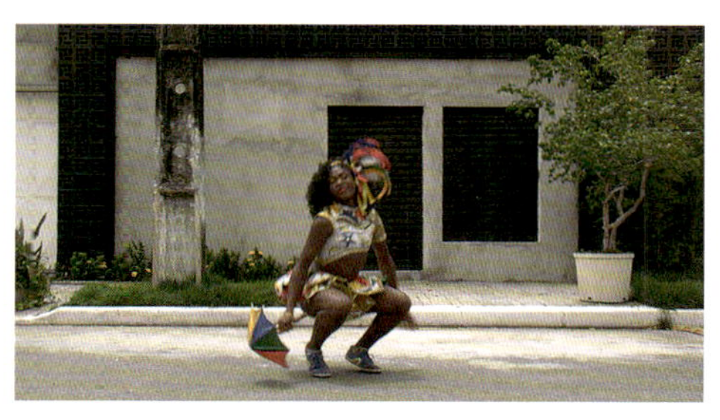
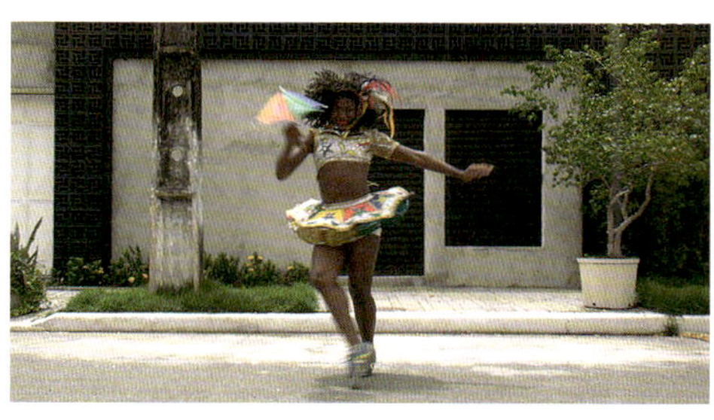
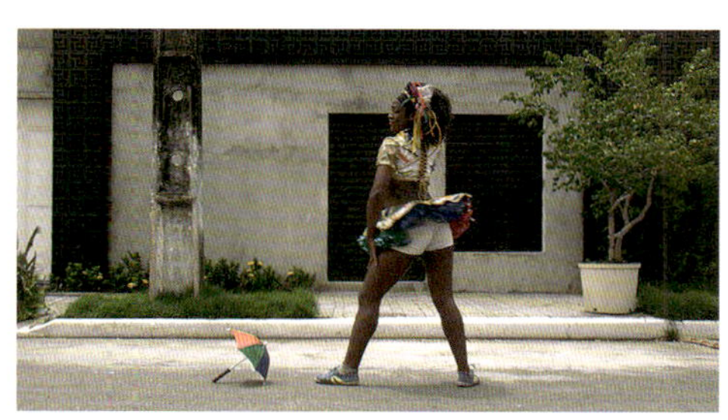
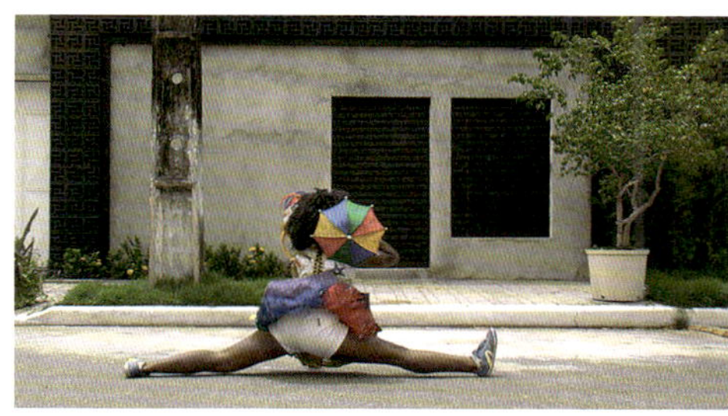
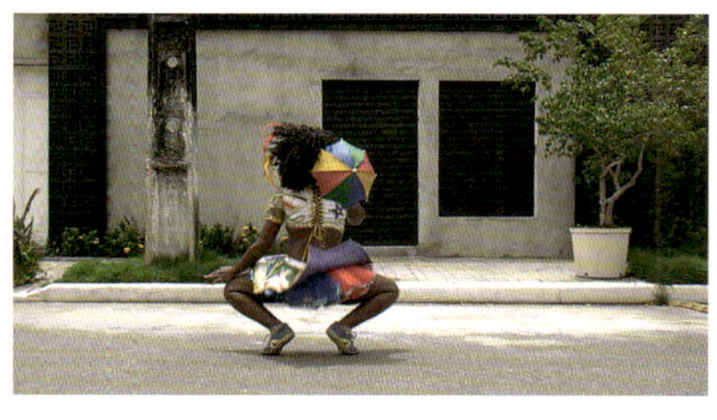
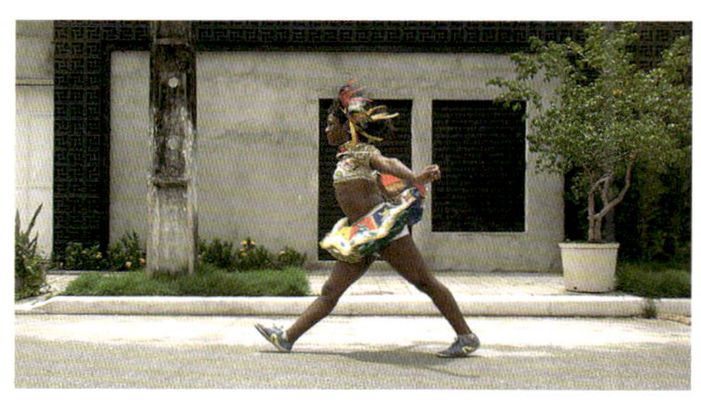
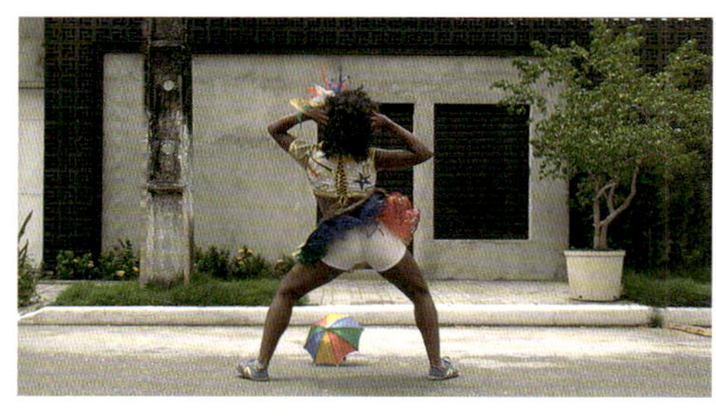

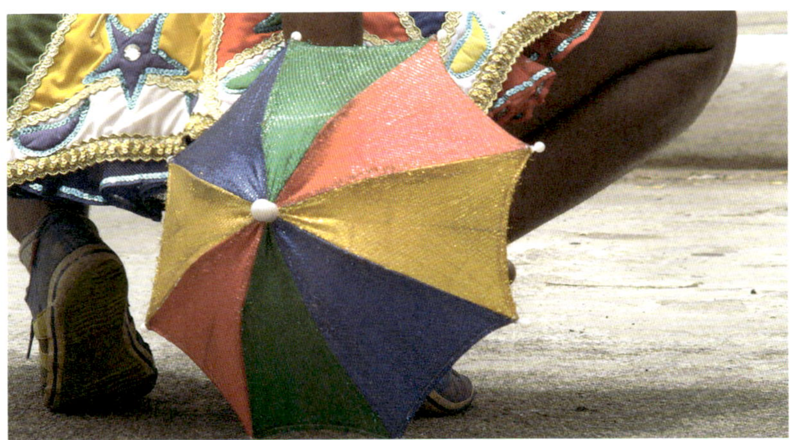

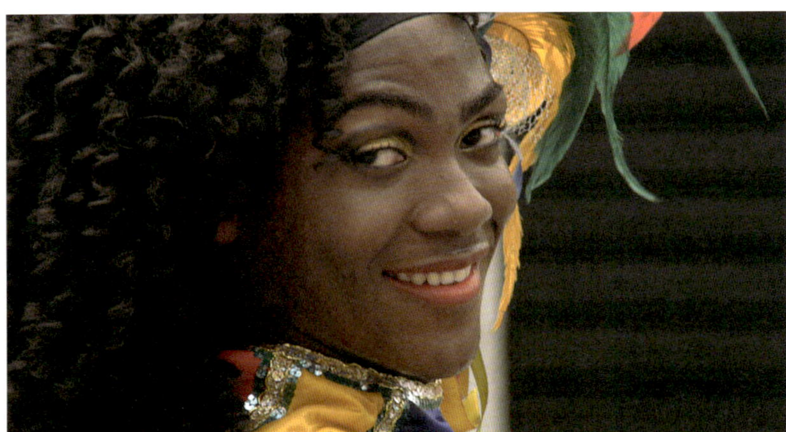

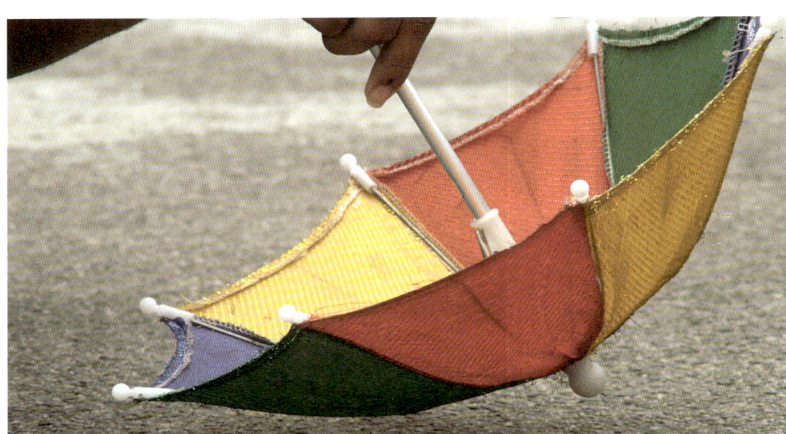

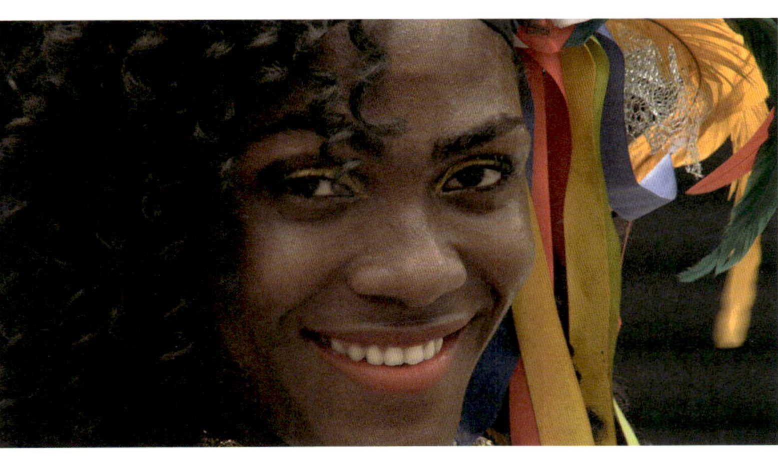

Identity, disjuncture and transformation are at the heart of Bárbara Wagner and Benjamin de Burca's short film *Faz Que Vai* (2015). In the opening sequence, a tall drag queen, wearing a long blonde wig, a silver crown and a short pink costume embellished with rhinestones and fringe, emerges from a dilapidated building, her entrance accompanied by an extended drum roll. She sashays in high heels, taking her place in front of a conspicuously unglamorous façade; the sign on the door behind her reads 'depósito de cimento' (cement depot). Surrounded by detritus, including a large, dusty plastic tub and a rusted metal barrel, this regal figure struts, turns and poses. Each time she taps her sceptre on the ground, a different version of herself materialises – initially relinquishing her crown and whipping her hair, then shedding her wig and assuming an altogether more boyish guise in a black-and-white outfit with trainers and twirling a small umbrella. With each transformation, the performer's footwork becomes more energetic and recognisable as frevo, the Brazilian dance and music style from the northeastern state of Pernambuco.

A centrepiece of the Carnival in Recife, which was added to the UNESCO list of intangible cultural heritage in 2012, frevo is a fusion of styles deriving from capoeira, military marching bands, polka and other late nineteenth and early twentieth-century genres. The artist duo Wagner and de Burca, who trained in journalism and fine art, respectively, began researching frevo in the archive of the Joaquim Nabuco Foundation in Recife. They discovered early photographs of frevo from the first half of the twentieth century showing male dancers with double-breasted jackets, wide trousers, hats and large umbrellas as well as a music score by Nelson Ferreira to accompany the frevo dance step 'Faz que vai, mas não vai' and a short film about the history of frevo by Fernando Spencer. The latter shows how frevo had its roots in the Brazilian military marching bands in Recife. Capoeirista martial artists were employed to protect the bands from rivals, but had to disguise their movements as dance and their umbrellas served as weapons. Techniques and steps were codified through the efforts of dancer Nascimento do Passo and the frevo academy that he established in 1973, but Wagner and de Burca are interested in the fluidity of frevo, from its roots in Afro-Brazilian and European traditions to its ongoing evolution.

In 'Faz que vai, mas não vai', which gives the film its title, the dancer rhythmically shifts weight between the back and front foot, pretending to go, then shifting tactics and pulling back. It is the instability and the potential of changing direction that interests the artists. *Faz Que Vai* embodies these principals as it cycles through a sequence of short dances set to frevo music that is stripped of its brass instrumentation so that it is entirely percussion. Wagner and de Burca collaborated with the dancers to decide on location, costume and how the camera would capture their routine. The movements of Edson Vogue, a shirtless dancer in simple brown trousers filmed on a rooftop in front of an empty building, are a blend of the stylised poses of voguing and the martial stances from frevo's origins in military marches and capoeira. The dancer's jerky movements, reminiscent of Michael Jackson's zombie shuffle in the music video for 'Thriller', and the percussive soundtrack unify the two dance styles. The dancer Brunno Henryque adds samba hip movements to his acrobatic frevo routine. Exuberantly dancing in a gold and white costume with a ruffled collar, he takes a turn and catches in a small parasol that matches his outfit. He spins this essential frevo accessory and passes it between his legs while executing jumps. Dressed in a cropped top, short skirt and headpiece, all in the colours of the flag of Pernambuco, the final dancer Eduarda Lemos is most closely aligned with the traditional elements of frevo and this performance is unmistakably marked by non-binary gender identity, returning full circle to the opening act of drag queen-cum-frevo dancer Ryan Neves. The high-spirited performances that make up *Faz Que Vai* attest to how fluid notions of identity are transforming frevo.

Lydia Yee

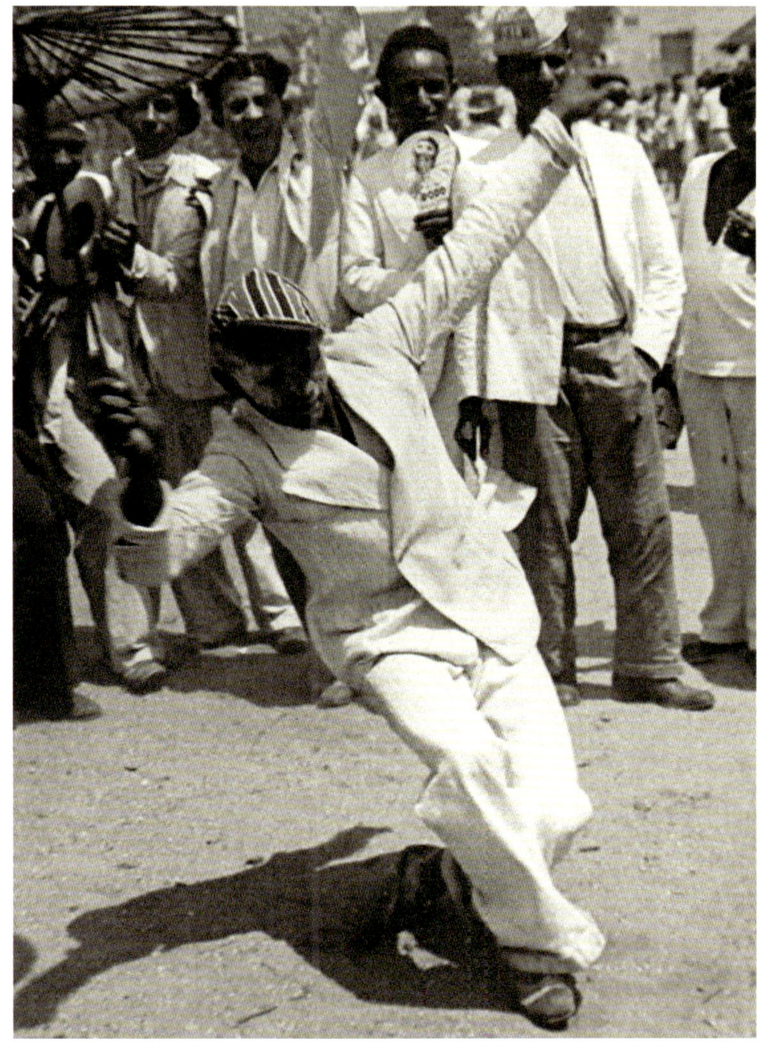

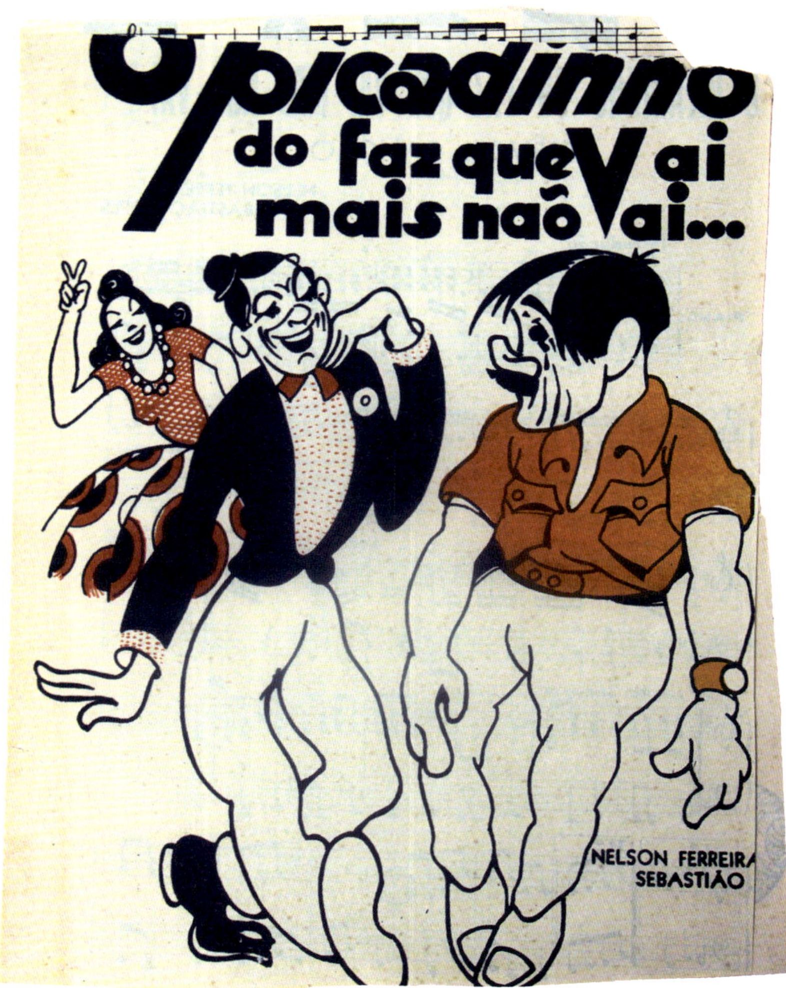


Nelson Ferreira and Sebastião Lopes, *Picadinho Do Faz Que Vai Mas Não Vai*, c.1940–45, sheet music of unpublished frevo song

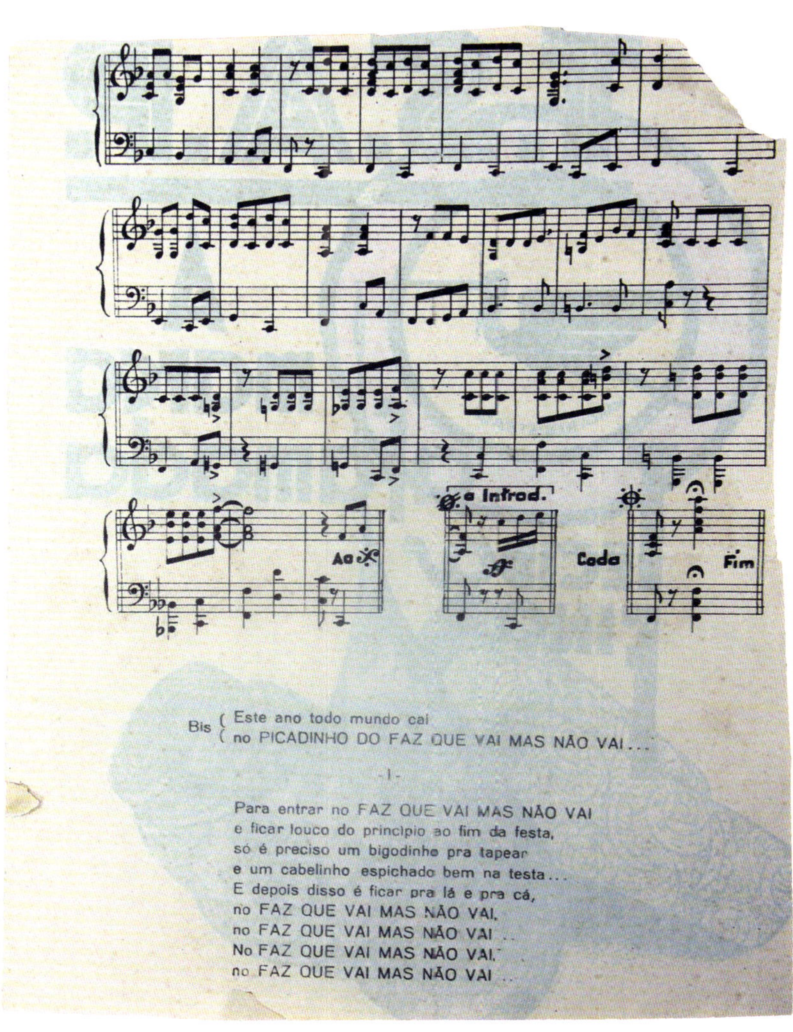



Bis {
Este ano todo mundo cai
no PICADINHO DO FAZ QUE VAI MAS NÃO VAI...

-1-

Para entrar no FAZ QUE VAI MAS NÃO VAI
e ficar louco do princípio ao fim da festa,
só é preciso um bigodinho pra tapear
e um cabelinho espichado bem na testa...
E depois disso é ficar pra lá e pra cá,
no FAZ QUE VAI MAS NÃO VAI,
no FAZ QUE VAI MAS NÃO VAI...
No FAZ QUE VAI MAS NÃO VAI,
no FAZ QUE VAI MAS NÃO VAI...

Fernando Spencer, *Trajetória Do Frevo*, 1988, 35mm (transferred to digital), colour, sound; 9 minutes

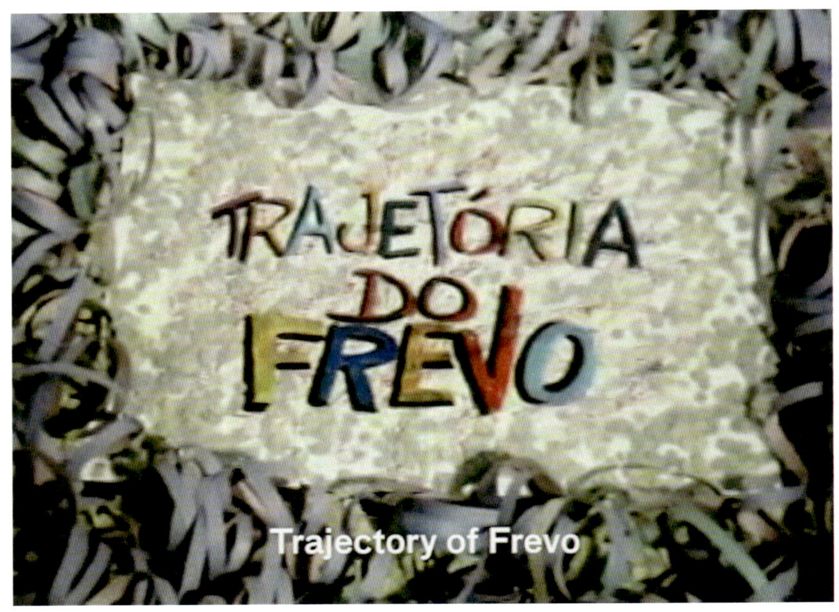
TRAJETÓRIA DO FREVO
Trajectory of Frevo

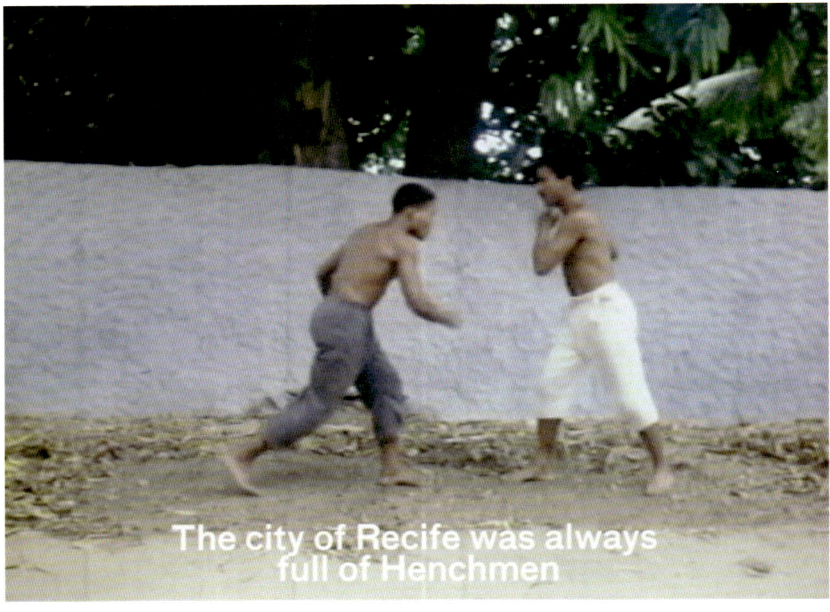
The city of Recife was always
full of Henchmen

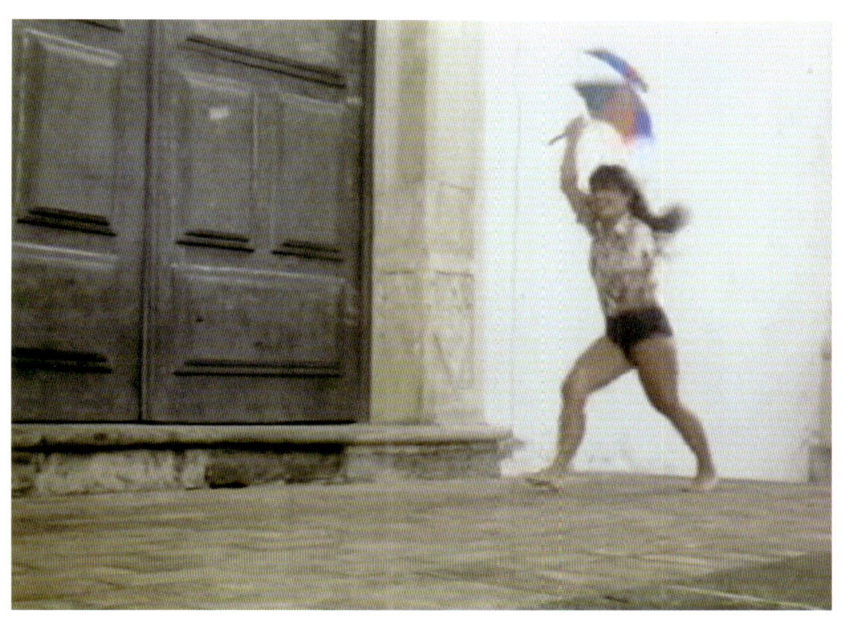

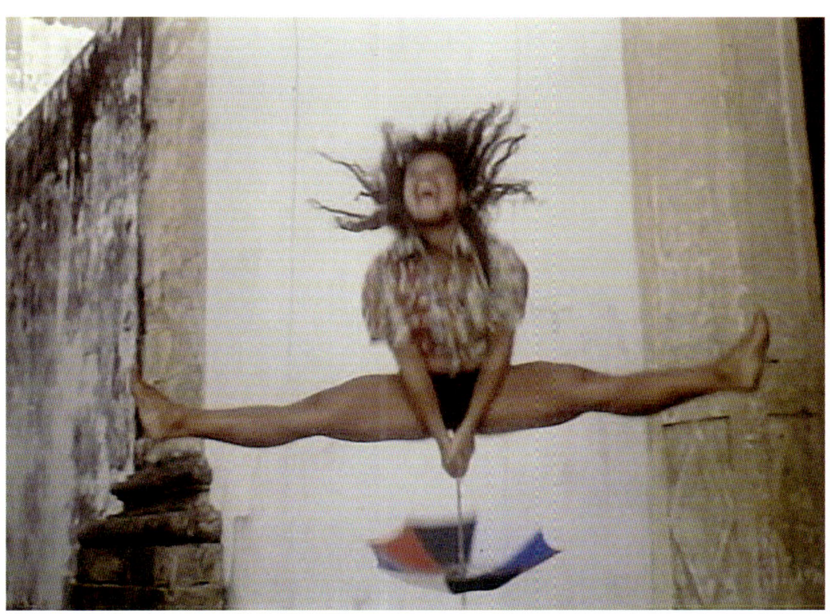

**Alberta Whittle**
*RESET*, 2020

**HD video, colour, sound;
32 minutes**

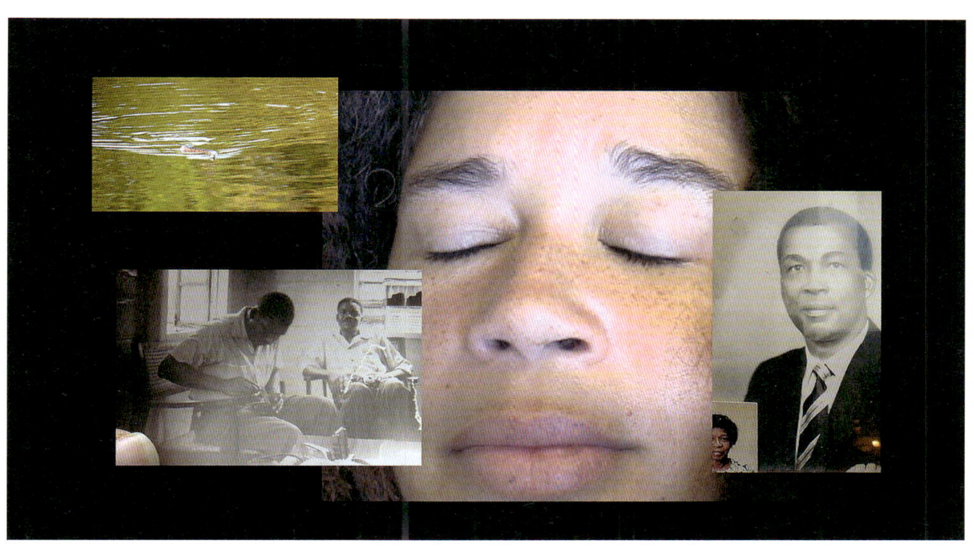

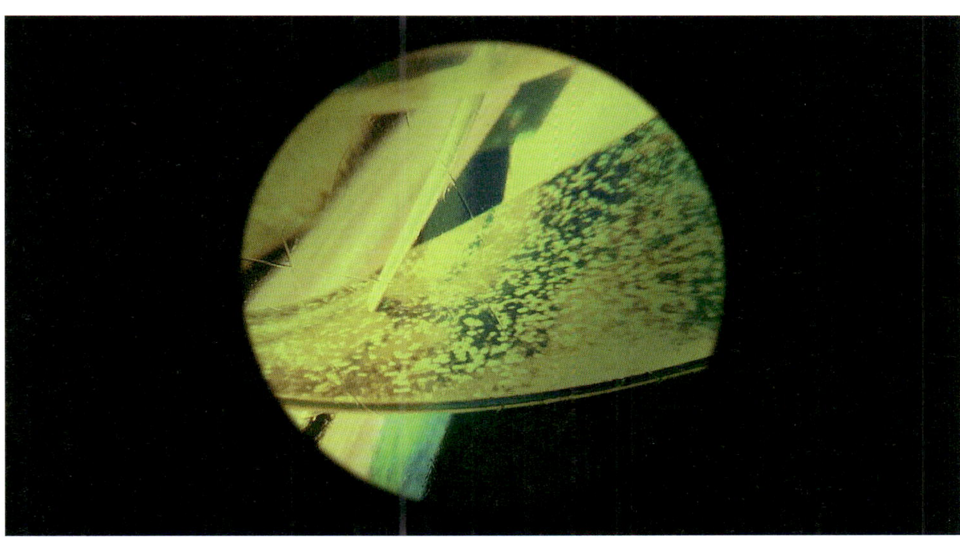

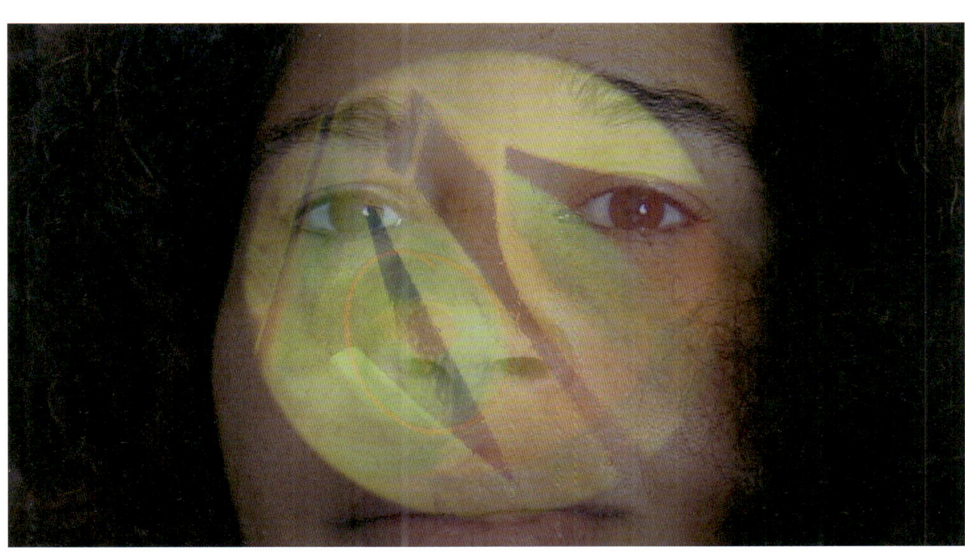

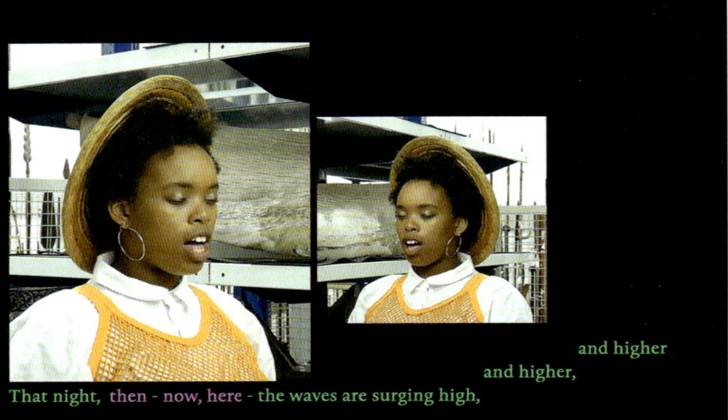
and higher
and higher,
That night, then - now, here - the waves are surging high,

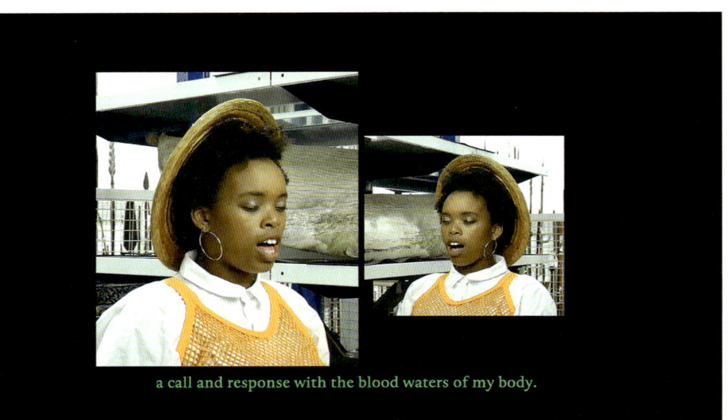
a call and response with the blood waters of my body.

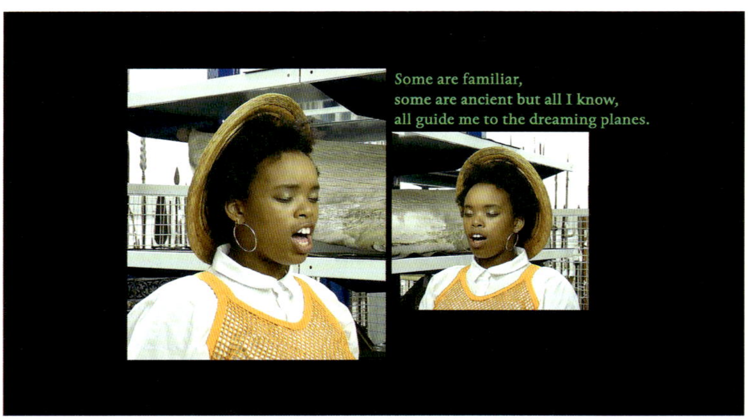
Some are familiar,
some are ancient but all I know,
all guide me to the dreaming planes.

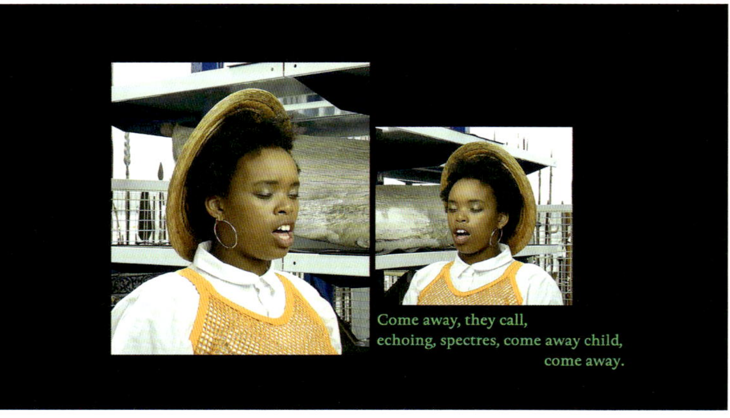
Come away, they call,
echoing, spectres, come away child,
come away.

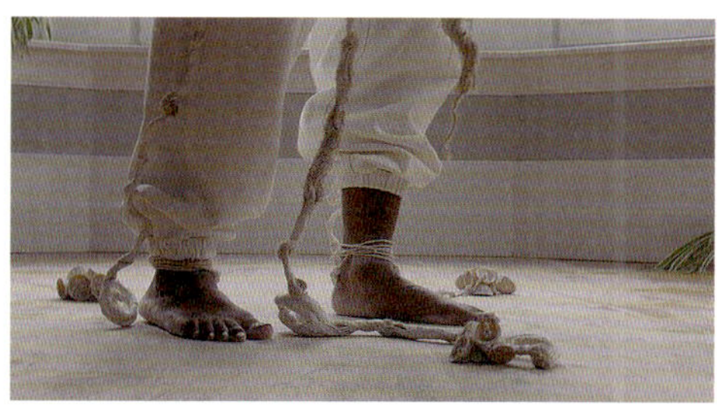
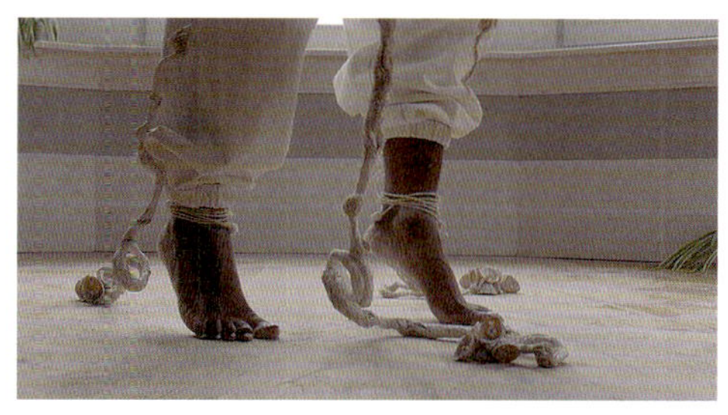
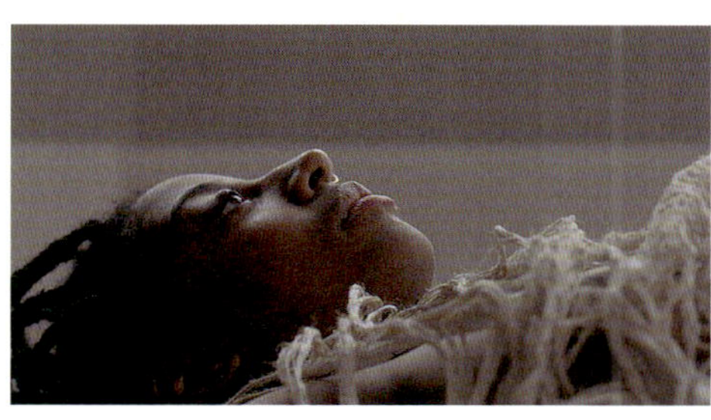
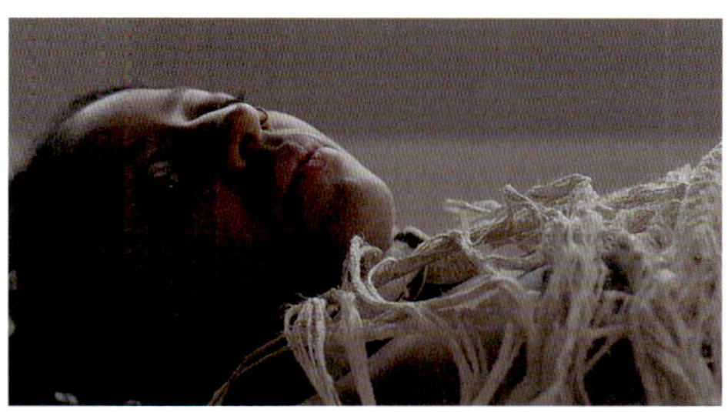
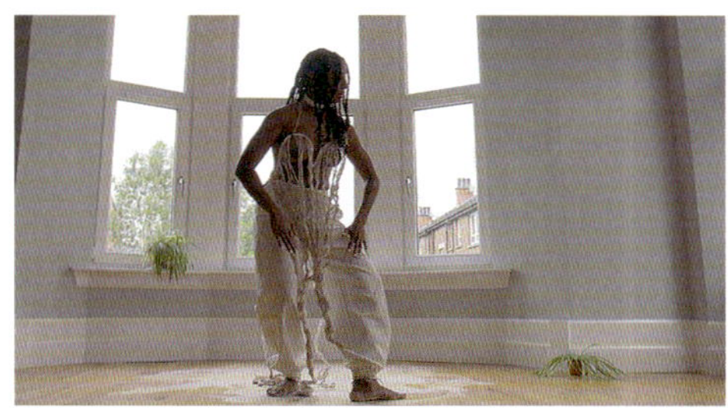
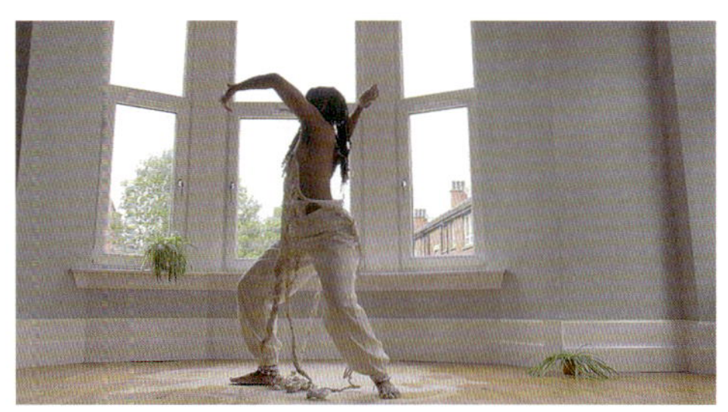
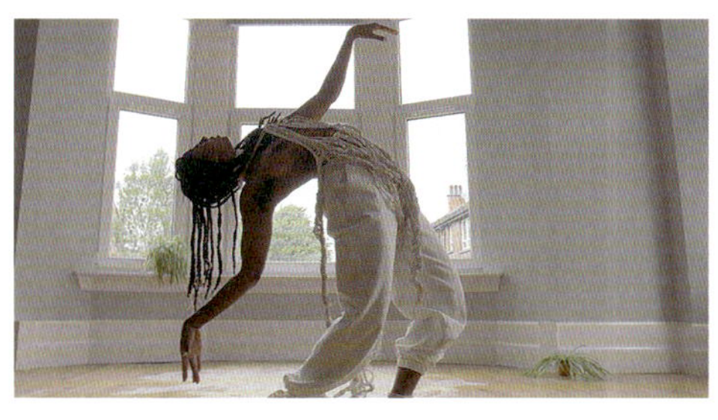
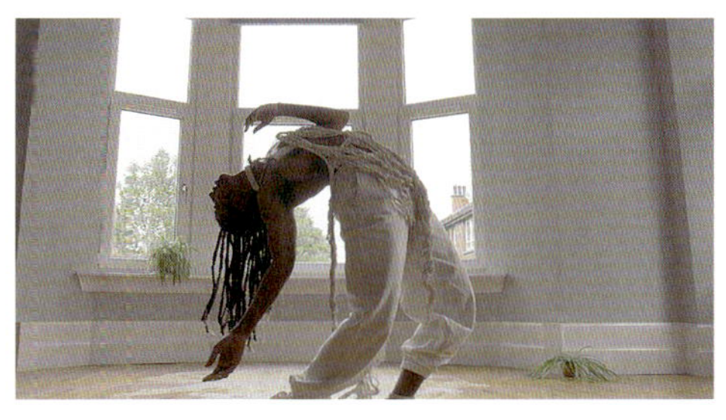

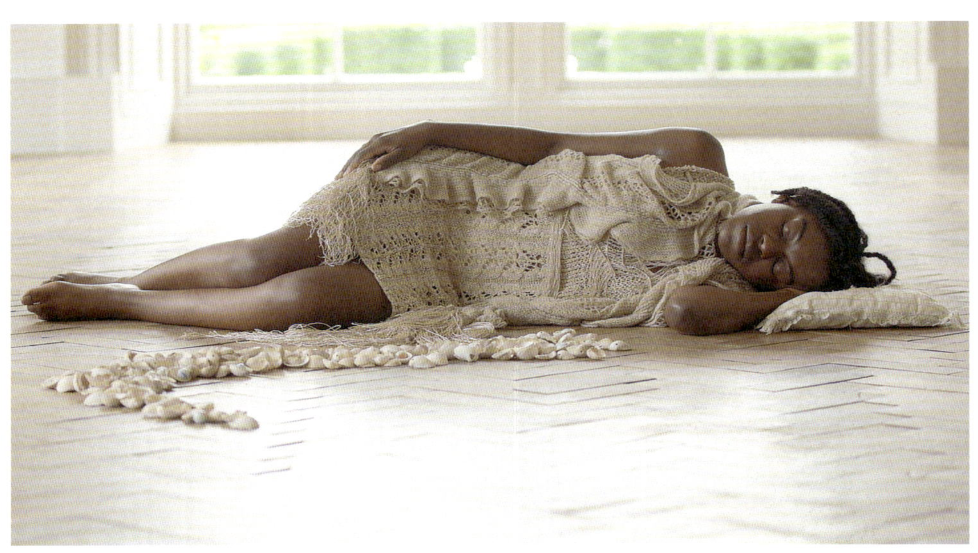

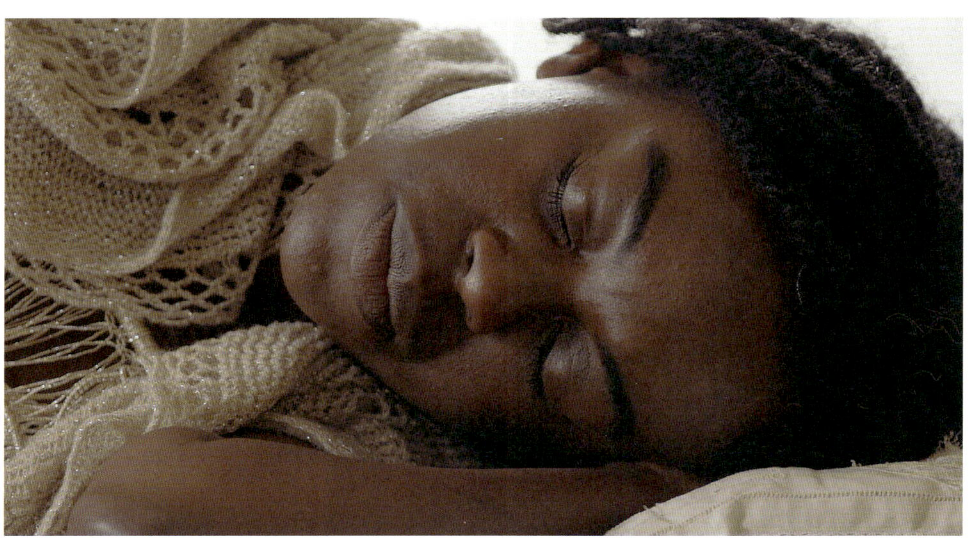

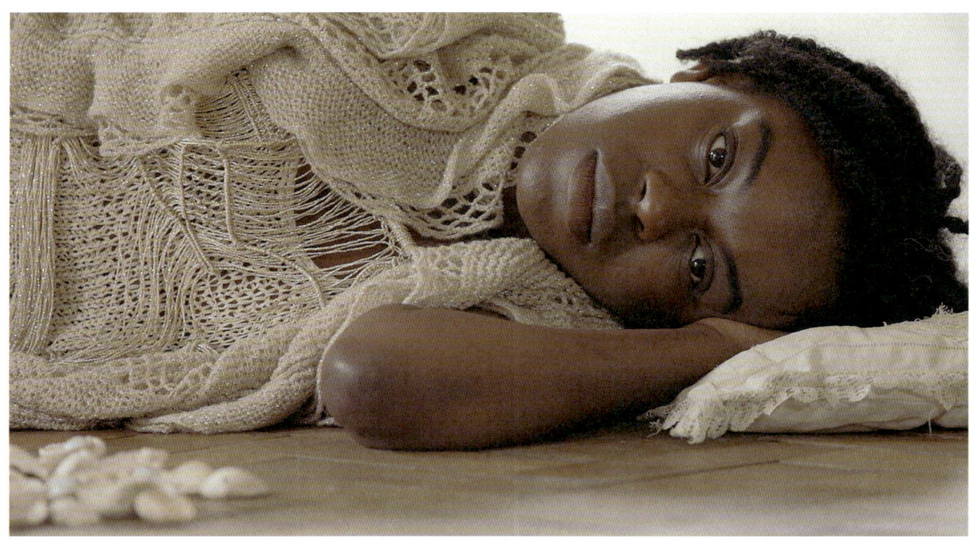

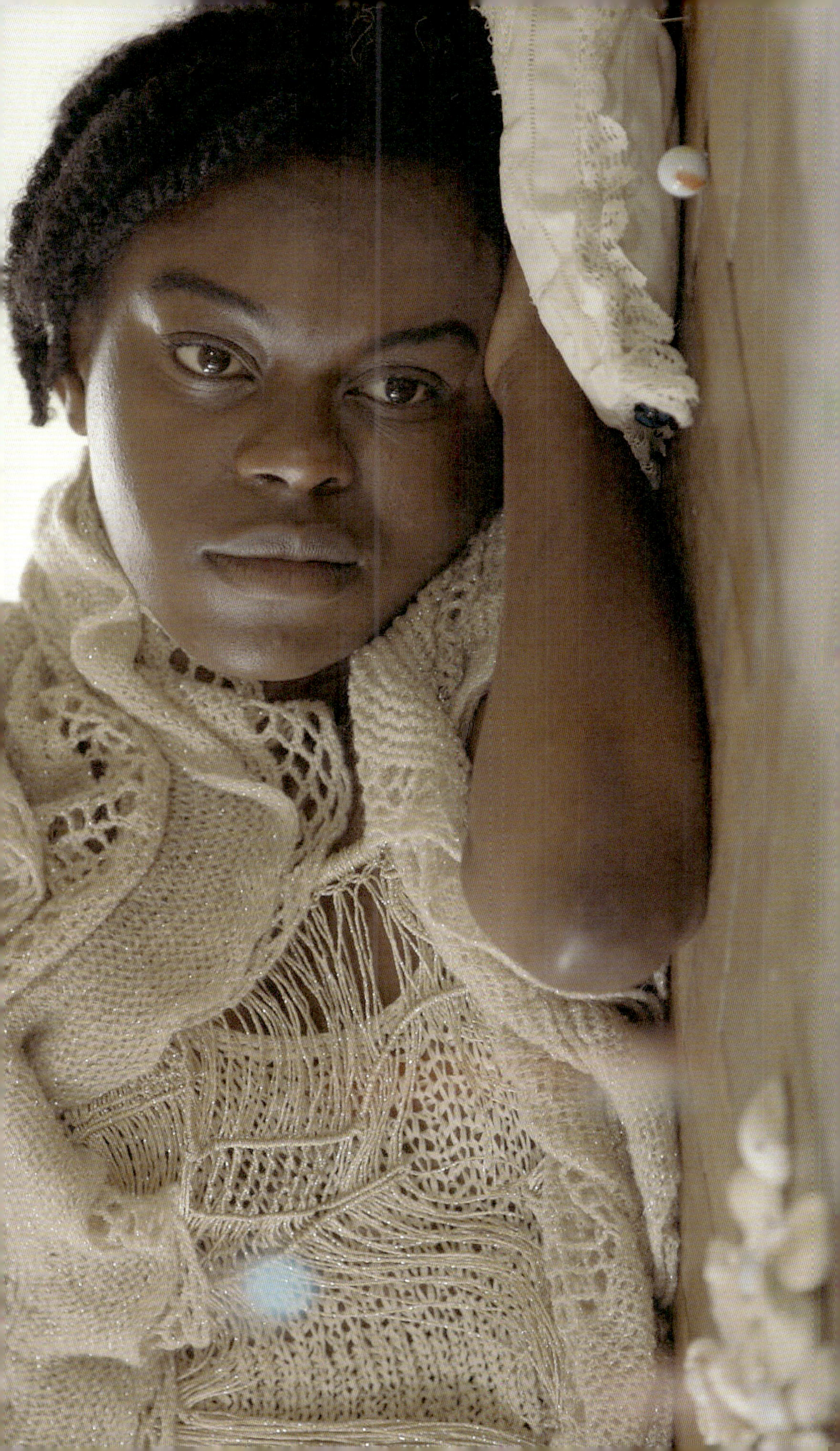

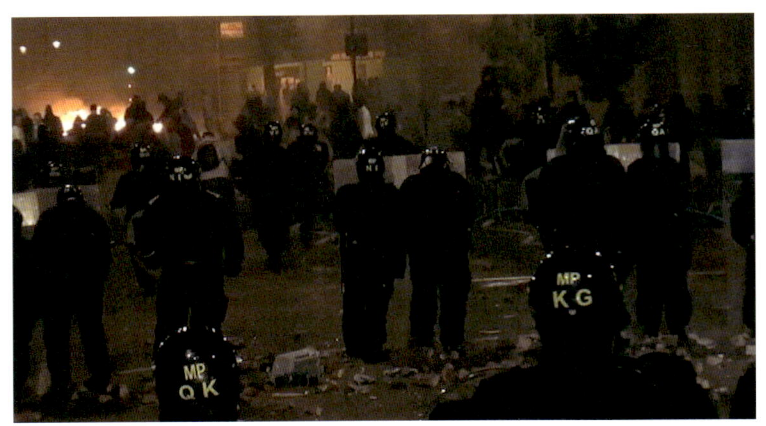

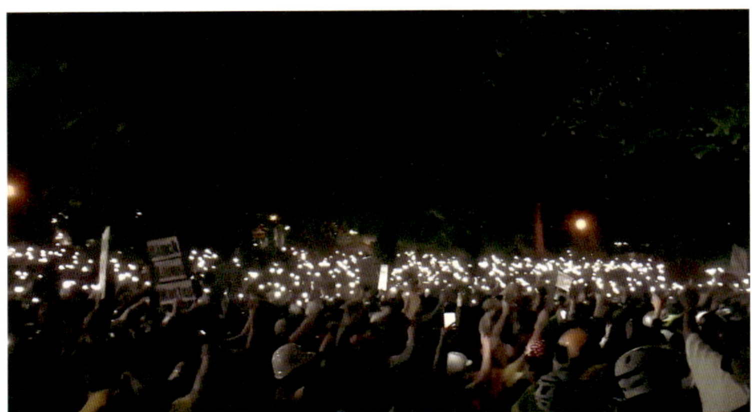

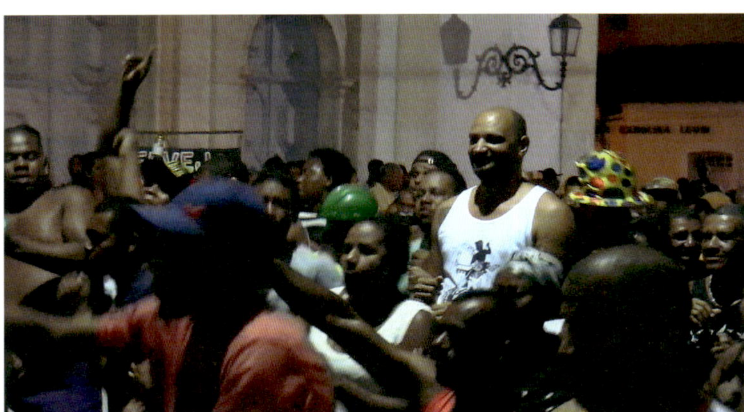

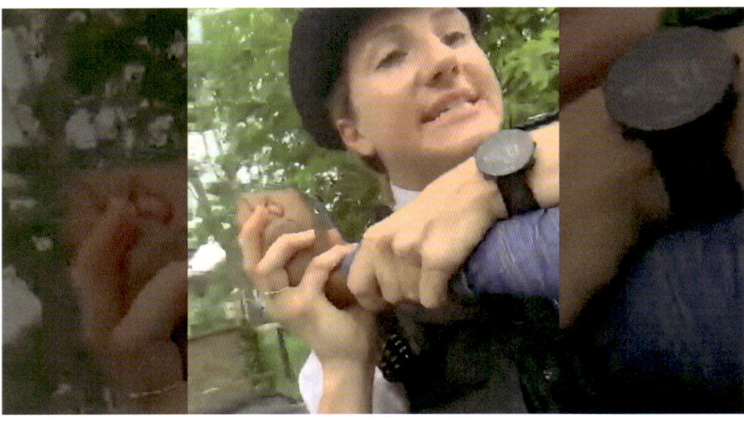

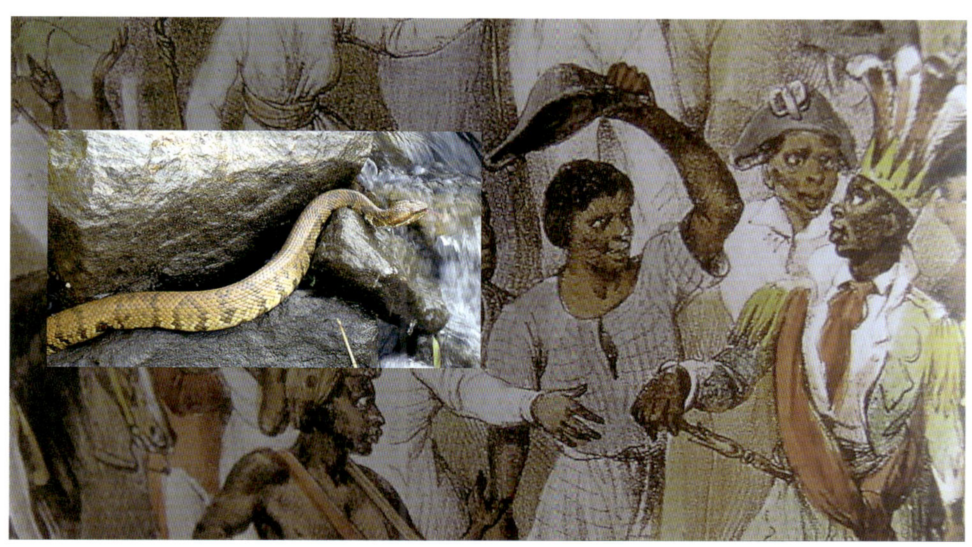

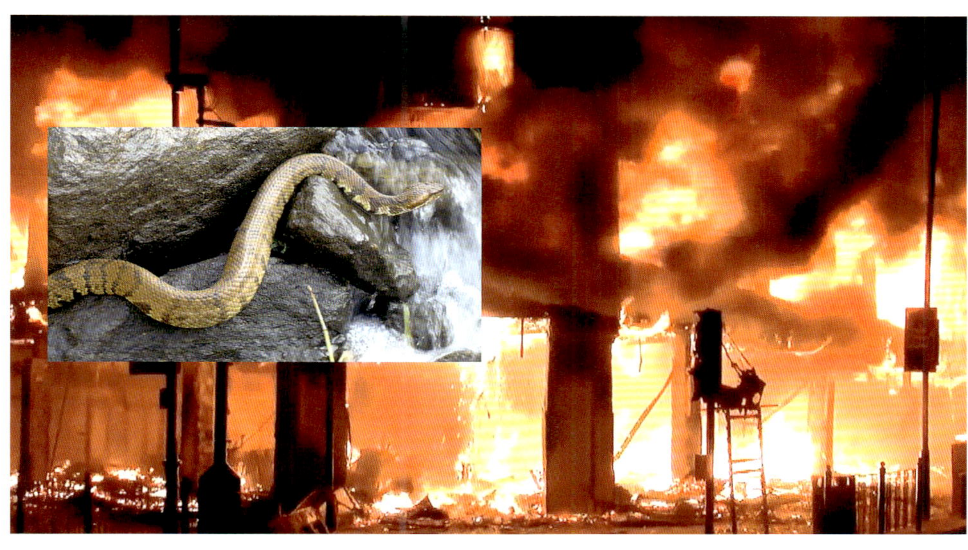

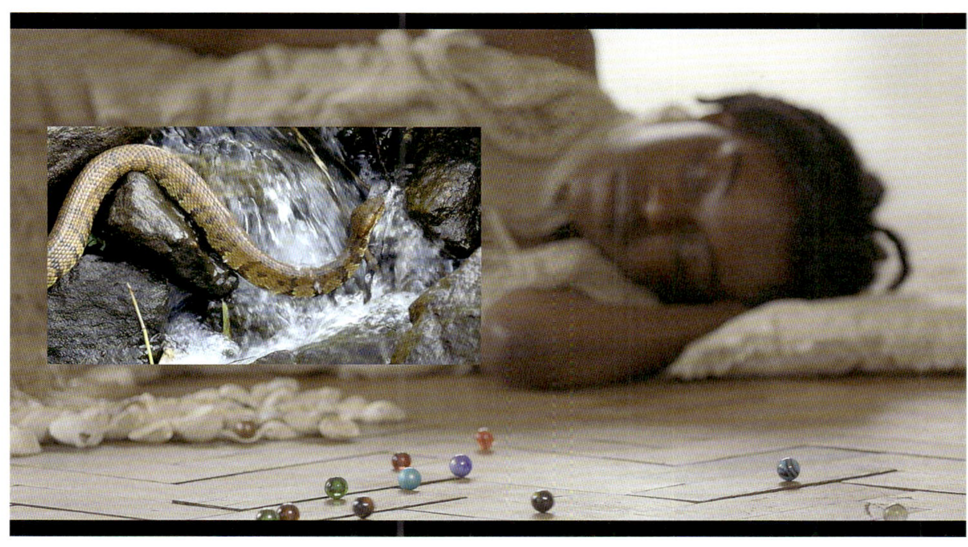

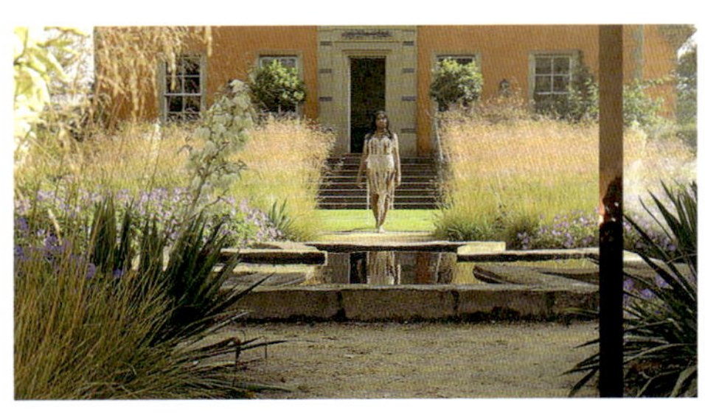
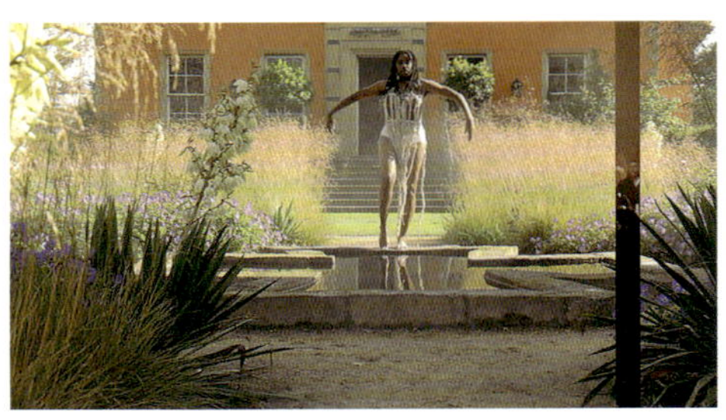
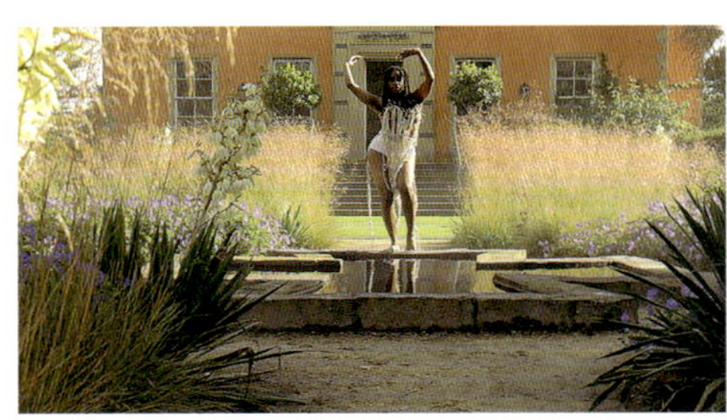
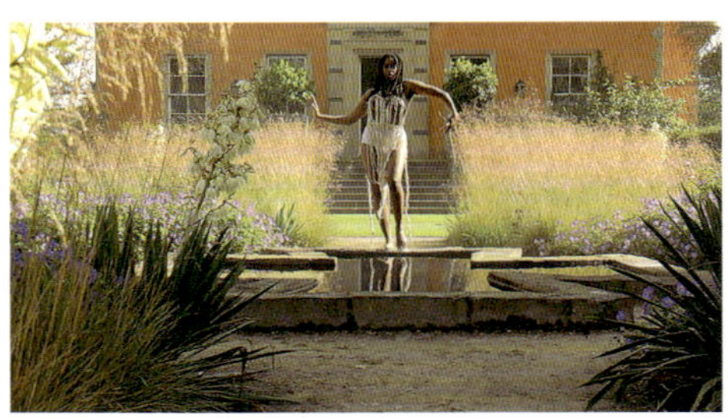
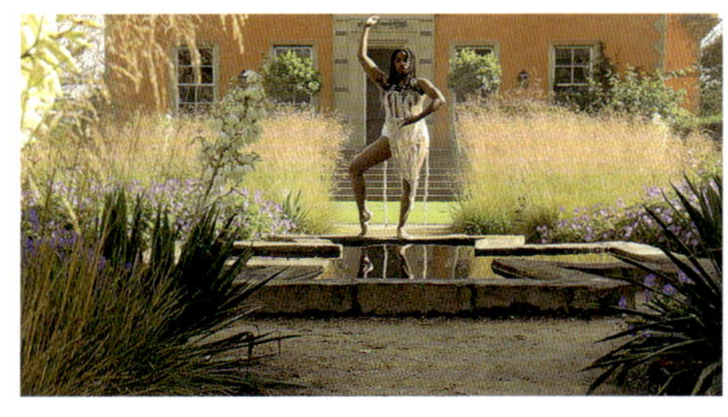
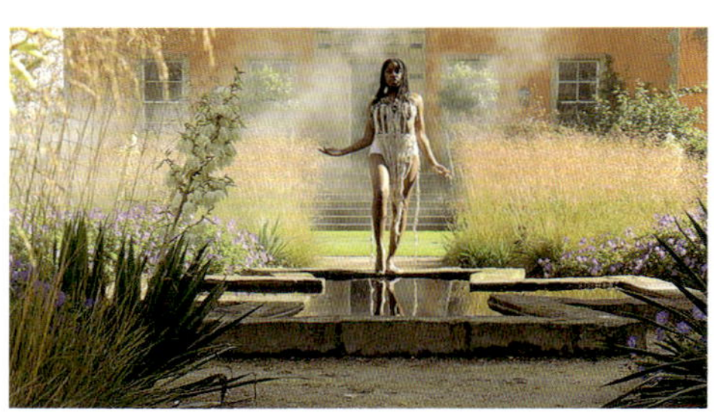
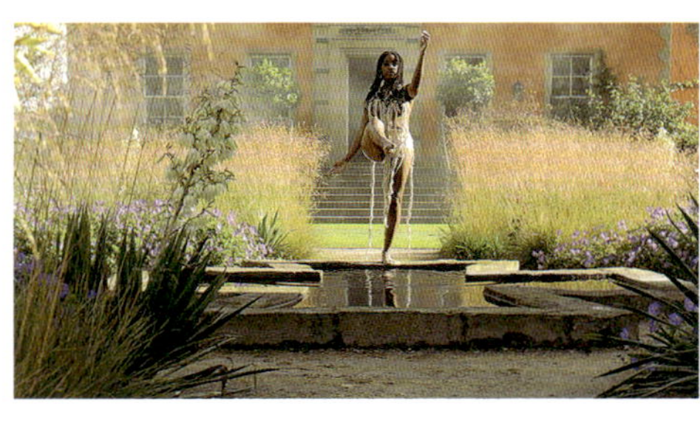
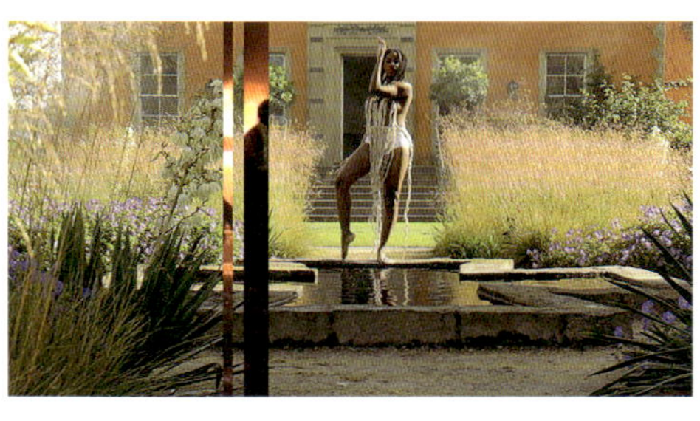

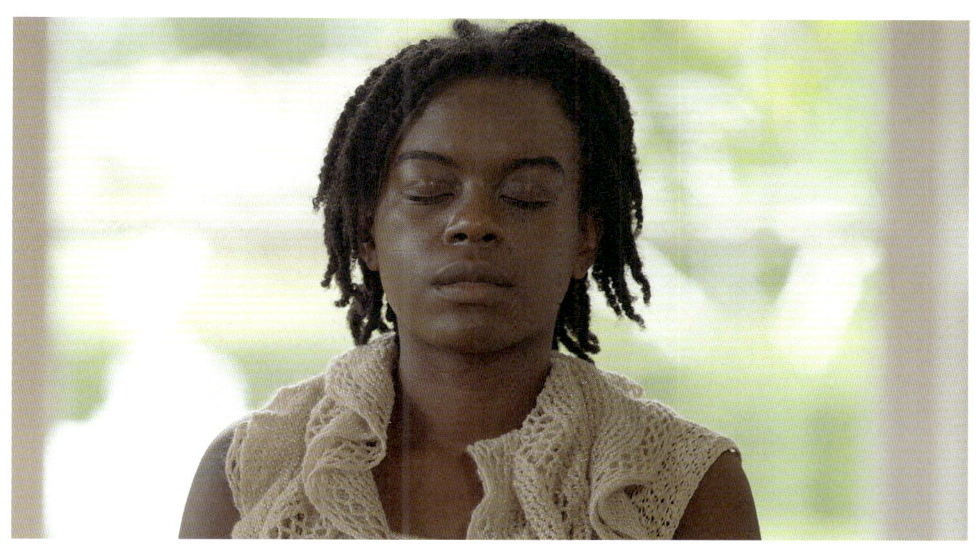

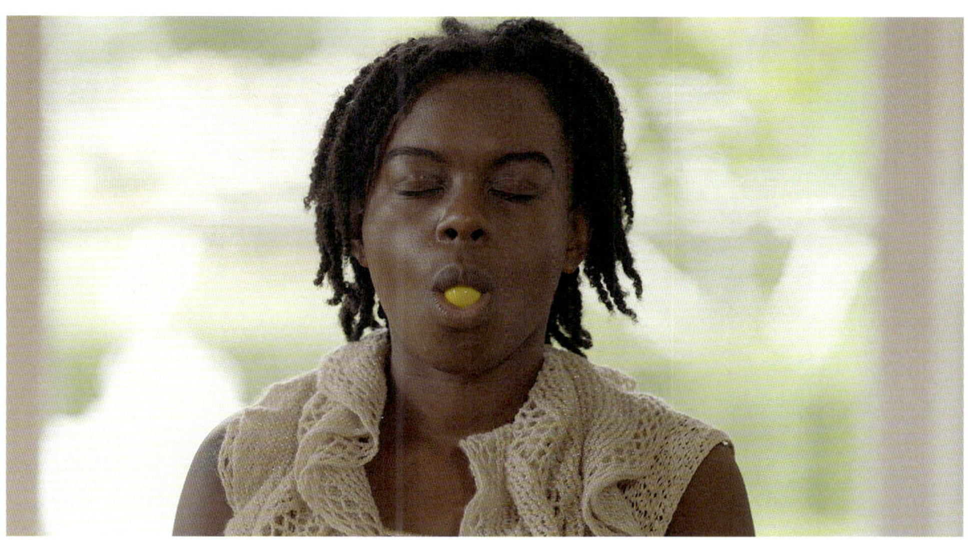

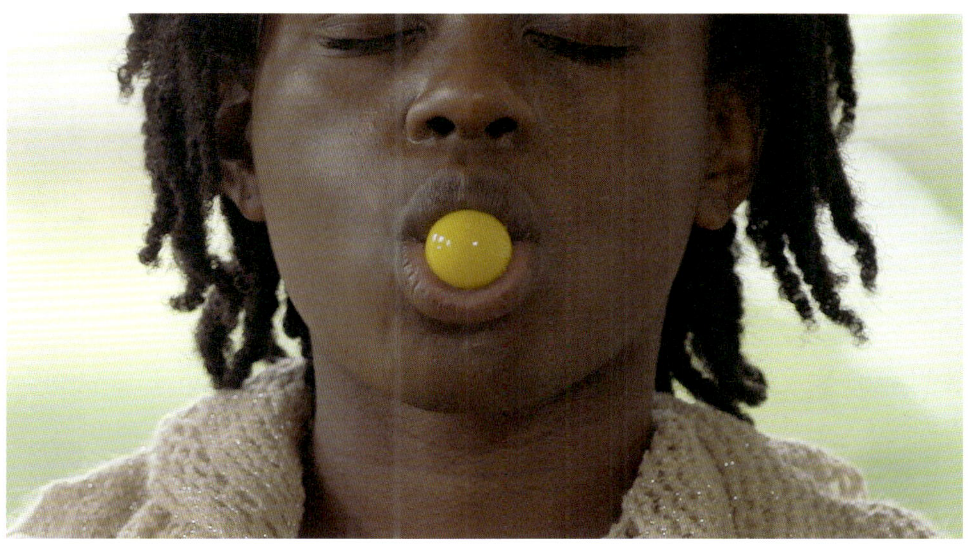

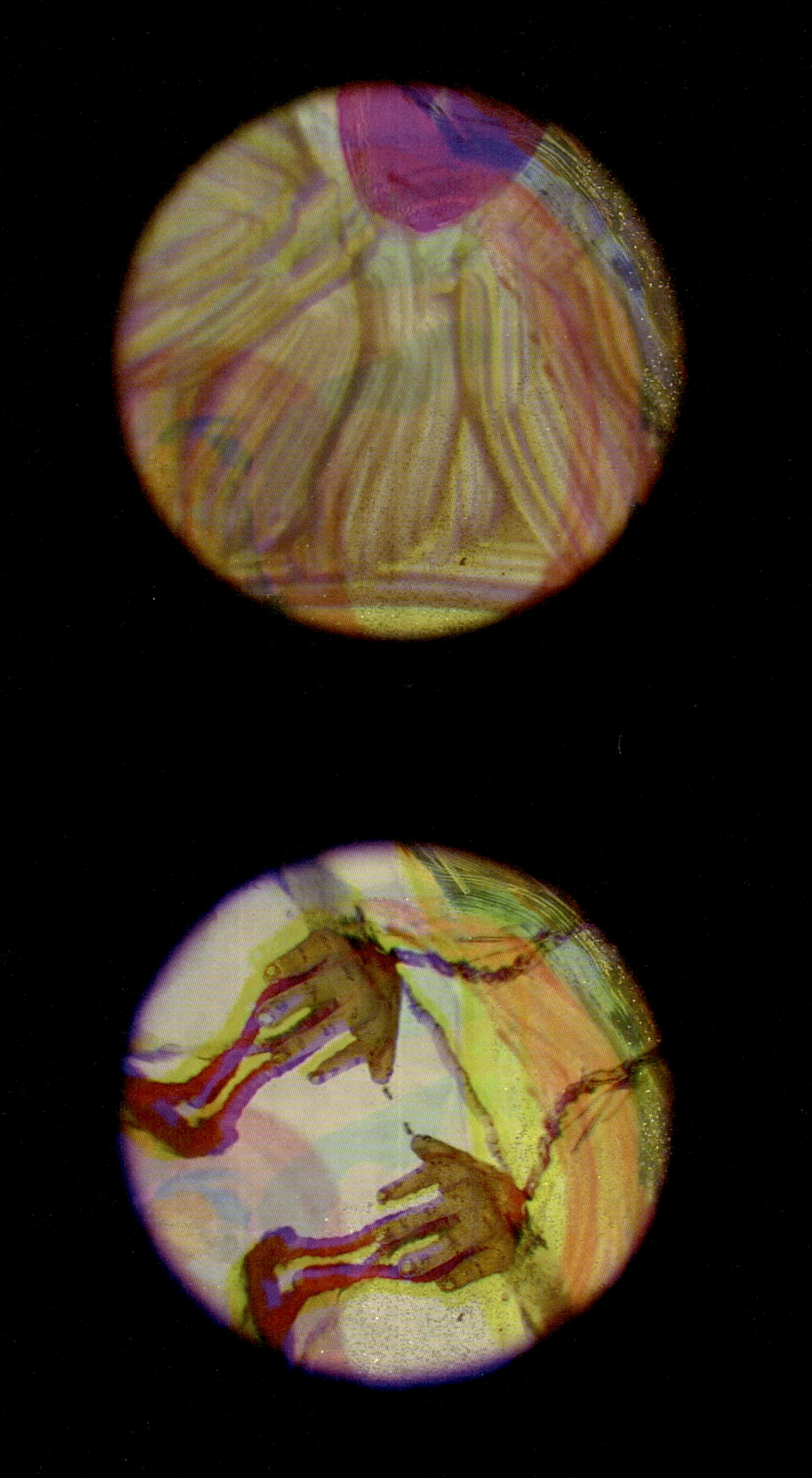

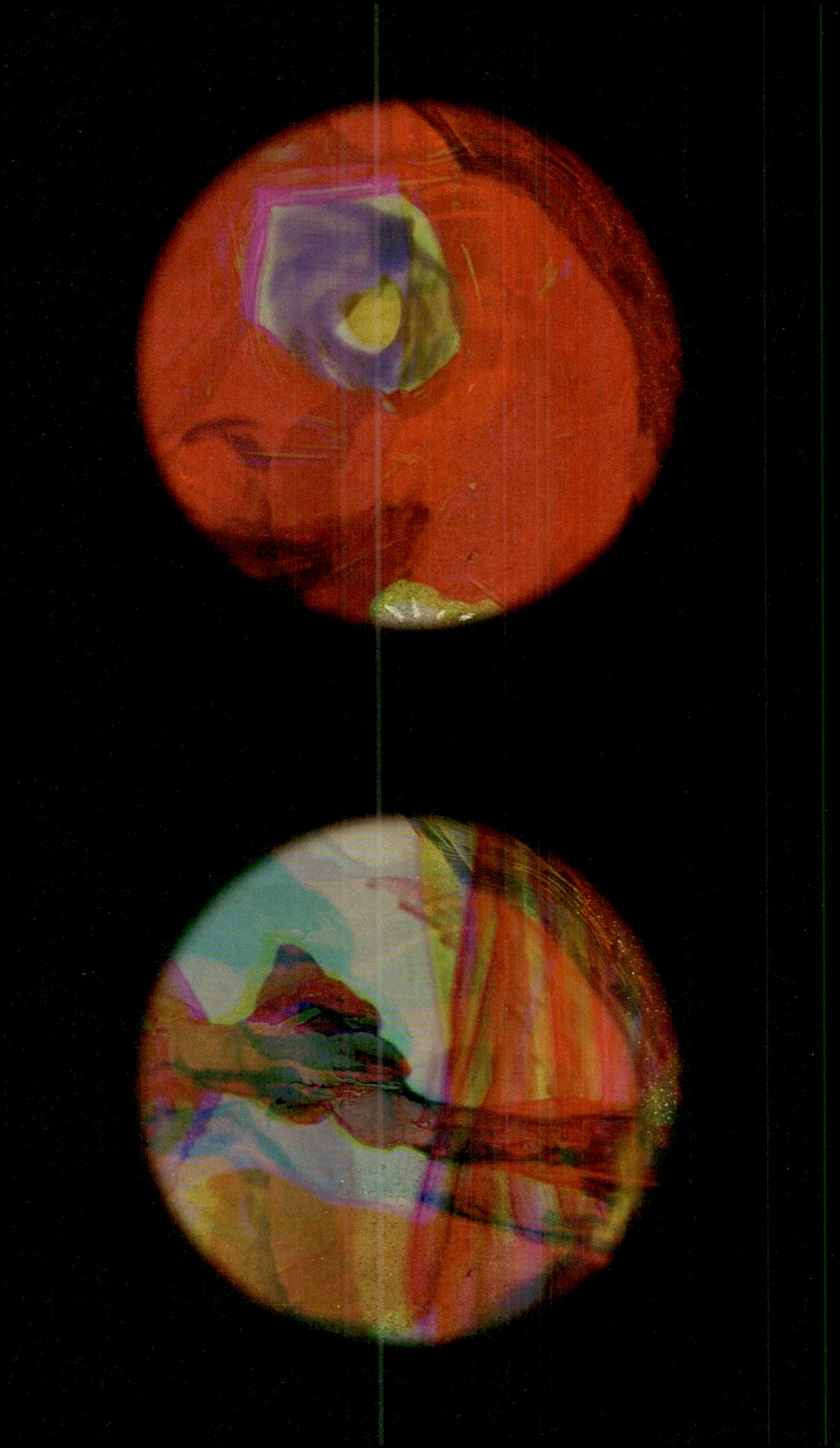

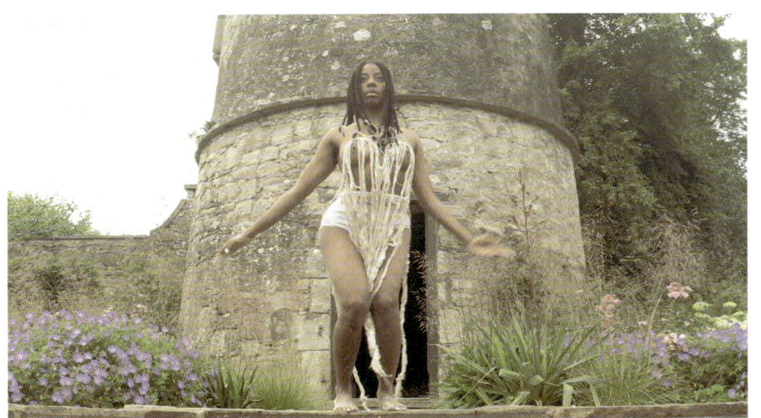

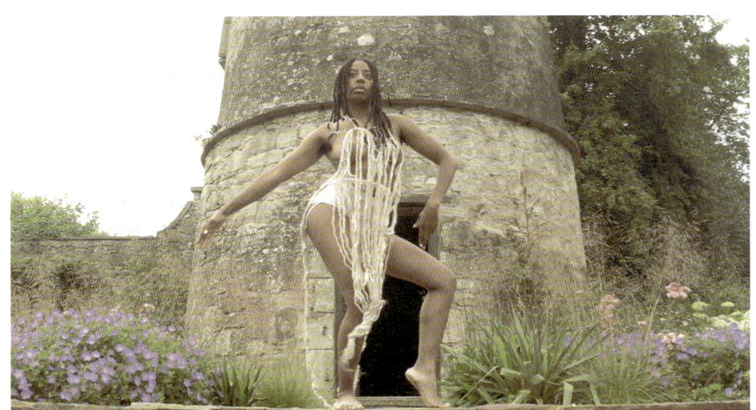

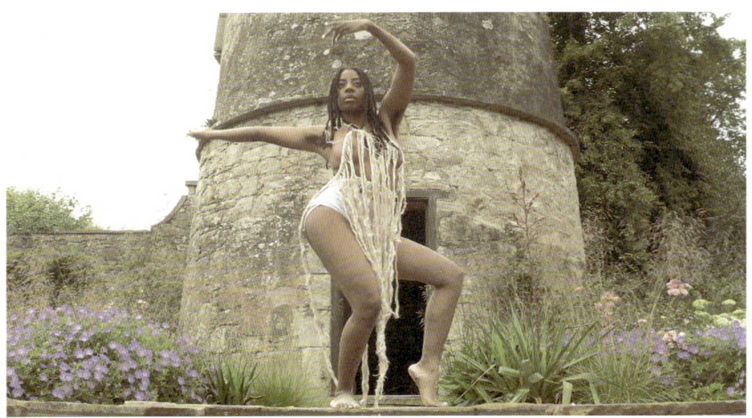

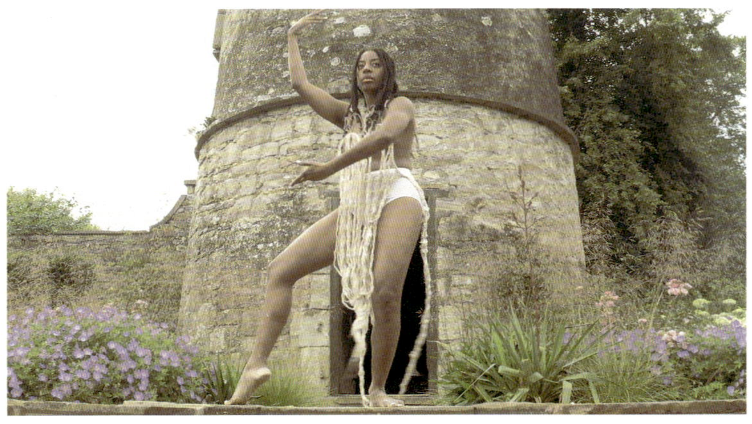

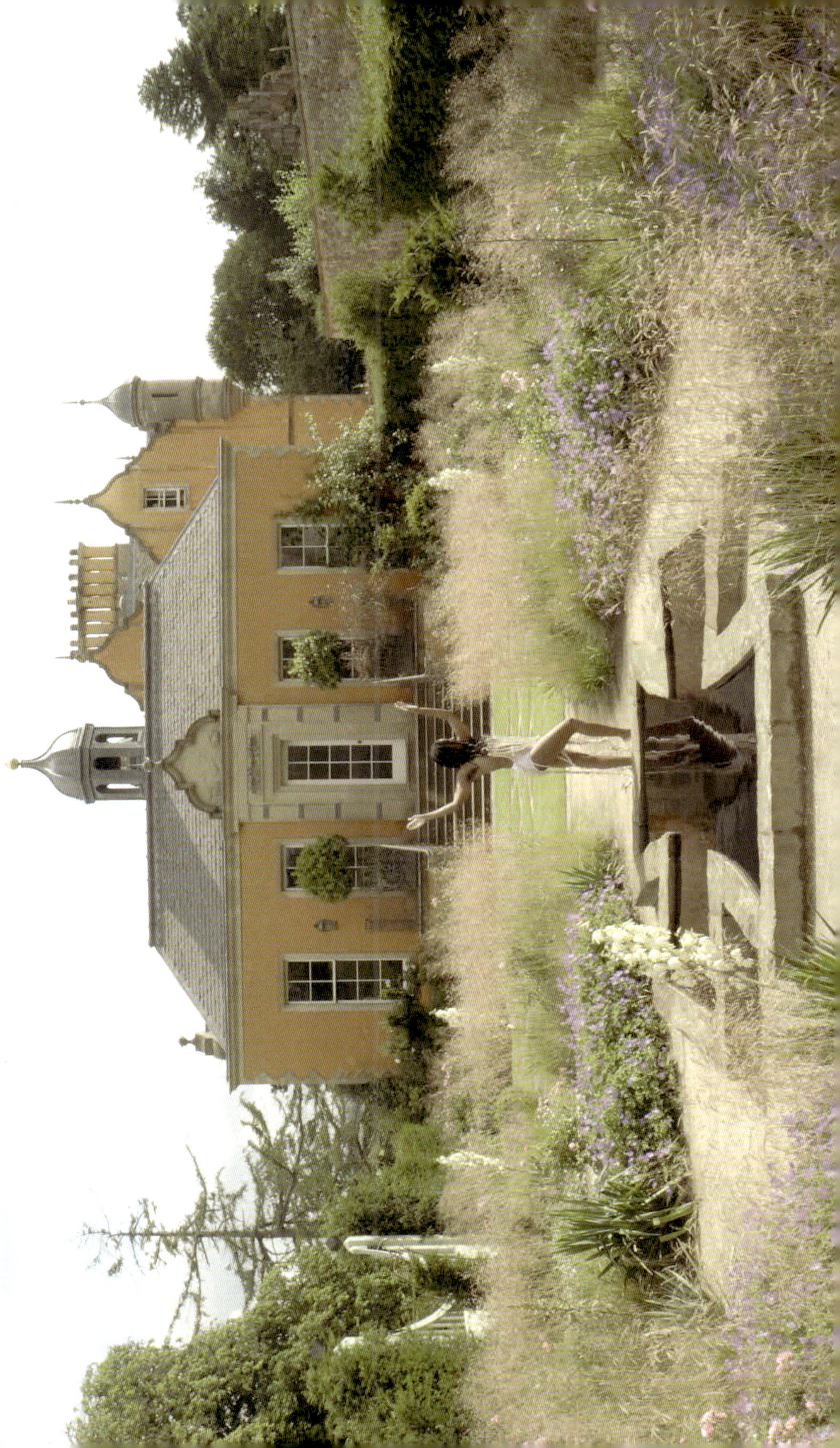

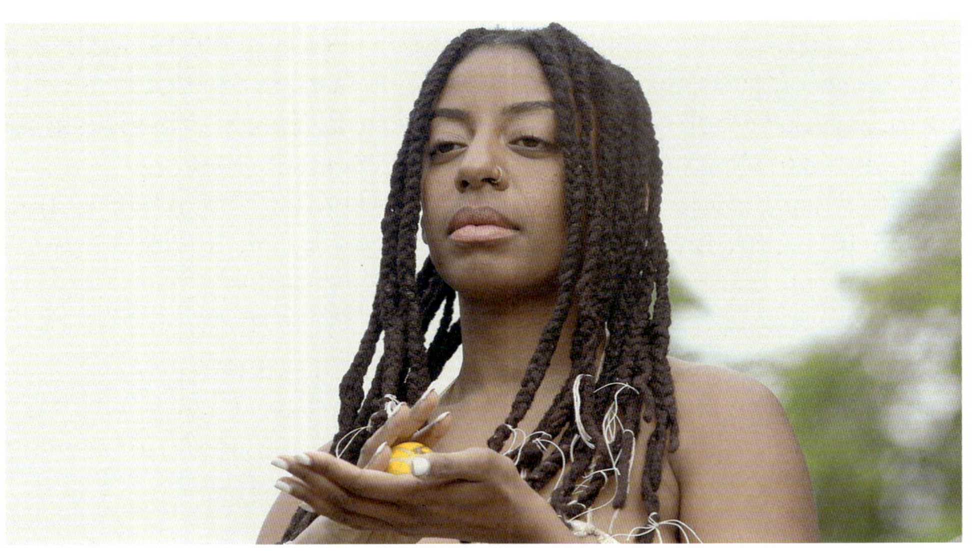

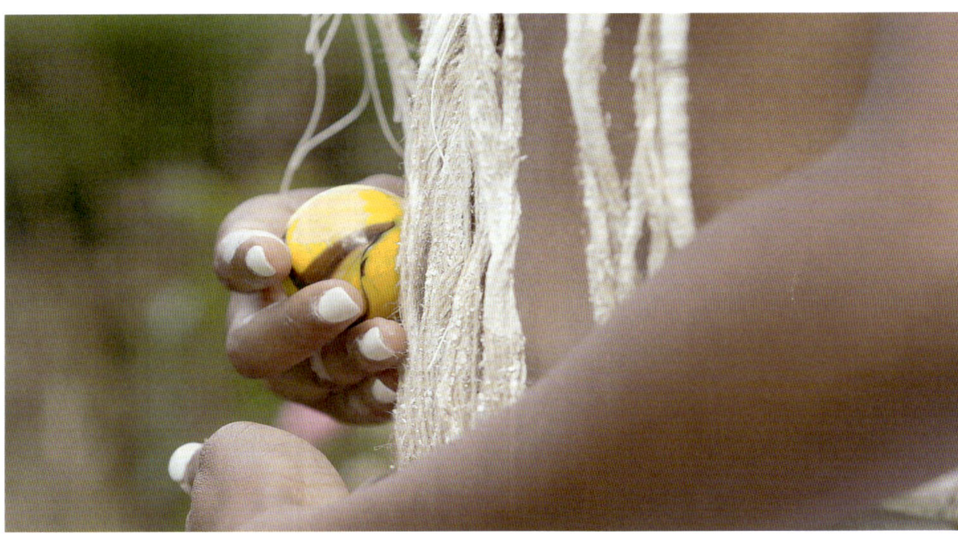

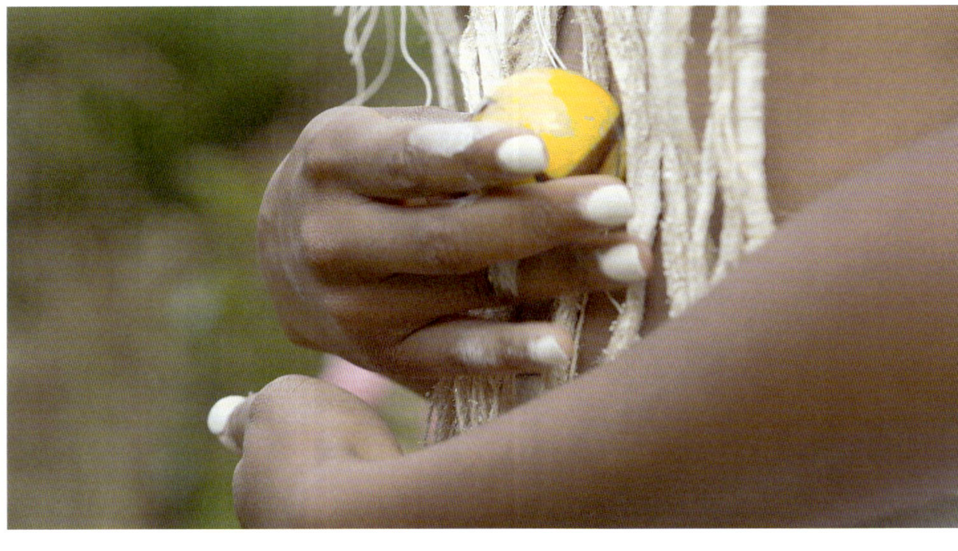

Alberta Whittle's research-led practice is concerned with the legacies of slavery and apartheid, the erasure of Black people from everyday society through the avoidance and suppression of Black histories and perspectives, and ecological emergency. *RESET*, filmed in Scotland, South Africa and Whittle's native Barbados, is a polyvocal journey organised as a series of three lessons: 'Reparable impulses under conditions of anticipatory grief', 'everyday ululations' and 'August 1st 2020 Emancipation Day'. Visual and aural motifs from the natural world – the sea, palm trees, snakes, birds and the moon – recur throughout and collage together the different sections. A hypnotic soundtrack titled 'Maroon Rage', composed by artist-activist St Mozelle aka Yves B. Golden and developed in collaboration with Whittle, forms the spine of the film. This is interwoven with a text titled 'On Touching' by writer and artist Ama Josephine Budge, which speaks of transnational memory, longing and liquidity, fragments of which appear on the screen in alternating green and purple text and are also read aloud by Whittle. The rhythm of the film is punctuated by the treatment of images which are spliced, juxtaposed and overlaid.

The text and score act as a catalyst for performances by artist and curator Sekai Machache, choreographer and performer Mele Broomes and artist Christian Noelle Charles. The second lesson opens with handbells being rung while Charles is pictured hocketing in two videos, as she holds and alternates between long notes. Later, Broomes is pictured alone in a sparse domestic interior wearing a costume of braided seagrass weighted down with seashells, referencing the sea and tidal memory. She performs a solo dance to flute music. Her movements are serpentine and poised, yet glitchy, her trajectory and gaze always moving and looking upwards. In subsequent scenes, directed over WhatsApp when Whittle was unable to travel from Barbados due to COVID-19 restrictions, Machache and Broomes are filmed inside the house and grounds of the sculpture park Jupiter Artland in Scotland. Machache is pictured sitting on the parquet floor of the former ballroom wearing a knitted costume, reclining with her eyes shut, as a cluster of coloured marbles fall to the floor in front of her. At the end of the film, Broomes performs a statuesque dance, moving through the landscaped gardens, with the ochre facade of the Jacobean house and doocot visible behind. This depiction of Black performers moving through and resting inside a British stately home suggests a reclamation of space associated with whiteness, privilege and the legacy of slavery, while the garden represents a utopian space of re-learning and resetting.

Whittle also includes scenes of bodies in motion, in footage she captured spontaneously in the UK and Barbados and material found online, which speak to 'the weight of the histories of violence' described in Budge's text. In one scene at a peaceful Black Lives Matters march, protesters hold up their mobile phones, torchlights on, illuminating the night sky. Subsequent clips show police officers forcefully restraining and handcuffing a protester and armed with shields amidst flames in scenes of conflict, against a soundtrack of thunderclaps. Whittle also includes a graphic of a body breathing on a ventilator, recalling the murder in 2020 of George Floyd, who repeatedly told the white police officer kneeling on his neck 'I can't breathe'. In another scene, which Whittle encountered by chance and filmed on her iPhone, a man is pictured repeatedly playing limbo, leaning back and ducking low under a parked car. This scene refers to the history of limbo as a dance which emerged in Trinidad in the nineteenth century and brings to mind enslaved Africans who were transported to the Caribbean on crowded ships and would have squeezed through tight spaces when entering low galleys.

Whittle's film also shows a consideration for the body of the viewer. In the opening sequence, she invites viewers to 'take a deep breath', pause and join in a meditative exercise to focus on their bodies and their breathing. As the film unfolds, she urges the audience to become active rather than passive spectators by calling for healing, rest and community at a time of inequality. Footage of a snake moving in water appears at numerous points throughout the film, representing the ouroboros, 'synonymous with eternity and cyclical return', which for Whittle offers hope, 'becoming a way to trace genealogies of kith and kin, and to signify communion with love and community'.[1]

Grace Storey

1.  Inês Geraldes Cardoso, 'Interview with Alberta Whittle: "RESET"', *This Is Tomorrow* (11 November 2020), http://thisistomorrow.info/articles/interview-with-alberta-whittle

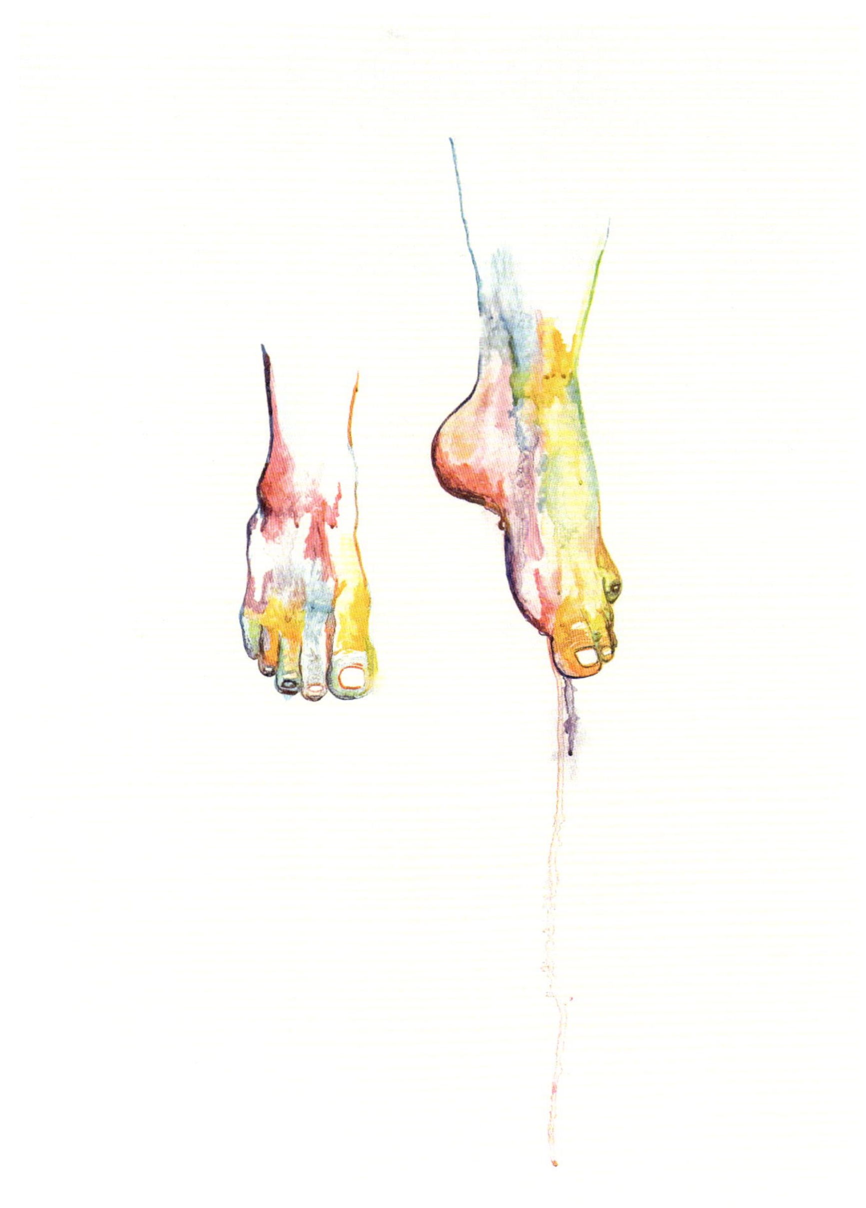

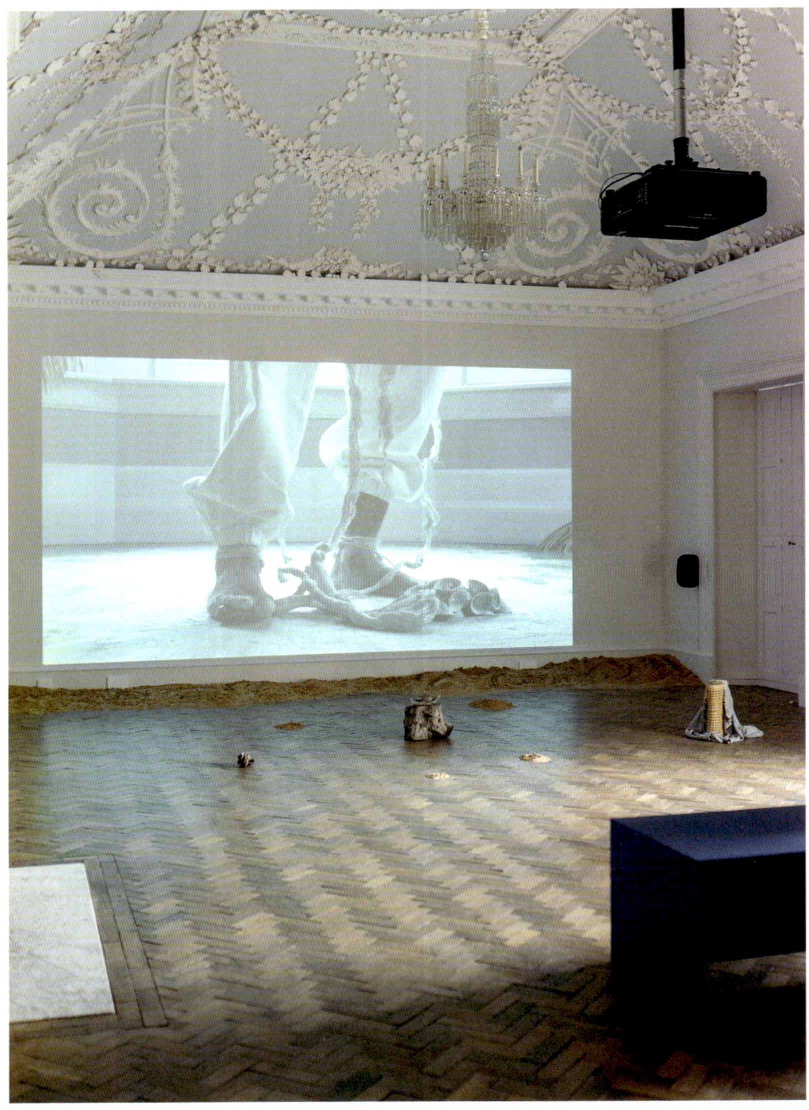

Alberta Whittle, *RESET,* installation view, Jupiter Artland, Edinburgh, 2021. Costume designed by Sabrina Henry

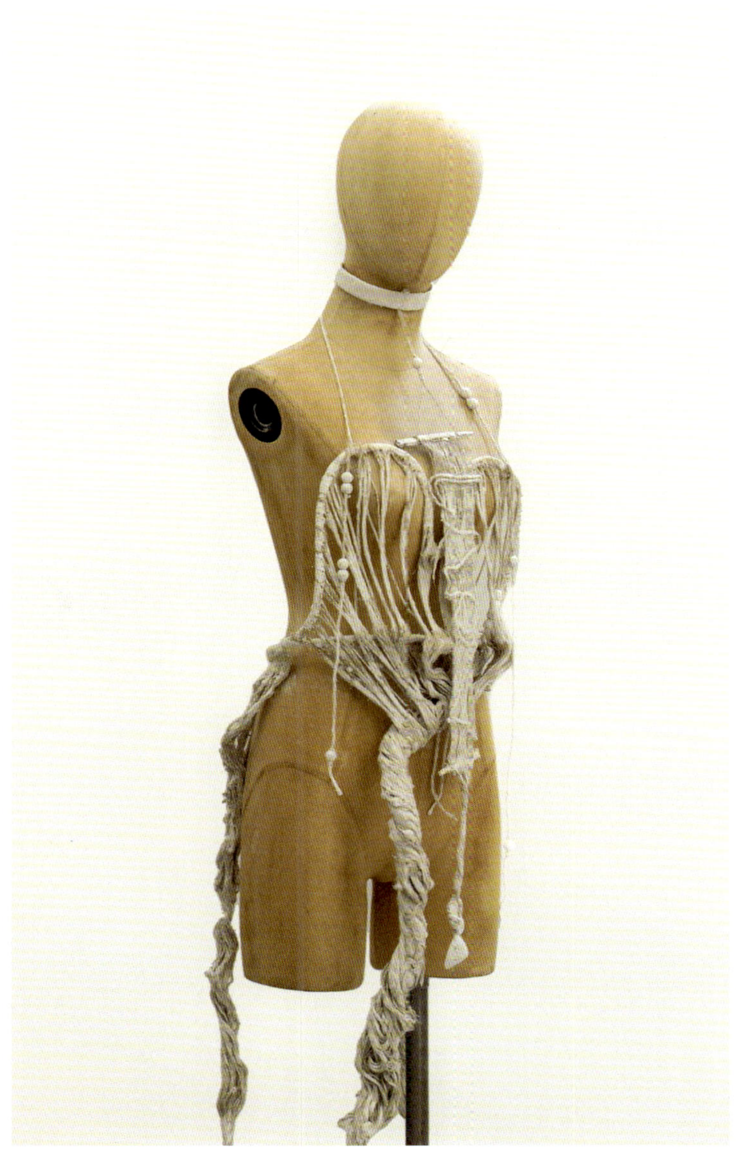

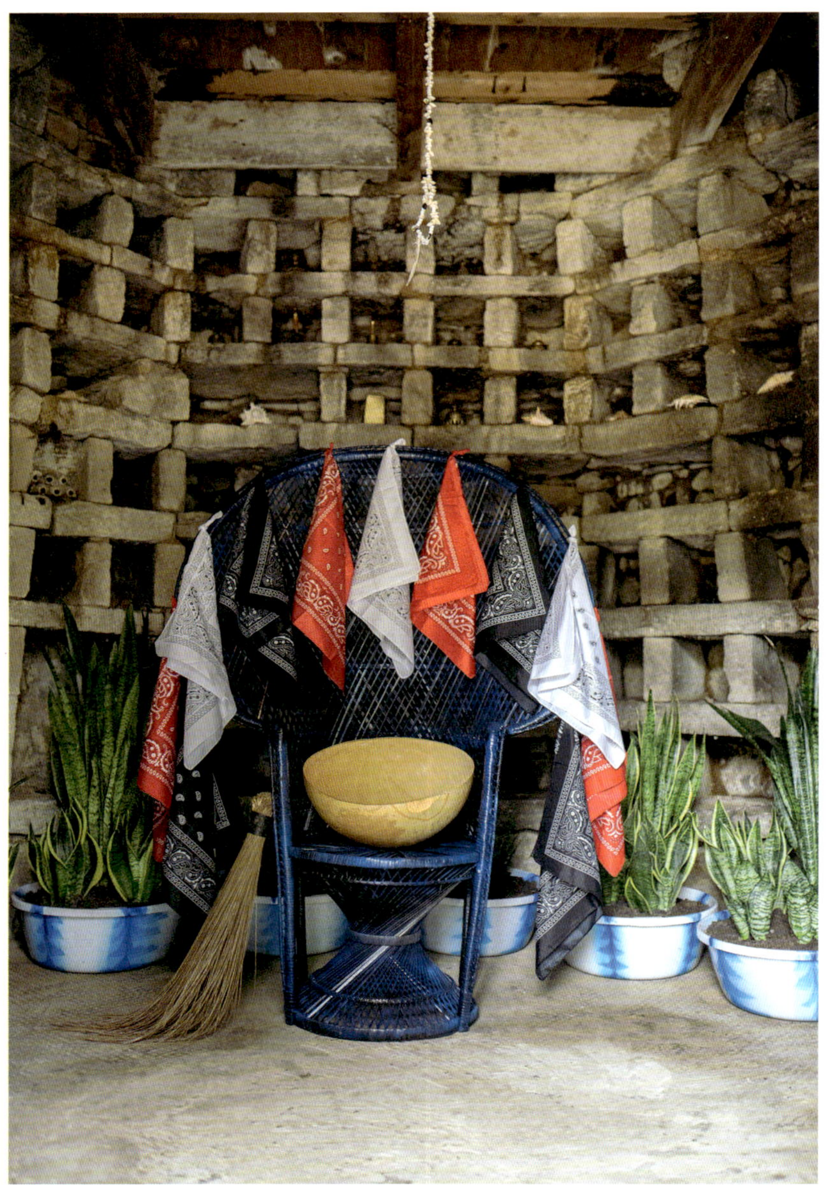

The night I went dreaming in the waves, I held sixteen marbles deep in my womb nestled there by sheer power of will.

When the water was black enough, echoing my own, and I could hear my great grandmothers tidal singing, I allowed them to slip and slither out, **one, by one, by one** at a time as the moon turned slowly to full. If I had let them go too quickly, or without a reverence measurable by lengths of wheat and seagrass, she might not make her turn at all. Such is the journey of a wave daughter: never alone, never touching.

For those of us who wear our atoms outside of our bodies can breathe here, anywhere, **but touch nowhere, everywhere, nothingness** at once.

Such is the weight of histories of violence, no touch ever the same, no touch free of it, of them, of us. Ever a haunting, a yearning, an ecstasy unfulfilled.

That night – **then, now, here** – the waves are surging high, and higher and higher, a call and response with the blood waters of my body. More voices now, voices join my grandmothers. Some are familiar, some are ancient but all I know, all guide me to the dreaming planes. Come away, they call, echoing, spectres, come away child, come away.

*Away from what?*
        *From where?*
                *To what?*
                        *To where?*

These questions are not mine to ask, only to hide, to pretend this dreaming journey is all I've ever dreamed of, to hide the whispers in my soles of rich seductive silch and sediment. The wracking longing to be seen as only myself, not just as only, as a vessel of ages, not the all that is a wave daughter, perhaps only one, or two or three, lapping lives, touching shore and leaving love knots of seafoam, even if only for a moment, once a month, once a tide, once a full moon. **Once in a lifetime.**

Yet we have no one land but the ocean, the largest land of all, and it is not our way to long for stasis, solidity, beginnings, middles, endings, we understand that all are at once, always.

*Don't we?*

Now voices mixologising with the waves guttural ululations, taking over my body with spasms of ecstasy I can no longer not want, or want, I am no longer myself. I find the last of remnants missing that I haven't felt for millennia,

*Missing what?*
> *Who?*

*Who is witnessing this? Me – the little here that is me?*
> > *You?*

How strange to close ones eyes, ones nose, ones mouth, to sink below and into everything, electrons reaching as they were made to do for everything, and thus for themselves. They used to call this a perversion.

How strange to lose the spaces of solidity, of ones own boundedness and still touch…***nothing***…and still be.. a… all… a… all… a… all… a…**lone.**

I exhale the last vestiges of oxygen, of sky, of *up there.* Now all is depths and peace.

The moon shows her belly swollen and full
with marbles.

Epitoky.
Climax.
Exhale.

Recuperate on the seabed, caressed by
bottomfeeding invertebrates. Fecundating me
slowly with each brush of their mulchy clitellum.
Almost touching, not quite. This is the closest I
get to soil, to surface, to standing still. And the
pieces of me regathering over decades weeps
with the joy of it, and the inadequacy.

I feel you.

I know you.

I miss you.

And oh,
**how it aches.**

# Biographies



**Alexandra Bachzetsis** (b. 1974,
Zurich; lives in Zurich) is an artist and
choreographer who has created more
than two dozen pieces for theatres,
festivals and public venues since 2001.
Recent solo exhibitions include:
Kunsthaus Zurich (2022); Mudam
Luxembourg – Musée d'Art Moderne
Grand-Duc Jean (2020); Art Institute
of Chicago (2019); Centre Culturel
Suisse, Paris (2018); Centre Pompidou,
Paris (2018). Group shows and biennials
include: Schirn Kunsthalle, Frankfurt
(2018); documenta 14, Athens and
Kassel (2017); 'Biennale of Moving
Images', Geneva (2014); documenta 13,
Kassel (2012); 5th Berlin Biennial
(Berlin, 2008). Bachzetsis is a recipient
of the Migros Kulturprozent Jubilee
Award (2007), the Swiss Art Award
(2016 and 2011) and Swiss Performance
Prize (2012).

**Pauline Boudry / Renate Lorenz**
(b. 1972, Lausanne and b. 1963, Berlin;
live in Berlin) have been working
collaboratively since 2007. Recent solo
exhibitions include: Palacio de Cristal,
Madrid (2022); CA2M Museum Madrid
(2022); Kunstraum Innsbruck (2021);
Frac Bretagne (2021); Centre Culturel
Suisse, Paris (2018) and Contemporary
Art Museum Houston (2017). They
represented Switzerland in the 58th
Venice Biennale (2019) and have
participated in numerous group shows
and biennials, including at the Walker
Art Center, Minneapolis (2019);
Hayward Gallery, London (2019);
Fundacion Jumex, Mexico City (2018);
Gwangju Biennale, South Korea (2016);
New Museum, New York (2017);
Contemporary Art Centre, Vilnius
(2014); Palais de Tokyo, Paris (2012);
Aichi Triennale, Japan (2010).

**Eglė Budvytytė** (b. 1981, Kaunas,
Lithuania; lives in Amsterdam). Solo
exhibitions and performances include:
The Renaissance Society, Chicago
(2019); Kiasma, Helsinki (2018);
Contemporary Art Centre, Vilnius
(2016). Group exhibitions include:
Riga International Biennial of
Contemporary Art (RIBOCA 2), Riga
(2020); Baltic Triennial 13, Riga (2018);
South London Gallery, London (2018);

Haus der Kulturen der Welt, Berlin (2018); Palais de Tokyo, Paris (2017); Moderna Museet, Malmo (2014). Budvytytė's work was also included in 'Milk of Dreams', the 59th Venice Biennale (2022). Her work is held in collections including National Gallery of Art, Vilnius; Moderna Museet, Malmo; Stedelijk Museum, Amsterdam and MO Museum, Vilnius.

**Éric Minh Cuong Castaing** (b. 1979, Seine-Saint-Denis, France; lives in Marseille) graduated from Gobelins l'école de l'image, Paris, and worked as an animation designer before discovering hip-hop and turning to choreography. Castaing was associate artist at the Ballet National de Marseille from 2016–19 and in 2007 founded the dance company Shonen, where he works closely with a group of dancers, playwright Marine Relinger and co-choreographer Aloun Marchal. Castaing's works have been exhibited at visual arts institutions including Le Bal, Paris (2022); La Villa Kujoyama, Kyoto (2020); Palais de Tokyo, Paris (2018); Centre Pompidou, Paris (2017) and performing arts venues including Festival de Marseille (2021, 2018 and 2016); tanzhaus nrw Düsseldorf (2021); Charleroi danse, Brussels (2020) and Viernulvier, Ghent (2020).

**Alia Farid** (b. 1985, Kuwait; lives in Kuwait and Puerto Rico). Solo exhibitions include: Kunsthalle Basel, Basel (2022); Kunstinstituut Melly, Rotterdam (2020); Portikus, Frankfurt (2019). Recent group shows include: the Whitney Biennial 2022, New York; The 10th Asia Pacific Triennial of Contemporary Art, Brisbane (2022); Lahore Biennale, Lahore (2020); Yokohoma Triennale (2020); MoMA PS1, New York (2019); Sharjah Biennial 14 (2019); the 12th Gwangju Biennale (2018); the 32 Bienal de São Paulo (2016). Forthcoming solo exhibitions include: The Power Plant Contemporary Art Gallery, Toronto and Chisenhale Gallery, London (both 2023). Farid is nominated for the tenth edition of the Artes Mundi Prize, 2023.

**Hetain Patel** (b. 1980, Bolton, UK; lives in London) works in video, performance, sculpture, painting and photography. Solo exhibitions include: New Art Exchange, Nottingham (2022); John Hansard Gallery, Southampton, (2021); John Hansard Gallery, Southampton, (2021); tanzhaus nrw Dusseldorf (2018); Manchester Art Gallery (2017); C-Mine, Genk (2014); . Group exhibitions include: British Art Show 9, Aberdeen, Wolverhampton, Manchester, Plymouth (2021–22); Asia Society Triennial, New York, (2021); Devi Art Foundation, Delhi (2019); Asia Pacific Triennial, Brisbane (2015–16); Ullens Centre for Contemporary Art, Beijing (2012). Patel has also presented live events and screenings at National Gallery, London (2021); Barbican, London (2019); Sydney Opera House (2019); Institute of Contemporary Arts, London (2019); Sadler's Wells, London (2015); National Gallery of Modern Art, Mumbai (2015); Serpentine Galleries, London (2014), Tate Modern, London (2012).

**Bárbara Wagner and Benjamin de Burca** (b. 1980, Brasília and b. 1975, Munich; live in Recife, Brazil) have been working together on films and video installations for the past decade. Solo exhibitions include: New Museum, New York (2022); De Pont Museum, Tilburg (2022); Institute of Contemporary Art, Boston (2022); Stedelijk Museum, Amsterdam (2019); Pérez Art Museum, Miami (2019). They represented Brazil in the 58th Venice Biennale (2019) and have been included in group exhibitions and biennials including: Fotomuseum Winterthur, Switzerland (2019); Museu de Arte Moderno de Bogotá (2017); Skulptur Projekte, Münster (2017); Museu de Arte do Rio, Rio de Janeiro (2014); Museu de Arte Moderna de São Paulo (2010).

**Alberta Whittle** (b. 1980, Bridgetown, Barbados; lives in Barbados and Glasgow, Scotland). Solo shows include: Grand Union Gallery, Birmingham (2022); Nicola Vassell Gallery, New York (2022); University of Johannesburg Gallery, Johannesburg (2021); Jupiter Artland, Edinburgh (2021); Dundee Contemporary Arts, Dundee (2019).

Group shows include: British Art
Show 9, Aberdeen, Wolverhampton,
Manchester, Plymouth (2021–22);
Kunsthall Trondheim, Norway (2021);
Tate Britain, London (2021); Somerset
House, London (2021); Göteborg
International Biennial for
Contemporary Art, Göteborg (2021);
MIMA, Middlesbrough (2021). Whittle
is a winner of the Frieze Artist
Award and the Turner Prize (2020).
She represented Scotland at the 59th
Venice Biennale.

## Contributors

**Ama Josephine Budge** is a British-
Ghanaian speculative writer, artist,
curator and pleasure activist whose
praxis navigates queer explorations
of race, art, ecology and feminism. Her
installation, written and video art
works have been commissioned, exhibited and published internationally.

**Jemma Desai** is based in London.
Her practice engages with film pro-
gramming through research, writing
and performance, as well as informally
organised settings for deep study.
She is a practice-based PhD student
at Central School of Speech and Drama
thinking through the liberatory possibilities of abolitionist praxis to cultural
production, where she is working
on a thesis entitled 'what do we want
from each other after we have told
our stories?'

**Grace Storey** is assistant curator at
Whitechapel Gallery. Recent projects
include 'Paulina Olowska: The Travel
Bureau' (2022), 'Simone Fattal: Finding
a Way', 'Eileen Agar: Angel of Anarchy'
and 'Sol Calero: 'Desde el Salón' (From
the Living Room) (all 2021). Storey was
previously assistant curator at Kettle's
Yard, Cambridge, and studio manager
in New York for Camille Henrot,
realising Henrot's exhibition 'Days Are
Dogs' at Palais de Tokyo, Paris (2017).

**Lydia Yee** is chief curator at Whitechapel
Gallery. Her most recent exhibitions
include 'Theaster Gates: A Clay Sermon'
(2021), 'Radical Figures: Painting in the
New Millennium' (2020) and 'Is This
Tomorrow?' (2019). Yee was previously
curator at Barbican Art Gallery, London
and senior curator at the Bronx
Museum of the Arts, New York. She
also co-curated British Art Show 8
(2015–16) and Frieze Talks (2018–19).

# List of Works

**Alexandra Bachzetsis**

*An Ideal for Living*, 2018
Installation with two-channel video,
colour, sound; 22:46 minutes

*Catapult*, 2018
AirTrack gymnastics mats,
70 × 500 × 100 cm

Courtesy the artist and Experimenter,
Kolkata and Mumbai; Karma
International, Zurich; kurimanzutto,
Mexico City and New York; Meyer
Riegger, Berlin

Concept and choreography: Alexandra
Bachzetsis. Direction: Alexandra
Bachzetsis. Camera: Cristian Manzutto.
Editing: Sotiris Vasiliou. Performers:
Mia Born, Oleg Houbrechts. Movement
research: Thibault Lac. Costume
research: Cosima Gadient in
collaboration with Mia Born and Oleg
Houbrechts. Production management:
Anna Geering. Production assistant:
Daphni Antoniou. Production of All
Exclusive supported by Kooperative
Fördervereinbarung (Kanton Zürich,
Pro Helvetia – Fondation suisse pour la
culture, Stadt Zürich). Co-production:
Robert Rauschenberg Foundation
and Tanzhaus Zürich. Special thanks
to Athanasios Bachzetsis, Verena
Bachzetsis, Franziska Born, Bernd
Houbrechts, Shannon Jackson,
Catja Loepfe, Priska Morger,
Paul B. Preciado, Jannis Tsingaris,
Marco Walser.

**Pauline Boudry / Renate Lorenz**

*Les Gayrillères*, 2022
Installation with two-channel video
(projection and LED), colour, sound;
18 minutes

Courtesy the artists and Marcelle Alix,
Paris and Ellen de Bruijne Projects,
Amsterdam

Gayrillères choreography: Harry
Alexander, Julie Cunningham.
Additional choreography/performance:
Harry Alexander, Julie Cunningham,
Werner Hirsch, Nach, Joy Alpuerto
Ritter, Aaliyah Thanisha. Directors of
photography: Bernadette Paassen, Siri

Klug. Sound: Johanna Wienert.
Costumes: Heloise Mantel. Wig:
Dushan Petrovic. Stage production:
Wibke Tiarks. Dramaturgical
assistance: Renen Itzhaki. Sound
design: Rashad Becker. Colour grading:
Waveline. Music: Ivo Dimchev,
'Overrated' (home version), Desire
Marea, 'Tavern Kween', Anhoni, 'Be
my Husband', Tragic Selector (a.k.a.
Daisuke Tadokoro & Terre Thaemlitz),
'A Dialogue with Gravity' – produced,
mixed and arranged by D. Tadokoro
(piano) & T. Thaemlitz (fx), 2014;
licensed courtesy of Comatonse
Recordings; publishing T. Thaemlitz
(BMI). Co-produced by Kunstnernes
Hus Oslo, Desingel Antwerp, Arsenic
Lausanne. Supported by service des
affaires culturelles du Canton de
Vaud, Loterie Romande, Leenaards
Foundation, Ville de Lausanne, Göhner
Stiftung, Guggenheim Stiftung, Emilie
Gourd Foundation, Burgauer Stiftung.
Special thanks to: Callie's Berlin.

**Eglė Budvytytė in collaboration with
Marija Olšauskaitė and Julija
Steponaitytė**

*Songs from the Compost: mutating
bodies, imploding stars*, 2020
HD video, colour, sound; 29 minutes

Courtesy the artists

Director Eglė Budvytytė. Song lyrics
and voices: Eglė Budvytytė. Art
directing: Marija Olšauskaitė, Ona
Julija Lukas Steponaitytė. Solo dance
performed and choreographed by:
Mami Kang. Sound design: Steve
Martin Snider. Mixing and mastering:
Maarten Brijker. Camera: Vytautas
Plukas. Camera assistant: Martynas
Norvaišas. Editing: Bart Groenendaal
and Eglė Budvytytė. Colour grading:
Ona Julija Lukas Steponaitytė.
Special effects: Elena Permogorskaya
and Viktorija Obor. Performers:
Viktorija Zobielaitė, Evgeniy Kalachov,
Goda Motiejaitytė, Silvija Lileikytė,
Kipras Chlebinskas, Ona Julija Lukas
Steponaitytė. Special thanks to: Coda
dance school, Inga Briazkalovaitė,
Egija Inzule, Maria Tsoy, Antanas
Lučiūnas, Martynas Kazimierėnas,
Kęstutis Minderis, Indrė Dikavičiūtė,

Klaipėda Puppet Theatre, Curonian
Spit National Park.

**Éric Minh Cuong Castaing**

*Form(s) of Life – ÉLISE*, 2021
HD video, colour, sound; 7:39 minutes

*Form(s) of Life – KAMAL*, 2021
HD video, colour, sound; 5:58 minutes

Courtesy Éric Minh Cuong Castaing,
Shonen

Conception, realisation: Éric Minh
Cuong Castaing, Shonen.
Video director: Victor Zébo.
Co-choreography: Aloun Marchal
& Éric Minh Cuong Castaing.
Dramaturgy: Marine Relinger.
Performers: Aloun Marchal, Kamal
Messelleka, Nans Pierson, Élise Argaud,
Yumiko Funaya. Sound design: Renaud
Bajeux. Costume: Silvia Romanelli.
Technical direction: Stanislas Kopec.
Sound engineers: François Charrier,
Samuel Poirée. Chief editor: Lucie Brux
Calibration: Alexis Lambotte Label 42
studio. Production: Claire Crova.
Administration: Tiffanie Sebbag.
Production manager (films): Scarlett
Garson. Stage management (filming):
Samuel Tuleda. Co-producers: Festival
de Marseille, Prix le BAL de la Jeune
Création avec l'Adagp 2021 (Paris),
Vooruit Ghent (BE). Points communs,
Nouvelle scène nationale de Cergy-
Pontoise et du Val d'Oise, Pôle Arts
de la Scène – Friche la Belle de Mai
(Marseille), Ballet National de
Marseille, Résidence Co-laBo/les
ballets C de la B (BE), Charleroi Danse
(BE), tanzhaus nrw Düsseldorf (DE),
Fonds Transfabrik (FR / DE), Carreau
du Temple - dispositif PACT(e) (Paris),
ICK Amsterdam (NL), Scène
Conventionnée Le Vivat (Armentières),
Dublin Dance Festival (IR), Ministère
de la Culture Délégation à la Danse –
dispositif Filmer la danse, C.N.C.
DICRéAM, Conseil départemental des
Bouches-du-Rhône – «Ensemble en
Provence» et «Centre de création en
résidences», Région Sud – Carte
Blanche aux Artistes 2020, ARS Paca
– Agence Régionale de la Santé / DRAC
Paca – Direction régionale des affaires
culturelles Dispositif «Culture et

Santé», Fondation Porosus (Paris),
Fondation Handicap et Société (Paris).
Art & Health partners: Centre de
soins palliatifs La Maison (Gardanne),
Hôpital Ste Marguerite APHM
(Marseille), Hôpital Bretonneau
APHP (Paris).


**Alia Farid**

*At the Time of the Ebb*, 2019
HD video, colour, sound; 15:43 minutes

Courtesy the artist

Nowruz Cast I. Shushi: Yahye Irani,
Hassan Chabok. Shtoor (camel):
Mohammed Poozan, Mohammed Karoi.
Asb (horse): Shoja Chabok, Mohammed
Tolandi. Shir (lion): Salim Daryai. Siyah
poosh: Abdurahman Irani. Rooba
(white bird): Mohammed Tamakhrah.
Saroom (herder): Mohammed Ali
Chabok. Booye saroom (herder's son):
Abdulla Irani. Nowruz Cast II. Shushi:
Yahye Irani, Abdulrahman Poozan.
Shtoor (camel): Ali Poozan, Ali Hasmi.
Asb (horse): Shoja Mahmood Shadman,
Ahmed Shadman Roob'e. Rooba
(white bird): AhmedShadman. Saroom
(herder): Akbar Deghani. Booye Saroom
(herder's son): Huma Irani. Music:
musicians convened by Baba Gholam.
Solo dance: Farzad Draye. Film crew.
DoP: Reza Abya. Producer: Mahmoud
Sani. Co-producer: Farah Al Adsani.
Sound recorder: Ali Alavi. Camera
assistant: Sajjad Karimi. Still
photographer: Huda Abdulmughni.
Director: Alia Farid. Edit: Alia Farid
and Cristian Manzutto. Sound edit
and mix: Cristian Manzutto. Color
grading: Francois Nobecourt, Cristian
Manzutto. Post-production studio:
estudio de producción.


**Hetain Patel**

*Trinity*, 2021
HD video, colour, sound; 23 minutes

Courtesy the artist and Chatterjee
& Lal, Mumbai

Film by Hetain Patel. Written by Hetain
Patel and In-Sook Chappell. Produced
by Sophie Neave. Cast: Vidya Patel:
Mina, Sudha Bhuchar: Samanya (mum),
Raffie Julien: Amy. Director of pho-
tography: Lorena Pages. Editor: Oliver
Parker. Music: Amy May. Production
designer: Bobbie Cousins. Costume
designer: Sarah Mercade. Hair and
make-up designer: Cosima Crowley-
Roth. Sound recordist: Jack Cook.
Choreographer: Chirag Lukha. Sign
language and story consultant: Louise
Stern. Avatars casting: Eva Martinez.
The ancestors: Saju Hari, Iris Chan,
Melanie Ingram, Jaki Wilford, Roshan –
Nirmal Chohan. A Tilt Films
Production commissioned by John
Hansard Gallery, New Art Exchange,
Sadler's Wells, Gulbenkian and
Motwani Jadeja Family Foundation.
Supported by Hayward Gallery Touring
for British Art Show 9 and Arts Council
England. Made with the support of
Anurang Tyagi and Skinder Hundal.
1st assistant director: Carlotta Beck
Peccoz. Production manager: Caermen
de Witt. Production assistant: Anna
Argiros. 3rd assistant director: Sunija
Mullick. Floor runner: Zarife Sevin.
Additional floor runners: Gwennaëlle
Counson, Amy Madden. 1st assistant
camera: Riaz Ahmed, Rushil
Choudhary, Chris Steel. 2nd assistant
camera: Joe Salkey. Digital image tech-
nicians: Ellie C. Bright, Gabriel Tineo.
Camera trainees: Jake Phillips, Shayne
Thomas-Gordon. Steadicam operator:
James Thomas. Gaffer: Krunal
Saadrani. Spark: Dimitros
Mavrogiannis. Spark dailies: Rob
Gifford, Johnjoe Besagni. Art director:
Sofia Secomani. Construction: Jasper
Levine. Graphics: Maria Sacomani.
Art department assistant: Hugo Harris,
Phin Shaughnessy-Symons. Costume
assistant: Anisha Fields. Makeup
and hair assistant: Amber Hoskins,
Amy Luthwood-Graham. Sign
language intepreters: Jade Odle, Helsa
Borinstein. COVID-19 supervisor:
Wojciech Czarkowski. Stills photogra-
pher & BTS videographer: Gabriel
Tineo. Postproduction: Colour & finish-
ing services: Cheat. Colourist: Jack
Mcgnitiy. VFX artist: Tim Mellem.
Sound mixed at Soundnode. Sound
designer: Martin Schulz. Sound editor:
Daniel Jaramillo. Re-recording mixer:
David Crane. Foley by: Clap Studios.
Foley artist: Sebastián Vázquez Garzón.
Foley recordist: Juan Pablo Saldarriaga

Alaguna. Foley supervisor: Daniel
Jaramillo Gutierrez. Studio coordina-
tor: Sebastián Alzate López. Additional
music and mixing by: Matt Whittington.
Violin: Charlie Brown. Viola: Amy May.
Cello: Ben Trigg. Vocals: Leela Patel,
Verity Quade, Suzy Robinson, Amy May.
Camera equipment supplied by Fava
Rental. Lighting equipment supplied
by SHL Lighting Locations. Catering
provided by CGI Catering. Rehearsal
studios provided by Sadler's Wells.
Insurance: Tysers. With special thanks
to: Eva Martinez, Louise Tanoto, Laura
Patay, Toke Broni Stranby, Julie Perry,
Lola Perry, Chaterjee & Lal, Shwetal
Patel, Holly Waddington, Gwen Van
Spijk, Cambridge Junction, Thomas
Owoo, Callina Pearson, Queens
Crescent Community Centre, Jessica
Feely & Gustav. Filmed on location in
Kentish Town and Hackney, London. In
memory of Kunverben Patel (Mamai)
1918-2014 and Lakshmiven Patel (Baa)
1928-2017. A Tilt Films Production
© 2021 Hetain Patel. All rights reserved.


**Bárbara Wagner and
Benjamin de Burca**

*Faz Que Vai* (Set to Go), 2015
HD video, colour, sound; 12 minutes

Courtesy the artists and Fortes D'Aloia
& Gabriel, São Paulo and Rio de Janeiro

Cast: Ryan Neves, Edson Vogue,
Bhrunno Henryque, Eduarda Lemos.
Cinematographer: Pedro Sotero.
Camera assistant: Raphael Malta
Clasen. Electricians: Alexandra Aranha,
Fernando Marinho. Production
Assistant: Bia Lima. Makeup artists:
Rodrigo Cavalcanti, Eva Venenosa.
Editor: Eduardo Serrano. Colorist:
Pablo Nóbrega. Sound: Cícero Batom,
Wellington Jamaica, Waltinho d'Souza
Orquestra Popular de Bomba do
Hemetério. Recording and mixing:
Jeferson Japa. Shot in Recife,
Pernambuco, Brazil. Produced in Brazil.

**Alberta Whittle**

*RESET*, 2020
HD video, colour, sound; 32 minutes

Courtesy the artist and The Modern
Institute/Toby Webster Ltd., Glasgow
Co-commissioned and co-produced
by Frieze and Forma for the Frieze
Artist Award 2020.

*On Touching:* Fragments from
a commissioned new text by Ama
Josephine Budge.

*Maroon Rage:* Collaborative score
by St. Mozelle aka Yves B. Golden
and Alberta Whittle.

Assistant director: Matthew Arthur
Williams. Produced by: Chris Rawcliffe,
Carolina Ongaro, Marina La Verghetta.
Players: Mele Broomes, Christian
Noelle Charles, Sekai Machache.
Director of photography: Basharat
Khan. Cinematography: Nick Whittle.
Camera assistant: Jim Rusk.
Animation: Anushka Naanayakkara.
Animation previz: Dan Brookes.
Costume: Sabrina Henry.
Choreography: Mele Broomes. Sound
editor and sound mix: Richy Carey.
Sound engineer: Mark Readhead.
Location support: Nicky and Robert
Wilson, Claire Feeley and Jupiter
Artland, Martin Craig and Glasgow
Museums, Molly-Mae Whawell
and Diana Stevenson, Andre Hoyte
and National Cultural Foundation
of Barbados.

Additional thanks to: Kitty Anderson,
Arts Council England, Centre for
Research Collections: The University
of Edinburgh, Rachel, Gus, Sancho,
Telmo and Isidro Crespo-Bonney, Eoin
Dara, Eva Langret, Forma London,
Frieze London, Fenella Gabrych,
Glasgow Women's Library, Angela
Johnstone, Katherina Ka Yi Liu, Eva
Langret, Thulani Rachia, Himali Singh
Soin, University of St Andrews, Leigh
and Violet Weatherhead, Louise
and Francis Westerhout, Lisa Williams,
Nicole Yip, the Barkers, the Whittles
and those who have crossed over.

# Acknowledgements

'Moving Bodies, Moving Images'
is generously supported by

swiss arts council

**prohelvetia**


**Special thanks to**

Harry Alexander; Moacir Anjo,
Fundação Joaquim Nabuco; Ard.works –
Guillaume Chuard and Michela Zoppi;
Aqsa Arif; Alexandra Bachzetsis;
Pauline Boudry / Renate Lorenz;
Mele Broomes; Ama Josephine Budge;
Eglė Budvytytė; Éric Minh Cuong
Castaing, Claire Crova, Alice Gabay,
Tiffanie Sebbag, Shonen; Karolina
Dankow and Geraldine Belmont,
Karma International, Zurich; Julie
Cunningham; Jemma Desai; Alia Farid;
Melanie Isabel García, Tanya Leighton
Gallery; Sven Gareis; Orit Gat;
William Lunn, Copperfield Gallery;
Hetain Patel; Chris Rawcliffe and
Carolina Ongaro, Forma, London;
Ellie Royle, Modern Institute, Glasgow;
Franziska Schmidt; The Swiss Arts
Council Pro Helvetia; Mike Sperlinger;
Wibke Tiarks; Ana Varella and Ligia
Carvalhosa, Fortes D'Aloia & Gabriel,
São Paulo/Rio de Janeiro; Bárbara
Wagner and Benjamin de Burca and
Alberta Whittle.

Regen Projects
Galerie Tanit Munich-Beirut
Tavolozza Foundation
Laura & Barry Townsley
The Whitechapel Gallery
Commissioning Council
White Cube
and those who wish to remain
anonymous


**Education & Community
Programmes**

Aldgate Connect BID
Art Fund
The Arts Society Westminster
Dorota & Olivier Audemars
Capital Group
Clore Cultural Learning Fund
Julie & Debashis Dey
GPE
Paul Hamlyn Foundation
Phillips
ZVM Rangoonwala Foundation
Alex Sainsbury
Dasha Shenkman
Swarovski Foundation
Tower Hamlets Arts & Music Education
Service (THAMES)
The London Borough of Tower Hamlets


**Public Events Programme**

Aldgate Connect BID
GPE
The London Borough of Tower Hamlets
Stanley Picker Trust


**Capital Renewal Programme**

The Headley Trust
Culture Recovery Fund, Heritage
Stimulus Fund – Historic England
The Wolfson Foundation


**Whitechapel Gallery Corporate
Patrons and Members**

Bloomberg Philanthropies
Frasers Property UK
Gazelli Art House
Lisson Gallery
Phillips
David Zwirner

**Whitechapel Gallery
Corporate Supporters**

Abbotts Flooring
Aldgate Connect BID
Bloomberg Philanthropies
Burgess & Leigh
Champagne Castelnau
Crozier Fine Arts
Dior
FRAME London
Hiscox (Artworks Insurance Partner)
Jayhawk
J&C Joel Ltd
Max Mara
Collezione Maramotti
Omni Colour (Signage Partner)
Phillips


**Future Fund**

Mahera & Mohammad Abu Ghazaleh
Sirine & Ahmad Abu Ghazaleh
Swantje Conrad
Mr Dimitris Daskalopoulos
Maryam & Edward Eisler
Luigi Maramotti
NEON
Dominic Palfreyman
Catherine Petitgas
John Smith & Vicky Hughes
V-A-C Foundation
Sir Siegmund Warburg's Voluntary
Settlement
Arts Council England Catalyst
Endowment Fund


**Whitechapel Gallery
Commissioning Council**

Dorota Audemars
Erin Bell
Emilie De Pauw
Heloisa Genish
Leili Huth
Irene Panagopoulos
Nicole Saikalis Bay


**Whitechapel Gallery Patrons' Chair**

Francis Outred

**Whitechapel Gallery Global Circle**

Elyse and Lawrence B. Benenson
Charitarian Foundation
Yan Du
Peter & Maria Kellner
Elie Khouri Art Foundation
and those who wish to remain
anonymous


**Whitechapel Gallery
Director's Circle**

Erin Bell & Michael Cohen
Dirk Boll
Pilar Corrias
Aud & Paolo Cuniberti
Julie & Debashis Dey
Rami Kim
Bimpe Nkontchou
Katie & Felix Robyns
and those who wish to remain
anonymous


**Whitechapel Gallery
Curator's Circle**

Cherry Cheng
Mark Harris
Soo Hitchin
Marcelle Joseph
Adrian & Jennifer O'Carroll
Oba Nsugbe
Ralph Segreti & Richard Follows
Dasha Shenkman
Audrey Wallrock
and those who wish to remain
anonymous


**Whitechapel Gallery Patrons**

Cedric Bardawil
Keith & Helen Clark
Sadie Coles HQ
Beth & Michele Colocci
Swantje Conrad
Francesca Consigli
Michael & Elizabeth Corley
Xiaochi Dong
Dunnett Craven Ltd
Sarah Elson
Sian Emmison
Belinda de Gaudemar
Joanna & Alan Gemes
James Green
Richard & Judith Greer
Sarah Griffin

Pippy Houldsworth
Crane Kalman Gallery
Marie Krauss
Frank Krikhaar
Gerrit & Tilman Kristen
George Loudon
Xi Liu and Yi Luo
Di Luo
Kate MacGarry
Pat Maugüé
Mary E McNicholas
Heike Moras
Jacqueline Nowikovsky
Reine Okuliar
Indi Oliver
Maureen Paley
Dominic Palfreyman
Darryl de Prez & Victoria Thomas
Maria-Cruz Rashidian
Eugenio Re Rebaudengo
Paulina Rider Wilhelmsen
Steve Ruggi & Gilda Williams
Marina Ruiz-Colomer
Jackie Russell
Alex Sainsbury & Elinor Jansz
Cherrill & Ian Scheer
Elisabeth von Schwarzkopf
Henrietta Shields
Matthew Slotover & Emily King
Karen & Mark Smith
Bina & Philippe von Stauffenberg
Nayrouz Tatanaki
Christoph and Marion Trestler
Vanessa Vainio
Samantha Wainstein
Eleanor Warnock
Kimberley Williams
Sharon Zhu & Michael Tian
and those who wish to remain
anonymous


We remain grateful for the ongoing support of Whitechapel Gallery Members.

The Whitechapel Gallery is proud to be a National Portfolio Organisation of Arts Council England.

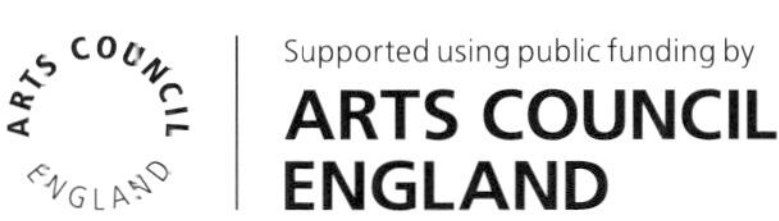

Published on the occasion of
'Moving Bodies, Moving Images'

Whitechapel Gallery, London, UK
12 October 2022 – 8 January 2023

**Whitechapel Gallery exhibition**

Chief Curator
Lydia Yee

Assistant Curator
Grace Storey

Head of Exhibition
Design and Production
Christopher Aldgate

Gallery Technical Manager
Alejandro Ball

Senior Operations and AV Officer
Sam Williams

**Publication**

Editors
Lydia Yee and Grace Storey

Head of Publications
Francesca Vinter

Copy Editor
Orit Gat

Designed by Ard.works
(Guillaume Chuard, Michela Zoppi)

Typeface
Rhymes by Jakub Samek (Maxitype)

Printed by Musumeci

ISBN 978-0-85488-311-0

First published 2022 by
Whitechapel Gallery, London

© 2022 Whitechapel Gallery and
the authors

Whitechapel Gallery
77–82 Whitechapel High Street
London, E1 7QX
whitechapelgallery.org

**Image credits**

Pp.37–8 © Marc Domage for Centre
Culturel Suisse, Paris. Courtesy Alexandra
Bachzetsis; pp.39–41 Marianne Wex,
'Let's Take Back our Space': "Female"
and "Male" Body Language as a Result
of Patriarchal Structures (Frauenliteratur
verlag Hermine Fees, 1979). Courtesy
Marianne Wex; p.57 Courtesy Pauline
Boudry / Renate Lorenz. Photographer:
Bernadette Paasse; pp.58–9 © Pauline
Boudry / Renate Lorenz. Courtesy the
artists; p.77 © Eglė Budvytytė. Courtesy
the artist; pp.99–101 © Éric Minh Cuong
Castaing, Shonen. Courtesy the artist;
p.119 © Alia Farid. Courtesy the artist;
p.137 ©Sarah Mercadé. Courtesy Hetain
Patel; p.138 (top) © Sarah Mercade.
Courtesy Hetain Patel; p.138 (bottom),
p.139, p.140 © Bobbie Cousins. Courtesy
Hetain Patel; p.141 © Amy May. Courtesy
Hetain Patel; pp.159–163 Courtesy Coleção
Fundação Joaquim Nabuco | Ministério
da Educação do Brasil; pp. 181–4 © Alberta
Whittle. Courtesy the artist and The
Modern Institute/Toby Webster Ltd.,
Glasgow. Photographer: Amelia Claudia.



The editors and publishers gratefully
acknowledge the permission granted to
reproduce the copyright material in this
book. Every effort has been made to trace
copyright holders and to obtain their
permission for the use of copyright material. The publisher apologises for any
errors or omissions and would be grateful
if notified of any corrections that should
be incorporated in future reprints or
editions of this book.

A catalogue record for this book is
available from the British Library.

Distributed by
Thames & Hudson
181a High Holborn
London, WC1V 7QX
+44 (0)20 7845 5000
sales@thameshudson.co.uk

Whitechapel Gallery

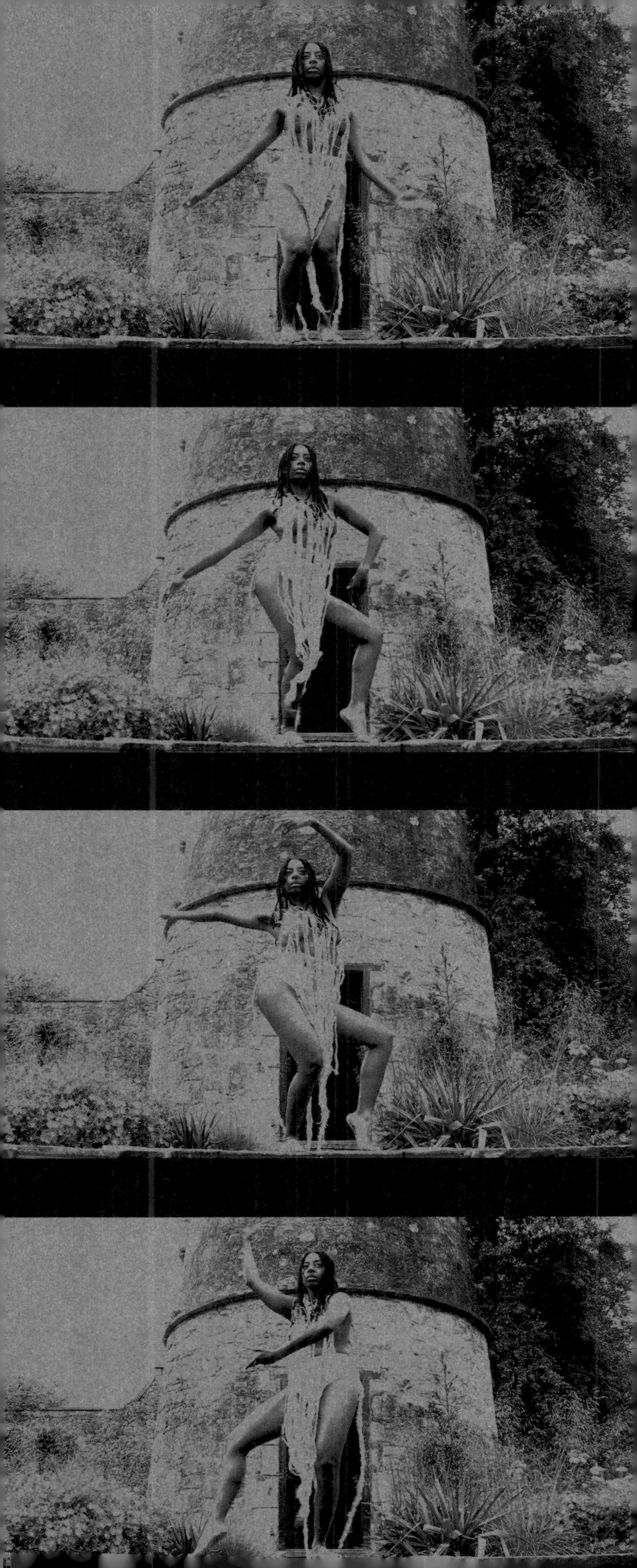

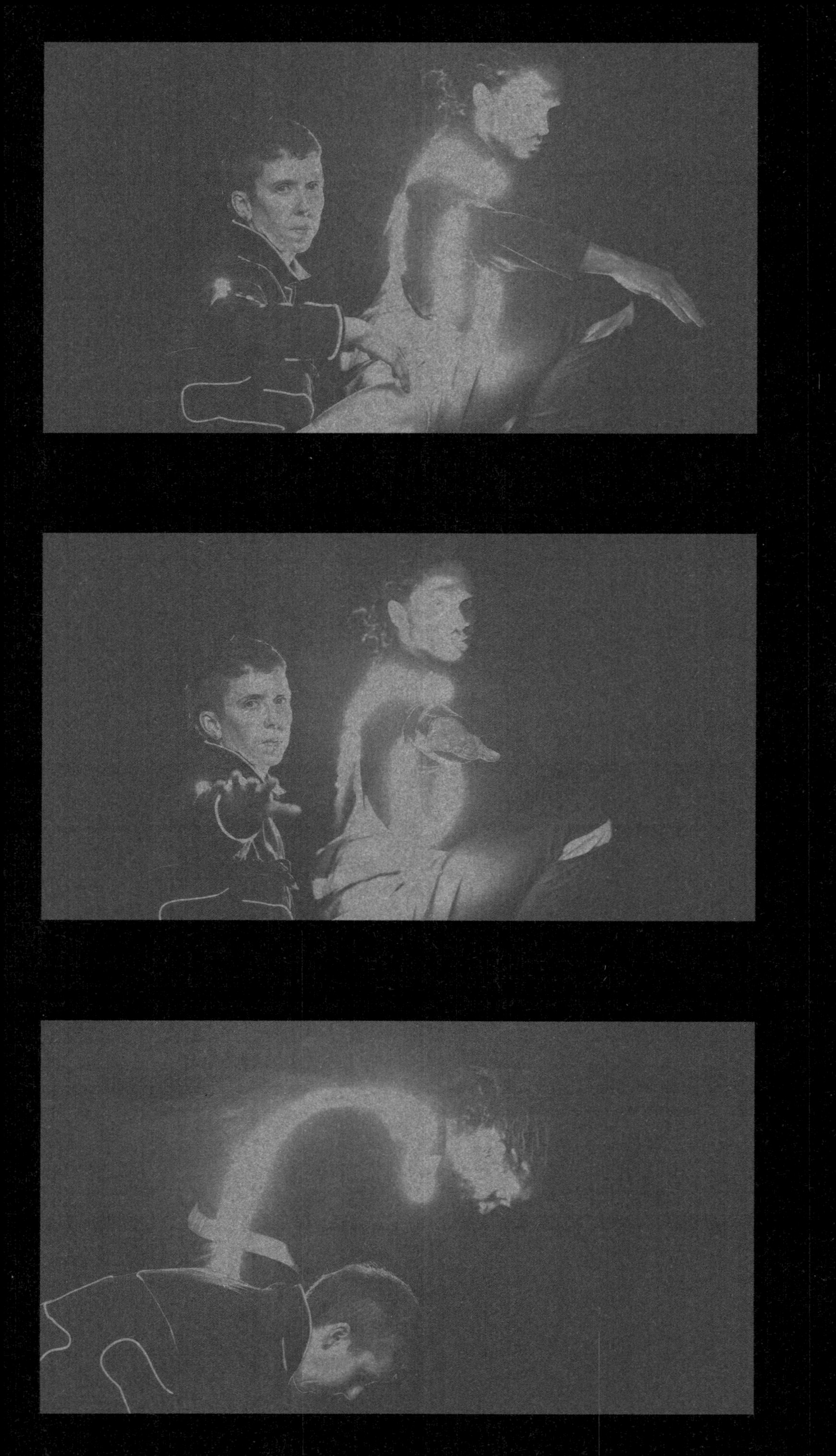